ONLY LOVE CAN BREAK

YOUR HEART

Also by David Samuels

The Runner

Only Love Can Break Your Heart

DAVID SAMUELS

THE NEW PRESS

NEW YORK
LONDON

Requests for permission to reproduce selections from this book should be mailed to:
Permissions Department, The New Press, 38 Greene Street, New York, NY 10013.

Please see pages 371–72 for original publication information
on the pieces in this book.

The author would like to thank Ben Metcalf, Lewis Lapham, Henry Finder,
Anne Fadiman, William Whitworth, Daniel Zalewski, Kyle Crichton, Mark Healy,
Susan Dominus, Tom DeKay, Sloan Harris, Zoe Pagnamenta, Andrew Wylie, and
Sarah Fan for bringing these stories to print.

Published in the United States by The New Press, New York, 2008
Distributed by W. W. Norton & Company, Inc., New York

LIBRARY OF CONGRESS CATALOGING-IN-PUBLICATION DATA
Samuels, David, 1967 Mar. 3–
Only love can break your heart / David Samuels.
p. cm.
Collected magazine articles.
Includes bibliographical references.
ISBN 978-1-59558-187-7 (hc.)
I. Title.
PN4874.S2685A25 2008
814'.6—dc22   2007034994

The New Press was established in 1990 as a not-for-profit alternative to the large,
commercial publishing houses currently dominating the book publishing industry.
The New Press operates in the public interest rather than for private gain, and is
committed to publishing, in innovative ways, works of educational, cultural, and
community value that are often deemed insufficiently profitable.

www.thenewpress.com

Composition by dix!

Printed in the United States of America

2   4   6   8   10   9   7   5   3   1

For My Parents

I know a wind in purpose strong—
It spins against the way it drives.

—Herman Melville,
"The Conflict of Convictions"

Contents

ONLY LOVE CAN BREAK

YOUR HEART

The Golden Land of Mini-Moos
(a Preface)

When Tom Wolfe insisted that journalists were writing the American novels of today, he may have been secretly dreaming of writing novels. But the observation that there is something in the warp of American reality that resists the rule-bound nature of fiction was true, is true, and has always been true, and will probably continue to be true, in obedience to the eternal laws of nature that govern the movements of the stars and the curvature of our planet. Americans, individually or in groups of greater or lesser size, have sent men to the moon, invented a vaccine against polio, obliterated the past and large hunks of the present, and attempted to remake large chunks of the world in our own image. Walt Whitman wrote journalism. Hawthorne wrote journalism. Edgar Allan Poe wrote journalism, nearly all of which turned out to be fake. Herman Melville wrote *Moby-Dick*, which was both a novel and an extended riff on the philosophy and practice of fact-based reporting, written by a man who began his career by making up a true account of his life on a Polynesian island and ended it by becoming a poet. Ernest Hemingway wrote journalism. So did Saul Bellow. Nearly every notable American writer of the modern era has at least tried his or her hand at a stray magazine piece or two to pay for that precious vacation in Corsica or the Galapagos Islands. But that is not what concerns me here.

It hardly comes as news to even the most casual fan of the mongrel art of writing literature on deadline that the great American magazines are dying or dead. At some point around the year 2000 A.D., as future historians of the blogosphere will relate, the great wheel began to turn. Writers continued to write, of course. They wrote memoirs and novels and learned treatises. They wrote crime fiction and op-eds. The magazines that once recorded the results of the headlong collision between literary style and personal affection—what I once called a furious human wave assault on the far shores of reality—lost their audience to art forms like cable television dramas that attempted to bridge the ever-widening gap between traditional storytelling and literary aesthetics and the protean, mind-blowing nature of an uncontrolled experiment in space and time inhabited by starry-eyed inventors, shit-heeled yokels, strong-arm men, hip-hop gangstas, rock stars, and other more or less distinctive types. It is startling to imagine that every one of the magazines that send out literary-minded ladies and gentlemen to chronicle the American scene, like *Harper's* and *The New Yorker, Esquire,* the *Atlantic Monthly,* and even the *New York Times Magazine,* was once a profit-making enterprise supported by hosts of paying subscribers. Today, each of these magazines survives in whole or part thanks to the generosity of a wealthy individual or corporate patron who is content to cover losses incurred by writers and editors who have lost their connection with the public. Add to that the stifling legal constraints imposed by large corporations and lawyered-up big shots, and it has become harder and harder for freelancers like me to have any fun.

The magazines that people actually read, like *Us Weekly,* or the various shopping and lifestyle publications put out by the well-heeled corporate editorial brains of the Condé Nast empire, are hardly magazines in the ancient or not-so-ancient senses of the word. Rather, they are creations of talented people who work together in fancy offices with designer cafeterias, bottled water on tap, and free limos home to tiny apartments in downtown Manhattan or Park Slope. Their job is to shape a product according to the dictates of the people who sell ads—not too long and not too short, on subjects of fleeting but general interest. The result is a glossy, highly reflective environment populated by photographs of brand-name designer clothing, perfume bottles, skinny models in cigarette ads, fast cars, and private jets. The professionalism that this kind of environment prizes is nothing to be ashamed of. But it's not the same thing as writing well.

I don't mean to seem ungrateful, but the truth is, I am. Being ungrateful is the first rule of magazine writing, the second and third rules of which are to issue sweeping pronouncements about people and places that you know very little about and to never, ever miss your deadlines. It is also a fact that the best magazine writers hit their peak within a decade or so of leaving college. By the time you make it to your late thirties, you should be thinking about getting a paying job and supporting a family somewhere outside New York. Magazine writers who survive into middle age are marvels of nature, or independently rich, or half-crazy, retailing fables about government secrets which are in turn part of larger conspiracies that never quite make their way into print. My advice for young writers who think about writing for magazines is to stay at home and sponge off your parents. Marry rich. Get thee to a gym. Spend a month holed up in some miserable Holiday Inn in the sticks, and then another two months trying to make sense of the sodden squiggles in your notebooks and dozens of hours of stoned conversation, and you'll wish that someone like me had offered you this advice much earlier, and that you had chosen to pursue a career in accounting like your Uncle Maury.

The problem with the current setup does not lie in the generosity of the wealthy individuals who sponsor America's money-losing, once-great print publications, but in the fact that these enterprises continue to lose money, which is another way of saying that they are completely detached from reality. It is no offense, I hope, to say that the world billionaires and their high-paid retainers inhabit bears not one iota of resemblance to the lived experience of most Americans. The inhabitants of Literary Cloud-Cuckoo-Land are concerned with very important subjects, like lesbian couples who raise mixed-race children conceived through artificial insemination, or Upper East Side private school kids who savor uni and rock shrimp at after-school courses designed to enliven tiny palates. But enough of all that.

During the course of the decade-long journey that is captured in these pages—which contain my best magazine writing, beginning in the year of Bill Clinton's reelection campaign and ending at a dog track in St. Petersburg, Florida—I lost five girlfriends, two stereo sets, stopped smoking at least half a dozen times only to start again, and was evicted or otherwise physically removed from no fewer than six apartments. The promise that I made to my subjects and my readers is that I would stay open to the full and actual range of human experience—my own experiences, and those of the people I was trying to write about. Every writer I know shelters a truth somewhere deep inside that informs the stories they write, the best of which are often told slantwise. My story has something to do with our national gift for self-delusion and for making ourselves up from scratch, which is much the same thing as believing in the future.

In order to propagate my truth as far and wide as possible, and as a hedge against forgetting, I have prevailed on The New Press to publish *Only Love Can Break Your Heart* together with its sister volume, *The Runner.* It is my hope that this joint publication will serve as my final good-bye to the dying industry that has paid my bills in a sporadic if generally well-meaning fashion for the past decade. So long, and God bless you all—editors, publishers, copy editors, and fact-checkers. I wish you all the best with your children, in making the payments on your homes and apartments, and with your commutes from the suburbs in Westchester, Connecticut, New Jersey, and the Hudson Valley. I appreciate all the effort and hard work you put into the work that appears in these pages. I never meant to hurt you. I never meant to make you cry.

My failings as a writer are obvious to anyone who has been cursed with being on the receiving end of one of my incredibly sloppy first drafts. I can't spell. I often meander. I am like a moonstruck adolescent when it comes to famous American musicians. When I met David Crosby in San Francisco—he was examining a chunk of jade at a jade emporium that he frequents on an average of once a month in the lobby of the Fairmont Hotel—I stammered and stuttered until he put a gentle, restraining hand on my shoulder. Because I require assistance in separating significant details from the larger field of my perception, I have had fights with every editor who was ever generous enough to spend his or her evenings and weekends straightening out the logical flaws in my arguments or trimming my riffs back down to a sane, publishable length. There are passages in every one of these articles that make me flinch, or wince, or might otherwise disturb my composure.

Only a fool insists on making the same mistakes twice. I have therefore allowed myself the liberty of adding passages that had been cut and reworking sentences that had been flattened or mangled. Thanks to these labors, which the scold in me condemns as the sneaking equivalent of colorizing movies or using the reset feature to win at *Doom,* I can recommend these articles as the very lightly airbrushed work-product of a reporter who often drove seven and eight hours to conduct an interview that one of my better-mannered colleagues would have wrapped up in a jiffy over the phone.

Somewhere around the millennium, when the thrill of long night drives wore off, I holed up in a seaside house on the coast near New Bedford, taking long baths and working on a novel whose desiccated corpse stays locked in a drawer at the foot of my bed. I smoked cigarettes and went to the gym, ate spaghetti for dinner, and read *Outerbridge Reach* by Robert Stone. Late one night, while reading a spooky and familiar-seeming description of a house on the coast of Massachusetts inhabited by a woman who had lost her mad husband to a solo voyage across the Atlantic, I realized to my horror that the gabled house that the author was describing was visible from my upstairs window.

It is plainly ridiculous for me to blame my fractured and unstable mental condition on anyone besides myself. To be young in what will surely be known to our posterity as the Golden Nineties was to inhabit a historical sweet spot so creamy and rich and frosted with so many layers of delusional thinking that dwelling on that moment for too long is guaranteed to induce an immediate diabetic coma. Knit together by an invisible web of beneficent new technologies like cell phones and e-mail, everyone in the world was getting rich. The Soviet Union had vanished into the ether. Only a few troublesome hot spots resisted the siren song of free Internet and the Almighty Dollar. Arriving back in New York after covering the war in the Balkans on a freelance basis, I remember sitting at the counter of my local diner and being entranced by the large number of gold-foil-covered creamers that came in a bowl along with my coffee. In America in the nineties, an abundance of Mini-Moos was there for the taking. Everything was free. Getting into a cab, I remember feeling a sudden black terror at the thought that the violence and disintegration that I saw in the former Yugoslavia might come rushing in through the driver's-side window. Snipers would pick off pedestrians from the safety of tall buildings. Buses would blow up in the streets of

Manhattan. I saw a psychiatrist to calm my fears, smoked some dope, and set off across America, in the hopes that I would find people and places that would match up with the free-floating weirdness inside my own head. I can picture myself at the tail end of the decade, with pen and notebook in hand, frantically smoking cigarettes, wearing a blindfold, and trying my best to get straight with the natives. My thoughts were strange but entirely my own. Or maybe not.

The shipwreck of great hopes is a story that belonged to our parents. The stories that I shared with my peers, who grew up in the seventies, were about working mothers and fathers who got angry, absented themselves, or got divorced. We joined together in a generation-wide regression to a version of childhood where we could at last feel safe, because we were now adults and were no longer living at home. We ate Kraft macaroni and cheese for dinner and stayed up late and got high and watched whatever crap was on television. We watched episodes of *Branded* with Chuck Conners, which started and ended the same way each time, together with reruns of *Seinfeld*. The world outside our living rooms in Brooklyn was peopled by believers in Christ who awaited the day that they would be sucked up to heaven by a celestial vacuum cleaner. The smart money designed software gadgets for Microsoft, in what was presented as a great religious adventure but which never struck me as any more exciting or adventurous than stereo sales.

The revolution that took place in magazine writing during the nineties was largely the result of the work of a number of inspired editors at *Harper's*, starting with the editor-in-chief, Lewis Lapham, who made it possible for some of us to say our piece. His goal was to create a place for young writers to tell stories without buying into the more loathsome aspects of the celebrity culture or the self-enclosed space of "news" reporting that managed to miss nearly every meaningful story of the decade in favor of a steam-table buffet of progressive-style bullshit and telephoto-lens shots of skinny blonde actresses with fake boobs. The idea that a scene filtered through the individual sensibility of a writer was more telling, more informative, more real, than the supposedly objective accounts of the news provided by the *New York Times* was another revolution that properly belonged to our parents' generation. Still, *Harper's* emboldened a new cadre of writers who took risks to invent new kinds of sentences and off-kilter rhythms that were more in tune with the contemporary American reality—the hype, the coloniza-tion of language by Web-based sales, and more self-conscious, aca-demic approaches to reality. The low-key rebellion of the individual sensibility that *Harper's* pioneered was directed as much against the undisciplined and contextless sloganeering by disembodied talking heads as against some black and white idea of objective reality. What beguiled me most of all was the promise of the golden ticket, which meant that you could go anywhere you wanted. Still, it was hard to imagine a movie like *Pretty Woman* being made about a journalist with a heart of gold, who receives presents from a handsome stranger and becomes rich.

The America I knew and loved was a more or less innocent place, one big green cow pasture, where the kids cut school, their older brothers smoked meth, the farmer was being driven off his land by the bank, and the farmer's wife was losing the family's life's savings at online poker. I met a man who lowered nuclear bombs into holes in the desert in Nevada at the end of his crane. I met a few hundred people whose lives intersected with my own and whose shadows fall here and there on these pages, the rip-off artists and the people they hurt. I acquired a coin bucket from the Sands Hotel and Casino in Las Vegas; a collection of anarchist wall posters from Eugene, Ore-gon, circa 1999; a fake letter from President John F. Kennedy; a col-lection of dog-eared novels by Robert Stone and Haruki Murakami. I thought I knew where the story was going, about a country without external enemies disintegrating into interstellar dust—a story about my own psyche as much as about anything real.

What follows, then, can best be read as a kind of screwball narra-tive, proceeding from the raw sewage and violence of Woodstock 99, to the antiglobalization radicals of Eugene, Oregon, to a visit with my childhood hero, Red Sox pitcher Bill Lee. Above these scenes hover darker angels like James Kopp, who murdered Dr. Barnett Slepian for aborting fetuses from the wombs of frightened teen-agers. A true believer, James Kopp was equally a child of the sixties, horror-struck by the disintegration of what conservatives call a moral center. What we all shared in common was the search for a point where inner and outer equilibrium could find a proper balance.

Writing for magazines, I learned, is a game that is played by different rules than the game of literature. The collision between sensibility and reality is in part a function of speed. You have to be ready to roll when you hit the ground, spring to your feet, notebook in hand, and start writing. A person can absorb these repeated impacts only a limited number of times. I went to California and found pyramid schemes which rooked Russian immigrants into selling high-priced phone time to their friends and neighbors. I went to rehab and found crack-smoking monkeys locked in cages.

My premonitions in cabs and diners that there was something weird in the air was proven right—but I was looking in the wrong places. Around the corner from my apartment in Brooklyn was the mosque where the first World Trade Center bombing plotters used to meet. I never believed in politics as the answer to anything. The terrorists didn't believe in politics, either. They believed in murder. After the attacks on September 11, 2001, I first made sure that my brother was okay, and then I went to the broken Pentagon, where the secretary of defense described what lay ahead as a second Cold War, a statement that led the nightly news in Germany but was not reported at home. I sat at home for a year and listened to records, and got married to the girl I was with when the planes hit the towers. I love her so much. When she got pregnant we went to Montana, which is truly the most beautiful state.

As the world changed, I began to experience what I did for a living as both difficult and shameful, a combination which left me feeling misunderstood. Exploring a complicated story in depth for four or five months, I would return to Manhattan and feel ashamed because the world that I saw was so different from what my editors saw. I felt ashamed at my mastery of the mimic's art of throwing my voice just a bit to the side so that I might sound enough like the other writers to keep my work in print. I felt ashamed when I gave in on small points of fact and style that changed the meaning of what I saw and wrote. I felt ashamed at the fact that I was in my late thirties, and my bank account was empty. I felt like a sucker.

What I came to believe by the end is that the American gift for forgetting is both the strongest and the weakest point of our national character. We forget what the rest of the world have no choice but to remember. The Goodyear airship I flew back on from the Super

Bowl was named "The Spirit of America." When I shook the president's hand at a fund-raiser in Texas, I was impressed by his athletic grip. The mall where the fund-raiser was being held, the Houston Galleria, was famous for its full-length ice skating rink where the skaters did waltz jumps in the middle of July. These are some things that I remember. If it wasn't for oil, and the price we are willing to pay for oil, the Saudi Arabian jihadists who flew the planes into the towers would still be living out their fever dreams of godly perfection in goat-skin tents in the Arabian desert. I see the jihadists as the savage cousins of the hippies who lived in buses in the woods in Oregon. Only the holiest of the enlightened ones would survive the death throes of a dying planet. It sucks to be raised on a diet of tofu and rice.

What's exciting about writing for magazines is the knowledge that the game can be won or lost in the last two minutes, as the copy editor jams up the rhythm of the opening paragraph, or the fact-checker discovers that the opening scene of your article was described with a somewhat different slant in one of your notebooks. Writing, the kind that appears in novels and poems, aspires to aesthetic perfection—to the formal beauty of a painting or a photograph. Writing for magazines is like playing sports. Nothing ever goes exactly according to plan, but sooner or later, you may experience a few moments of perfection in the middle of the scrum. My magazine-writing career is officially over, but I will continue writing for magazines, of course, provided that my employers continue to publish my work. The sad truth is that I don't know any other kind of life.

—August 2007

Woodstock 1999

As the candlelight flickers over the hand-painted murals and the wrought-iron patio furniture, the concert promoter Michael Lang, in his fifties, with the long curly hair and dreamy good looks of a gracefully aging teen idol, is telling me about his dreams. Michael Lang is a man whose dreams have a strange way of reflecting the mood of his generation. They have included, in no particular order and to varying degrees, the Woodstock Arts and Music Festival in 1969; a traveling exhibition of treasures from the Kremlin; a head shop in Coral Gables, Florida; a concert at the Berlin Wall in 1989; the Rolling Stones concert at Altamont, where a fan was stabbed to death by Hell's Angels; and a movie based on the Mikhail Bulgakov novel *The Master and Margarita,* with a script by Roman Polanski. Tonight, Michael Lang is telling me about Woodstock 99, the latest reincarnation of the 1969 festival, which he has organized with John Scher of the Metropolitan Entertainment Group and the Irish rock-business mastermind Ossie Kilkenny, and which will open here, at Griffiss Technology Park, a decommissioned air force base in Rome, New York, in exactly one week from today.

"The goal is to create a space where people feel safe, secure, un-guarded, open," the promoter explains. "Somehow in this circum-stance people seem able to do that. And to do that you need to feel vulnerable. And the result of feeling that vulnerability is that you come out of the experience feeling less alone."

As Michael Lang talks, I am lulled into an ingratiating stupor by the repetitive motion of his fingers through his curls and the steady mechanical pulse of the crickets in the empty campgrounds below. At the end of the runway, past the control tower, is the main festival stage that will present twenty-five brand-name rock bands, including the Red Hot Chili Peppers, the Dave Matthews Band, Metallica, and Alanis Morissette, to an expected audience of a quarter-million concertgoers. A skeletal assembly of prefabricated steel beams, the stage rises above the open fields to our right like a giant erector-set project whose builder has been called home to dinner early by his mom. Directly in front of us, beyond the runways, are the camping areas, paved with wood chips and strung with yellow plastic construction lanterns, surrounded by a half-finished "Peace Wall" decorated with murals of unicorns and B-52 bombers morphing into doves. Twelve feet high and 16,000 feet long, the Peace Wall is only one component of a comprehensive security plan that also includes 500 state police officers and a second perimeter fence, topped by coils of razor-sharp wire.

"We were maybe a little more serious," he says, comparing the spirit of his generation with that of my own. "We were very impressed with what we could accomplish, the freedom marches, the civil rights movement, demonstrating against the war." Through his nearly transparent blue eyes I can see the album jackets of *Sgt. Pepper's Lonely Hearts Club Band, Workingman's Dead, Disraeli Gears, Goats Head Soup, Big Brother & the Holding Company,* and all the other long-playing albums my parents bought when they were still young. "We showed people that there was a business with the power to draw these people in far greater numbers than anyone had ever imagined," he remembers. "And rock and roll was never the same." When I ask him to describe his perfect vision of next week's event, he slouches back in his chair and clasps his hands behind his head.

"The temperature would be between seventy-five and eighty degrees," he says. "Light showers in the late afternoon . . . no bad traffic jams. I have a lot of faith in the production being together." The contrapuntal coherence of his dream reminds me of the lyrics to a really good rock song. "And people would be connected in a meaningful way," he continues, pointing out over the runway to the campgrounds beyond, where one hundred bands will play rock and roll, a couple will get married, at least four women will be raped during shows, two people will die, and some portion of the 225,000 concertgoers will finally riot after living in and around lakes of raw sewage for three days and three nights, "in a vulnerable, connected way, feeling like it's their space."

I am standing in my red, white, and blue "Kill Rock Stars" T-shirt on the Griffiss field runway with tens of thousands of kids trudging around and past me, bearing knapsacks and suitcases and black plastic garbage bags and kicking up dust like a herd of dispossessed extras in a made-for-MTV version of *The Grapes of Wrath*. Unfolding nylon sporting-goods tents in the designated camping areas and spreading out sugar- and calorie-rich stashes of Snickers bars, Pringles, and Wonder Bread on the grass, the faces of a generation look tired, having driven five, ten, fifteen, or thirty-eight hours to see band after band play live from morning to midnight on two main stages and an emerging-artists' stage that will also host late-night raves. Since I visited the site a week ago, the runways of Griffiss field have been transformed into an encampment of white canvas tents doling out pizza and burgers under the supervision of the Ogden Corporation, one of the largest event-related food-service providers in America, capable of serving an estimated 425,000 hot dogs, 2 million sodas, and 5 million packages of condiments to the hungry crowd.

Wandering through the carny landscape of empty pizza boxes and crushed plastic Sprite bottles that the Ogden Corporation has created are college kids on summer break as well as their less fortunate peers, who have taken long weekends off from their jobs reshelving videos at Blockbuster outlets and serving the $5.99 breakfast at Denny's. When asked which bands they are excited to see, most mention brand-name touring acts like the Red Hot Chili Peppers, Dave Matthews, or Korn without any greater enthusiasm than they show for videos by these same groups, which they also like. Sullen, bare-chested guys push through the crowd with the elastic waistbands of their boxers pulled up hip-hop-gangsta-style above baggy shorts from Polo and Tommy Hilfiger. Their macho appearance is undercut by smooth-shaven chests, a style that has less to do with any deep embrace of a gay male aesthetic than with the fact that men and women no longer occupy their age-old roles as hunter and hunted in the sexual chase. Despite the reversal, or because of it, the men seem more than usually invested in the practice of total, absolute conformity. They walk the same and talk the same and fuck the same and eat slices of gooey pizza from cardboard boxes at the price of $12 for a small pie. Bare-midriffed girls counter the dirty-girl allure of their tight shorts and white, pink, and blue baby-doll T-shirts by hunching their shoulders and staring blankly down at the melting asphalt in the ninety-degree heat, lost in a haze of sexual discomfort that makes me feel like the worst moments of my adolescence have been captured in some highly concentrated form and sprayed out over the runway like cheap perfume.

Above the crowded runway, beneath cream-colored table umbrellas, Michael Lang's porch is an oasis of shade and calm, filled with the middle-age vibe of the brave generation of lifestyle pioneers who own houses near Woodstock, drive Volvos and Saabs, and are watching their children graduate from college after more or less successfully enduring years of psychotherapy. As I sit gratefully sipping from my Evian water bottle, I notice a woman walking from table to table pouring polished river rocks from a plastic bag into decorative earthenware bowls. She is in her late thirties or early forties, with a wholesome aspect to her face that reminds me of the inside of a loaf of freshly baked bread. Her name is Mary Fellows. Like most of the people here, she has a real-life job back home, which in her case consists of designing and selling bedding for Little Merry Fellows, her semi-eponymous line of organic children's bedding. Before that, she worked for rock promoter Ron Delsener designing dressing rooms, which is why Michael asked her to come here. Rock stars are interesting people, she says. Her favorite rock-star request came from Barbra Streisand, who asked that her dressing-room toilet at Madison Square Garden be filled with gardenias. When the plumbing at the Garden proved unable to accommodate whole gardenias, Fellows says, she picked rose petals off the stage and had them arranged inside the bowl so that Barbra Streisand could pee.

Framed in the plate-glass window above Mary's head, Michael Lang is responding to some new crisis on the phone while a sad-faced older man relaxes on the couch. He looks like a faculty member from the Ringling Bros. and Barnum & Bailey clown school in Florida, his face topped by a halo of thinning reddish-brown hair, his burlap-green clown suit covered in five-pointed stars. Famous as a member of the Hog Farm commune, which warned the original Woodstock crowd not to take bad acid, Wavy Gravy—the clown on the couch—now lives in Berkeley, California, where he commutes between his home, the Hog Farm, a clown camp for kids ("Camp Winnarainbow"), and college-lecture dates arranged by his manager. He is more than happy to share a bottle of Evian and talk.

"We were trying to evacuate New York because two of our people had been busted with one-quarter of a gram of marijuana ashes," he says. "Ashes." He pauses for a moment, then two, then describes the Hog Farm's blocklong loft on the top floor of a building owned by a Dutch woman named Elizabeth-something in lower Manhattan, where a man named Stanley Goldstein appeared one day on a mission from Michael Lang.

"Goldstein comes to the kitchen table and he says, 'We've been watching your style,'" Wavy Gravy remembers, spreading his fingers wide as he drops into the role of his younger, more heavily publicized self:

" 'We're in New Mexico now. We've got some land.'

" 'No problem. We'll fly you out in an Astrojet.' "

Wavy Gravy's eyes are starting to lose focus, but by this point in the conversation, I have enough experience to help him maintain.

"An Astrojet," I say.

"An As . . . tro . . . jet," Wavy Gravy happily responds. He takes another sip of water.

"So we're in New Mexico and Kesey had just arrived," he says. "It was the summer solstice. And it had never occurred to us that beer could be electric. They had just invented screw-top caps for beer, you see. So we're all flying, and Stanley shows up again with his aluminum briefcase. He had all kinds of stuff in that briefcase."

"He had money in the briefcase," I say.

"We couldn't be paid for Woodstock," Wavy Gravy answers. "We were so pure. We got six grand in the end for clearing some pasture. Never again, man. Never again."

As the music from three stages booms over the runway like a B-52 bomber, it occurs to me that I really have time to take in only so many well-practiced tales from the sixties while reporting on an event that really has nothing to do with the original Woodstock at all.

Wavy Gravy senses my impatience. "There's a lot of bullshit about Woodstock being a free concert," he relates, wiping the sweat from his forehead with a star-spangled sleeve. The real story of Woodstock, he says, his voice dropping down to the conspiratorial whisper that aging hippies use when passing on certain kinds of historical tips, like the fact that George Washington smoked hemp with his slaves at Mount Vernon, is that the gates were up before the concert began, and that Michael Lang told him and fellow Hog Farmers Ken Babbs and Tom Law to clear all 50,000 early arrivals from the field if they didn't have tickets. "We looked at each other and Law asked him, 'Do you want a good movie or a bad movie?' " he says, giving me a full eyeball-to-eyeball stare for at least thirty seconds before he completes the story. "Because we knew they had signed their big movie deal with Warner Brothers, you see. And to their credit, it took them maybe ten minutes to decide."

More than 200,000 people have already made it to the site by late Friday morning. Inside the Woodstock 99 press tent, a few hours before the concert is officially set to begin, reporters and cameramen wander through the big top picking up colored information folders to guide them through the event, setting up laptops at long wooden tables, or resting digital video cameras on folding chairs for a few moments before heading back into the heat and the dust. Gray, black, and red cables snake across the floor like the elongated ganglia of some low-budget fifties science-fiction movie brain. But the analogy is sadly out of date. Woodstock 99 is not so much a movie as a prepackaged Information Age Happening, streaming from this room and the video trailers parked out back into millions of brains in multiple formats, with pay-per-view, MTV, newspapers, magazines, local and national news, and the Internet adding value to the Woodstock brand and making the promoters, artists, record companies, and associated vendors happy.

The hierarchy inside the tent resembles that of the average American high school, except for the fact that it is more precisely and geometrically defined. The flacks from Los Angeles are skinnier, better looking, have better clothes, and wear square all-access passes that allow them to go anywhere they want, including the stages. In jeans and black T-shirts, or flannel-patterned cotton shirts, or comfortable shorts from the Gap, the reporters and cameramen are in their late twenties and early thirties, or a good ten years older than the average age of the crowd outside. They bustle around the walkie-talkie-wielding flacks, fondling triangular backstage passes which permit access only to a designated interview area near the main stage and tossing out hard questions about a reported drug overdose in the campgrounds last night and the fact that the band Sugar Ray has backed out of their slot on this afternoon's bill. Then they lower their voices, shift from foot to foot, smile, and ask for five or ten minutes with Alanis Morissette.

On the runways outside, temperatures are now climbing back into the nineties, and the Ogden Corporation vendors are doing a thriving business, as evidenced by the sea of garbage that has been gathering around the food-service tents since yesterday. Dodging the blizzard of Dove Bars, Frozen Lemonades, Iced Mochas, Orange Mango Drinks, Sprites, Pepsis, Cokes, Nachos, Tenders and Poppers, Jelly Buns, Fat-Free Soft Serve Ice Creams, Gourmet Butter Salt Potatoes, Caramel Apples, Jelly Bellys, Doughnuts, and Arepas, I make my way to the center of the lawn, which has exploded in a sea of beads, T-shirts, necklaces, sarongs, and Tibetan rugs, promiscuously mixed in with more corporate and orderly tented booths for Columbia House records and the Woodstock 99 Platinum MasterCard. The crowd of a few hundred people gathered outside the Body Painting and Piercing booth is being whipped into a low-grade strip club frenzy by an MC, who chants, "Look at her! Look at her!" while female concertgoers with painted chests and pierced nipples are paraded on a makeshift stage.

In the middle of the crowd, a girl with silver rings through her nipples and a purple butterfly painted across her bare chest is having her picture taken with groups of smirky, camera-happy guys. She has a wonderful smile—the smile of someone who believes that a really great smile can make all the difference in someone's day and that even in the darkest midnight hours her inner light will continue to shine. Her name is Brandy Parkinson, she says as she sits down beside me on the grass. The butterfly on her chest means that she is free. She is eighteen years old, comes from Rockford, Illinois, and she drove twelve and a half hours in her Hyundai to be here, because she didn't want to regret not going. At home she works two jobs—as a cocktail waitress and in telemarketing—and lives with her boyfriend, who has two kids, and whom she met while waitressing at a Denny's. Her favorite band is Godsmack. "I crave," she explains. "They say it. It's so absolute, so desperate and needy." She also likes Alanis Morissette; inside and out, Alanis Morissette is a beautiful person. She doesn't go to the movies that often, she says, because working two jobs and taking care of her boyfriend's kids doesn't leave her much time. For breakfast this morning she had a frozen strawberry slushie. What all of this adds up to in my mind is the impression that Brandy Parkinson is a nice person who makes bad decisions, and that if her judgment doesn't improve she might wind up married to her boyfriend, or hitching a ride one night with a friendly well-spoken stranger who has been featured on *America's Most Wanted* for leaving mutilated bodies in ravines across three states. I want to warn her against these possibilities, especially the latter, but I have no idea how or where to start.

Half a mile away, on the main stage, Woodstock 99 has officially begun. A man with a megaphone is standing on top of an RV and shouting to the crowd that has gathered to watch. "You guys are awesome partygoers!" he informs them. Standing beside him, several girls in bathing suits and T-shirts are squirted with water guns as they bare their breasts to catcalls and applause from the crowd. Looking up at the bright orange blimp hovering over my head, I wonder whether its message—FRIED DOUGH—might be some kind of key to the deeper meaning of this event. If the original Woodstock was about peace, love, music, and making a good movie instead of a bad one, Woodstock 99 is about feeling the grease soak through the paper and onto your fingers. The guy in the San Diego Padres cap standing next to me screams, "Show us your tits!" His face is turning red with the effort. He is screaming himself hoarse. "Show us your tits!"

On the main stage, James Brown is already halfway through the concert's opening set. Beneath Peter Max's hundred-foot-tall psychedelic mural, the hardest-working man in show business is wiping the sweat from his brow and strutting across the stage to the tune of "Sex Machine," embellished by a Vegas horn section in blue tuxedos and a trio of backup singers in spangly showgirl dresses whose job includes nailing the words "James Brown" to the downbeat at the end of each and every line of the song. If their timing is off on even one "James Brown," the looks on their faces suggest something bad will happen to them after the show. Since my view of the stage is blocked by the forty-foot-tall plywood camera tower in the center of the lawn, I watch the action on the tear-drop-shaped JumboTron screen implanted in the center of Peter Max's mural like an alien mind-control graft onto the shopworn trope of psychedelically altered reality.

"Everybody over there, put your hands in the air," James Brown instructs. I can feel the shirtless kids pressed in around me near the stage weighing the pros and cons involved in obeying his order. When the set is over, only a few of the people around me applaud. They respond with far greater enthusiasm to the Offspring, who hit the stage in outfits that look like they cost a thousand dollars apiece in the glam-rock boutiques of Los Angeles, and whose punk-inflected pop songs incite the crowd to hurl empty Sprite bottles into the air, an effect that suggests that an army of translucent grasshoppers is attacking a field of unprofitable wheat. Even more impressive is the crowd's response to Korn, a rap-metal band whose songs all sound aggressively the same and are popular among fourteen- and fifteen-year-old boys. Korn's lead singer, Jonathan Davis, wears a black-rubber restraining garment and a kilt, which I take to be some inscrutably youth-specific symbol of sexual deviance, but which he justifies later in his set by serenading his fans on the bagpipes.

The message of Woodstock 99 goes something like this: rock and roll is a moment of instant and lasting communion between the generations, a source of half-remembered trivia like the name of John Lennon's first wife or The Who's second drummer drifting through the pot-clouded haze of wall-to-wall-carpeted rec rooms with "When the Levee Breaks" by Led Zeppelin or something cool by Pavement cranking through monster quadraphonic speakers as you make it for the second or third time with your high school girlfriend on the suburban orange shag rug. In the heat and the dust beneath the stage, the past and the present are one. Onstage, beneath the mural, heroic banks of amplifiers dwarf the band members, who scurry like animated cartoon ants in flouncy shirts and spandex tights while rocking out on the latest guitars from Martin, Fender,

Rickenbacker, and Gibson, shown in the pages of *Guitar Player* magazine in airbrushed beaver-shot detail next to the article on mastering diatonic sequences with Yngwie Malmsteen, whose high-speed noodlings remain a byword for genius among generations of adolescent boys launching masturbatory riffs through the wood-paneled basements of Long Island.

Flashing my shiny, laminated triangle, I pass through the security gates to the tented interview area, where I wait for forty-five minutes before I find a flack in sunglasses with an all-access pass who agrees to walk me through a second set of gates. The artists' compound, or the artists' village, as Mary Fellows prefers to call it, consists of a gray carpet running through what is actually a glorified trailer park. Absent here are any of the signs of life, like outdoor barbecues, screaming babies, and domestic disputes, that might make a trailer park an interesting place to spend my afternoon. The only sign of life I see is a lone musician from the group Jamiroquai, deep in conversation with another musician about a house in Tucson, Arizona, that he may or may not rent next fall. Otherwise, the streets are empty and silent, save for the anonymous hum of twenty window-unit air conditioners all going at once.

Mary Fellows is glad that I came, and she is happy to show me around the artists' house, a mix of earthy pastels and design-studio touches that would feel right at home in the more upscale neighborhoods of Tucson. Artists visiting the house can enjoy four Sony PlayStation suites upstairs, a large-screen color TV set, a foosball table, a pinball table, and an air-hockey set. The trailers where the rock stars actually hang out offer little evidence that a rock star's life is any more glamorous or less depressing than my own. The trailer assigned to George Clinton, the dreadlocked leader of Parliament-Funkadelic, is pretty much representative of the other trailers I visit, with wood-veneer-paneled walls, linoleum floors, wicker chairs, a white futon branded with the Woodstock 99 logo, and air-conditioning turned all the way up to create the impression that a perishable product is being stored inside at well-controlled temperatures. Clustered on the craft-service table by the window are food items personally requested by George Clinton himself, including tea, honey, a bag of assorted Hershey's miniature chocolates, a jar of

Hellmann's mayo-mustard combination spread, a loaf of white bread, a bottle of Jack Daniel's, and an even bigger bottle of Sunsweet prune juice. The expected rock-star touches, such as leopard-print fabrics, mounds of cocaine, or a powdered drink in space-age silver pouches, are nowhere to be seen. When I ask Mary Fellows why, she explains that profit margins in the rock business today no longer allow for willful excess. The concert business, she says, is currently divided between two companies that guarantee the bands a large chunk of money up front for each show and then squeeze expenses as tightly as possible.

As we walk back through the trailer park, past the wide-bodied construction-site monster currently inhabited by the rapper DMX, I realize that Woodstock 99 is a perfect microcosm of the greater world beyond. Rock stars are wealthy, privileged people who live just like other wealthy, privileged people do, protected by gates and uniformed security guards from the danger, filth, and darkness of a world where everyone wants to be rich and famous and loved. They have come to Woodstock 99 because it's the biggest concert event of the summer, a place where they will be loved by 200,000 people. Instead, they find themselves penned up in a gated community of people like themselves, cut off from wherever it was they came from, with a loaf of processed white bread on the table to remind them of who they truly are.

By the chain-link fence at the far end of the enclosure, George Clinton and his Parliament-Funkadelic orchestra of freaks are having their picture taken by the official Woodstock 99 photographer. There is the bassist Bootsy Collins, Bernie Worrell, the rapper Humpty Hump, a guy wearing a white diaper, and a witchy violinist with curly black hair who looks to be more or less my age. Her name is Lili Haydn, she is from L.A., and she was trained as a classical musician. She likes playing with Parliament-Funkadelic, she says, because the band is made up of expert musicians. Otherwise, she listens to Brahms. Wendy Weisberg of Mammoth Records, Parliament-Funkadelic's publicist, standing by the gate to the artists' compound with a red all-access pass around her neck, is a more recognizable type. She wears her platinum-streaked hair in pigtails that stick out little-girl style from either side of her head and black-framed rock-nerd glasses, an unmistakable reference to the three years she spent as a college radio station DJ. "You went to Smith, you do fucking PR for rock bands, big fucking deal," she says when I ask her to describe her feelings about her work. "Then I think, music gives so many people pleasure."

It is now past midnight, and Michael Lang is running his fingers through his hair while talking on the phone and I am doing my best to concentrate on whatever it is that he is saying over the heavy beat from the runway below, where 15,000 ravers are waving glow sticks and bobbing their heads in a scene that reminds me of a New Year's Eve event at Club Med. "I love having built this, seeing people blown away by it," he says. The phone rings again. A promoter named Brian Lash has issued fake credentials, which are being seized by event security. A few minutes later, the credentials turn out not to be fake. Or maybe they are.

In the eye of the storm, Michael Lang will remain even-tempered in his K-Swiss sneakers and Banana Republic bush jacket whether the credentials are fake or not. This morning, he surveyed the site from the air in a helicopter. He saw James Brown but missed Korn. One thousand cases of water were delivered to first-aid stations. At seven-thirty he attended a meeting at which the concert's grand finale was discussed. He smiles like a magician whose bag is not yet empty of tricks. "I had a rotoscope of Hendrix's performance from 1969," he explains, "and we had it turned into a laser hologram projection. There's a little dialogue, and then Jimi plays 'The Star-Spangled Banner,' and then he rises up into the sky."

Why has Michael Lang spent a year organizing this event, I wonder, when he could live off his licensing profits from the Woodstock name, or start a software company, or produce movies, or pursue any of the other avenues by which ex-hippie entrepreneurs make money? "This is for a moment," he says when I ask him. "It's not an institution. It's not something permanent."

Permanence is bad, Michael agrees. "It's a mirage. It doesn't have a chance to get crusted, mundane, trivialized, a caricature of itself." But maybe there is evidence on the other side too. What if permanence is not trivial or mundane but something powerful and real in the world? Michael Lang will be getting married in October. I wonder how he squares his beliefs about institutions and permanence with the actual facts of his life.

Michael Lang invites me onto the balcony to watch the rave, and the air outside is pleasantly cool. Below us, the crowd on the runway looks nothing like the crowd that was gathered there earlier today. The kids are inside the music, and the sound seems like it is coming from somewhere inside their bodies, leaving no clear division between the music and the dancers. There is only the undivided communal experience of a beat that goes on for hours with no beginning and no end, and no three-minute sections that can be excised from the moment and played on MTV. As I perch on the rail, dangling my legs over the side to the deep bass boom of the airplane-hangar speakers, kids in sunglasses circulate through the crowd selling glow sticks and pills, and exhausted dancers stagger out of the crowd to pass out by the wall. Two girls sit facing each other in a circle of light beneath a trailer, a white girl in a peasant-print skirt and an Indian girl with big brown eyes. The white girl is rocking back and forth while the Indian girl touches her face over and over in a steady, rhythmic, calming motion, feeling her skin. A few minutes later, a long-limbed boy steps out of the crowd, picks up a canteen from the ground, unscrews the top, and pours a stream of water into his mouth. Then he lies down on the ground next to the girl who is rocking back and forth, and they start rocking back and forth together. She licks his face. He runs his hands up and down her body as if he is feeling something that has nothing to do with the girl at all. He gets up and takes another drink of water and dances back into the crowd.

The next day in Michael Lang's office, Lee Blumer, a friend of Michael's, is working the phones and trying to get someone to deal with the trash. "Let's deal with the situation now, before diphtheria breaks out," she says. Lee Blumer is a woman in her midfifties with curly black hair who used to work for Bill Graham at the Fillmore East and who sounds like she grew up in a large Jewish family in Brooklyn, which, as it turns out, she did. When I ask why the campgrounds are covered in trash, she shrugs, then jerks her thumb back over her shoulder to signify that dealing with the trash is the kind of thing that big-shot promoters never want to handle, which is why they keep women like Lee Blumer around.

"Have you met Lisa Law?" she asks, gesturing toward the couch.

In a blue denim dress and a straw hat, with the weather-beaten look of someone who left home in Appalachia at age nineteen to ride with the Hell's Angels, Lisa Law is an American counterculture legend who tried to feed half a million people at the original Woodstock concert on bulgur wheat cooked in five-gallon pots, served with soy sauce, and on muesli for breakfast, with rolled oats, almonds, and wheat germ. "It was cheap," she says. "And it was a way of educating people, to help them learn about healthy food." A member of the Jook Savages commune during the sixties, she still gets stoned a few times a month and remains a fervent believer in overthrowing traditional modes of social and family life in order to create a new and better reality. She is happy to help out with the trash.

Commandeering a golf cart, we load fifty boxes of trash bags on the back, and Lisa Law puts the cart in gear. As we drive down the runway, where the temperature is now approaching 100 degrees, the sound of the bands is all but drowned out by a group of thirty or forty kids who have taken an equal number of green-painted garbage cans from the midway to form a drum circle. Beating on the cans with their hands and fists, they have found a way to open up a space within the staged event so that they can participate in the action. The sounds they make suggest a cut-rate garage where something bad is being done to a car. To the left of the circle, a bare-chested kid with a heavy black beard lifts a garbage can over his head and smashes it down on the asphalt. As the drumming continues, he lifts the can up, then smashes it down again on the runway, over and over, until the can flattens out into a sharp-edged metal pancake. Still, the shape seems too defined, too flat or too round. He picks up the metal pancake and smashes it again, lost in a private ritual of destruction that will continue until the shape of the can matches the misshapen thing in his head.

From the backseat of the golf cart, where I am attempting to hand out trash bags, the campgrounds look like a relief area crammed with sullen refugees from a distant civil war. The attempt to establish any semblance of order collapsed long ago, and the streets with names like Penny Lane and Abbey Road have vanished in a claustrophobic tented mass. Buried beneath heaps of pizza boxes, Sprite bottles, Pringles cans, and navy bags from the Gap, the corridors between the tents have been turned into estuaries of trash that ebb and flow with the occasional sluggish breeze off the runways.

"Help keep your area clean!" Lisa Law encourages the kids closest to the runways. Lying in their underwear inside their tents, or sitting cross-legged and stoned in the heat by the runway, only a few of them volunteer to help out. After a few minutes of this, Lisa Law adopts a new tack: "Help keep your area clean!" A kid in a Korn T-shirt runs behind the golf cart, making wavy, trippy motions with his hands as he follows the trash bag I am holding out. When we stop to press the point more directly, a kid with dyed blond hair says, "I paid $150 to come here. You clean up my fucking trash."

To the left of the runway, a row of twenty Porto Potties is leaking raw sewage into a stream of running water that is in turn flowing into the tent areas and collecting there in a series of small pools or lakes ranging in size from ten to thirty feet across. Raw sewage is not an easy smell to ignore. As the smell gets stronger, I notice that there are still people inside the tents, apparently awake and unbothered by the smell, which is so strong that I instinctively cover my nose and mouth and breathe in and out through my sleeve. It is hard to imagine why anyone would organize a festival of peace, love, and music where kids spend three days camped out in sewage. On the other hand, it is hard to imagine why anyone who found himself camped out in sewage wouldn't ask for his money back, or at least move his tent.

While Ice Cube raps his ten-year-old hit "Fuck tha Police" from the East Stage, the first-aid stations along the runway are filling up with hundreds of kids who have passed out in the heat. Water costs $4 a bottle at the concession stands, and there simply isn't enough to go around. As I approach the campgrounds exit, I pass two concertgoers walking together, as fast as they can, each completely unaware of the other. The first is a hippyish man in his late forties or early fifties, with a long brown beard, wire-rimmed sunglasses, and a tie-dyed T-shirt with a peace sign. Above the peace sign is the word "Imagine." Next to him is a well-muscled guy in his early twenties, wearing shorts, a pair of Nike sneakers, and a navy T-shirt that reads, "I'm here about the blow job."

•   •   •

Ossie Kilkenny, the second of the three Woodstock promoters, is an accountant from Ireland who makes deals for a long roster of English and Irish bands, including U2, and who is supposedly the sharpest business mind in rock and roll. I have been trying to talk to Kilkenny for the last two weeks. I climb the stairs to Michael Lang's office, sit on the couch, and at least a half-dozen phone calls later, following various crises and disputes, a report of a drug-related death, and rumors of radiation poisoning on the site, Ossie Kilkenny has still not shown up. So I talk to Lee Blumer instead.

"We wanted to get out of Brooklyn," she says, when I ask her about the dreams of her youth. "We all did. We wanted to get out of the Catskills. To create our own world. It was going to be fun and funny. We would do away with racism, with classism, with all the gossipy, parental stuff that people thought was love. Everything was focused on expansion, even the drugs. It all had something to do with improvement, with improving yourself, improving the world." She leans back in her chair and sighs an imperious-old-Jewish-lady sigh. "Then somehow we gave birth to that," she says, gesturing out the window toward the trash-strewn campgrounds and the noise of the bands and the kids on the runway still beating on the trash cans. "And the thing that puzzles me is—how?"

Outside the office, fifteen or so people are sitting on couches in front of a giant color TV set and watching Alanis Morissette, who stands before the camera with her long hair in braids, her shoulders hunched, and her eyes trained on the ground, the same way any of the young women watching her would pose if they found themselves standing onstage in front of 200,000 people. She holds tight to the microphone, makes spastic, grabby hand gestures at the camera, and lets her eyes roll back in her head. She is entering a trancelike state that makes it okay for her to declare her most intimate thoughts and feelings in public, a choice that might otherwise seem unsympathetically selfish to her fans. "How 'bout no longer being mas-o-chis-tic?" she sings. "How 'bout unabashedly baw-ling your eyes out?" There is something patterned and obvious about her performance, I think, but when I look at the screen again the pose makes sense: the embarrassment is real. Alanis Morissette is embarrassed to be looked at, I understand, because she is so unnaturally beautiful. She has the deep, unselfconscious physical beauty that

movie stars kill for, and she is embarrassed by it, because beautiful
women aren't supposed to feel insecurity or self-hatred or anger or
any of the other emotions that her fans connect to in her songs—
which in turn makes her beauty okay, opening up a common space
where the performer and her audience can coexist on the same
emotional plane of hunched-shouldered embarrassment.

Ossie Kilkenny arrives an hour or so later, a white-haired man in
his fifties who looks like a college professor or an Irish newspaper
editor, despite the fact that he is wearing a Missoni T-shirt and a
rumpled linen suit shot through with golden threads. It seems only
fair to say that I like him immediately. I like the fact that he comes
off as shy, and that he is in fact smart, and that the Missoni T-shirt
and the gold suit are not just part of a studied attempt to dress the
part of a big-time promoter but are also items of clothing that he
truly likes to wear. He talks about his rock-star clients like U2 and
Oasis with the discretion that people of means would expect from
their accountant. If he controlled the Woodstock name, he adds, he
would concentrate on developing a presence in recorded music. He
would also donate money to socially responsible movements and
groups, "which in turn strengthens the Woodstock brand."

Because he was two and a half hours late, and because he is a
thoughtful and interesting man who grew up poor in Dublin and
who is now directly responsible for the very Irish brew of bad food,
overflowing toilets, and lousy music in which I have been immersed
for the last two days, I decide to give Ossie Kilkenny a piece of my
mind. I mention the absence of any effort to reach out to the audience, and he nods and says, "We're giving the masses what they
want." When he was growing up in Dublin, he loved to listen to Otis
Redding and Ray Charles. He quotes a few lines from the poet John
Betjeman. Then he tells me about his house in Dublin and his other
house on the lakes and the two seaplanes with all the original details
that fly him from one house to the other. He loves planes, he says,
and he is embarrassed that he doesn't know how to fly them himself.
He talks about how much it means for a kid from Dublin to be part
of the biggest rock concert in the world. I ask him what the audience
has learned here, if anything, and he looks down at the runway,
where kids continue to beat on the cans.

"Did we get anything across to people?" he wonders. "I don't think that we did. Which is an amazing admission to make, after bringing 200,000 people together in one place and spending $38 million."

Thick clouds are moving in fast overhead, and as I push toward the main stage I can feel the disconnected energy of the last three days starting to assume some more definite form. After three days of wandering through the midway drinking bottles of water, stepping through piles of trash that are never cleaned up, sitting out the heat in clouds of cigarette and marijuana smoke, breathing in the sewage-tainted dust that hangs over the densely packed campgrounds, the crowd smells sour and stale. They have had enough. Up onstage, Fred Durst, the lead singer for the rap-metal band Limp Bizkit, is sharing this mood. He plays with the crowd's anger, proclaiming that "there are no rules" and urging them to "smash stuff" and not to mellow out, because "that's what Alanis Morissette had you do." The closer I get to the stage, the uglier the vibe becomes, with bare-chested guys raising their fists in the air and smashing into one another with a full-bodied force that is meant to cause physical damage. This is not a good place to be. As I turn and head for the exit to the left of the stage, someone plants an elbow hard in my lower back, and I go flying into the kid standing next to me. His nose is broken, and his face is sticky with blood from his nose to the bottom of his chin. To the right of the stage, bodies are being carried out of the crowd on makeshift plywood pallets torn from the camera tower and from the wall around the stage.

As the set ends, I make my way backstage and head through the crowd to the VIP bleachers to hear Rage Against the Machine. Notable for a heavy, abrasive machine-shop sound that blends metal-inflected guitars and rap-derived textures, Rage Against the Machine is also the only band at Woodstock 99 with its own reading list, an eclectic mix that includes *State and Revolution* by V. I. Lenin, *The Culture of Narcissism* by Christopher Lasch, *Play It as It Lays* by Joan Didion, *What Is Communist Anarchism?* by Alexander Berkman, and *The Lorax* by Dr. Seuss. They are also the only avowedly Marxist rock band to have a number-one album on the Billboard charts. The cultural contradictions involved in playing agitprop to a $150-a-ticket crowd are evident from the band's first song, "No Shelter," a Marcusian anthem and also the band's contribution to the soundtrack for the movie *Godzilla*. It is at once an angry grad-student rant, denouncing the cultural myth that "buyin' is rebellin'," and also proof of the near-infinite capacity of that culture to absorb any criticism as long as it features kick-ass guitars. A bare-chested guy wiggles his head of long black hair in the VIP aisles below me next to a well-muscled Woodstock 99 security guard as Zack de la Rocha prowls the stage and declaims:

> *Coca-Cola is back in the veins of Saigon*
> *And Rambo too, he got a dope pair of*
> *Nikes on*
> *Godzilla, pure muthafucking filla*
> *To get your eyes off the real killa.*

As Rage Against the Machine socks it to the Man, a woman near me pushes her blonde curly-haired toddler daughter back and forth in a stroller while complaining bitterly about the non-VIPs who are being allowed into the bleachers by the security guards and about her husband, who took her son off somewhere in the crowd and left her alone with her daughter in the bleachers. She takes out a joint and lights up, hoping the pot will calm her down. At the sight of the joint the child's eyes go wild. Twisting around in the stroller, she tries to grab it from her mother's hand. Her mother moves the joint a fraction of an inch and continues puffing angrily away. Rage Against the Machine's set is just about over. At the end of their last song, they burn an American flag onstage.

"If the rain comes, stay away from the towers. Stay away from the towers." The voice belongs to John Scher, Michael and Ossie's partner, the man who put the concert bill together. He is worried about the safety of the crowd but is also really getting into the role. John Scher standing onstage and warning the crowd to stay away from the towers is a scene from the movie playing in the promoter's head. Past midnight, the band Metallica comes onstage and chants, "So what! So what! Who cares? Who cares?" while launching long, slow guitar riffs into the night.

I get up from the bleachers and walk through the VIP gate into the parking lot behind the stage, where the raw, mind-bending power involved in bringing so many rock bands to an air force base is nakedly visible. Clamped to the top of mobile production trucks, or to thin metal poles, the few production lights throw dark, uneven shadows across the asphalt, making the parking lot seem bigger and emptier than it does during the day. In front of the All Mobile Video truck, ten or fifteen people are sprawled on the pavement, watching a thirteen-inch color television set wired into the pay-per-view feed from the stage. In the shadows are hundreds of empty buses, parked in double rows stretching out for at least a quarter of a mile. In the darkness behind them are the oversize tractor-trailer trucks, the kind that transport forklifts and boilers and other heavy industrial equipment on superhighways at night. Nearly thirty feet tall and a hundred feet long, they rise off the asphalt like enormous hi-tek basketball sneakers, with sleek curvy lines crafted from cold impenetrable steel. Standing here, I sense a tiny but still recognizable element of danger, the slightest fractional expectation that two or three seconds from now the headlights will turn on, the motor will roar to life, and the truck will accelerate forward, crushing everything that gets in its way. If this expectation is proof that paranoid fatigue has set in, it also expresses the more rational thought that there is a power in this world that operates just outside the horizon of our understanding and whose motives and actions have little if anything in common with my own.

———

California is buggy, buggy, buggy, buggy.

At 3:00 A.M., the airplane hangar is still filled with kids on ecstasy drinking water and twirling glow sticks and dancing to the music of DJ Norman Cook, a tall, balding, stoop-shouldered man who appears on the video screen above their heads in grainy, black-and-white stop-action shots that show the DJ with his arms spread wide like a cable-access-show prophet in a dirty raincoat, his eyes rolling back in his head.

California is druggy, druggy, druggy, druggy.

My energy has definitely turned manic, and dancing to the music of Norman Cook seems as good a way as any to come down. An hour later, when I am feeling tired and my heart rate has returned to normal, I sit down on a folding chair on the tarmac. Within a two-minute interval I note:

A shirtless guy with a Chinese dragon tattooed across his chest.

An unhappy-looking girl in tight denim shorts.

A couple having sex under a trailer.

A fat guy in a gray "Woodstock Athletic Department XXL" T-shirt.

A bearded kid in a bright orange jumpsuit who is stripped to the waist, exposing a large, unhealthy-looking gut.

T-shirts advertising Nike, Puma, Adidas, the Grateful Dead, Abercrombie & Fitch, and Graffix bongs.

A pudgy crew-cut kid, fourteen or fifteen years old, who pauses by my chair for a moment and retches a mouthful of water at my feet.

I meet Sara, twenty-two, and Tammy, twenty-three, from Morristown, New Jersey. (Perhaps because of the drugs around, or because of the simpler shame of having paid so high a ticket price to wallow in garbage and feces for three days, some of those I speak with refuse to provide last names.) They greet me with the unapproachable glare of a pair of cheerleaders in a high school lunchroom. I ask them if they have enjoyed camping out. "It's not really camping," Tammy answers. "Camping, you have your own area, and a grill."

An hour later, I see a man about twenty-five years old, with marble-white skin and perfectly proportioned limbs in which every last muscle is visible. His fellow concertgoers, returning from the rave with black balloons filled with nitrous oxide, give him a wide berth, because he is stark naked and obviously out of his mind. Standing in the middle of the runway, he whirs his arms over his head as if signaling to his fleet of invisible helicopters that it is time for them to land. As I stand and watch from a distance of twenty feet away, he walks up to two frat boys in T-shirts and starts talking excitedly about something. After less than a minute, the bigger of the two frat boys has heard enough. His eyes go wide, he looks down at the boy's exposed genitals, then draws his fist back and punches him hard in the face. *Splat!* I can hear the sound very clearly from where

I am standing as the boy's nose bursts open, and then I hear *Crack!* as he hits the pavement facedown.

"Bro, he's dead," one of the concertgoers says as he passes. The kid isn't moving, and his face is turning blue. People stop to snap pictures with disposable cameras, but no one stops to help. A medic arrives and radios for help, then tries mouth-to-mouth resuscitation. By this time, a crowd has gathered to see whether or not the kid is dead. They argue with an older poncho-wearing hippie couple, a husband and wife who live in the area and who have come to Griffiss Park to help out.

"You've got to help people like that," the woman is saying. "He's stoned out of his mind. He's not aware of what he is doing." The kids around her are unconvinced.

"Fuck him. He's crazy, man," answers one of the frat boys.

The guy standing beside me, wearing a fishing hat and a red plaid shirt, mutters something in disgust. His name is Andrew ("just Andrew"), he is twenty-three, and he is majoring in political science at Virginia Tech. "There's no brotherhood at this event at all," he says. A team of medics have arrived on the scene, and as they bend down to check the kid's pulse he stirs, turns over on his side, and releases a stream of urine onto the runway. Andrew came to Woodstock 99 as a volunteer, he says, and when he arrived he helped decorate his station with flowers and paintings and a poem he wrote about giving back to the people who came to Woodstock before. His eyes are red, he explains, because two nights ago someone offered him a bong hit while he was making his rounds of the campgrounds, which he accepted, and which was laced with PCP. Twenty-four hours later he is just beginning to come down. Which doesn't matter much, he adds, because there is nothing for the volunteers to do except watch kids freak out on bad trips or sell drugs or punch one another in the face.

Ten feet in front of us, the kid on the runway has regained consciousness and is flailing away at the medics, who are trying to pin him down.

"That's not the right way to handle him," the hippie woman in the poncho is shouting. As the medics tackle the kid and then tie him to a stretcher, other kids with cameras continue snapping pictures.

"This is the promoters' fault," Andrew says, when I ask him why he thinks tonight was so bad. Scheduling three heavy-sounding bands one after the other was wrong. "It incites people to beat the shit out of each other," he says. "They built people up to be in a frenzy. They should have calmed people down before sending them out here to be with each other."

We stand and talk by a pool of raw sewage, which appears to be twenty feet long and perhaps a foot deep, and which is flowing downhill into the closely packed tents to our left. As we talk, kids are wading through the stream to get to their tents without appearing to notice or to care, as if they have somehow been convinced that wading through raw sewage is just a normal part of the Woodstock experience, like the heat and the dust and the drugs and the $4 bottles of water and the bands. Andrew walks over to a metal gate, and together we pull it out of the ground and lay it flat across the stream, so that the kids can cross without stepping in shit.

On my way to the backstage press area the next morning, I find two young kids sitting cross-legged in the dirt with a disposable lighter, burning sticks of incense and looking like they have washed up on the island from *Lord of the Flies*. The taller one is Patrick Kraus, fifteen, and the shorter one is Ben Smith, thirteen. They are from Shelter Island, New York, and they are wearing expensive-looking sunglasses. Ben Smith's sunglasses are the coolest, they agree. "They're Oakleys," Ben says, before he corrects himself. "Faux-kleys," he says. "They aren't real." They came here with someone's older sister, as a reward for getting good grades last semester, and have been consuming pizza and buffalo wings, along with the Nutri-Grain bars, fresh peaches and pears, potato chips, and the two six-packs of bottled water that they brought with them from home. People on drugs are scary, they say. Naked men are scary, too. The bare-breasted women are okay, they blushingly admit. They are well-spoken and obviously responsible, and so it makes sense that their parents felt safe sending them off to a three-day-long rock concert with somebody's sister. One of their fathers went to Woodstock in 1969, they say, and told them how a vendor was charging too much for hot dogs, and so the crowd burned down his stand.

In the backstage press area, the rapper Everlast, his broad knuckles covered with tattoos, is being interviewed in the Woodstock.com tent. He looks exhausted but speaks passionately for a few minutes about how it is wrong for the promoters to be charging $4 for a bottle of water. A few minutes later the sky opens up and it starts to pour. I run for the shelter of an empty canvas tent, where I am joined two minutes later by John Entwistle, my least-favorite member of The Who, my favorite band in junior high. The spider around his neck, he says, was a gift from Who drummer Keith Moon. What John Entwistle actually says, however, is really anyone's guess, since it is impossible to piece his statements together into sentences that reasonably scan.

"Thirteen dogs," he says, bending forward and tipping his sunglasses down, so that I can gaze deep into his rock-star eyes. "Gloucestershire. Thirteen dogs. New band. Deep-sea fishing."

"I draw serious ass," he adds.

"I draw seriographs," he repeats, when I look puzzled. "I draw cartoons. Of rock stars."

The secret I have learned is hardly surprising. After thirty-five years of standing next to banks of amplifiers on concert stages with the loudest band in the history of the world, John Entwistle, a gentle, intelligent-seeming man, is basically stone deaf, and mumbling sentence fragments is simply his way of answering whatever question might have been asked. I shout my next questions into his ear, and he smiles, grateful that he no longer has to mumble.

"Why is this concert so awful?" I shout.

"Festivals always are," he says. "There's no sound check. You're lucky if the equipment works. The first Woodstock was horrible, too."

A few minutes later, we shake hands, and John Entwistle and his new bandmates pile into the back of a red Ford Taurus and drive off through the sheets of rain to meet with John Scher, perhaps the one person, out of all the thousands gathered here, who might be able to tell me exactly what went wrong.

John Scher is a short, balding guy in a sports shirt who looks and talks like an average suburban New Jersey dad. "It's been an awesome experience," he says. "I'd say the third time was the charm." Because my laminated reporter's pass doesn't allow me onto the stage, he is standing on a metal walkway five feet above me and shouting down into my ear. And because John Scher is not a bad guy, he eventually steps down off the platform, takes my arm, and guides me through the crush of people with all-access passes, past the Red Hot Chili Peppers, the show's final act, to the parking lot, where we can talk face-to-face. I ask the promoter what exactly went right here.

"Nobody got in for free," he says. "I think the Wall itself set a great tone. The kids really responded to the Wall. They saw that so much love and care went into the Wall."

I ask if there is anything that he might have done better.

"Commercial opportunities were not exploited as fully as they might have been," he says. "If there was one really big corporation . . . ," he says. "The right tasty, big corporation that could help underwrite the whole event. . . ." He is really flying now, his expression suggests, his eyes alight with the vision of a series of brand-name concert events occurring like clockwork every five years and lasting until the end of time. "I mean, it's a great opportunity for someone," he says. "What's page A-1 of the *New York Times* worth? A-1 of the *Daily News*? You answer me that."

I admit that the front page of tomorrow's newspaper will probably be worth a lot.

"That's editorial," he says, underlining the distinction between advertising and content that the universe of events like this one has all but erased.

The Red Hot Chili Peppers are moving smartly through their closing set, but John Scher is still standing out in the parking lot, giving generously of his time, caught up on a white-capped wave of euphoria that comes at the end of a day that has most likely made him several million dollars richer. "It's an emotional rush unlike anything else," he says, moving from the emotionally connected language of Michael Lang to far-seeing business-speak to his own more earthy and sentimental vocabulary as a tall man in a navy shirt comes up beside him and waits until his answer is done. "In this plugged-in, technologically driven world, a world that's becoming more and more impersonal, well, you can't get any more personal than this. And a million people watching this on TV who know that there are real, living, breathing human beings on the other side. It's euphoric. And you can say, 'Schmuck, you don't know if you've made money yet.' But it is euphoric to know that in 1999 this can still happen."

The man in the navy shirt is growing more and more impatient, and finally he interrupts.

"John, they've turned over a Mercedes in front of the house. Ten guys turned it over." The meaning of the sentence is clear. "The house" is theatrical jargon for the crowd. John Scher looks interested for a moment, and then he turns his attention back to me.

"It's an older Mercedes," the man in the navy shirt continues. "But still, John, that's a nice car."

John Scher shrugs. That an older Mercedes has been turned over near the stage doesn't make sense to him. Why should one lousy German car ruin the enjoyment of standing at the exact center of the loudest, biggest, most powerful, marketable, attention-getting, historically resonant rock and roll event on the planet?

"Where?" he asks.

"In front of the house."

John Scher turns back to me. "You get to do something that hardly ever gets done," he explains. "And not only did no one get in for free but almost no one tried."

I thank John Scher for his time and walk out into the crowd, where the kids are now holding tens of thousands of candles in the air. Close to the stage, not so far from where the Mercedes was turned over, the fires have already started, and the crowd rips down sections of the camera tower and the Wall to feed the flames. I stand in the crowd for a little while longer, until the Red Hot Chili Peppers end their set and lead singer Anthony Kiedis appears onstage again and peers out at the fires in the crowd. "It looks like *Apocalypse Now* out there," he says.

Twenty feet away from where I am standing, the flames are licking at the camera tower. The camera teams are already gone. To my right, the crowd has broken through the barrier that divides the concert lawn from the backstage area, rendering all the many varieties of laminated passes obsolete. A thin line of policemen is moving across the field, driving the crowd away from the fires. A shirtless white kid with a beard is standing nearby, gathering debris from the ground to feed the flames. I ask him what he wants, and he looks at me for a moment, then shrugs, as if the answer should be obvious to anyone who has spent the last three days and three nights in this place.

"I'm going to burn it down," he says, and as I think to myself that it is hard to argue with that, he catches my eye and raises his fist before heading back to the fire.

Through the flames I can see the eyes of hundreds of concert-goers, mostly white, mostly male, with goatees and baseball caps, looking nervous, or frightened, or panicked, or alight with the simple anticipatory pleasure of throwing another piece of wood on the fire. Over by the runway a crowd is plundering food-service trailers for free cans of Sprite. The scene around me will be described in newspapers the next morning as a riot. Yet what is happening now feels oddly light. The real riot happened over the last three days, not as a single, chaotic, explosive event but as a slow-motion disintegration of the bonds that might hold 225,000 people together. What happened isn't really that hard to describe. With nothing larger to hold them together, the crowd endured the heat, and the sewage, and the trash, and the drugs until all that was left was the feeling of standing in a tired, dirty crowd of people at the end of the day and knowing that you are alone. The selfishness and irresponsibility of the promoters are obvious: that they have created this particular scene, of bonfires burning on a darkened field beneath Peter Max's gigantic mural, is really no better and no worse than what most other people here would have done in their place. As the line of policemen in blue uniforms pushes forward, I realize that it is time to leave.

Speeding south on the interstate in the luxurious isolation of my borrowed Volvo S80 sedan, built like a leather-lined sarcophagus with eight tiny, cunningly concealed speakers blasting rock and roll, it is hard to imagine a better ride. As the publicity materials in the folder messengered to my house by Volvo Cars of North America have assured me, the S80 sedan is the safest car that Volvo has ever built, equipped with features that make reckless driving apparently risk-free. If I am sideswiped by a Honda, or plow my Volvo S80 sedan into the concrete median around the next curve, a sensor-activated Inflatable Curtain (IC) hidden inside the roof lining of my car will deploy in a maximum of twenty-five milliseconds to cover the upper side of the doorside interior, and the WHIPS seat folds back at an angle of up to fifteen degrees, reducing acceleration forces by as much as 50 percent.

What I am thinking now is that safety is an illusion that we use to cover up some larger absence in our lives. The real causes of the

Woodstock riot, if that's what it was, are larger than personal ir-responsibility, or bad music, or poor planning, or greed. The riot is a footnote to a larger story. Thirty years ago something vital and lasting—an idea of the good life and how to live it, what marriage meant, what to eat, what family and community were for, and who was supposed to take care of the kids when the parents both work—broke apart, and now, thirty years later, that sense of connection, of some overarching narrative frame for our lives, still hasn't been repaired or replaced.

Notes from Underground

Outside the air is thin and cold, and behind the porthole-shaped sheets of double-thick Plexiglas the landscape of northern California looks like a string of yellow Christmas lights floating on a featureless sea. Inside the cabin, at a height of 30,000 feet, I have stowed my tray in its upright and locked position, and a drawn but efficient-looking stewardess in a navy-blue jacket has brought me a plastic cup of water with ice. As we pass over the Silicon Valley to the San Francisco Bay, the ground below lights up with the jewellike sparkle of tens of millions of Americans flipping lights on and off, watching TV and operating personal computers, using phone lines and digital cables to access the information-age bounty of words and images and other digitally rendered information speeding across thousands of miles in fractions of a second. I sip the water and look out the window and admire the millennial promise written on the ground below, a glowing geometry of vertical and horizontal lines laid out like circuits on a microchip. No one will ever be lonely. No one will ever be bored.

The red light flashes overhead, and the plane descends 25,000 feet in only a few minutes through the bad-weather clouds that muffle the runways of Portland, Oregon, six months out of every year. The optimistic tenor of my airborne thoughts is darkened by a sudden burst of paranoia, triggered by the noise of the engines and air filters and the flicker of the in-flight movie screens. It is the modern-day equivalent of a belief in magic, I am thinking: the expectation that in a minute or so the plane will touch down lightly on the rain-slicked runway instead of exploding in midair. If a blind trust in the operation of complex technological systems is a necessary part of modern life, it has only recently become the rule. Twenty years ago, most Americans could still fix their own cars and build their own radio sets. The wing of the plane is silhouetted against a bank of heavy fog, and jutting out from the edge are antennae transmitting data relating to the speed of the plane and the angle of descent. Inscribed on the wing is a black-bordered warning, "Do not walk outside this area."

Outside the Greyhound station in Portland, a knot of six or seven dispossessed-looking men stand in the rain smoking cigarettes, waiting to board the bus to Eugene. The nylon gym bags at their feet advertise the brand names of Adidas and Nike. After thirteen hours in the air, I am happy to get on the bus and sit in the dark, the nighttime conversation washing over me like the sound of a television set coming through the walls of a neighboring apartment. Every few minutes the channel changes. There is the blonde woman behind me, who left home at fifteen and who is now twenty-five and who ordered grilled-cheese sandwiches at the station for her two young children. She is leaving town to stay with her mother and to escape her old man. Behind her is a pretty girl in a red flannel shirt, a long-haired traveler, a group of Mexican laborers, and a well-muscled guy with a shaved head and bulldog features. His black nylon sweat suit whispers in the dark whenever he moves. "He is a known drug user with a known propensity for violence," he reads out loud from a copy of a restraining order obtained by his girlfriend. He has lost everything he owns, he tells me, including a split-level ranch house worth $140,000, and now he is headed for Las Vegas. His nylon sweat suit is emblazoned with the Nike swoosh.

Eugene is an old logging town in the Willamette River Valley, forty minutes by car to the Oregon coast and an equal distance from the Cascade Mountains. The Greyhound there from Portland takes approximately two and a half hours, and listening to the rise and fall of the voices on the bus, I can still taste some slight residue of anxiety left over from my hours on the plane. Most people I know have similar moments of dissonance, when some snippet of reality suddenly seems unfamiliar and strange. The frame slips by a fraction of an inch, just enough to admit some new possibility that wasn't there a moment before and that usually vanishes again a moment or two later. What is revealed in the gap, between these moments is that the world you perceive is actually the result of a more or less complicated bargain that you strike with yourself over time. If the slippage happens often enough, and with enough force behind it, your experience of reality can shift in a permanent way.

In the late sixties and early seventies, Eugene became the favorite destination for thousands of middle-class sons and daughters of California and elsewhere who arrived in hand-painted school buses and VW vans to search out unspoiled nature and live close to the land, practice communal living, manufacture handicrafts, smoke pot, meditate, chant, and raise a generation of children outside the corrupting norms of American consumer culture. It is a place where you go when your angle on reality shifts and the slippage becomes too great to sustain your previously settled approaches to life.

I am going to Eugene today so that I can see how the new age of human interconnectedness and beneficent globe-spanning technologies looks from a weird angle that first attracted public notice on November 30, 1999, when several hundred black-clad anarchist demonstrators materialized out of a protest march in Seattle, smashing windows, spray-painting anticapitalist slogans on walls, fighting running battles with police, and otherwise turning the birthplace of Bill Gates into the Waterloo of the World Trade Organization (WTO). Three weeks before the World Trade Organization met, Eugene's chief of police, James Hill, warned the Seattle police of the likelihood of violence by Eugene anarchists, who had attacked the local NikeTown the previous fall and tossed boxes of sneakers into a fountain. At home the anarchists' tactics had ranged from the familiar to more disruptive and original expressions of alienation. They smashed the windows of a local restaurant and health food store, spray-painted graffiti on walls, and disrupted a city council meeting by vomiting on Eugene's mayor, Jim Torrey. On June 18, 1999, nearly 400 demonstrators smashed computer screens and stereo equipment, and then snake-marched through downtown Eugene, attacking the local Taco Bell and several local banks, spray-painting slogans and throwing rocks at police.

By November 30, Eugene's anarchists were a phenomenon of global interest and concern. "The black bloc was a loosely organized cluster of affinity groups and individuals who roamed around downtown," a communiqué from the ACME Collective later explained, "pulled this way by a vulnerable and significant storefront and that way by the sight of a police formation." Using spray paint, slingshots, sledgehammers, crowbars, paint balls, eggs filled with glass-etching solution, and other devices, the black-masked demonstrators attacked storefronts bearing the logos of brand-name corporations. Their message was a spirited blend of radical environmentalism, leftist anticapitalist sentiment, and slacker disdain for consumer culture. Their targets included "Levi's (whose overpriced products are made in sweatshops), McDonald's (slave-wage fast-food peddlers responsible for destruction of tropical rainforests . . .), Starbucks (peddlers of an addictive substance . . . harvested at below-poverty wages . . .), Warner Brothers (media monopolists), [and] Planet Hollywood (for being Planet Hollywood)."

What the pictures from Seattle captured was an anger whose true sources had less to do with Nike's treatment of its third-world labor force or other objectionable practices than with a broader, more unreasoning sense of being trapped in a net. My favorite picture from Seattle showed a group of kids perched on top of the entrance to NikeTown, using hammers and chisels to pry off the brushed-steel letters that spelled "Nike." At least one of the kids was wearing Nike sneakers on his feet.

The logic expressed in the photograph from Seattle is familiar to all of us. It goes something like this: You can't help wanting Nike sneakers. At the same time, the desire to smash the windows of NikeTown makes sense, too. Not because Nike sneakers are bad, or because they are manufactured in Third World countries by slave-wage labor, but on the more general principle that someone should be held responsible for the feelings of absence and compulsion that overwhelm us all at some point or another in our lives and that are not our fault, or even the fault of our parents. Rather, they are the products of the addictive vacuum that has manifested itself through the combined karmic energies of millions of flickering cathode-ray tubes and flat LCD screens and soothing advertisements whose carefully screened and focus-grouped vocabularies and images have insinuated themselves into the weave of the generational unconscious almost since birth. These advertisements—of children swimming and laughing in the Technicolor playgrounds of Aetna, and of twenty-somethings in khaki swing-dancing for the Gap—are powerful magnets for human desires, for health, human companionship, good times, and eternal consolation.

Advertisements are our secular prayers. And when our prayers aren't answered, the spiritual energies released by so many unmet desires focused on a single photograph or frame of film can result in a kind of corporate-sponsored low-pressure system, a Bermuda Triangle of the emotions whose human inhabitants feel abandoned and alone.

The Whiteaker neighborhood, where most young radicals in Eugene live, is a working-class district of 6,000 people, with a 20 percent minority population and perhaps an equal number of disenchanted white bohemians in their twenties and early thirties. Because of the city's location west of the Cascades, the temperature in Eugene rarely falls below thirty-five degrees, but the darkness and the damp combine to make it seem much colder. The rain begins in late October and lasts through the end of April. The streets are often shrouded in fog, and the sky is gray for six months out of the year.

In the Whiteaker police substation, Officer Tod Schneider sits at his desk and tries to explain what has happened to the neighborhood where he lives. A stoop-shouldered man whose liquid eyes and sensitive features make him an unlikely candidate for police work in most areas of the country, he still vividly remembers the moment when the slippage began. "When it first went sideways for me," he says, "was two years ago, when somebody, a self-titled anarchist, decided to attack me personally, as a representative of the police department and of their own projections of what police represent in the world. That involved smashing my windshield, spray-painting my car, slashing my tires, and so on."

As he recites a litany of facts relating to the destruction of his car, it is easy to forgive Tod Schneider his most apparent human weakness, which is his desire to be seen as a decent, well-meaning, liberal person. He doesn't carry a gun, he says, and is puzzled that someone might target him as a representative of repressive authority. After arriving in Eugene wide-eyed and broke as a nineteen-year-old hippie in 1971, he went to the University of Oregon and then spent the next ten years working for the White Bird Free Clinic and other local social-service agencies, caring for burnouts, acid casualties, and other needy members of the community. In 1986, after joining the police department, he cut his hair short and bought a modest wood-frame house in Whiteaker, where he lives with his wife and children. The books above his desk, including an oral history of the civil rights movement and *Common Ground* by J. Anthony Lukas, suggest the personal library of a middle-aged sociologist at the nearby U of O.

Like everyone else in Eugene, Tod Schneider is puzzled by where the anarchists came from. His account includes the radicalization of local environmental activists after a two-year-long occupation of a tract of forest land at Warner Creek; the violent response of local police to a 1997 demonstration against Symantec, a high-tech company that had moved into Eugene and cut down forty trees; the influence of a local anarchist writer named John Zerzan; the fact that Eugene is now the third least affordable housing market in the United States; and the closing of Icky's Tea House, a refuge for local anarchists, street kids, and punks. At night, the streets of downtown Eugene are home to a floating population of approximately 400 street kids, many of whom were abandoned by their parents. The kids sleep in shelters, under highways, in cars, in $30-a-night motel rooms on Sixth Street, in newspaper-recycling boxes outdoors, and in the woods. Two years ago a local teenager named Kip Kinkel shot and killed his parents, and then opened fire on his classmates at school.

"The forces that used to be right there, the people sitting on their front stoops and watching the neighborhood," Schneider says, propping his worn Hush Puppy loafers up on a corner of his desk, "that kind of world is all but gone. You don't feel comfortable telling some kid you don't know, 'Hey, knock that off,' because you're afraid that you're going to get sued or accused of something. Kids are taught not to talk to strangers, which is one of the worst crime-prevention errors in the history of the country, since 90 percent of offenses against kids are committed by relatives, not strangers. Strangers are the guy running the corner grocery store or the neighbor across the street who maybe you could turn to and say, 'I need some help.'

"The more those things go away there's less of a sense of trust and safety in the community and more of a sense of isolation," he continues, gesturing out the window to the darkened storefront across the street. "Isolation is one of the things that makes people go crazy. That's why you punish prisoners by putting them in solitary confinement. And we do that in our culture by isolating people from each other."

Houses in Whiteaker are often drafty and poorly insulated, and the warmth of the old-fashioned steam radiators and electric heaters is rarely strong enough to make much of an impression on the weather. After only a few days of unending damp, bundled in Levi's jeans and a hooded sweatshirt, I become aware that the distinctive generational emotions of foot-dragging anger, thwarted desire, and suicidal disconnection familiar to fans of brand-name Pacific Northwestern rock bands like Nirvana and Pearl Jam in the early nineties, as well as to partisans of Nirvana's more current and folkishly introverted cousins on the Olympia-based Kill Rock Stars label, have at least as much to do with the rain and fog and cold as they do with the decay of the American social fabric or the anomie-inducing properties of an Internet-based society. The weather here is enough to make anyone miserable. The cold and the damp enter into your body, and after a while it is impossible to stay warm.

Randy and Kari's apartment, on the first floor of a wood-frame house in Whiteaker, is a warm and cozy oasis of silk-covered cushions on the floor and printed cloth tapestries that hang from the ceiling. With the silk cushions and the tapestries and the array of Christmas lights blinking from an assemblage of tree branches in the corner, it feels like a cross between an artist's loft and a Moroccan tent. Nearly everything in the apartment is made by hand.

"The helicopters show you where the action is," Randy explains. A videographer who grew up in Eugene as the child of hippie parents, he now goes by the name Tim Shadowalker, or Shade. He shot the footage we are watching on a handheld camera, as part of his ongoing attempt to capture the experience of the Whiteaker community in its own language, free of commercial sponsors and ads. The hour-long films he makes are shown on Sunday nights at the Grower's Market under the title "Simmeren Stew."

Lying on the floor, in a heavy woolen sweater and a black wool watch cap to keep warm, Randy looks like a hip but scary children's book character with a mournful face and unwashed, shoulder-length hair. Images of smashed windows and policemen in riot gear fill the screen above his head as Kari steams vegetables in the kitchen. Next to the sink is a plastic container for vegetable matter to be used as compost for the nearby community garden.

"It was the ultimate paintball game," Kari says, entering the living room with a plate of steamed broccoli, as the camera pans across the storefronts belonging to Starbucks Coffee and Fidelity Investments. "No real bullets. The gas does get to you after a while."

Below a spray-painted anarchy sign on a wall is the message WE ARE WINNING. The camera pans to a shot of the front page of the *Seattle Times,* with the headline "Shoppers Barred in Retail Core," and everyone laughs. The camera glides to a boarded-up Urban Outfitters, then to a long, artistic zoom-in shot of the McDonald's golden arches enveloped in a floating cloud of tear gas. The people in the room have seen this tape before. They are spellbound by the images on the screen, by scenes from a fairy tale in which good conquers evil and the edifice of American consumer culture comes crashing down. The evil empire of Starbucks and McDonald's, with their bad food and soul-sucking corporate architecture, is conquered by the forces of sustainable living and tofu pâté.

May the force be with you!

Which is not to say there is anything wrong with the idea of crafting your own life, spending time with close friends, buying only what you need and walking lightly on the earth in torn sneakers. It's only that the fantasy of escape from the market is part of the logic of consumer society, and anyone who thinks different is likely to get screwed.

Seeking refuge from the dizzying logic of late-stage capitalism, I wander into the bathroom of Randy and Kari's apartment, where I find a painted scene of swimming dolphins whose peaceful, intelligent gaze draws attention to the toilet, whose unflushed basin testifies to the importance of saving water. The mirror is decorated with dried leaves and a handmade relief that asks, "Why is it called Black Market?" and answers, "Because it's Beautiful." The dolphins look down their bottle-shaped noses from the wall. It is only a matter of time, they are thinking. Global warming is real. In a thousand years the polar ice caps will melt, the cities will be flooded, and the virgin forests of the Cascades will be buried underwater. Nike sneakers,

McDonald's wrappers, computers and television sets, and all the other detritus of human civilization will petrify at the bottom of a vast and all-encompassing ocean ruled by dolphins with brains two or three times the size of the vanished race of dirty human beings.

In front of the television set, Randy sips apple-ginger juice from a Mason jar. He is talking about his parents' divorce and about the recession of the late seventies, when the national housing market crashed and the mills in Eugene shut down.

"I remember once it was a cheese factory," Randy says of Eugene's attempt to attract new industries. "Everyone was bummed out about the cheese factory not coming to town. After that it was a chocolate factory. I remember seeing people lined up around the block, waiting to fill out applications at Taco Bell."

Thanks to tax breaks offered to Symantec, Hyundai, and other local high-tech employers, Eugene is now a magnet for highly paid workers from the Silicon Valley who drive BMWs and Land Rovers through town and enjoy facials and massages at the Gervais day spa down the street. As Randy and Kari see it, Eugene has become the regional headquarters of a rapacious consumer culture that destroys the environment, exalts material values, and pacifies benighted slobs by filling their minds with corporate-sponsored sludge. Beneath the handmade aura of their lives you can feel a powerful undertow of anger at a world that they feel powerless to change. They will always be the losers, because they are virtuous but weak, and their opponents—Starbucks, McDonald's, and Nike, the Eugene police force and the local yuppies—are ruthless and strong.

"I love to use a lot of the TV stuff as a mirror reflecting back on itself," Randy says, as the riot policemen onscreen club a knot of peaceful demonstrators who have chained themselves to a post. "I want people to walk down the street and freak the fuck out. I want them to walk into McDonald's and look around and wonder, 'How do I get the fuck out of this system?' "

After a week of lead-gray skies and the chill and the damp, it becomes difficult to separate the readings on my internal barometer from the influence of the weather. The weather is everywhere, inside and out, throwing a depressive blanket over the streets and erasing the divisions between my own depression and the fog outside. John Zerzan, Eugene's leading resident anarchist theorist, keeps his apartment immaculately clean, with a pile of correspondence stacked neatly on his desk and a television set turned to face the wall. He is a clear-eyed man in his fifties, with a gray beard and an intellectual stoop to his shoulders, who graduated from Stanford University in 1966 and then spent the rest of the sixties in Haight-Ashbury, working as a social worker and later driving a cab. He is the favorite teacher of Eugene's anarchist youth. "Everybody was happy, aren't we happy, let's watch the Nelsons and listen to the canned laughter," he says, recalling his childhood in the suburbs of northern California. "And I remember thinking as a kid, 'I'm being strangled here. I don't get it. I don't like it. Goddamn, what a death trip this is.' "

What Zerzan wants is a total collapse of industrial society, which will bring about a return to a primitive state where men will be at one with nature. "It's becoming unbearable," he says, "the real emptiness of this society. I think it's been emptied out by technology . . . the erosion of the moral self, the erosion of personal responsibility . . . you get to a place where all kinds of horrors are possible. . . . You're just an object of the micromarketing stuff, and there's no real attempt to give anybody the truth about anything, because, after all, what does it matter?" He is patient and well-spoken, referencing the works of Jacques Ellul, Herbert Marcuse, and Exene Cervenka, lead singer of the LA punk-rock band X. Still, there is something in the tilt of his head, in the Slavic cast of his features, and in the gentle despair in his voice that makes me think of a candlelit character in a novel by Turgenev or Dostoevsky. The words all seem to run together, to the sound of the rain falling on the wet ground outside. "Now everything is so mediated, real experience is being evacuated at a dizzying speed," he continues. "People wonder why there are forty million people on antidepressants. The kids are just getting dosed up on this stuff, because Ritalin isn't enough, and the teenage suicide rate has tripled in the last decade."

There is something unbalanced in his argument, in his desire for radical industrial collapse, that is causing my attention to wander from the television set facing the wall to a nearby Exer-Cycle to a neat pile of correspondence on his desk. "I felt a real connection with him, in an almost mystical way," Zerzan says of his most famous correspondent, Ted Kaczynski. In addition to writing to Kaczynski, he also visited the Unabomber several times in jail. "There were just a whole bunch of biographical parallels," he explains. "We were both kind of whiz kids in school, we both renounced the academic route, we had brothers who were social workers, our fathers both died of cancer. . . ." He sees Kaczynski as an ideological ally and as a modern-day John Brown. "They ain't innocent," he says of Kaczynski's victims. "Which isn't to say that I'm totally at ease with blowing them into pieces. Part of me is. And part of me isn't."

Zerzan lived a quiet life in town until one night three years ago, when he gave a speech at the University of Oregon in defense of his friend. Among the audience of more than six hundred people were two local high school students who soon began coming over to Zerzan's house after school. Anarchist graffiti began appearing on the walls downtown, along with flyers calling for Kaczynski's freedom. An anarchist newsletter, the *Black-Clad Messenger*, followed a few months later, along with the attack on the local Nike store and the conversion of a number of older radicals to the anarchist cause. The resurgence of the radical activist spirit in the Whiteaker neighborhood reminds Zerzan of the late sixties. It has also caused problems in his relationship with his adult daughter, who lives in Eugene.

"To her, well, the sixties were about a lot of people who didn't grow up, and then they had kids, and they didn't do right by them," he explains sadly. "When I was living in the Haight, I wasn't mature enough, and if I might say, her mother wasn't either." Their daughter's childhood, he readily admits, was not a happy one. It was the generic childhood lived by a generation whose parents' attachment to the dogmas of freedom and social justice and personal fulfillment meant a wholesale abandonment of the responsibilities that traditionally go along with getting married and having children. No child would ever willingly choose to be a part of such an adventure, no matter how righteous the cause. The big ideas and the lighthearted fucking were not entirely meant for their benefit. Even a nine-year-old could understand what was happening, even if her mother took longer to figure out the score.

"She and her mother disappeared, " Zerzan remembers, "and for some years I didn't know where they were." A gentle man, he is still pained by the memory of losing his family. "The bottom line is, I wasn't there when she was a kid," he says. "She sees me, rightly, as a fraud."

Seekers, drifters, and train-hopping street kids often make their way to one of Whiteaker's communal apartments, where they can meet like-minded people and find a bed for a night or a week before moving on. It is the kind of world you can build in when you are in your twenties before you have kids and no one is particularly inspired, a place where rents are cheap and people work part-time jobs as waiters or telemarketers, ride their bikes, and cook at home. You change your name. You stop eating meat. You stop drinking milk. Everything you own fits comfortably in the pack that you carry from town to town and from apartment to apartment. Most of the apartments you live in have no furniture. The Ant Farm is home to Food Not Bombs. The Pleasure Palace is the local anarchist house. Environmental activists often wind up at the Ranch House, home to the leaders of Earth First! or at Bipi's House, a center for the tree-sitters at Fall Creek who have built a network of platforms two hundred feet above the forest floor. Broadway House is home to a floating collection of radical activists, and Blair House is a magnet for punks. Underground houses shelter activists affiliated with ALF and ELF and other radical animal-liberation and environmentalist groups responsible for raids on animal-research labs and incendiary attacks like the one that burned the Boise Cascade timberlands management center to the ground. A large number of people in town wonder if they're under police surveillance. You might meet someone five or six times before you invite him over to your house.

At Out of the Fog, a local vegan coffee shop, a bearded wanderer who calls himself Air takes careful sips from a glass of steamed soy milk as he describes his recent tree-sitting experience at Fall Creek. He spent eight or nine days in the forest and has spent the last month in town sleeping on a friend's porch. Before that he worked for a year on a farm in Maine, then traveled in a motor caravan across the country, promoting opposition to the WTO. He is thirty years old, polite, and soft-spoken, and wears a black woolen watch cap pulled down low over his brow. "I'm someone who works for a positive transformation in society," he explains as three local environmental activists heatedly discuss the latest episode of *The X-Files* at the next table over. It takes a while for Air to feel comfortable enough to talk. He grew up in Chicago, he says, where he went to a private boarding school and then to the University of Illinois. His movements over the past ten years are a map to the confluence of urban radicalism and the environmental movement, taking him through Berkeley, Minneapolis, New York, Austin, San Francisco, and Philadelphia to the environmentalist blockades at Headwaters and Warner Creek. In 1998, at Grizzly Creek in northern California, he was sitting in the forest with another activist named Gypsy when an angry logger felled a tree in their direction. Gypsy died. "The highest path is to put down roots somewhere, grow your own food, and lead a connected life," he says. "At the same time, I seem to fit in really well with a traveling lifestyle."

Working your way into the radical activist network in Eugene takes patience and time. The community is private and suspicious, and operates on many levels, reaching out to new arrivals through a variety of formal and informal institutions that also function as a sifting process separating the committed activists from the floating population of transients, addicts, unstable personalities, and possible spies. The literature on local activities and causes available at local coffeehouses and vegan restaurants welcomes newcomers into an alternate universe of affiliations that celebrate the pleasures of commercial-free consumption. "You hear the most amazing stuff on RFC," explains a leaflet for Radio Free Cascadia, the local pirate radio station. "Paranoid rants, out-of-print jazz albums, talk shows on anarchy, drunken tales of bondage, news from Cuba, erotica read over techno beats, and stolen movie dialogue."

The *Black-Clad Messenger*, the leading voice of anarchism in Eugene, serves up a peppery blend of anarchism, environmentalism, and animal rights mixed with the unwashed aroma of a roomful of fifteen-year-old kids who are enjoying their very first experience of punk rock. One author indicts "the Nuclear family—incubator for imbecility," while others call the WTO protests "a carnival of reformist lies" and provide instructions for making "a Paraffin-Sawdust incendiary" that is "almost as effective as napalm against combustible targets, but it is slower in starting." A parable entitled "Ship of Fools" targets the errors of reformist liberalism. The author is Ted Kaczynski. The radical end of the environmental movement is well represented, too. "Not only will the American people be robbed when the Anti-Forest Service steals their trees and sells them to Zip-O Lumber of Eugene," an anonymous tree-sitter warns from Fall Creek, "but all the creatures who live here will have their homes stolen . . . to please a handful of fat-ass-evil-eyed money-mongruls." An essay entitled "Beyond Civil Disobedience" by "Snap Dragon" puts the radical environmentalist case in more sober terms. "Most [civil disobedience] campaigns require enormous amounts of time and resources but achieve very little," the author writes. "Making these compromises would be justifiable if we were getting something significant out of it, but we don't."

Once you are past the age where everything unmistakably matters, it is easy to lose track of time, most often with the more general goal of escaping from your life. There is the thrill of dropping in from the sky to unfamiliar places. There is the excitement of meeting new people and forming instantaneous bonds that allow you to penetrate their personal thoughts and record them on tape. There is the practice of emptying out your own center to create whatever space is necessary, a process that combines a zenlike appreciation for the void with the interpersonal dynamics of carnival sales. Or the no less false and manipulative but still emotionally connected position that allows you to shut off your empathic radar, disengage, and turn the people you meet into characters whose dreams and aspirations are revealed in a sentence on the page. The sense that time is slipping away is plastered on the telephone poles and on the walls of the Blair Street Free Space. "On time? Are we? What if we weren't?" a poster asks. "Losing track of time is so common many humans carry a 'time keeping' device."

When I start to feel really bad, I rent a room at the Eugene Hilton, which has a minibar and a color television set, and where I can lie under the blankets with the heat turned up as far as it can go. I listen to the rain on the window, and talk to friends in Los Angeles and New York about new apartments, professional successes, marriages and break-ups, the stuff of the life I have left behind me. I watch the actress Winona Ryder interviewed by Charlie Rose. Winona Ryder has a willful fragility that suggests that she might lose track of time or forget her own name, or conversely, that she might enjoy hurting others. Charlie Rose, the thinking man's talk-show host, is impossible to watch without wincing—he is the incarnation of the self-satisfied pretender who prides himself on speaking into the mirror every morning to properly enunciate the names of the faraway places where Americans are spreading the Gospel of Peace. Without the parade of certifiably successful people who appear on his show every evening, discoursing on a stunning variety of subjects like guests at a dinner party in a fever-dream, where no one speaks the same language or has read any of the same books, Charlie Rose would be just another drunk old man with a thing for young actresses. But there is still hope. Charlie Rose, if you are listening, why not give Eugene, Oregon, a try?

On the other hand, it is also true that people who spend their lives performing for the camera are trained to use their features to express a very limited range of emotions, a kind of universal sign language that links our modern media rituals to the ancient arts of Kabuki or Noh. Bare of traditional masks, their faces act like powerful magnets, attracting millions of stray emotional particles charged with envy, hatred, boredom, and fear. The incessant bombardment by these particles cannot help but have a negative karmic impact. Imagine what it would be like to be a famous actress, or the actor David Cassidy, whose comments on the mutually emasculating aspects of celebrity in the final issue of *Ben Is Dead* keep me up for a few more minutes after Charlie Rose goes off the air. *Ben Is Dead,* which I purchased at Green Noise Records before checking into the Hilton, is a kind of twentysomething samizdat publication that has a lot in common with the anarchist literature I have been reading in Eugene, and might qualify as the decidedly unslick but equally celebrity-obsessed antithesis of Charlie Rose.

"They owned my likeness and put it on everything," the former teen idol recalled, below a picture of his dreamy, wondering, twenty-year-old face, "plastic guitars, pillow cases, trading cards, lunch boxes, dresses. My mom told me my aunt was riding the escalator at Macy's and as she got off there was a huge cut-out of me with these dresses hanging there. David Cassidy dresses."

". . . Was there ever a point [when] you felt unworthy?" the interviewer wondered. No trace of any hesitation can be found in the transcript.

"No."

On Sunday nights at 7:30, activists and new arrivals gather in the upstairs meeting room at the Grower's Market for "Simmeren Stew," Randy Shadowalker's weekly look into the community's collective unconscious. Sitting in the dark on folding chairs, or sprawled out on the carpeted floor, a packed house of approximately seventy-five people whistle and cheer as shots of smashed windows and menacing policemen appear on the screen. Images of the communal triumph in Seattle morph with dreamlike random logic into a *Hard Copy* segment denouncing electroconvulsive treatment, footage of the Gulf War, an air freshener ad from the seventies, buffoonish shots of Mayor Jim Torrey, and scenes from Nazi propaganda rallies cross-cut with ads for new cars. Yet beneath the more general mood of sitting paranoid and stoned in the bluish glare of a television set at four in the morning there is also a very serious message.

"The power of advertising," a talking head with a British accent explains, "is based on its monopoly of the cultural space within which we think about ourselves." He speaks in the serious yet off-hand tone that signals the presence of a truth received by all right-thinking people with a sympathetic nod of the head. The truth of these sentences is a powerful adhesive, bonding author and listener together in a common apprehension of superiority to the ignoble consumers of cable TV and Big Macs.

"Wow, my teeth feel really clean!" explains a chirpy blonde in a toothpaste ad. Everyone laughs. A dog wanders through the narrow aisles, making its way up to the front of the room to lie down at the foot of the screen.

Against the evils of television ads and consumer culture are hand-held shots of everyday life in Eugene, of familiar people and places that advertise the pleasure of removing yourself from the economy of fat-filled muffins and hormone-saturated cow's milk and entering a world where the muffins are all-natural and the soybeans are harvested by hand. A waitress at Out of the Fog explains the principles behind "Buy Nothing Day," when the cafe offers food and beverages for free. She is followed by scary infrared shots of shoppers at the

local mall and by a deodorant ad warning, "If he smells, it's over."
Freeing your mind from the grip of deodorant commercials is a step
on the road to true liberation from new car ads and Styrofoam con-
tainers and the even more subtle oppressions inherent in late-stage
capitalism. From the passivity inherent in television viewing. From
your parents. From the pain, fear, and boredom that are part of
everyday life.

Only Mother Nature is pure. "Prairie dogs are cooperative," explains tonight's feature, an hour-and-a-half-long film about black-
tailed prairie dogs. "They give off different calls for different
predators. They groom each other." The audience's appreciation for
the rodents' communal, crop-destroying behavior is matched by
their disdain for the human residents of the Great Plains.

"No!" someone shouts, as a rancher in a cowboy hat lines up a
prairie dog in the sights of his gun.

Huddled out in front of the Grower's Market, a small knot of new arrivals are discussing their plans for the rest of the night. "We can stay
at the Ant Farm or the Broadway House," a boy in a denim jacket offers. No one in the group is over twenty-five. They have come to Eugene, they explain, to join the tree-sit at Fall Creek. The boy in the
denim jacket came from Colorado. His name is Brian, and he heard
about Eugene from a guy at a punk show in Denver. He thinks that
Eugene would be a cool place to live.

Standing off to the side, staring out into the fog, is a blond guy in a
hooded patchwork corduroy sweatshirt. He is wearing the hood up
to obscure his face. When I ask him his name, he looks at me for a
long moment. When I ask him his name again, he answers, "A medley." He grew up in Massachusetts, he says, and went into military
intelligence when he was sixteen. He was discharged from the army
two years ago, he says, with a bone-marrow disease that costs $3.2
million to cure. Recently, he decided to stop taking medication.
There is something spooky in his manner that I can't quite place. He
is twenty-four years old, he says, and as I look into his eyes again I
can't help doing the math. Eight times four is thirty-two. Eight times
three is twenty-four. A moment later, he adds that his parents got divorced when he was younger. I ask him how old he was. He thrusts
his hands deeper into his pockets. He was eight.

"They thought I was trying to kill myself," he says of the night when he was living in Brooklyn, New York, and decided to climb the Williamsburg Bridge. "I told them that I wanted to see trees. You have to climb a bridge if you want to see the trees. That's why I came here."

In the forest outside Eugene, activists live on sheets of four-by-eight plywood with caches of food, wood-powered rocket stoves, and emergency cell phones 200 feet above the floor of an endangered stretch of old-growth forest known as Fall Creek. They have been sitting in trees for the last two years under the banner of Red Cloud Thunder, the environmental organization directed by Deane Rimerman, which has moved beyond the letter-writing campaigns and civil disobedience tactics of the mainstream environmental movement to the idea of a sacred community that will use any means necessary to defend endangered lands.

"When I first showed up in town in '95," Rimerman explains, "there was a whole community of people organized around defending Warner Creek." At Warner Creek activists blockaded roads by clipping their hands to buried concrete blocks until a court finally issued an injunction against cutting the trees, pending an investigation of claims that the forest was a refuge for spotted owls, whose territories are protected by the Endangered Species Act. In response Senator Slade Gorton of Washington attached the so-called salvage rider to the 1995 Recisions Act, releasing timber sales that were held up by the courts, "notwithstanding any provision of law."

It was then, Rimerman says, that environmentalists and anarchists began to come together. In March 1998, under the authority of the salvage rider and the Northwest Forests Plan, the Clinton administration approved the sale of the Fall Creek tract to Zip-O Lumber of Eugene. The first tree-sitters were discovered on April 20, 1998. Rimerman's goal now is to save the forest and to build a community of younger activists who feel comfortable operating outside mainstream environmental campaigns and, when necessary, outside the law.

"They are basically kids who are searching to find something in their lives," Rimerman explains. "They are coming out of typical American families, which are broken families." Some are mentally imbalanced. Others are young addicts who come to the forest to get straight, or street kids who vent and scream and start fights in order to get attention. "Most of the kids that come out here visit once and leave," he says. "They don't have the social skills. They are much more pissed off at the world." Fall Creek offers these kids a sense of community, a place where they can work, cook, and live together as defenders of pure and ancient forest lands.

"Trees and forest symbolize unconditional love," Rimerman explains. "That's not something that many of these kids have felt before in their lives. You take them out of this hate-filled society, and you give them a place where they can be free."

You have to believe that trees have a life of their own to see why the environmental movement is such a powerful magnet for the innermost dramas of a generation that grew up talking to their television sets. As objects of one's own internal process, the trees stay pure and absolute forever. Trees represent freedom, or the love of your parents in its most perfect and ideal form. Every tree is the same. You can become one with the trees in a way that would be much more difficult to accomplish with the poor and oppressed. What you are left with in the end is a pure and unbounded field for projection. You can erase the boundaries that exist between yourself and the world, and vanish completely inside your own head.

In an anonymous apartment in Whiteaker, with beige wall-to-wall carpeting in the living room, bare mattresses on the floor, and a copy of *The MIT Guide to Lock-Picking* in the bathroom next to a tube of Tom's of Maine toothpaste and a bar of Residence Inn soap, a group of activists is talking about the direction of their lives. "Right now there are people living in trees, because it's something they believe in," explains a crew-cut young activist in a red T-shirt and denim overalls who gives his name as "Free." He is limber, fidgety, and charismatic, in his late teens or early twenties. He speaks with a clarity of purpose that he carried with him from the suburbs of Los Angeles, where he grew up, to the forest at Fall Creek.

"I'm not fucking happy," he says when I ask him about his state of mind. "I'm not sitting in fucking trees in the cold because I'm happy. Going to jail doesn't make me happy. Going to jail is a bad experience. We're out there because we know we're right."

Two years ago Free was the first activist to enter the forest at Fall Creek and climb a tree. "I have a very close relationship with my parents," he says. "They're very supportive." His father was a federal officer who retired to spend more time with his children. While Free was sitting in a tree at Fall Creek, his parents led a write-in campaign that sent 15,000 e-mails to Bill Clinton and Al Gore asking them not to cut the forest. His relationship with his parents is close, he says, because he and they agree on many issues, and perhaps also because his older brother killed himself at eighteen.

"I was the rebellious one," he says. "And I know that they treated me in certain ways to prevent me from ending up like my brother."

His embrace of anarchist philosophies, he says, began on the first day of his Introduction to Sociology class at Cal State Long Beach, when the professor walked into the classroom, put his books down on his desk, and delivered a speech that has stuck in his mind ever since.

"The reason you are here," his professor explained, "is because we live in a society that can't find meaningful, constructive, engaging work for enough of its members. So we made up this thing called college to delay your entry into society for four or five years while training your minds to accept a system of discipline and control that benefits a very small percentage of the population. When you graduate, most of you will wind up working as waiters or dishwashers, or in other mindless, dead-end jobs. You will come home at night, get drunk, and watch television. Welcome to sociology."

The other activists in the room had similar moments of radical disconnection, when they realized that government was a form of oppression, or that politicians lie, or that their parents' lives were empty, or that the culture around them was too fragile and meaningless to support the true weight of a life. "We can live off dumpster garbage, and we do, and we still live better than 90 percent of the world's population," one activist says. They don't want to give their names because they were present in Seattle and are involved in other activities at which the authorities might look askance. Seattle was the culmination of months of careful planning and organization. "It went just like the instructions said it would go," one activist says.

"My mom shops," another activist offers. "She creates scenes at the stores. It's embarrassing. She likes to buy the latest technological gadgetry for the home."

"They all know the latest character in Pokémon, that stupid fucking game."

"They all know that the pink Teletubby is gay."

Kooky, an activist in a tall mohawk, red long johns, and overalls came to Eugene three years ago after following the Grateful Dead. His given name is Steven Hesline. "The society we're living in now is so fundamentally rotten," he says, "that it's become almost commonplace for kids to walk into school with guns and murder their classmates, or for people to walk into work and open fire on their coworkers." His interest in social change, he says, began with jobs at the Ralph Nader–inspired network of Public Interest Research Groups, or PIRGs, which took him to Massachusetts, New York, and nearly a dozen other states. As a member of OSPIRG, he spent a year of his life working to expand the Oregon state bottle bill, which promised consumers a nickel for every bottle they returned to stores.

"The Snapple bill," he says, reclining on the floor. "That's what broke me. The beverage industry slammed us with their stupid, misleading ads. It left me feeling ripped off. What I realized after that was that my life spent as a liberal activist was so full of contradictions and hypocrisy that I couldn't recognize myself anymore. Do I believe that affirmative action is good? Do I believe in gun control? In my mind I was always against state regulation of firearms, but I would open my mouth and out came the usual liberal bullshit party line."

At the same time, Kooky admits, the life of an activist in Eugene is hardly free of contradictions. "People here are unwilling to acknowledge their privilege," he says. "So we create this nice alternative universe of organic community gardens and vegan restaurants and places to have coffee, because we have the luxury of doing that, and it's nice. But it doesn't really answer the question of how to live a life."

The fantasy of total secession from the corruption of human existence is what brought the hippies to Eugene in the first place, and after a week there I find an old, gray-haired hippie named Skeeter, who lives in a single room with a futon on the floor. His gentle, scratchy voice, mellowed by years of meditation and smoke, reminds me of an old record. A mosaic of handwritten notes and elephant pictures covers nearly every square inch of space, as if the inside of his head had exploded onto the walls.

"We sent groups of people in VW buses up to Oregon, looking for land," he explains. "We were saving money, putting our money into a bank account, that was the scene." As a student at San Jose State, Skeeter belonged to an audiovisual collective that filmed protests, engaged in street theater, and demonstrated against the war in Vietnam. In 1971 the collective picked up en masse and moved to a three-story farmhouse in Eugene, where they worked the land and made their own tofu and mayonnaise. He later became a child-care worker and looked out for many local kids who are now his neighbors in Whiteaker. He sees their mood as similar to his own but filled with a lot more darkness and despair.

"I threw my rocks," he says. "I threw rocks at Nixon. And all these years later part of me is still bummed out that I did. I threw rocks through windows in San Francisco," he continues, "and there were secretaries behind those windows who had nothing to do with corporate power or the Vietnam War. Someone might have gone blind."

No matter how many times I nod, as I gently try to change the subject, Skeeter stays focused on the rocks he threw thirty years ago, which appear to be symbolic of some deeper trauma or disturbance that he wants to set right. A young anarchist leader named Marshall Kirkpatrick, a bearded kid in his early twenties, listens attentively from a seat on the floor. Skeeter flutters his fingers and fixes Marshall with a drawn-out hippie stare. He takes another drag on his hand-rolled cigarette, then turns to me and launches into a story about watching a group of long-haired hippies stomp a man into the sidewalk one evening in Berkeley on the suspicion that he might be a cop.

"So there's a bunch of freaks beating on this guy, and I'm saying, 'Are we going to lynch the guy? Are we going to kill him?' It scared me," he says. "I worry now about the people I might have hurt. As I've gotten older, I worry about people taking things into their own hands."

• • •

The world outside of Whiteaker is an ocean of false desires, summoned up by sorcerer-like technologies and by the destructive greed of big corporations. Under the circumstances, the best thing to do is to ride your bicycle to work, scale back your desires, and lead a modest life in which no one gets hurt. Thou shalt not eat meat. Thou shalt not buy new clothes. Thou shalt not dominate or oppress. The commandments prevailing here have less in common with anarchism than they do with the teachings of Jesus Christ, or with the absolutist psychology of children whose parents split up or sold out or otherwise succumbed to the instability inherent in modern marriage, as amplified by the social experimentation of the sixties and the selfish and self-satisfied individualism of the seventies, eighties, and nineties.

Eric and Whitney are in their early twenties and live together in a ground-floor Whiteaker apartment, where they spend a lot of their time. They work at the tofu factory in town. Whitney draws and plays the piano. Eric watches television and reads. One of the major questions they face is how to reconcile their emphasis on personal freedom with the possibility that someone else might get hurt.

"Eric's a lot more free with where he places things," Whitney says, in her precise way of speaking. "My space is my space, and I like it a certain way."

"Whitney lets stuff build up inside her," Eric says, rubbing the reddish stubble on his chin. "She'll get mad about a lot of things and say nothing."

Eric's parents divorced when he was four years old. He left home at fifteen. "I remember distinctly sitting there in freshman math class and thinking, 'My parents don't have any money, I'm not going to college anyway,'" he says over the low throb of the stereo. He moved into a rooming house, where his neighbors included a guy who wrote for the *Earth First! Journal*, a crazy guy who wandered the streets, and a recent graduate of the University of Oregon with a bachelor's degree in science who worked as the day manager of a Carl's Jr. franchise and was happy to have the job. The gentleness in Eric's voice is the type that conceals some deeper anger. "Today I spent an hour watching a Q and A with reporters who covered Governor George W. Bush in Texas," Eric says. "They were all talking about George W. Bush. The big question was whether George W. Bush has the gravitas to be president."

What seems most obvious about Eric and Whitney is that they are bound to each other by a shared love and by a shared anger. "My mom is one of the true Silicon Valley drunks," Whitney says of her childhood in Cupertino, California. Her father runs a high-tech firm. "He makes bank, but that wasn't what he wanted to do," she says. Their Puritan renunciation of unsavory appetites and impulses is matched by an emphasis on personal responsibility, which they contrast favorably with the attitudes of their parents. "They've been able to be okay with society," she explains. "They are happy with that and with the cost of what they bought, and I truly admire that in a way, that they have the necessary level of ignorance to make that work."

The life that Eric and Whitney make together, they believe, will be free of all hypocrisy and compromise. They will be honest and straightforward with each other. Poverty, imagination, and strength of will will help keep unruly desires in check. They will stay pure in a compromised world of superflammable materials made with slave labor in Third World countries, where half the people on the planet live on incomes of less than two or three dollars a day.

"I make fifteen thousand dollars a year before taxes," Eric says. "I try to spend my money in the neighborhood. I try not to buy new stuff. Which accomplishes nothing, sadly. I ride my bike to work." He leans back on the couch, taps the end of his hand-rolled cigarette, then talks some more. After a while, the simple, declarative sentences in which he sums up his life take on the solemn aspect of a hymn to the saving grace of limited desire. A palpable sense of release accompanies his words. By limiting his own desires, he has found a way to rebuke and strike back without hurting anyone else.

"I work in my little job," he says. "Spend my time with little people. Try to be as light on the earth as I can. As light on other people as I can." There is something Christlike in this approach, and also something sad and scared. I want to tell Eric that boredom, fear, and crushing disappointment are simply part of life, and that it is better to live in the world as it is than to shut down inside and live in a cave. In an hour or so, at three-thirty in the morning, I will return to the Hilton, turn the heat up too high, and fall asleep with the television on.

The Spaceman Falls to Earth

It feels great to be back in Montreal, that wonderful old city, where the French girls sashay past the stony gaze of the apostles in cheap cotton dresses that show off their fine round asses, on the way to one of the great old bars on St. Catherine's Street, where the writers, drug dealers, and old-timers hang out and everybody still loves the Spaceman. Stretch, breathe in deep, flatten your back against the fake green grass, look up for a moment at the space-age retractable roof of the stadium, then raise your arms over your head and touch your knees to your chin. The Spaceman winces. He gazes up at the empty white vault of Montreal's Olympic Stadium, which he once compared to a giant bidet.

Everybody loves the Spaceman. They love the Spaceman in Montreal, Alberta, and British Columbia, and they love him in Boston, Maine, Vermont, and throughout New England, Puerto Rico, Venezuela, and everywhere else where the Spaceman played baseball. In the seventies, a decade when the nation and its national pastime came unstrung, the Spaceman was a hero to Mitch Melnick and to every other kid in North America who liked to get stoned and watch baseball. The Spaceman made the All-Star team with the Red Sox; followed Nixon to China; sprinkled marijuana on his organic buckwheat pancakes; championed public transit, Zen, and zero population growth; and underwent a vasectomy. When Cincinnati Reds' manager Sparky Anderson announced, before the sixth game of the 1975 World Series, that Reds' pitcher Don Gullet was so good that he would wind up in the Hall of Fame, the Spaceman was ready, as always, with an answer.

"Gullet is going to the Hall of Fame," he said, "and I'm going to the Eliot Lounge," a famous old-time Boston dive that, as it happened, was owned by my uncle, who presented me on my eleventh birthday with a Bill "the Spaceman" Lee autographed baseball, which I kept on a windowsill by my bed. The baseball helped me sleep better at night. The Spaceman shared my dislike for coaches, teachers, parents, and other authority figures at a time when the eternal, unvarying laws that kept the adult universe in motion had lost whatever cosmic sanction they might have formerly enjoyed. The Spaceman was bigger than baseball. He salted interviews with lines from his favorite songs by Bob Marley and Warren Zevon, who returned the favor by transforming one of the pitcher's acerbic postgame commentaries into "Bill Lee," a poetic assessment of the condition of man:

You're supposed to sit on your ass and nod at stupid things
Man, that's hard to do
And if you don't, they'll screw you
And if you do, they'll screw you, too.

Still, it was hard for any Red Sox fan to ignore the darker side of the Spaceman's approach to the game. Up three to nothing during the sixth inning of the seventh game of the 1975 World Series, Lee experimented with an "eephus ball," or "Leephus ball," a lazy zen blooper that took forever to reach home plate, allowing hitters plenty of time to drive themselves nuts by contemplating the limitless possibilities for embarrassment inherent in a pitch that any Little Leaguer could hit out of the park. They swung and missed, or lifted harmless flies, then slammed their bats to the ground and cursed at the Spaceman. This time, however, Reds' first baseman Tony Perez waited for the ball to arrive, timed his swing perfectly, and launched the Spaceman's pitch over the right field fence, costing the Red Sox the World Series. The Spaceman was funny and smart, but he was also a fuck-up. In 1981, the Red Sox traded Lee to the Expos, who released him after he walked out one afternoon to protest the trade of his second baseman, Rodney Scott.

Alone in the infield on a weekday afternoon, Bill "the Spaceman" Lee is a boyish-looking fifty-year-old man with a lopsided grin that leads directly to his vulnerable belly, grown fat with decades of free lunches and beers. When he is finished stretching, he ambles over to

the dugout, changes into a bright Hawaiian shirt, and heads over to
first base to tape a few spots for the Montreal Expos' pregame show
with his producer Mitch Melnick, whose second daughter was conceived on a beautiful evening at the Spaceman's home in the mountains in Craftsbury, Vermont.

"God, he loves baseball more than anything," Melnick says. "But
he was smarter than the people who ran the clubs." He sticks out his
foot, and looks down at the fake green grass beneath his patent
leather shoes.

"So I guess his career never ended on his terms," he says. "And I
don't know if he ever really got over it."

The Spaceman loves driving. He knows the roads of Vermont like
the back of his hand. "That's Mount Mansfield right through there,"
he says. "That's the highest point in Vermont." On our way back
from Montreal, he calls out the names of every tree that he passes,
oak, maple, birch, lemon spruce, white pines, a Whitmanesque
litany that leads him in turn to naming the different types of rocks
that make up a mountain, which leads in turn to the deeper subject
of geological time. Man is only a speck in the universe, he observes,
before returning back to earth. "That's a sugar house," he says.
When you find a moth in your syrup bucket, he adds, that's when you
know that maple syrup season is over.

The house the Spaceman built in Vermont is light and airy, perfectly situated on a hill to take advantage of the surrounding 270-de-
gree wraparound views of the mountains. The air smells like cow
shit, and the woods are loud with mating frogs. At the top of his
driveway is a garden, which is guarded by a battered scarecrow in
an old baseball jersey with "Lee 37" printed on the back. A lot of
ex-spooks, CIA types, have moved up to Craftsbury, he says. They
are scared of cancer, the big C, and they need someplace to grow
their pot. "They need it for the chemo," he explains. He clenches his
jaw, and out comes the nasal sound of a suffering ex-spook holed up
in the woods. "I need some of that Acapulco Gold," he croaks. "I
need some of that good stuff to take away the pain." Nails cost a
nickel a piece, he says, as he leads me around the house to admire
the construction. A dried-out three-foot-tall marijuana plant is
nailed to a beam inside the garage.

In the kitchen, the Spaceman's wife, Pam, is carrying a tray of burritos past the brushed steel refrigerator, which is covered with a jumble of magnetic letters that have combined to spell out "Anna loves Jason." Anna is seven years old, with light blonde hair, perfect features, and a bright, determined smile.

"Did you have a nice trip?" Pam asks. She is an attractive woman in her late thirties who looks like an older version of her daughter, with a wider face and darker, dirty-blonde hair. Taped to the counter where she's preparing dinner is a photograph of the Spaceman dancing in a bar. Underneath the picture Pam has written a poem:

Swing your pig
Round and round
Don't let your gut
Hit the ground.

Lee points out the poem and shrugs. On the drive back from Montreal, the Spaceman had casually mentioned that the Lees are getting divorced in six weeks, after which Pam is planning to move to Atlanta to be with her boyfriend, a pilot for Delta Airlines. The Spaceman's new girlfriend lives in Calgary. They met a month ago, and they are now completely and totally in love.

"You better tell your lawyer to stop sending me those stupid letters," Pam says. The Spaceman's answer is lost somewhere in clanging of pots and pans.

"What was that?" Pam asks.

"Nothing," the Spaceman answers.

"You think that you've said something funny, and that I won't think it's so funny," Pam says. "That stupid grin is what gives you away."

Then she shows me to the spare bedroom, where she fluffs out a pillow and apologizes for being bitchy. Bill sleeps down the road, she explains, at the house of a farmer named Bruce Reed, who met the Spaceman at a Red Sox fantasy baseball camp and sold him the land on which they built their home. In the morning, the Spaceman comes over to read the paper, drink his morning coffee, and see his daughter, Anna.

"He lives in his own universe," Pam says. "He walks into my house, drinks my coffee, and takes a shit in my bathroom. There's something wrong with his connection to reality. What he doesn't understand is that in six weeks we're getting a divorce, and then I'm taking Anna to Atlanta. I have no idea what's going through his head."

"Pitching is a cardiovascular thing," the Spaceman says. "It makes you secrete endorphins, and the endorphins get you high." As the Spaceman paddles his canoe down the river, his faithful dog Winnie paddles along by his side. "There are three mallards, big long drakes, jumping up there," he says, pointing in to the marshes. "Yes, pitching is a great way of getting high."

The Spaceman's aunt played professional baseball for Fort Wayne, Indiana, and Minneapolis in the forties and fifties. She was also a pitcher, and by the time the Spaceman left Little League she had taught him to throw a curve, a changeup, and a sinking fastball. He went to USC, and became a star. "We made so many great comebacks," he remembers. "You get this feeling of immortality, and you want to keep on going forever." Then he switches course. "Two players went to the University of Southern California," he says, as Winnie flushes two more drakes from the marsh. "Two players graduated in 1968. Two players were All-Americans, and two players led their teams to national championships. They both wore the number 32." He raises his paddle from the water. "Me and O. J. Simpson."

Two years later Lee was pitching in the majors. "Everyone was wearing sport coats and pinstripes," he remembers, "and I thought I was back at USC in my college days. Baseball was very Southern, very conservative. It didn't really reflect what the rest of the country was all about." The only college graduate on the Red Sox, the Spaceman earned his nickname after he shared his enthusiasm for the latest Apollo landing with reporters after a win in Cleveland. The Spaceman's enthusiasm for the moon landing struck the Red Sox beat reporters as odd, as did his enthusiasm for organic food and Zen Buddhism. When Judge Arthur Garrity announced his determination to bus poor black children to schools in the city's white neighborhoods, the Spaceman praised the judge as "the only man in Boston with any balls," which made him a hero to the liberals in Cambridge, but did little to increase his popularity in the city's Irish bars.

Another factor, of course, was the drugs. If ballplayers have always liked to drink, and older players took speed to cure hangovers, the drugs that players took in the seventies did little to improve their performance on the field. A dentist from Lexington provided the Red Sox with a connection to Malindrot, the licensed Swiss manufacturer of pharmaceutical cocaine. Players smoked pot and dropped acid. None pursued the nightlife of the seventies more avidly than the Fraternal Order of the Buffalo, a tight-knit society made up of Red Sox pitchers Lee, Rick Wise, Jim Willoughby, Ferguson Jenkins, and outfielder Bernie Carbo. The Order was also united by their lack of affection for Don Zimmer, the Red Sox manager, a crew-cut throwback who loved the dog track and had a metal plate installed in his head. If the Order was baseball's equivalent of Hogan's Heroes, Zimmer was their Colonel Klink.

"We're coming into Anaheim," the Spaceman remembers, "and Willow got paranoid about something, and he ate his stash. So we're standing in the outfield, and he can't move. He's catatonic. And Al Jackson comes by, and says, 'Jesus Christ, what's wrong with Willow?' And we say, 'Oh, he'll be all right.' And he says, 'We'll get him out of here. Don't let Zimmer see.' So we put him in the bullpen to keep him safe. The day goes along, and he still can't move. He's paralyzed. Finally it's late in the ball game, it's eleven o'clock at night, and Zimmer calls and says, 'Get Willow up.' Willow throws maybe six or seven warm-up pitches, and then comes into the ball game. He staggers, throws one pitch, and the guy hits into a ground ball double play. From a coma to a save."

Don Zimmer would have his revenge. One by one, the members of the Fraternal Order of the Buffalo were traded until only the Spaceman remained. On December 7, 1981, the Spaceman was traded to the Expos for a reserve infielder named Stan Papi.

"I cried," he remembers, as we load the canoe back onto the top of his car. "I probably would have been mayor. I would have banned the private vehicle from downtown Boston and turned it into a walking city. I felt betrayed."

The Spaceman remained confident that he would always pitch in the majors, even after he was released by the Expos. "I was a left-hander, I could throw strikes, I never walked anybody," he says. "My shoulder was back. I was in great shape." He wrote letters to every team in the National League. Only Hank Peters of Pittsburgh wrote back.

"He said, 'We've got enough problems without you,' " he remembers. The Braves promised a plane ticket to spring training, but the ticket never arrived. Dick Williams, who managed Lee in Boston, promised a tryout with the San Diego Padres. When the Spaceman arrived at the Padres training camp in Arizona, he found that he had been barred from the field by the team's owner, Ray Kroc, who objected to the Spaceman's public defense of marijuana.

"They can't do that," the Spaceman answered.

"I'm sorry, Bill," the manager said.

"What happened next," the Spaceman remembers, "was that I went back to the van where Pam was waiting. Now we had stopped at McDonald's on the road, and every time Pam eats McDonald's she has to shit real bad. So she had shit in the McDonald's bag. I took the bag, and I threw it over the fence onto the field. And that's how we left Yuma." After that, the Spaceman sold his house and went down to Venezuela, moving on to Moulton, New Brunswick; Red Deer, Alberta; and Sydney, Nova Scotia. When the Senior League started up in Florida, he went down to Winter Haven to serve as player, coach, and general manager, and to bring the Fraternal Order of the Buffalo together again for one last hurrah.

"They gave us twelve days to get in shape," Lee remembers. "We were all thirty-five, forty years old, mostly forty and older. We were the oldest team down there. Cuellar got hemorrhoids, so he was on the DL. I lost both my catchers on opening day. They both blew hamstrings." Bernie Carbo was a drunk. Jim Willoughby was a diabetic and couldn't play. The team lost on opening day, and then they lost again.

"Then we had a big game out in St. Petersburg, but our left fielder was totally worn out or hung over, and he got sick, and was throwing up, and I wanted Carbo to go out to left field," he remembers. "And he started crying. He was all strung out, and all he could say was, 'I didn't bring my glove.' So I had to play left field. The first ball hit to me, I do a cross-over step, I didn't tie my shoelaces, and I hog-tie myself and fall flat on my face."

On the way back home, he tells me about a dream he had, in which he shot Pam's boyfriend in the balls. The shotgun shells were filled with McCann's steel-cut oatmeal.

"Then he went down on his knees with his hands in front of his nuts," the Spaceman says, "and I shot him right in the hands. And then I ejected the third shell, and then I butted him right in the mouth. And I pulled out his incisors. And I said, 'That is for alienation of affection.' "

The Spaceman pauses. "I didn't want to kill him," he explains. "But he ends up dying of blood poisoning. So they bring me in front of the magistrate, and they said, 'How do you plead?'

"And I say, 'I plead not guilty.'

"And they say, 'But you murdered this guy.'

"And I said, 'But I didn't know he was allergic to oatmeal.' "

In his dream, the Spaceman's sentence is suspended. He leaves the courthouse a free man.

After dinner, Pam and I go for a walk together with the Lees' golden retriever Winnie, after which she has promised to find me some marijuana. A little marijuana after dinner is a time-tested way to take the edge off the weirdness, she says. Living in the Spaceman's house in the middle of his divorce is definitely a weird experience. Winnie romps down the logging road, a muddy trail leading deeper into the woods and then up into the mountains. During the height of the marijuana-growing season, Pam says, you see the spotter planes flying low over the mountains and the fields. A few weeks later, the men go out with their pickup trucks and return with a harvest that might bring in enough cash to sustain their families through the winter.

When she first met the Spaceman, she says, she was working in a dentist's office in Montreal. She was twenty years old. Her father, the former head of the Bathhurst International Paper Company, had died of cancer the year before.

"That was when cocaine was big," she adds, in the matter-of-fact voice of someone who lived through the eighties. It was the Spaceman's last season in the majors, and she would go to the ballpark for half an hour, and then cut out to a local bar and snort some lines.

When the Spaceman was released by the Expos, they went to play in Alberta, and then Argentina. The towns got smaller, and their bank balance shrank.

"He needed a stage," she says. "He needed to play baseball." The small towns didn't bother him, she says. "The smaller the town, the more attention he got," she says. We stop at a clearing with a pond, another place for Winnie to swim. Pam tosses a stick, and Winnie paddles into the middle of the pond to retrieve it. Winnie is a retriever. She will chase the stick as long as her master continues to throw. Pam talks about moving from city to city and the fights they would have in the lobbies of provincial hotels, and how Bill's voice would always get louder whenever he had an audience.

Over Christmas, she says, she ran up $2,600 on Bill's credit card when he was in Calgary. Vermont is her home, and it is scary to think of being alone in the world, with no education and no job experience and a seven-year-old daughter.

"I've known him my entire adult life," she says. "So I can fight with him as good as anyone." She tried to bring the Spaceman down to earth and failed, and now she is angry with herself because she should have known better. By the time we get home it is dark. Anna is resting her head on her father's shoulder. Pam takes Anna up to bed. The Spaceman seems distracted. He hurt his thumb playing basketball earlier, and he winces whenever it touches the ice. There is a ball game on television, and by the time it is over we have finished two bottles of wine.

"She says, 'Daddy, why don't you sleep here,' " he says, as I walk him outside to the driveway, past the old BMW with the "Earth" sticker on the rear bumper, and then he turns around and blows me a kiss goodnight. The Spaceman's problem is that he needs to be loved, I am thinking. It hurts too much to need love that bad.

Anna Lee's birthday is Sunday. She is having a party. She is scared of the rooster. "Don't ever turn your back on the rooster," she instructs, as she chases the bird back to the coop. "My father taught me that. Don't even let the rooster see that you are scared." I push Anna in the tire swing while her father mops up the deck.

"See how great it looks?" the Spaceman asks. He stands outside and surveys his tattered menagerie. This morning the rooster attacked Winnie and lost a few feathers. There is Winnie, the rooster, a chicken, two cats, a turtle, a girlfriend in Calgary, his ex-wife in Mississippi and their three children. There is Anna and Pam.

"Now Mommy has to help," Anna says.

"Mommy is busy," says a voice from inside the kitchen. Anna goes inside, and comes out a few minutes later. Her mission is a failure. We drive to the store in Craftsbury and buy some party favors. When we come back home her mother is on the phone to the garage.

"I told them the divorce is final in June," she says, "so I want the most expensive set of summer tires you can get. I told them to order them from out of town." Anna locks Winnie in the rooster cage. Her father has to come outside to let the dog out.

Sunday morning, after breakfast at McDonald's, we visit Agway, a dark, warm place that smells like feed, and where they keep baby chicks in a cage by the register. Anna loves the baby chicks. She wants them for her birthday.

"And the baby ducks!" Anna says. "And the baby turkeys!" The ducks are the nicest, with wide, blunt bills that give their faces a quizzical expression. The turkeys are mean. The Spaceman is a soft touch. We gather up the baby chicks, the ducks, and two baby turkeys, and load them in the back of the car along with a sack of feed.

"That's lovely, dear," her mother says. "That's one of those gifts where you should really ask the person who has to take care of them." She isn't mad at Anna. She's mad at the Spaceman. He expects other people to clean up his mess. Or maybe he doesn't mind the mess, and expects other people to feel the same way. Anna takes the birds upstairs to her mother's bedroom.

"Those are the cool ones," she confides, in the flat, truthful voice that seven-year-olds use before they have learned how to lie to themselves. She peers into the box, and points at the turkeys. "See how they peck at the others. And then they stand in the corner by themselves."

Anna's friends start arriving around noon. In addition to the baby chickens, turkeys, and ducks, she gets a tub of chalk, a Beanie Baby rabbit, a box of stationery, a curly headed doll, and a battery-powered jump rope with a radio inside the handle that lights up when you jump. Anna hits Jason, and then they make up. The rooster gets loose and the children get scared. "That chicken is the dominant male in this household," the Spaceman says. He picks up two sticks, and he chases the rooster back into its enclosure. A few minutes later the pony arrives. There are eight kids at the party, and everyone gets to ride the pony twice. At the end of the party, the kids sign their names on a plush black stuffed pony with a white pen in honor of Anna's birthday. Someone hands the pony to the Spaceman, and he signs too.

"Jesus Christ, Bill," Pam says, when she looks at the signature. "She's your daughter."

The Spaceman picks up the pony, turns it over in his hands, and finds the place where he has written "Bill 'The Spaceman' Lee, Earth 2001.' "

"Habit, I guess," he says.

"He wouldn't remember his kids' own birthdays if I didn't remind him," she says. "He'd never send a postcard." The Spaceman's refusal to fight back is only making her madder.

"I had this dream last night," the Spaceman says as we drive up a logging road after dark. It's our last night together, and we have celebrated with a few more bottles of wine before taking my rental car up into the mountains. "I always have this dream about going back to winter ball," he confesses. "I end up on this island, like the lost Island of Atlantis. I've got to get there, and I don't know if I can make the ball club. This time, Tug McGraw was there." The island is somewhere off the coast of Puerto Rico, he says, where he used to play ball in the winter. His eyes shine with the memory of playing winter ball.

"It's a chance to get your shit together," he says, his voice low and relaxed over the crunch of half-frozen gravel. "You've had a bad season, you're on the disabled list or you didn't get a chance to play, you're a prospect, you feel like your summer's been wasted. Now it's late fall, and they tell you can play again in a Caribbean paradise. You get a nice little apartment. You buy a *media kilo* of *hamburgesa* and some buns. You live on the beach and meet the fishermen, and you play baseball every day." The last time he played baseball with

Tug McGraw, he says, was at a fantasy camp on the island of Captiva. Pam was pregnant with Anna.

"I think I always have these little dreams, they're always about baseball, and playing, and not getting to play," he explains. "I think that's about the mortality that is part of being human—also the fact that one eventually has to find some other form of gainful employment, which I find hard to digest."

Life isn't bad. He is the only player to hit six home runs in six consecutive at bats in Colona, British Columbia. "The fire department wouldn't play us after that," he says. Next week the Spaceman is going to Cuba. Baseball brings him a sense of peace.

"You wake up in the night, and you don't know where the bathroom is, because all the hotel configurations are different. You wake up and say, where the hell am I. But you're by yourself, there's no TV, there's no refrigerator, so you can't put on weight, you read books, anything you want to read. You're by yourself, and it's great. It's a lot like the rodeo circuit or old-time horse racing," he adds. He points out a deer camp, and then a stand of ash, the wood that baseball bats are made of. The wheels of the rental car are grinding hard against the frozen trail. Where the trail has thawed out there are patches of deep mud.

"You always play in pain, it doesn't matter whether you're old or not," the Spaceman answers, when I ask him what he's learned over the last two decades of his life. It's a question that I've been particularly eager to ask. "You have to do your stretching every day," he continues. "I've learned that you gain patience only when you get older. When you're younger, you're always trying too hard and getting hurt." He tells me the myth of the three fates, Aptos, Lethos, and Pathos. "The first one spins, the second one measures, and third one cuts the string," the Spaceman says. "And you don't have any say in the matter. You really don't. You never know when a moose is going to run across your path. I can't believe we haven't seen a moose yet." The grinding of the wheels is getting louder. The car shudders and swerves. Then it stops. We are stuck dead in the mud at the top of the mountain.

"Oh, shit," the Spaceman says.

The Making of a Fugitive

Doris Grady's rambling Victorian house in Pittsburgh has seen more than its share of would-be saints. Of all those who have passed through, she says, crowding into her wood-trimmed living room and sleeping on the tufted couches and bare wood floors, none was more gentle and devout, more sincerely devoted to nonviolence, than James Charles Kopp. A shy, red-haired man in his forties, with a quiet sense of humor, she recalls, he traveled the country with other activists opposed to abortion, rescuing babies before they could be ripped from their mothers' wombs, torn apart, and flushed into sewers. He loved classical music, books, and old movies. His favorite time to visit was the fall.

It was just last summer, Grady says, that they watched *The Usual Suspects,* a film about a criminal mastermind who assumes a dizzying succession of disguises. "It's a real mind-game movie," she explains. "Jim would say: 'Oh, listen to that. That was really smart.' "

The ease with which the prayerful defender of life has since eluded a federal-local task force of more than fifty agents, assisted by authorities in Canada, Mexico, and overseas, suggests that Jim Kopp's interest in disguise may have run deeper than he let on. Kopp is wanted on a federal material-witness warrant in connection with the fatal shooting of Dr. Barnett Slepian on October 23, 1998, in Amherst, New York. In a sealed affidavit supporting the warrant, Kopp is identified as the man seen running near Slepian's house on the day of the shooting. A car registered in Kopp's name was seen near Slepian's house, and hair taken from Kopp's last known residence, an apartment in Jersey City, has been matched in DNA tests with a hair found near the scene. The Slepian shooting has also been linked to three shootings of doctors who performed abortions in Canada, in 1994, 1995, and 1997, and to a fourth in Rochester.

"All of us who were into rescues, we have a criminal mind," Grady explains, taking a matronly sip from her tea. " 'How can I get into this building without being detected? How can I get past the guard?' " She reaches for a napkin and presses it gently to the corners of her mouth. "So you definitely exercised the criminal part of your mind. But it was for peaceful, nonviolent purposes."

Living in two worlds at once, the religious and the profane, the nonviolent and the criminal, as Grady defines it, is a way of life for those who devote themselves to rescuing the unborn. They believe in God and in the divinity of his son Jesus, in the reality of divine reward and punishment, in the literal truth of the story of Noah, in the miracle of the loaves and the fishes and other proofs of God's presence in a corrupted world. And as clearly as Kopp believed in God's kindness and mercy, he believed that the people responsible for the legalized murder of more than a million babies in America every year had no scruples at all.

" 'With Clinton in there and Janet Reno, you know they're after us,' " Grady recalls him saying during one of his visits. " 'You're going to hear about them pulling me in on something. That's going to be it. They're going to get all of us one way or another.'

" 'Blowing something up' is what he said," she recalls, her hands clasped tightly together on top of her dining-room table. "He said: 'If you hear something like that, don't you go believing anything. You talk to me first.' " But by the time agents of the Federal Bureau of Investigation arrived at her door, soon after the Slepian murder, the mild-mannered man who liked to walk through the parks when the leaves changed colors was long gone.

I. The Making of a Missionary

Jim Kopp did not travel alone. The story of how a deeply religious man became the object of an FBI manhunt is also the story of how a movement that proclaimed the sanctity of life became a forcing ground for terror and killing. While Kopp's connection, if any, to the Slepian murder remains to be determined, his path from religious commitment to blocking clinic doors, to participation in even more extreme forms of resistance, mirrors the experience of thousands of other protesters who became involved in the movement during the 1980s.

Though abortion remains a divisive issue in the national politics of the 1990s, the organized grassroots resistance to abortion had largely disintegrated by the end of 1992. Kopp's descent into the movement's increasingly violent and deadly underground was to some extent a result of this collapse. While outwardly gentle, he was by most accounts a tortured man who found in religion a relief from the pain of death, divorce, and romantic disappointment.

Like the members of the Black Panthers and the Weathermen at the tail end of the 1960s, the most passionate opponents of abortion understand themselves to be at war with a society blinded by material wealth and grown fatally corrupt. The results of that faith are easy to measure. Since 1993, when Dr. David Gunn was shot and killed by Michael Griffin in the parking lot of Pensacola Medical Services, six doctors and clinic workers have been shot and killed. The movement has also been linked to fourteen attempted murders, as well as hundreds of incidents of trespass, assault, acid attacks, and bombings. As sickening as these numbers are even to many who oppose abortion, violence may well be succeeding where nonviolent protest did not: between 1992 and 1996, 338 fewer hospitals, clinics, and physicians performed abortions.

The child of a successful corporate lawyer and a nurse, James Kopp grew up riding his skateboard through the well-kept streets of Marin County north of San Francisco. He entered the laid-back University of California at Santa Cruz for reasons that had less to do with lifestyle or politics than with the university's proximity to his home. He lived there with his girlfriend, Jennifer, in an off-campus apartment. After graduating in 1976, he attended California State University at Fullerton, where he earned a master's degree in biology in 1982.

He considered following his father and becoming a lawyer, or even a doctor. Yet for Kopp, as for many graduates of Santa Cruz, the idea of professional success was ultimately less compelling than the call to serve a higher good. The cause that he found was not the environmental movement, or any of the personal liberation movements that swept through California in the '70s and '80s, but the promise of personal salvation through Jesus Christ.

That Kopp would turn to religion in the early 1980s—after his sister's death, his parents' bitter divorce, and the end of the only love affair of his life—was not surprising. He was a shy and gentle person who demanded that suffering and pain serve some larger purpose. That search took him from California to L'Abri (the retreat in the Swiss Alps founded by the father of modern Protestant fundamentalism, Francis Schaeffer) to the South American missions of the Wycliffe Bible Translators.

His growing religious conviction also found expression in the emerging movement to stop abortion. Beginning on April 8, 1984, Kopp was arrested nine times outside San Francisco clinics on charges ranging from trespass to aggravated assault. But the movement alone did not satisfy his spiritual yearning. Raised as a Protestant, Kopp converted to Catholicism in the mid-eighties and in 1986 joined the Missionaries of Charity, an order established by Mother Teresa and housed in a former convent located two subway stops from Yankee Stadium. He woke up every day at 4:30 A.M. to feed the homeless, crack addicts, and others who gathered at the order's soup kitchen to take their meals.

When not feeding and ministering to the poor, Kopp spent his days in a rigorous routine of prayer, meditation, and study. He abjured frivolous conversation, sexual contact, material possessions, and most direct communication with his family. He owned three sets of clothes: the clothes he wore the previous day, the clothes he would wear tomorrow, and the clothes on his back. Because appliances were forbidden, he learned to wash his clothes by hand in a bucket, a practice that, like his vows of poverty and chastity, he would maintain throughout his life. "He had a seriousness, a certain quietude about himself," recalls the Reverend Richard Nielsen, a witty and gentle priest who heard Kopp's confessions and helped direct his spiritual growth. "His primary focus was to discover God's will for himself, and to discover that will at great personal cost."

Leaving the Missionaries of Charity after about six months, Kopp set out to bring his evolving spirituality and capacity for self-sacrifice to bear on the movement to end abortion. For Kopp, the movement to stop abortion was more than a profession of belief. Abortion was a touchstone for the most painful events of his life.

The idea that abortion was murder, plain and simple, and must be stopped was a reflection of a world in which right and wrong were clear, absolute, and unchanging. It was a promise that a world that had been broken apart by death, divorce, and the failure of love could be made whole again in accordance with the will of God.

The record of his years in the antiabortion movement is a kind of *Pilgrim's Progress* in reverse, a trail of arrests and driver's license applications that, together with grainy surveillance footage and the memories of his family and friends, tells the story of one man's plunge into the heart of the deadliest internal conflict that America has seen since the end of the Vietnam War.

II. A Family at War

On July 4, 1984, a woman named Lynn Hightower, a pretty forty-six-year-old legal secretary, was getting ready for a party at a country club near Dallas when the telephone rang. She did not recognize the voice on the other end of the line. "He said, 'I understand you're a close friend of my father, Charles Kopp—is that right?' " she says. "And I said yes. And he said, 'Well, my mother is upset at the letters that my father has been receiving.' "

Hightower had been corresponding with Charles Kopp ever since the two met during a trial in Dallas four years before. She had seen him often and couldn't imagine why Kopp's mother would be upset. "He said, 'Why would you think that?' And I said, 'Well, they're divorced.' " As the conversation continued, it turned out that Nancy Kopp and Lynn Hightower both had good reason to be angry. Charles Kopp was not divorced. He was leading a double life, conducting an affair as an unmarried man while living with his wife of almost forty years in the house where they had reared their children. Jim "wanted to pray about it," Hightower remembers. "And I was sitting there seething at what he was saying. He was saying things that were inappropriate. 'God help this woman who destroyed a marriage' and things like that."

No one factor drives a person to a celibate life or to devote himself to the diamond-hard clarity of the belief that abortion is murder. Yet the disintegration of his parents' marriage was clearly traumatic for Jim Kopp. Within a year, Charles Kopp divorced his wife and married Lynn Hightower, while Nancy Kopp traveled across California informing her husband's friends and associates of his infidelity. The children learned of their father's new marriage through a printed announcement they received in the mail.

If the bitterness that Lynn Kopp's stepchildren showed toward their father was not surprising, it did change her impressions of the family and the man she had married. Lynn Kopp knew her husband as a gentle, straight-backed ex–Marine lieutenant who loosened up after a few drinks and portrayed his family as a northern California version of *Father Knows Best*. Yet the father her stepchildren remembered was a distant authoritarian figure, a heavy drinker who often disciplined his children as if they were raw recruits. Of all the children, Lynn Kopp says, Jim appeared to have the least connection to his father and the hardest time understanding his parents' divorce.

A year after his remarriage, Charles Kopp suffered a stroke, brought on, a doctor told Lynn, by alcoholism. He stopped drinking, and his personality changed. "He was very sharp-tempered after that," Lynn remembers. "He was not the nice, easygoing fella I married." When the Kopp children visited, she says, they were uncommunicative and rude, appearing to delight in the fact that the forbidding father of their childhood had been stripped of his authority.

Happy divorces are rare, of course, but what made the Kopp family unusual—and relevant to Jim Kopp's later career in the movement—were the fierce arguments over abortion in the years before the divorce from Nancy. "It was like their own civil war," remembers a cousin of Kopp's who attended Santa Cruz around the same time as Jim.

At Thanksgiving dinners and other occasions, Jim, his sister Anne, and mother, Nancy, would passionately insist that abortion was murder, while Jim's twin brother, Walt, his sister Marty, and their father argued that it was a woman's right to choose. In part, these arguments reflected the family's guilt over the early and painful death of the Kopps' youngest child, Mary, a schizophrenic who died of leukemia at the age of twenty-one. They also reflected a deeper division of faith. Nancy, Jim, and Anne were devout Christians. Marty was an atheist and a committed feminist, while Walt and his wife gave money to Planned Parenthood.

For Jim Kopp, the family arguments over abortion must have been especially compelling because of an event that marked the end of the one sustained romantic relationship of his life. Throughout his years in the movement, those who knew him well remember, he often spoke of his love for his college girlfriend, Jennifer. "I was committed," he told Doris Grady. "This was going to be my commitment for my life."

What he didn't tell Grady, according to Lynn Kopp, was that Jennifer had an abortion before the couple broke up. "His father confided to me that Jim was very, very upset about it," she says. "He was upset because it was his child and he was not consulted. It just broke him. When he found out about it, it just flipped him out."

Sometime during the mid-1980s, a female prisoner in the Florida state correctional system received a long and admiring letter from a man she had never met. The prisoner, a Catholic activist named Joan Andrews, was serving a five-year sentence for having trespassed at the Pensacola Ladies Center in 1986. Entering the clinic in the company of a local man named John Burt, she had found the room where abortions were performed and thrown herself at a suction curettage machine, furiously tearing at tubes and cords until police arrived to restrain her.

At the time of her arrest, the usual penalty for illegally entering an abortion clinic was little more than the cost of a speeding ticket: a thirty-day suspended sentence and a $50 fine. When Andrews refused to recognize the legality of her trial, however, the judge sentenced her to five years in prison, where she continued her posture of noncompliance until prison authorities locked her in solitary confinement for forty days in the hope of breaking her will. They failed.

As the first living martyr of the antiabortion movement, Andrews was accustomed to receiving letters from strangers, some of them proposing marriage and others referring to her as "Saint Joan." By contrast, the letter she received from Jim Kopp seemed entirely sane. "It was about the helpless mode of being in jail and noncompliance," she remembers. "He was very interested in that."

As his letter probably conveyed, Kopp's interest was more than speculative. In San Francisco in 1984, he had established a "crisis pregnancy center," where women were encouraged to come in for pregnancy testing and counseling and then were shown photographs of aborted fetuses. Drawn to Pensacola in 1986 by the Andrews trial, he was arrested again, for blockading the entrance to the Ladies Center with a truck on a day when abortions were performed. "He was one of a relatively small group of prolife activists who had been working to get stuff started around the country," remembers John Cavanaugh-O'Keefe, the recognized leader of the rescue movement in the late 1970s and early 1980s. "He was a very likable guy with bright eyes and a big smile, and it was a delight to be around him."

Like Kopp, whom he met in Washington in 1984 during the first widely publicized protests against abortion, O'Keefe did not fit easily into the pigeonholes generally reserved for abortion opponents. As an undergraduate at Harvard in the late '60s, he became active in the antiwar movement and then joined a commune in the New Mexico desert from which he emerged as a devout Catholic and an apostle of Mahatma Gandhi and Martin Luther King Jr. The movement he led was small and composed almost entirely of Catholics who followed centuries of church teaching that the soul exists from the moment of conception.

Yet even at its beginning, the movement was torn by passionate disagreements over O'Keefe's commitment to nonviolence. And if Kopp was among the most enthusiastic advocates of more extreme methods of peaceful protest, like using locks and chains to block clinic doors, O'Keefe recalls, he was also consumed by another passion that struck the movement's leader as equally dangerous. Nonviolent protest opposes force with passive resistance, secrecy with openness. "I was then, and am now, extremely troubled by some of Jim Kopp's behavior," he says. "Locks were one thing. Secrecy was another. A lack of candor is not the same as violence in Gandhi, but it is closely allied."

In 1985, Michael Bray, a young evangelical pastor and protégé of

O'Keefe's, was arrested in connection with the bombings of ten clinics in Maryland, Delaware, Virginia, and Washington. A darkly handsome former Annapolis midshipman who had dated the future Kathie Lee Gifford in high school, Bray brought to the movement a dash of the worldly charisma that its professorial leader lacked. Misled by Bray's proclamation of his "innocence"—a word whose biblical connotations can be at odds with its meaning under the law—O'Keefe leapt to his defense, denouncing the arrest as a plot to discredit the movement. When Bray entered a no-contest plea to federal conspiracy charges, O'Keefe's nonviolent protest movement collapsed.

The display of innocence and suffering that Kopp would act out year after year, chaining himself to clinic doors, banisters, tables, and gurneys, was also an enactment of a personal drama in which Kopp was both blameless victim and avenging angel. It was the opportunity to enact this drama on a larger stage that drew Kopp in 1988 to the burned-out industrial city of Binghamton, New York, where an evangelical street preacher named Randall Terry was preparing to project his own mixture of righteousness and suffering into living rooms across America through the vehicle of Operation Rescue.

While Operation Rescue's founders drew on the language of Gandhi and King, their real inspiration came from the imperative of Proverbs 24:11: "Rescue those who are being taken away to death; hold back those who are stumbling to the slaughter." As the core group of Operation Rescue organizers in Binghamton planned a major rescue for Atlanta during the 1988 Democratic National Convention, Kopp's personal drama was about to take center stage under the heat of national television lights, applauded by religious leaders like John Cardinal O'Connor and Jerry Falwell and by politicians like Ronald Reagan and Henry Hyde.

Randall Terry quickly persuaded Jim Kopp to serve as his liaison to America's Catholic churches. In addition to their devotion to the movement, the two men shared a common grounding in the writings of Francis Schaeffer, who taught that evangelicals had a responsibility to enter politics, write books, and otherwise rescue a dying culture from secular humanist unbelievers. Schaeffer's influence on

American evangelicals during the 1970s is hard to understate. And the issue that occupied Schaeffer more than any other from his mountain retreat at L'Abri before his death in 1984 was abortion. "When all avenues to flight and protest have closed," he wrote in *A Christian Manifesto* (1981), a blueprint for the rescue movement that Randall Terry was preparing to lead, "force in the defensive posture is appropriate."

While Kopp impressed the leadership in Binghamton with his dedication to saving the unborn, his greatest passion was for the construction of ever-more-intricate combinations of locks that stretched from minutes to hours the time it took for police to remove protesters, thereby forcing clinics to cancel procedures or shut down for the day. "He had two locks welded together so close, like a dog collar, to the point where it was pretty dicey about whether you could get it off without slicing his throat," one organizer remembers. The only way to get the collar off was with a high-powered grinder that shot sparks up into the wearer's face.

Not satisfied with ordinary Kryptonite bicycle locks, Kopp spent days and weeks building cardboard models that he sent to a locksmith in New York. Surrounding a Kryptonite lock with steel pipes, he found, stretched removal time up to six hours. When that was too fast, Kopp added tars, glues, and abrasive materials and inserted metal rods inside the pipes, so that the grinder would foul with tar and glue and its blades would spin until the motor burned out.

While Operation Rescue did not officially endorse the use of locks and chains to blockade clinics, its leaders were more than happy to refer interested parties to Kopp and to the growing numbers of other protesters who were raising such tactics to the level of an art. "They were friends of mine," recalls Jeff White, who was Randall Terry's right-hand man and the leader of Operation Rescue-California. "I sent a lot of people to them." The particular group to which White refers, the Lambs of Christ, would serve as the shock troops of the rescue movement throughout the 1990s. The Lambs' founder, the Reverend Norman Weslin, knew Kopp from his days with the Missionaries of Charity. The two men would soon meet again, in the summer of 1988 in jail in Atlanta.

III. The Army of God

Francis Schaeffer's vision of an army of believers marching forward to reclaim the corrupted secular culture was brought spectacularly to life in the streets of Atlanta. And for the 1,200 men and women who were arrested, the moment was one for which they had been waiting their entire lives. "Even more than excitement, there was almost a peace about it," one participant recalls. "Because you knew at that moment in time you were doing everything you could do. You were acting in accordance with your beliefs." And with several Supreme Court justices who had supported abortion rights set to retire and Republicans securely in charge of the White House, it seemed as if it was only a matter of time until abortion was banned for good. "I remember thinking—five years," says Barbara Magera, one of the original Operation Rescue organizers from Binghamton, "five years and this thing will be turned around."

The caution born of years of marginal struggle gave way to an intoxicating expectation of triumph and cleansing among the believers confined in the Fulton County jail. The atmosphere was reminiscent, in its way, of that in the jails of Birmingham, Alabama, which had helped to shape the civil rights movement in the 1960s. "It was the greatest experience of my life," says Henry Irby, a Baptist minister known in jail by his nickname, Boss Hog. "There was preaching two or three times a day, and preaching like you don't hear in churches. When we left Fulton County Jail, a lot of the regular prisoners cried."

For Jim Kopp, the moment must have seemed like a particularly sweet reward for a life that, to some members of his family, seemed to have spun dangerously out of control. No longer a lone activist, he was an important and admired figure, a man to whom other prisoners turned for advice. "Jim had done stretches in jail before," Barbara Magera's husband recalls. "He was kind of our in-house expert on how to deal with jail situations."

The prison routine, the closeness of the prisoners, and the atmosphere of prayer and teaching may have reminded Kopp of his days with the Missionaries of Charity. It also called on his desire to help others. In jail in Fulton County, Kopp could indulge his passion for anonymity while also serving as a central figure within a tight-knit group of believers, as an expert on medicine and the law. He also found an eager audience for his impromptu seminars on the use of locks and chains.

It was at this time, if not before, that Kopp met the person or persons who would become known as the Mad Gluer, who edited and contributed to the *Army of God Manual,* a handbook for violent action that would shape the movement in the decade to come. Its apocalyptic tone is palpable from the first sentence: "This is a manual for those who have come to understand that the battle against abortion is a battle not against flesh and blood, but against the devil."

What follows is an excursion through the darker passages of the movement's id, in a voice that mixes profound hatred for secular culture with biblical references, instructions for making bombs, and descriptions of laughing babies floating above a courtroom. "The only rational way to respond to the knowledge of an imminent and brutal murder," the manual instructs, "is direct action." If "direct action" includes the use of locks, chains, glues, and acids, these methods are secondary, the author suggests in "Operation B.R.I.C.K." or "Babies Rescued Through Increased Cost of Killing," to the larger purpose of making the practice of abortion too costly to sustain.

A blueprint for the campaign of terror and violence that would wreck the rescue movement in the 1990s, the *Army of God Manual* was also a logical outgrowth of the understanding that abortion was murder and that the struggle to end abortion was a war. And if Kopp's affinity for this message was obvious, the importance of his connection to the manual would become clearer in the years to come. The Mad Gluer never refers to activists by their proper names. Some of the aliases he uses appear to have a more personal significance, like the "ultra special thanks" given to "the wonderful Gamma Ray Queen who is my close friend and loves Jesus and the babies and me, too." The acknowledgment of Shaggy West would acquire its share of significance in 1993, when the woman behind that alias, an Oregon housewife named Shelley Shannon, walked up to Dr. George Tiller in the parking lot of his clinic in Wichita and shot him six times with a .25-caliber revolver. The person to whom Mad Gluer proclaimed the greatest debt, however, was Atomic Dog, better known outside the movement's emerging violent underground as James Charles Kopp.

After his release from jail in Atlanta, Kopp returned to Binghamton, where he came down with severe pneumonia and possibly hepatitis. He returned to northern California to recuperate and then went back on the road, locking himself to clinic doors in cities across the country, from Houston to Milwaukee to Burlington, Vermont. The Burlington rescue was led by Father Weslin in his new capacity as leader of the Lambs of Christ.

Like the *Army of God Manual,* the Lambs of Christ was the product of the intense emotional currents that swept through the Atlanta jail. "It occurred to me after I got out of jail in 1988," Weslin remembers, "that the only way to stop the murder of God's babies was to become victim-souls for Jesus Christ." When the Lambs were arrested by the police, he says, they would bear witness to the helplessness of the aborted fetus. "We become babies when they arrest us," Weslin explains. "We can't walk, because the baby can't walk. The baby can't give a name. We don't have names." The Lambs would sometimes adopt more extreme measures, including taking emetics before their arrest and lying passively for hours in their own filth, as a baby would under similar conditions.

Weslin's strong personality may have held special appeal for Kopp. Like Kopp's father, Weslin was an ex-military officer (responsible for the nuclear air defense of New York City), and as the leader of the Lambs, he did not easily tolerate dissent. "Of their own free will, they choose to gather with us," Weslin says, referring to the estimated several hundred Lambs. "And we are interested only in those who of their own free will would submit themselves totally and completely to the Lamb concept, which places a shepherd in charge. And that shepherd calls all the shots."

The night that Jim Kopp arrived in Burlington, he stayed with a local sympathizer along with twenty-odd members of the Lambs and other out-of-town rescuers. Janet Cocchi, a woman from Pittsburgh who stayed in the house with Kopp, remembers finding his clothes hung out to dry. "I thought, 'My God, he's going out in the morning in the snow in wet clothes,'" she remembers. "I knew that Mother Teresa's people hang their clothes out to dry, but I wasn't bound by whatever vows he took with her. So I threw his clothes in the dryer." At the rescue the next morning, the Lambs staged a "lock and block," locking themselves to a rusted-out car in the driveway of the clinic. Kopp wore dry clothes and a Kryptonite lock around his neck. The police pulled on the lock so hard, Cocchi says, that Kopp's face turned red and he started to pass out.

At the time of his arrest and during his subsequent trial, Kopp identified himself only as Baby John Doe. On April 6, 1990, he signed a handwritten affidavit to Judge Matthew Katz in which he wrote: "My jury and/or judge must hear, to rule fairly, my evidence about FORCED ABORTIONS being performed in the mill. I refuse to be stifled when talking about Jesus, His babies and the justification defense." Katz sentenced Kopp to fifty-one days in prison. Katz's name would later appear in the Nuremberg Files, the sinister online data base that provides the names and home addresses of doctors who perform abortions and other enemies of the movement and that is plausibly seen by some as a hit list. In February, an Oregon jury awarded $107 million in damages to Planned Parenthood and others in a lawsuit filed against those responsible for creating and maintaining the site.

The approximately hundred protesters arrested in Burlington were kept in a former mental hospital in Waterbury. For Cecil King, a rescuer who had driven up to Burlington from Pennsylvania with Kopp, the experience was a discouraging one. "We didn't see public opinion sway too much or see much help to the babies," he says. "I was of the mind that I would take some time off and think this thing through again, and I think a lot of other people did, too."

Jim Kopp decided to stay on in Vermont. He lived in a farmhouse in St. Albans, a small town in the heart of the Champlain Valley, a region of dairy farms and dirt roads. A twenty-minute drive north of Burlington, St. Albans is also close enough to the Canadian border that half the songs on the radio are in French. His host, Anthony Kenny, was arrested with Father Weslin and the Lambs in Burlington. On the door of their farmhouse, its raw red shingles and gray trim battered by the harsh Vermont winters, is a hand-painted sign with the word "Welcome" on top and a picture of an innocent-looking lamb underneath. Kopp lived here for two years, working construction and other odd jobs. The Kennys' son Eric, then in his early teens, remembers him fondly. "He was a nice guy, kind of like an uncle to us," he told an interviewer. "He'd sit around and play video games with us and make us model planes out of wood."

Kopp also registered two cars to the Kennys' address in Vermont, a green 1977 Dodge Aspen and a black 1987 Chevy Cavalier. According to published reports, the Cavalier crossed the border around the time the three Canadian doctors were shot. The black Cavalier, license plate BPE 216, was recovered at Newark International Airport in December 1998, about a month after the warrant was issued for Kopp's arrest by the FBI.

IV. The Collapse

The promise that the divide between the religious and the profane might be erased through a movement that would awaken the American conscience to the evils of abortion did not end the way Operation Rescue's leaders had expected. In June 1992, Republican-appointed justices on the Supreme Court joined with their liberal colleagues in the Casey decision to reaffirm a woman's right to abortion.

At about the same time, the National Organization for Woman and the federal government began to threaten Randall Terry and other movement leaders with prosecution under RICO, the federal statute designed for crushing organized crime. In the face of RICO's treble damages, many grassroots activists dropped out, unwilling to risk losing their homes and life savings. "We were not prepared for defense at all," remembers Michael McMonagle, an Operation Rescue leader from Philadelphia. "The rescue movement effectively stopped by the end of 1993." The threat of federal prosecution also had the effect of depriving the rescue movement of what public support it had enjoyed from Jerry Falwell and others who feared being named as co-conspirators in lawsuits and having church property seized by the government or awarded to Planned Parenthood.

The end of the rescue movement, like the end of the civil rights or antiwar movements before it, marked the beginning for many activists of a descent to the plains and valleys of everyday life. "The nature of activism for me was that the motor was running," says Gary Leber, the Operation Rescue organizer from Binghamton. "If all of a sudden you feel like a rug is pulled out from under you, there can be a sense of disorientation, a sense of loss." The transition took Leber over a year. "All that required a tremendous help from God," he says. "I was disappointed that things didn't go the way we thought they would go."

Alone, without a job or a family or a church to go home to—and with no house or life savings to lose—Jim Kopp refused to give up. He rescued with Joan Andrews in Europe and then in the Philippines. He rescued with the Lambs in Milwaukee, Green Bay, and other locations and often served as the Lambs' advance man, surreptitiously entering clinics to acquire intelligence about their layout, operations, and personnel.

In 1991, Kopp applied for a Wisconsin driver's license. The address he gave, 1414 North 27th Street, for a two-story warehouse in Milwaukee, is the same one used by members of the Missionaries to the Pre-Born, some of whose leading members have advocated violence against abortion providers and the police. The Missionaries' founder, Matt Trewhella, was videotaped at a 1994 convention of the U.S. Taxpayers Party calling on America's churches to form militias and for parents to do "the most loving thing" by buying their children "an SKS rifle and 500 rounds of ammunition."

Yet Kopp's journey into the militant fringe was not simply a response to the movement's failure to reach a public that seemed more and more inclined to regard the protesters as a dangerous nuisance. It was also an attempt to win the respect of his father, the lawyer and ex-Marine.

Announcing himself as Mad Dog, Kopp would call collect from jail in order to seek his father's advice. When Kopp went to visit, he would tell stories about his time on the road. During one of these conversations, he spoke of having passed through Quantico, Virginia, on the way to a rescue. "Chuck had been there during the war, in officer's training for the Marines," Lynn Kopp explains. "And Jim said he had stopped and gone by the places where Chuck would have been, the parade ground and things like that. And Chuck would just go, 'Uh-huh, mmm-hmmm.' "

That Jim Kopp was trying to connect to his father through his service in an army dedicated to stopping abortion was obvious to his stepmother. Yet years of arrests and beatings had also made it clear that there was no going back to the life his father wished he would lead. In 1992, Charles Kopp suffered a fatal heart attack. Jim arrived at his funeral in Texas in the same frayed, ill-fitting clothes he always wore. His one concession to the occasion was to wear one of his father's ties to the service. Afterward, at the house, Lynn Kopp brought her grandchildren outside and gave them balloons. When they let them go, she said, they should say a prayer or make a wish. Jim refused to participate in what he considered a sacrilegious act. As the balloons rose into the air, his face went purple with anger and he turned his back on the ceremony.

"I said, 'Now, Jim, do something with your life,' " Lynn Kopp recalls of the week and a half the two spent together after her husband's funeral. " 'Your dad wanted you to do something.' And he said: 'My dad was proud of me. The last time I saw him, the look in his eyes, he just had this look of pride.' And I thought to myself, 'This is a lost cause.' "

Kopp would never be able to reconcile with his father. Moreover, the rescue movement, which might have provided him a measure of stability, instead grew increasingly isolated and bizarre. It was during the winter of 1992, while imprisoned in Fargo, North Dakota, that Father Weslin first noticed that the forces out to crush the movement had been joined by an otherworldly presence that manifested itself through unmistakable signs. "There was beating, jumping around on the bed like a fish, the head and the feet would be rising off the bed," he explains. "Their countenance would change to an ugly countenance, and they would issue forth guttural noises and curses, 'I'm going to get you, priest.' " When these Satanic interventions ended, he says, the afflicted Lambs would lie on their beds with peaceful smiling faces and proclaim that "the Blessed Mother was issuing little babies out of me, and she loves the Lambs of Christ."

Clues as to Kopp's state of mind during the period that he traveled with the Lambs can be gained from a surveillance tape shot of a November 1993 gathering outside the Buffalo clinic where Dr. Barnett Slepian performed abortions. A trumpeter plays the "Battle Hymn of the Republic" while the Lambs sing and pray. Also on the tape is a stoop-shouldered man with a thin build and light-colored hair who closely resembles Jim Kopp. He turns into the late-November wind, his face stern and his voice hoarse and crackling with emotion.

"It's like AIDS was a warning to homosexuals," the man on the tape begins. "He loves them, but he is trying to warn them to repent. Eternity in hell or eternity in heaven. You cannot escape death. We are all sinners. We all will die." The violent resolution of the sermon, in which the promise of God's love struggles with threats of damnation, is hard to miss. "God's commandment is 'Thou shalt not kill.' You are breaking God's law. God's wrath is getting ready to pour out. All the money you've made can't buy your way out of hell."

V. A Time for Killing

With the death of his mother from cancer in 1994, Jim Kopp lost the person who served not only as his anchor in the world but as his only consistent source of financial support. If Nancy Kopp's death made her son an orphan, the passage of the Freedom of Access to Clinic Entrances Act (FACE) in May 1994 destroyed what remained of the movement to which he had devoted his life. The new law might just as well have had Kopp's name on it. Instead of facing local misdemeanor charges, which carried sentences of thirty days or less, protesters who blocked clinic entrances or harassed clients would now be subject to full-scale federal prosecution.

Yet even before FACE, there was disturbing evidence that the remnants of the rescue movement had passed beyond the tactics that the law was designed to stop. On the morning of March 10, 1993, a handyman named Michael Griffin joined a demonstration in front of Pensacola Medical Services, not far from the clinic where Joan Andrews had been arrested seven years before. Walking around to the back entrance, he shot and killed Dr. David Gunn and then waited for the police to arrest him.

The first shooting in the movement's history would not be the last. Later that year, Shelley Shannon fired at Dr. George Tiller in Wichita, Kansas. In 1994, Paul Hill, one of Griffin's most outspoken defenders in the movement, killed Dr. Gunn's replacement, Dr. John Bayard Britton. In 1994, John Salvi shot up two clinics in Brookline, Massachusetts, with an automatic rifle, killing two clinic workers and wounding five more.

Even more surprising was the speed and enthusiasm with which movement leaders embraced the idea of killing doctors to defend the sanctity of life. The April 1993 issue of the *Life Advocate*, for example, opened with an article by Bernard Cardinal Law subtitled "Pro-Life Movement Is Inspired by God's Love." The May 1994 issue, by contrast, mentioned a "defensive action statement" defending the shooting of doctors, drafted by Paul Hill and signed by thirty movement leaders, including the magazine's publisher. The November 1994 issue included a column by Terence J. Hughes, who instructed that only "two people have actually risked their lives to save babies. . . . They are Michael Griffin and Paul Hill, and they saved the babies by shooting the abortionist paid to kill them."

The sniper attacks that would transform Jim Kopp into a hunted fugitive also began in 1994, in November, when a doctor in Vancouver was shot by a gunman with a high-powered rifle who fired through the window of his home. The shootings that followed—in Ancaster, Ontario, in 1995, in Rochester and Winnipeg in 1997, and in Amherst, New York, in 1998—all conformed to a similar pattern from which the outlines of the gunman's personality began to emerge. Most likely male, he was patient, organized, intelligent, and experienced in moving in and out of locations far from his home. By shooting doctors in their homes at night, he insured that "innocent" people would not be killed or wounded and increased the odds that he would be able to shoot again.

Even Kopp's closest friends within the movement agree that he is capable of acts requiring patience, intelligence, planning, and stealth. They also insist, in the strongest terms, that he is incapable of committing murder. "When you have a movement founded on religion, you tend to attract people who are fanatics," says Tara Blackwell, a New Jersey woman who has known Kopp for almost ten years. "Jim Kopp wasn't one of them." Blackwell adds that her husband is a Naval Reserve officer: when Kopp came over to their house in New Jersey for dinner last year, she says, he expressed surprise that anyone could hold—let alone fire—a gun.

Yet there is also one incomplete but tantalizing set of clues to the possible identity of the man who murdered Slepian. It is contained in an archive in the editorial offices of *The Hamilton Spectator,* a newspaper in Ontario, where the second of the five doctors was shot. According to Dana Robbins, *The Spectator*'s deputy editor, the first package arrived at the newspaper's offices on December 10, 1997. It contained a threat against the life of a local doctor. The name on the return address belonged to the police officer in charge of investigating the 1995 shooting in Ancaster.

The second package, received December 31, included the words "puzzle piece" handwritten on a photograph of the cover of John Updike's novel *Toward the End of Time*. It also included a warning that the next shooting would be fatal. The third and fourth packages were hand-delivered to *The Spectator* on May 14, 1998, and July 9, 1998, by a man who spoke with either an American or a rural Canadian accent. The packages contained dozens of photocopies with handwritten annotations and newspaper clippings, articles from the *Life Advocate*, protest posters, handmade collages, and apocalyptic warnings. After Slepian was shot, five more packages were sent, the most recent of which arrived at *The Spectator* on February 4.

Reading through the packages is like sifting through the fragmentary record of arrests, addresses, and conversations that Kopp left behind during his fifteen-year journey through the movement. "Army of God" is scrawled on articles torn from newspapers and magazines. It appears alongside a picture of Saddam Hussein, and it appears again next to a photograph of General Norman Schwartzkopf. In an accompanying article, the words "a more complicated mission" (than Desert Storm) are underlined, then referred to again in a marginal note: "We're these kind of people too."

The author also displays a particular hatred for Planned Parenthood, scrawling angry notes on leaflets, tracts, and a list of the organization's benefactors. There is a photograph of Dr. Barnett Slepian with an "X" drawn through his face. There are clippings from the *Life Advocate* and references to the Missionaries to the Pre-Born. In a recent package, a picture of a black man holding a rifle above the motto "By Any Means Necessary" is juxtaposed with the wanted photograph of Kopp issued by the FBI. The man who dropped off the two hand-delivered packages at *The Spectator* was identified by the two employees who saw him clearly as Jim Kopp. Still, it is quite possible that they were mistaken. Earlier this month, police in Ontario arrested another man in connection with the packages.

The question of Kopp's innocence or guilt is finally less absorbing than the consequences of his search for a higher good, sure and unchanging, to sustain him in a fallen world. It is a shared if unspoken premise of the world that most of us inhabit that absolutes do not exist and that people who claim to have found them are crazy. It is also a fact that Kopp's journey was shared by thousands of others who believed that abortion is murder and were willing to sacrifice themselves for their beliefs.

Perhaps sacrifice in the name of a higher good—God, Marx, freedom, or whatever the good of the moment happens to be—is admirable only as long as you support the cause. Or perhaps, in the absence of absolutes, we must judge beliefs not by their inherent righteousness but by their visible consequences. And the consequences of the path that Jim Kopp and the rescue movement followed for the last fifteen years are apparent even to the founders of the movement.

"A handful of prolife assassins have turned abortionists into heroes and martyrs," says John Cavanaugh-O'Keefe. "This is who we are. It's a devastating loss, and time is clearly not on our side."

James Kopp was arrested in a small town in northern France on March 29, 2001. He was extradited to the United States, where he waived his right to a jury trial. He told Judge Michael D'Amico that he had spent over a year planning the shooting of Dr. Barnett Slepian with the intention of wounding the doctor so that he would not be able to continue performing abortions. He is currently serving a sentence of twenty-five years to life.

The FBI believes that Kopp was also involved in four other incidents in the United States and Canada in which doctors who performed abortions were shot in their homes with a high-powered rifle.

In the Age of Radical Selfishness

I.

What little I know about the self, or at least my self, comes from a year that I spent living in air-conditioned hotel rooms while reporting on various subjects after giving up the lease I had held for five years on a one-room apartment in New York City. It was during this unsettling time, which began two months before I turned thirty, that I became seriously interested in the workings of the human brain. Is the brain a computer? Is the self a fictional construction of the mind? I remember very little of what I read. What I do remember is lying in bed late at night, smoking cigarettes, and reading abstruse arguments from university presses that I marked up in red and blue ink like a student cramming for final exams. The air in these rooms was artificial and cold. Along with scientific and philosophical treatises, I packed flannel shirts and heavy sweaters in solid colors. When I was finished reading, I called down to the front desk and requested spare blankets, which I piled on my bed for extra warmth.

The sense of absence and weightlessness that I experienced during this time was not entirely unfamiliar. I experienced the same feelings as a child, after my family moved from Brooklyn to New Jersey, where my parents wrestled with the pressures of four children, two careers, and their marriage, and where I carried a small transistor radio with me every day on the bus to school. The radio, a gift from my grandfather, was made of red plastic and received both AM and FM stations. I kept it with me all morning. By early afternoon I would begin to feel anxious, until I would finally sneak off to the first-floor boys' bathroom and tune in to 1010 WINS. "You give us twenty-two minutes," the announcer reassured me, "we'll give you the world." The Yankees won and the Mets lost. Water-main breaks in lower Manhattan were causing fifteen-minute delays outside the Holland Tunnel. I returned to class feeling calmer, if also slightly dazed. Eating a chocolate ice cream cone after school, I would feel the cold of the ice cream on my tongue, and then the sun on my arm would feel warm and nice. The pleasure of these moments was always mixed with the feeling that a ghost was leaving my body. I was eleven years old.

The next time I felt that way I was twenty-two years old, recently graduated from Harvard, and sharing a five-room apartment in the East Village with five other people. The apartment was a third-floor walk-up with five rooms separated by partition walls that provided separate living spaces for a transient population of slackers, pot smokers, and heroin addicts from widely mixed educational backgrounds. The room where I lived was a rectangular space carved out of the living room, with three doors and no windows, for which I paid $325 a month. There was an overflowing toilet down the hall. For lunch I ate spaghetti on a Formica table whose surface was crosshatched with the marks of many aimless generations of forks and knives. Countless people had sat here before me and imagined the moment when their lives would be filled with meaning and purpose. When I looked closer at the table, I saw tiny flecks of gold.

II.

The year I turned thirty, I was living with my girlfriend in a walk-up apartment on the Upper West Side. By Manhattan standards, at least, the apartment was a bargain. We had an old Danish sofa with a light plaid pattern, framed travel posters from yard sales in the country, a three-legged coffee table that wobbled, a cheap set of dishes, an oak-frame futon with a hump in the middle, paperback books, an old-fashioned school desk that I carried home from the flea market one Saturday afternoon, a color TV set, and an armchair covered in nubby green fabric.

My girlfriend and I had been together on and off for almost five years without getting married, despite repeated hints from our parents. They were liberal people who believed in their hearts that the pursuit of our careers, combined with the inherent selfishness of our natures, had led us into new and uncharted territory, a land of un-washed dishes and empty refrigerators swept by winds of frustration and delay. This territory is unique in the absence of landmarks like birth or death; it can be defined as the decade or so after graduating from college; it grows longer, if the statistics are right, with each passing year; and it promotes depression, for which Prozac and Zoloft are prescribed. Men and women live together for some in-definite period of time, with no real intention of having children and with only a vague commitment to getting married. Still, we were no more happy or unhappy than lots of other couples we knew, longtime friends and companions who have slept with, and often lived with, a long and depressingly unromantic succession of other partners.

When we stopped sleeping together, we were both too embar-rassed to talk about it. Four months later, when we finally discussed the matter with each other, we had learned that not having sex was a more common condition than either one of us would have guessed. "All couples go through periods like this," my girlfriend insisted. "Take Dan and Lizzy, for instance. Or Melissa and Tom."

New York does something bad to people, we agreed. It concen-trates too many restless, twitchy human atoms in too small a space. You could sense the same disorienting effect in the air at every Man-hattan cocktail party, an anxious communal whisper that rose up from the Pottery Barn couches and the overburdened ashtrays like the swirling background noise on the Beatles' "Day in the Life." That two people might feel more fully themselves by joining to-gether in a lifelong commitment, this sound suggested, was an obvi-ous and transparent emotional mirage. She might do better with a banker or a lawyer, and I might find greater happiness with the girl in the light blue dress by the door. Why bother with being faithful? Why bother with sex at all? Still, it was strange to think about, two representatives of our generation, brought up on Alex Comfort's *Joy of Sex*, trying and failing to get it on.

On the weekends we spent time with my girlfriend's parents. Her father was a modest, intelligent man in his early seventies who de-lighted in acquiring suits for $25 apiece, rummaging through the racks at local thrift shops for amazing, mothballed finds. Her mother was fifteen years younger. At dinner parties, her eyes gave out a pleasant but by no means elderly crinkle at the corners, and her brush-cut white hair seemed to stand on end, as if galvanized by the electric current of social possibility that ran through her living room on Riverside Drive. I admired them both. Offered the chance, who wouldn't want to spend night and day with the parents of my friends from high school and college—children of the Great Depression, witnesses to the civil rights struggle and the Vietnam War, who know how the bond markets work and who's up and who's down at Alfred A. Knopf? Who own nice apartments in Manhattan, and country homes in the Hamptons where, for the cost of a jar of fancy marmalade or a fresh-baked pie, I might spend a luxurious, life-restoring weekend tanning myself brown at the beach.

These weekends with her parents kept us together for at least the better part of a year. When the weather was nice, we went to the beach. On rainy mornings we went to yard sales, where we browsed through framed museum posters laced with spidery cracks, rickety end tables, ancient rowing machines, *Life* magazines from the 1950s, and paperweights with snowy scenes of the Manhattan skyline dulled by overenthusiastic shaking. Her parents had been together for more than thirty years, and they indulged in their fair share of complaints. Still, they loved each other, and it was impossible to imagine them on their own, or with other more attractive or successful partners. They were interesting together. They were whole.

Our inability to imagine a future together was not ours alone. It was a symptom of a larger fracture or collapse, I concluded, involving however many hundreds of thousands of people in their twenties and early thirties who seemed to lack any sense of necessary connection to anything larger than their own narrowly personal aims and preoccupations. In the aftermath of the civil rights movement, women's liberation, the movement from the cities to the suburbs, the birth of rock-and-roll, and other changes, basic laws of social gravity had lost their pull. We were free to be white or black, gay or straight, grow our hair long, shave our heads, meditate for days on end, have children or not, drink bottled water, work out at the gym, watch television until three in the morning, and otherwise exist outside the traditional roles and the close, gossipy communities that had burdened and constrained our parents growing up in Brooklyn or the Bronx.

This freedom from the gravity of age-old constraints was accompanied by a weightless feeling that attached itself to even the most fundamental human decisions. Why bother? Why get married? What are families for? What was new about these questions was that they didn't have answers, or that the answers they did have were so multiple and contingent and arbitrary that they never really felt like answers at all.

Six months later, after another failed relationship, I bought a cellular phone and a portable computer, packed the contents of my apartment into boxes and moved them into an eight-by-ten-foot aluminum-walled storage locker by the West Side Highway. I was amazed that my eleven boxes of books, along with my share of the furniture from our apartment and two army surplus duffel bags containing sweaters and jeans and CDs and a stack of expensive white shirts from Barneys that I hadn't really been able to afford, could fit into such a small space. I hailed a cab, and as I rode back to my near-empty apartment, I thought again about what my freedom would feel like. I would sleep late and go wherever I wanted. If I wasn't happy, I would pick up and leave. I would spend the next year on the road, writing and reporting and visiting friends, without obligations or commitments, living in borrowed apartments and hotel rooms, none of which could be called home.

When I arrived at my old apartment for the last time, I found a TV reporter sipping coffee next to a mobile news truck across the street. I knew exactly why the truck was there. The five-story red-brick building was the scene of a front-page murder that had occupied the city's attention for weeks. The victim, a schoolteacher named Jonathan Levin, was a Trinity graduate and the son of Gerald Levin, the chairman of Time Warner. Instead of using his father's name to make a career in the entertainment business, he chose to teach in the New York City public schools.

As the case played out in the tabloids and on the local news, the murder of Jonathan Levin became the story of a powerful and wealthy family that had been touched by tragedy. The choices that Levin made, and the consequences of those choices, had no necessary place in the story. Why was a rich white kid teaching public school in the Bronx? Did he really believe in social justice for the poor? Was he rebelling against his father? The attorney for his killers had suggested in court, without a shred of supporting evidence, that Jonathan Levin had used drugs. However outrageous this suggestion was, it also made a strange kind of intuitive sense. His choices didn't connect to any larger narrative about the hopes and dreams of the society in which he lived. It was a story that seemed left over from the headlines of an earlier era, like civil rights marches in Birmingham or hippie runaways found strangled in Golden Gate Park.

Climbing the stairs to my apartment, I tried to remember what my neighbor had looked like. I remembered a serious-looking young man in his late twenties. Perhaps he had a beard. The picture of his killer, Corey Arthur, taken the day of his arraignment, stayed with me in greater detail. As the photographers pushed forward, and the policemen propelled the suspect down the stairs, he met the camera's eye and executed a perfectly timed series of physical maneuvers. First he twisted his body around to show the well-defined muscles in his shoulders. He wanted their perfection to show. Then he tilted his chin defiantly upward against the pressure of the policeman's hand on the back of his neck. Around his lips, in the middle of the scrum of policemen and photographers, I saw the ghost of a smile. It was a shadow from his childhood, I thought, of a swivel-hipped boy dancing backward away from a gang of tormentors with his middle finger raised high in the air. Fuck You All.

During the '60s, my father worked in the Bedford-Stuyvesant neighborhood of Brooklyn, setting up a community college named after the civil rights leader Medgar Evers. It was one of the major commitments of his life. Our family lived in a two-bedroom apartment in a red-brick building by the Brooklyn Bridge. Our neighbors were other young families without money and the working poor. One morning, on my way to school, I noticed spray-painted graffiti on the side of our building. A week later I found a syringe when I was playing in the sandbox. My mother told me to put it down. The sanitation department went on strike, and bloated garbage bags piled up on the curb. It was the middle of the summer. The garbage stank, and there were rats in the streets.

The message was clear. My parents started looking at houses in New Jersey. When we finally did move to New Jersey, I remember listening to the crickets outside my window and the hiss of the sprinkler systems throwing water on the empty lawns at night. The suburbs were empty. They were safe. In Brooklyn, students now graduated from Medgar Evers College without being able to read simple texts in English. That was part of the equation, too.

"That was a different time," my father said, when I talked to him about the Levin murder and Medgar Evers College on the phone. Upstairs, in my empty apartment, I flipped through a coffee-table book I bought for $5 on the street, a shrink-wrapped greatest-hits package of news photography from the '60s. There were pictures of LBJ and the Beatles and Woodstock, and of a screaming boy lying in an Asian jungle with the word "Mom" painted on his helmet and half his leg blown off. Flipping through the pictures, I couldn't decide whether to bring the book with me or leave it behind. I stopped at a picture of a poncho-wearing hippie standing with her two small children outside a half-finished cabin on a rural road. What exactly were they after? I wondered. How exactly does this story end? The woman is making scented candles in Vermont for the tourist trade, or writing a memoir about her experiences. Her children are waiting tables and pregnant, or writing screenplays in Hollywood like everyone else.

III.

With my belongings safely in storage, I drove from New York to my aunt and uncle's house on the southeastern coast of Massachusetts. It is a beautiful house, decorated with sailing ships and nautical charts and 270-degree wraparound views that fill the rooms with coastal light. A lawn the size of a football field slopes gently down to the sea. My aunt and uncle move down to the house from Boston for July and August. In the fall and winter, they make their house available to poor relations like me.

When I was a child, my aunt and uncle were my favorite people in the world. They were glamorous and tall. My uncle was rich and raced sailboats. My aunt was beautiful and smart, had a PhD from Harvard, smoked cigarettes, and drank Tab. They went out dancing at Studio 54. They were people who acted without any responsibility to others, my father told us. They were never on time to family occasions. Sometimes they didn't show up at all. Their apparent selfishness, their willingness to defy the expectations of a family of strong-willed people, made me love them all the more.

Seven years ago my uncle was in a bicycle accident that left him paralyzed from the waist down. The speculation inside the family was that the marriage might be in trouble. Instead, their relationship appeared to grow stronger. The accident gave a weight to their marriage that it didn't have before.

On weekends my aunt and uncle came down to visit. During the week I would sit and read and write. I missed my family. I ate a bowl of Frosted Flakes cereal every morning for breakfast. It was my favorite cereal when I was a child. I dipped my spoon back into the milk, brought the spoon up to my mouth, and swallowed. The cereal was crisp and sweet, a condition that lasted for approximately a minute and a half before the sugar coating melted off the flakes and they became soggy. The whole experience could turn sour in an instant. The milk in the bowl was already turning blue.

I worked in a room looking out on the water with a single shelf of books and a high-end stereo, where I listened to records by my favorite college-rock bands—Pavement, Superchunk, and Nirvana. The distorted guitars always sounded to me like the authentic sound of emotional blockage. Next door was a brand-new supersize color TV that took up half the room, like the kind you see in a hospital or an old-age home. After dinner, I sat outside on the porch and looked over the ocean and talked to my friends in New York and Los Angeles. They wondered whether I was happy, and whether my choice to leave New York City wasn't really a symptom of some greater disturbance.

Listening to their voices as I sat in the dark, I wondered at the miracle by which the latest technology could link us in the most profound of dissatisfactions: ourselves. We were all graduates of good universities, bearers of elite credentials that would smooth our way in the world, leading lives detached from any real public or private passion. One friend told me about the $2,000 suit that he had bought at Barneys. It was a great suit, he said. He talked about the suit for half an hour. Another friend was living at home with her parents in Los Angeles. She spent her days smoking cigarettes, reading magazines, and going to the gym. An actor friend in Los Angeles had a child with a woman he had met at Bed, Bath and Beyond. That is what actors do, I reasoned. He hoped that having a child would provide a sense of consistency and purpose to his life. It was something to do. It was what all of us were doing, looking for a way to fill up the empty spaces at night. A girl I liked had moved down to Florida to work in her family business. She worked out at the gym every morning, ate steamed vegetables, and studied Judaism with a rabbi in Miami Beach.

My friend Ben, who is also a writer, had recently been out to Los Angeles. The people we both knew from college were all writing comedy for television. One Sunday afternoon, Ben and his wife had been invited to brunch by a young married couple we knew, who wrote for a famous cartoon comedy show and had a house with an Olympic-size swimming pool in the Hollywood Hills. Ben hadn't been swimming for almost two years. He asked if he could use the pool. He went into the house, changed into a bathing suit, jumped into the pool, and swam a few laps, and then hung out and enjoyed the view. The view from the pool was truly spectacular. The other guests began to leave. Ben refused to get out of the pool. The moment he left the water, he explained, he would have to justify his belief that it was better to live with his wife and dog in a four-room walk-up in Chelsea, instead of sitting around a table with seven or eight people in Hollywood, spitting laugh-track-ready jokes into a tape recorder, and making a million dollars a year.

I told my friend in Miami that I wanted to move back to New York. She came back to the city only once or twice a month, so she offered me her apartment, and I moved in. Her building, on the Upper East Side just off First Avenue, was a magnet for young professionals who walked in the marble lobby past fake plastic ferns with their dry cleaning slung over their shoulders at eight or nine every night. The rest of the tenants were mostly over the age of forty-five, with a heavy complement of single women who dyed their hair blond, watched television, and watered the plants during the day.

The drilling began a week after I moved into the apartment. When I visited the apartment above me to find out when the noise might stop, I found walls torn down, concrete exposed, and tangles of wires tumbling loose from the ceiling. It was a gut renovation, the kind that would end in a marble-floored kitchen with custom appliances opening onto a loftlike living-dining area with hardwood floors that had been opened up to take full advantage of the limited East River view.

My friend B. came to visit me in New York. B. looks like a surfer, with strawberry blond hair and clear blue eyes whose zoned-out intensity suggest that he spent some good part of his life eating handfuls of hallucinogenic drugs. During college, we had dated girls who were roommates at Columbia. We both wanted to write. Now B. was living in Los Angeles and writing for television. On the weekends he surfed. He had just signed a deal with a movie studio to write four scripts over the next two years. He would receive $100,000 for each draft of each script, for a minimum of $400,000, in addition to the salary he received from television. He wasn't happy, either. He came to New York every few months. When he arrived, he was always in love.

His most recent obsession was a girl he had met at Columbia years ago and then had recently seen again in an elevator. She was standing with her shoulders down and her head tilted just a little, as if she was following a barely audible melody seeping in through the walls or the floor. There was something about the precise tilt of her head, or the look of intelligent involvement on her face, he insisted, that suggested she was actively listening to a song. The impression was so strong that, as he stared at the girl's face and tried to place her, he thought he could almost hear her humming along.

She wore a sleeveless T-shirt beneath a fuzzy red shirt that bunched up over her shoulders. On the evidence of her clothes alone, she looked like a composite portrait of a dozen girls you see every day, cutting class at NYU or living postgraduate lives as dancers or choreographers or painters, or as the next Tama Janowitz or Toni Morrison in the East Village, where a job as a waitress supplemented by modest contributions from a trust fund might buy you a 300-square-foot third-floor studio walk-up with the kitchen sink right next to your bed. On days when the boyfriend had band practice, or when the writing or the dancing or the painting wasn't going so well, you could see them gathered together in girlish knots drinking coffee from paper cups outside the Astor Place subway station and pretending they weren't twenty-five years old and scared. They wore black leather jackets over long shapeless dresses, sleeveless T-shirts to show off their tattoos, floral prints from Guatemala or Puerto Rico, fuzzy fall sweaters, rings through their noses or belly-buttons, with hair dyed black or platinum blond. The toes of their black leather boots were scuffed gray from dragging their feet and kicking at the curb.

The girl in the elevator, B. said, was nothing like that at all. She was flesh and blood and alive. She looked up for a moment without meeting his gaze, but not looking away exactly either. She was just comfortably inhabiting the place where she stood. When he remembered her name the silence would dissolve. There were twenty floors to go before they reached the lobby. The numbers flashed on and off over his head counting down the number of floors. There were fifteen floors left. He left the elevator without asking the girl her name. Once he remembered her name, he said, it would be easy to find her. He was sure that they would fall in love.

The idea was crazy. Then again, who knows? You meet a friend from Harvard or Yale or Brown or Columbia who is working for Paramount, or has started an online media company and is taking it public next week. Maybe you would like a job? The rules by which the new universe operates can seem random and scary, winners and losers rattling around together like the numbered Ping-Pong balls in the Lotto drawings on TV. The winners receive big paychecks and fame; the losers curse their luck and read about the winners in alumni bulletins and *People* magazine.

It is hard to put my finger on exactly when this change was set in motion, or what the larger forces behind it might be. Only that the old rules no longer apply, and that coherent narratives, the stories that tell us who we are and where we are going, are getting harder and harder to find. There is the decline of organized religion and the nation-state, the failure of politics, the reduction of human behavior to chemicals in the brain, the absence of the sense of common purpose that is often created by large-scale human suffering. There are Lotto drawings on TV. What is left behind is us. Or not us exactly, but a few hundred million loopy, chattering, disconnected I's. What is so new and radical about the present epidemic of selfishness is how widely, and unthinkingly, it is shared. We make up for our self-ishness with small but reassuring acts of kindness, like joking around with the man behind the deli counter or bringing the doorman a cup of hot tea.

IV.

A few months ago I bought a Walkman so I could listen to music when I walked down the street. It cost $39. There are people who object to the substitution of linear chord progressions, drum machine beats, and other market-researched components of a three-minute, twenty-seven-second pop song for the unprocessed reality of the streets, the rumble of cabs and trucks, honking horns, squealing tires, and the voice of the Indian woman at the newsstand in the red-and-orange sari who wants her son to get better grades in school. We have the freedom to rearrange reality more or less to our liking, as our brains synchronize the movements of the people around us in some relation to the songs that play in our heads.

I walk beneath the shady awning of the deli and into the air-conditioned interior, where the sawdust on the floor strikes a dry, sweet note above the assortment of fresh fruits and vegetables. It's nice and cool in here. Fluorescent light sparkles off racks of refrigerated soda cans. I stand with the yellow plugs in my ears, humming along.

My friend in Miami has a special theory about restaurants. Our parents went to restaurants to mark special occasions, to feel important and glamorous, to get out of their lives and to eat the food. What people our age want from restaurants, she says, is something heightened but warm. It's the Technicolor version of home. And because none of us are really able to create that feeling of home in ourselves, eating out in restaurants almost always ends badly. The food is poor, the room is bad, or the service is unfriendly and disconnected. If the restaurant is good, you feel high, like after watching too much television or doing too many drugs. When you come down, you feel even more depressed than before.

We had dinner in Miami with another couple she knows—I'll call them Ned and Laura. We sat together at a restaurant eating raw vegetables as they told us stories about the week they spent together at an ashram in the Berkshires last fall. All the people who went there were crazy except for Ned and his wife. They were seekers, psychotics, and divorcees in search of a dose of enlightenment and sharing. Breakfast lasted for half an hour. No one was allowed to speak. After breakfast, there were encounter groups and walks in the forest, along color-coded pathways laid out to make maximum use of the beneficial energies of the trees. The place sounded creepy. But to Ned and his wife, the week at the ashram was cool. It was a way to charge up depleted spiritual batteries. It was a chance to goof on the inner lives of people you would never see again, while taking power yoga three times a day followed by the hour-long deep-tissue massage.

As Ned finished his stories about the ashram, Laura held out her special health-snack mix, reverently packaged in clear plastic Ziploc baggies that suggested some really fine-leafed grade of Hawaiian pot. I took the plastic baggie from her hand. She smiled back.

"I can feel it working already," I said.

"If you want it to work, you have to eat it," Laura answered. "If you don't eat it, it doesn't work." Her voice was surprisingly strict. Now that she was married to Ned, she didn't have to take flak from anybody. Before Ned married her, he apparently lived on a diet of cheeseburgers and Cokes. Now he looked terrific. He had grown a beard.

"You should really try it," Ned said, smiling at Laura from beneath his new beard. Laura was a nice person. She had big brown eyes, even California-girl features, and silky, shampoo-commercial-perfect black hair that cascaded down her neck and served as a medium for her own personal form of self-expression, which involved scattering brightly colored beads and baby barrettes throughout. She was smarter than Ned. They were good people. They worked at togetherness. Still, it was hard to imagine myself in their place. When they talked about having children together, Laura referred to the children as "mine."

After months of talking every night on the phone, my friend from Miami and I were now in the early stages of a new relationship. We had known each other for five years. I was living in her apartment in New York. We talked about what it would be like if I moved down to Miami. Then she said she was serious. I said yes on the spot.

V.

I live on the thirty-second floor of a glassed-out apartment tower in Miami now, with a view of the sea. I can see long rolling waves, sandy beaches, palm trees, and a maze of traffic-filled roads that twist and turn according to no discernible plan. In Miami, the view can change in an instant. The sky goes from blue to gray and then the landscape disappears beneath sheets of water streaking down the glass. Half an hour later, it's sunny again.

I live in Miami now, but I fly between Miami and New York at least once a month. The other day, while waiting to board my plane, I thought again about my year in the East Village and my expectation of the moment when my life would become whole.

The gold flecks in the Formica table were a promise of something of value. It was a promise of something inside myself. The harder I concentrated back then, the hazier that promise became. Still, I recognized that the promise was real every time I sat down to lunch.

The problem is that the self isn't real. The self is a necessary illusion that allows us to function in time, to create law, and morality, and art, and the rest of civilization. But the self was never meant to save us from death, or imbue our lives with meaning and purpose. Selfishness is what makes us unhappy. Too much concentration on ourselves makes us anxious, because the self cannot support the weight. That is the difference between the self and the soul.

Rehab Is for Quitters

I.

The Great Coffee Debate at the Hazelden Foundation, in Canter City, Minnesota, was the type of controversy that is dear to historians, a seemingly trivial event that illuminates the hidden fault lines on which a group or a society might eventually divide. The debate began in the spring of 1994, when a majority of the counselors at Hazelden, which is the wealthiest and most influential twelve-step treatment center for alcoholics and drug addicts in the country, suggested that coffee be banned. Coffee is an integral part of most Alcoholics Anonymous meetings, a de facto sacrament. Members of AA have been known to make pilgrimages to Akron, Ohio, to view the coffeepot used by Dr. Bob, the cofounder of the organization. Nevertheless, the counselors at Hazelden decided that coffee was just another drug. "There was concern that some people could be using caffeine as a stimulant, three-bagging or four-bagging it," Russell Forrest, one of the leaders of the anticoffee camp, recalls. "What we were really dealing with, I guess, was a question of philosophy."

While a ban on caffeinated coffee was implemented at Hazelden, enforcing the ban was another story. "You had people bringing this stuff in from outside," Forrest recalls, "and there was an underground market, which, of course, you would point out to patients, and you'd say, you know, 'Doesn't this sound like chemical use?' People were opening up packages, and I saw what was in there. It was the strongest brew you could buy. Somebody was getting coffee from South America, and it was sticky and black, and I said, 'What is this? This is not Maxwell House from Bogota.' "

The black market in coffee grew at an alarming speed. Patients were brewing large quantities of coffee in their rooms and flushing the evidence down sinks and toilets. Soon the pipes were stuffed with coffee grounds, and the conflict between a fundamentalist approach to the tenets of AA and the practical demands of running a treatment center came to a head. As the plumbing at Hazelden became more and more clogged, the maintenance staff rebelled, and the coffee ban was finally and ingloriously rescinded.

Hazelden was disrupted for months by the coffee wars, which took place just as the foundation's president, Jerry Spicer, had begun to encourage the use of antidepressant drugs and other therapies that are not traditionally part of the twelve-step process. This was a controversial move, and several staff members had left in protest. Spicer's supporters also tended to support drinking coffee. Phil Kavanaugh, the head counselor at Shoemaker, one of Hazelden's six primary treatment units, was an outspoken proponent of caffeine. "The problem with the coffee, as I saw it, was that it wasn't strong enough," he says. "My proposal was that we should put in an espresso bar next to the dining area."

A true ideological crisis was brewing. The opponents of coffee were registering disapproval of drugs of all kinds, no matter how limited or benign (or therapeutic) their effects might be. The pro-coffee faction was willing to embrace caffeine and also antidepressants and other drugs that might help addicts get well. Among the new drugs are substances that are being engineered to act on addiction in much the same way that SSRIs (selective serotonin re-uptake inhibitors) like Prozac and Zoloft act on depression. The new research on addiction is a mixed blessing for Hazelden and other AA-based treatment centers. On the one hand, neuroscientists using advanced imaging equipment to observe changes in regions of the brain that are known to govern addiction have provided evidence that addicts do suffer from a physical disease, which is what AA has claimed all along. On the other hand, the idea that addiction is a disease with the same kinds of physical causes—and cures—as diabetes or clogged arteries challenges the premise of a spiritual cure on which Hazelden has operated for the past fifty years.

II.

The Hazelden Foundation sits on the shores of a small lake, surrounded by 488 acres of nature trails and tall pines. It looks like a well-run monastery or a small but fashionable resort. It was established in 1949 as a retreat for alcoholic priests by a local writer named Austin Ripley, author of *Minute Mysteries* and *Photo Crimes,* who named the property after his dead wife, Hazel. The original white-shingled farmhouse has been replaced by tan brick buildings, and the Hereford cattle that used to graze on part of the land are gone, but the addicts at Hazelden today, many of whom are wealthy and some of whom are famous, live much as patients did fifty years ago, recovering from what they are told is not only a disease of the body but also a profound disturbance of the soul.

Bill Wilson, who cofounded Alcoholics Anonymous with Bob Smith (Dr. Bob), was a member of the Oxford Group, a religious movement that attained its greatest influence in twenties and thirties. Wilson also drew on an eclectic variety of other sources, including, most significantly, William James's *Varieties of Religious Experience.* His intention in founding AA, he wrote to Carl Jung, was to make the conversion experiences that James described "available on an almost wholesale basis." The AA Big Book, compiled by Wilson and Smith, functions as the gospel of the twelve-step movement, and has sold over 13 million copies since its first publication in 1939. Chock-full of eclectic personal reflections and earnest testimonials, the Big Book is written in a plainspoken Midwestern fashion in which a sufferer in his last extremity might chance to hear the voice of a friend.

While sales of the Big Book have never been higher, its prose can also sound dated and grating to modern ears, in a way that can cause sensitive or finicky readers to doubt the reliability of the promised cure. "I remember we had a famous novelist in treatment, and we gave him the Big Book," Phil Kavanaugh told me. "The next day he said, 'I'm getting out of here. Because if you people think this is any good, then you can't help me.' " Supporters of drug therapy in the AA community also note that Wilson in his later years experimented with LSD and ignored or abandoned many of the homespun tenets of the Big Book; his eventual fixation on vitamin B_3 as a final cure for alcoholism led to a rebuke from AA's semisecretive governing organ-ization, the General Service Board.

Hazelden is legally, if not philosophically, independent of AA, and treatment there has long incorporated behavioral psychology and other less-than-spiritual methods. But, because AA does not run treatment centers of its own, Hazelden is the closest thing to the institutional voice of the AA-based treatment community. It is a nonprofit foundation, run by an independent board of directors whose members include George McGovern, Calvin Klein, and Ju-dith Moyers, and has a twenty-five-million-dollar endowment that is funded by big-name corporate donors including ITT, CBS, and Goldman Sachs. The publishing arm of the foundation brings in over twenty million dollars a year by distributing manuals and work-books to treatment centers across the country. It also publishes Melody Beattie's best-selling book *Co-Dependent No More,* which helped to expand the concept of the twelve-step cure to people who are in bad relationships, shop too much, eat too much, have too much sex, or suffer from other borderline behavioral disorders. The foundation has forty thousand alumni, who make donations and at-tend retreats and reunions on the peaceful and spacious Center City campus. The shelves of the Serenity Corner gift shop are filled with the everyday heartbreak of addiction, with Hazelden sweatshirts, children's coloring books entitled *My Dad Is an Alcoholic,* and base-ball caps with the Hot Seat logo stitched in red.

William Cope Moyers is typical of many recent Hazelden alumni. He was the troubled son of privileged parents, he overcame an ad-diction to crack cocaine, and he stayed in Minnesota, becoming a pillar of the AA community. Moyers went to Hazelden for the first time when he was twenty-nine years old. He is now thirty-seven, and he works as Hazelden's director of public policy. He appears to be a younger, faster-talking version of his famous father, Bill Moyers. As he speaks, it is as if the down-home cadences familiar from hun-dreds of hours of good-for-you public television viewing are being played back with one finger held down on the fast-forward button.

A former reporter for *Newsday* and CNN, Moyers has been in treatment for addiction to crack three times since 1989—twice at Hazelden and the last time at the Ridgeview clinic, outside Atlanta, in 1994. "I had been sober for three years and two months," he recalls, in a nasal prep-school drawl. "I was working at CNN. I named my second son after Tom Johnson, the president of CNN, because Tom had been really good to my family. And I stopped taking care of myself in recovery. And one day I decided, in the summer of '94, that I was never going to repeat the insanity of the past, because who would want to, but I might just try it my way. And I'll never, never forget holding the crack cocaine in my hand and thinking, this is going to last me a week. It lasted me four hours."

Several days later, he was removed from an inner-city crack house by the Atlanta police and taken to Ridgeview. "My family was very angry," he recalls. "My wife was very angry: 'How could you do this? Doesn't your family mean more?' And those are the questions that millions of people ask. And I couldn't explain it, except that I had stopped doing what I needed to recover."

As he reaches the summation of what he describes, in the AA language of the moment, as "my personal journey," Moyers spreads his arms wide. "There are two things more powerful than me," he says, his thick blond eyebrows rising high on his forehead and wiggling just a little to underline the point. "One is my disease. And the other one is God. God, disease, William Cope Moyers."

Thanks to AA, alcoholics and addicts are already the best-organized sufferers of any major disease. But the Twelve Traditions of AA appear to prohibit the kind of affecting personal stories that have become a staple of daytime talk shows and congressional hearings alike. Tradition Ten, for example, states, "Alcoholics Anonymous has no opinion on outside issues; hence the AA name ought never to be drawn into public controversy." Tradition Eleven instructs AA members to "always maintain personal anonymity at the level of press, radio and films." Hazelden is not the same thing as AA, of course. "I think there has been too literal an interpretation of anonymity," Jerry Spicer says.

Moyers's closest friend and mentor on the Hazelden campus is a soft-spoken, slow-talking Midwesterner named Bill Pittman who helps to run the treatment center's publishing operation, which shipped over two million books last year. The walls of his office are covered with old newspaper headlines and pamphlets that illustrate AA's distinctive dry sense of humor, the product of millennia of collective experience in dealing with addicts. Included on Pittman's shelves is a copy of *Eleven Years a Drunkard: The Life of Thomas Donner,* whose subtitle summarizes the story thus: "Having lost both arms through intemperance, he wrote this book with his teeth as a warning to others."

Pittman's easygoing manner belies his former career as a hard-living bar owner and a gambling machine operator who ran strippers on the side. His father was an alcoholic who committed suicide when Pittman was seventeen years old. He ended up at Hazelden at age thirty-two after losing his second marriage and his business, he says; his sober personality is the product of a profound renunciation of his old way of understanding himself as an all-powerful person who stood at the center of a world that he himself had created. Having been in the program for over three decades, he speaks in a detached but tolerant way about the tapers who sell recordings of their favorite AA circuit riders, like Clancy from Los Angeles, and the predictable enthusiasm of members who are two years sober and who take the Third Step very much to heart and insist that everything in the universe happens precisely according to God's plan. In his mellow old age, he is still suspicious of his occasional desire to play the slots, and his trouble sticking to a diet or doing anything else that requires moderation.

What Pittman likes best about AA, he tells me, is the instant and lasting fellowship that the society of ex-addicts provides, which acts as a gentle but constant counterbalance to his immoderate impulses. A convincing mix of Midwestern salesman, New Age Shriner, coin machine operator, and self-made Buddhist, he worries that William Cope Moyers's jones for publicity may threaten his friend's recovery by awakening the egocentric impulses that get addicts into trouble. Mostly, he takes the same easygoing, tolerant approach to Moyers's enthusiasm for passing bills in Congress as he does to those who see Moyers's high-speed promotional campaign as a violation of AA's historical insistence on anonymity. "We need those people in AA," he says. "We need people who relapse. We need people who insist on reading only conference-approved literature. The term in sociology is 'boundary maintenance.' A social movement needs differing opinions, it needs reformers and fundamentalists, and that's where we are at right now."

A confirmed believer in the AA method, Pittman also takes

Prozac to treat his depression. He is also suspicious of any attempt to explain how exactly Hazelden works or to export the treatment center's magic elsewhere. Leaning back in his worn leather chair, he indicates the sweep of the snowy landscape outside his window with a swipe of his broad, heavily calloused hand. "Somewhere on the property is a black box, and no one knows what's inside," he says. The irony of the recovered addict being grateful every day for the gift of no longer indulging in behaviors that most people think of as supreme pleasures is hardly lost on him.

"I think the best story is that a limousine pulled up in front of admissions late one night," he said, in an account that may be in part autobiographical, "and the night guy came out and opened the door. And the guy inside the limousine was in there naked with two beautiful girls, and there were booze bottles and drug paraphernalia all over the floor, and he was arriving that night to be admitted. And the night guy looked inside the car and he said, 'Son, you don't have to live this way anymore.' "

III.

The low concrete buildings that replaced the original farmhouse, known in Hazelden lore as "the old lodge," are linked by long, sloping passageways that branch off without warning into cinderblocked dead ends or open suddenly onto views of ice fishermen's huts on South Center Lake. Hazelden legend holds that the labyrinthine tunnels are a deliberate part of the therapeutic process, a reminder to addicts that they must ask for help if they want to get well. The most obvious signs of Hazelden's spiritual mission are square cardboard placards in the halls that say "Quiet Please: Fifth Step in Progress." The Fifth Step is as essential a part of the treatment process here as a radiology lab is to the operation of a modern hospital. The Fifth Step directs alcoholics to admit "to God, to ourselves, and to another human being the exact nature of our wrongs."

There are six treatment units at Hazelden, four for men and two for women, each named for a Hazelden founder or for one of the founders of Alcoholics Anonymous. When patients arrive for their twenty-eight-day stay, they are admitted to Ignatia, the detoxification unit. (Sister Ignatia was a Roman Catholic nun who helped Dr.

Bob dry out alcoholics.) At Hazelden, unlike the more literal-minded AA treatment centers, including the Betty Ford Clinic, many of the new patients are placed on Librium, or, at any rate, they have been since Jerry Spicer liberalized Hazelden's drug policy. A majority of the patients are also put on antidepressants. After a few days on Ignatia, arrivals are assigned to one of the treatment units for a twenty-eight-day stay.

Despite official claims to the contrary, each unit has a distinct personality, which tends to reflect that of the head counselor in charge. Thibout, named after Henry Thibout, the psychiatrist who treated Bill Wilson for depression in the fifties, would qualify, in a college setting, as the jock dorm. Silkworth, which places its emphasis on behavior modification techniques, is named after the physician who wrote the "Doctor's Letter," which enjoys pride of place in the AA Big Book as the first medically approved testimonial to the theory that alcoholism is a physical disease. Dia Linn, one of the two women's units, specializes in the treatment of eating disorders and sexual abuse.

Shoemaker, the unit at Hazelden at which I spent a week recently, is known for its ethos of self-government and emphasis on personal growth. It looks like a ski chalet, with an open common area where there are couches and chairs and a color TV, and a split-level kitchen with a coffee machine, two pay phones, and a large framed poster displaying the twelve steps. The unit is named for the Reverend Samuel Shoemaker, a leading Oxford Group publicist and the pastor of New York's Calvary Episcopal Church, where Bill Wilson attended missionary meetings before founding AA.

The patients, or "peers," as they are called, begin their day at seven-thirty in the morning with a period of meditation. They then go to a lecture down the hall, and return to the unit for a group discussion, or "process," before disappearing for individual counseling or relaxation sessions. The afternoon is devoted to "story time," in which the peers recount tales of their addictions and answer questions from the group. Contrary to current AA practice, the Oxford Group and the early AA meetings that evolved out of it did not place much emphasis on telling stories of past drinking and debauchery. "A man's sponsor and Bill W. knew the details," recalled Bob E., an early apostle of the twelve-step movement. "Frankly, we did not think it was anybody's business."

Phil Kavanaugh, a gentle, bearded man with a law degree and another degree in English literature, sees patients in his office, whose walls are lined with books by Pascal, John Berryman, Edith Hamilton, and John Milton. "What happens after five years in this job is that you realize that nothing you do works," he tells me. "And then all that's left is to tell people the truth. If those normal, good things in life meant anything to you, you wouldn't be here." He runs Shoemaker like a cross between an all-day graduate seminar and a New Age men's encounter group, quoting liberally from the AA Big Book and keeping things simple for his flock. "If you follow the program, we can guarantee sobriety," he says, a zenlike tautology that he repeats day after day and that many of the men grasp onto like a life raft. The plaque near the bulletin board lays out Kavanaugh's philosophy, whose main tenet is that it is important for addicts to learn that the same rules that apply to the rest of humanity might also apply to them:

"The unit expectations on the bulletin board are the expectations that have evolved over many years of self-government on this unit. Some of these seem silly and unnecessary, but so also do the rules, social mores and expectations out in the real world."

At times, the scene in Shoemaker suggests freshman week in a college dorm. Temporarily freed from their addictions, the addicts are like cartoon versions of themselves, with significant features exaggerated by their illness and the hothouse nature of the surroundings. Harsh criticism of others is the rule, accompanied by the telling and retelling of the stories of how they got here—the broken promises, failed relationships, all-night drinking binges, embarrassing blackouts, professional failures, lies told to spouses and parents. "What if you get sober and your girlfriend leaves you?" Bob the banker, a taciturn middle-aged man from the Midwest asks Mike, a hockey-playing broker from Connecticut. Henry the rare-book dealer from Madison, Wisconsin, has been in rehab thirteen times before. The longest he ever stayed sober was fifteen hours. He attacks Mike with a special fervor. "Listening to your story, I don't even know why you're here," he says with contempt. "You're not even an alcoholic."

Eventually, even the most active critics require a break from the soul-searching routine. One afternoon, I sat with Josh, an engineering student from Chicago who sat at the kitchen table with a navy wool watch cap pulled down low over his forehead as he meticulously folded sheets of lined paper into aerodynamic forms and sent them soaring out into the common room. Henry told stories of his thirteen prior attempts at rehabilitation to Rick, a self-made millionaire from Tennessee in a Caterpillar baseball cap and matching T-shirt. Don, a car dealer from Texas, was in his room reading aloud from the AA Big Book in the fervent Sunday morning voice of a revivalist preacher, while his roommate Mike, a nineteen-year-old from San Francisco with dyed blonde hair, listened peaceably to his Walkman. Card playing and television watching are banned before 4:30 P.M. The staff usually leaves around 5.

The threat of failure weighs heavily on the residents of Hazelden. For their First Step, they must surrender themselves to a higher power. "I just don't know how I feel about the higher power," Josh told me one afternoon in the Shoemaker lounge. If Josh failed to believe in a higher power, his counselor had told him, he would use drugs again and probably die. "A friend of mine was here with me, and he was having the same problem," he said. "And the day after he left he started to use."

The models for the arduous transformation of self that Hazelden demands are the counselors, most of whom are recovering addicts themselves, and former Hazelden patients who return to Center City in the evenings to talk to the current residents. Talks begin and end with the Serenity Prayer, attributed to Reinhold Neibuhr and known to J. D. Salinger fans as the prayer that Seymour Glass teaches his precocious siblings: "God, grant us the strength to accept the things we cannot change, courage to change the things we can, and the wisdom to know the difference." There is a sameness to the stories that the former patients tell—of lost jobs, broken homes, an inability to stop using drugs or drinking, difficulties in treatment, the moment of connection with the higher power, and the lifelong importance of attending AA meetings at least once a week.

It is hard to find a single person at Hazelden who doesn't appear to want sincerely to get sober, or who doesn't profess a strong belief in the tenets of AA. Yet nearly all the patients also admit to terrible cravings that go on for hours and threaten to obliterate any hope they have of staying sober. The intensity of these cravings is similar to those noted by Thomas De Quincey in 1822, in *Confessions of an English Opium Eater:* "Think of me as one, even when four months had passed, still agitated, writhing, throbbing, palpitating, shattered; and much, perhaps, in the situation of him who has been wracked. . . . My dreams are not yet perfectly calm: the dread swell and agitation of the storm have not wholly subsided."

One evening, a ponytailed biker named Jim related his difficulties finding work, confessed his desire to drink, and finally broke down in tears. Sitting on the long couches in the Shoemaker living room after Jim's talk, many of the peers seemed put off. "It's depressing," said Damien, a lanky young crack addict from Michigan. "If my dad knew that my treatment was going to consist of a bunch of crackheads and addicts like myself, he never would have spent fifteen thousand dollars to send me here." A few of the men wander off to watch a movie called *Malice* on television. When one of the actors refers to "a crack team of professionals," Josh makes his first joke of the week. "We have a pretty good crack team right here," he says.

Outside, the snow continued to fall. In the winter in northern Minnesota, snowfalls of up to a foot and a half are not unusual, blanketing the trees and the frozen lake. Gazing out into the darkness, it is easy to fall into a black depression, and to seek solace in a hot shower or another round of readings from the Big Book. Addiction is a line that some people cross more easily than others, and once you cross the line it is impossible to ever go back to being the same person that you were before. It's like having a parent die when you are young, or being sick for a long time as a child. Sometimes you feel better than you did a few hours earlier. Other times, you feel like you are going to die.

III.

One reason that Hazelden may find it difficult to accommodate the new drugs that some scientists now claim will revolutionize the treatment of addiction is that the AA philosophy fervently rejects the idea of a cure. Addicts are always "recovering," or "in recovery," regardless of how many years of sobriety they have attained. They are forever members of the AA community.

In the warm cocoon of Minneapolis–St. Paul, an hour's drive from Hazelden, AA members in need can find a meeting dedicated to almost any addiction at almost any time of the day or night. Young professionals in suits and ties gather at the Houses of the Holy on Grand Street in St. Paul. Hipsters and street kids gravitate to the Central Pacific Group in Minneapolis, which was started by disciples of the charismatic West Coast AA leader Clancy I., who denounces antidepressant users and coffee drinkers as being at odds with the spirit of the founders as laid down in black and white in the AA Big Book.

Recovering addicts with money settle down in spacious turn-of-the-century houses off Grand Street in St. Paul or near one of the lakes. They get married, raise children, and lead comfortable lives shadowed by the fear that old demons will be stirred up and the lives they have painstakingly constructed for themselves and their families will come crashing down in a moment of headlong impulsiveness that might send them racing out to Selby Avenue to buy crack from a dealer on the street. "It happens maybe two or three times a year," says Bob Ferguson, a recovering crack addict from New York who lives in Minneapolis with his wife and children. "It always begins with the thought, 'Wouldn't it be nice?' The complete scenario usually involves leaving everything I know, my wife, my family, my children, and going someplace halfway around the world where I can use."

On Sundays, Ferguson and his wife meet for brunch with six other couples, all in their thirties, in recovery, and with small children. Yet the shadow of addiction falls here, too. "You watch your kid take his first sip of Coca-Cola and go ballistic until you give him more, and you laugh about it," he says. "And then you pray to God."

New arrivals from Hazelden ease into the recovery community at Fellowship Club, a turreted Victorian mansion shadowed by the massive cylindrical tanks of the shuttered Landmark Brewery across the street. A Hazelden-run halfway house, Fellowship Club, costs close to three thousand dollars a month for a four-month stay. Fellowship Club residents attend individual and group counseling sessions much like those in the treatment units at Hazelden, and are expected to find full-time work within their first two weeks of arrival. The jobs they find, at the YMCA or Sam Goody, or at the Camp Snoopy amusement park in the Mall of America, often bear little relation to the jobs they held before.

Hazelden has opened halfway houses like Fellowship Club in Chicago, New York, and West Palm Beach. These new facilities are intended to act as incubators for the recovery culture, re-creating the close-knit atmosphere of Minneapolis–St. Paul in other cities. Not all patients can afford to stay in facilities like Fellowship Club, however. The day after Josh left Hazelden, we met at a halfway house called Crossroads, a converted motel by the side of a highway in Minneapolis. His room, which cost sixteen dollars a day, looked out on a parking lot. His roommate, who was lounging in a sleeping bag, chain-smoking cigarettes and stubbing the butts out on the floor, was barely nineteen.

Josh was alternately hopeful and subdued, talking about his love of mathematics at one moment and then quoting from the Big Book. When he left Hazelden, he said, he cried because he was afraid. At home, he had dinner with his mother. "It was difficult to see her," he recalled. "She was checking me out, looking at my face, trying to see some change that had happened to me while I was at Hazelden. She wanted to hear that everything is fine, that I've done good, and now we're ready to go and start up our life again. And that isn't how I feel. And the more I told her, I could look at her face and see her getting sad and disappointed. But I told her that I had to tell the truth. I'm not better. I'm sitting on the fence. And a little breeze could come along and push me over to the other side."

After dinner, he says, he went to shovel his old car out of the snow and found a crack pipe in the glove compartment and a rock of crack underneath the mat on the floor. "I took a little bite out of it to make sure it wasn't a salt pellet," he said, "and then I threw it out the window into the snow. Then I dug around, got it back, and called my AA sponsor and asked him what I should do. He told me to throw it back in the snow, and then he came and got me twenty minutes later. I could tell he was looking at me thinking, 'Maybe he smoked it.' But I didn't. And it was rough, you know."

There are few reliable statistics about how effective programs like Hazelden actually are, and the statistics that do exist are not particularly encouraging. In one recently completed, unpublished study, Pat Owen, Hazelden's director of research, was able to reach 71 percent of a representative sample of recent patients, a number just above the acceptable minimum-participant rate. Of that sample, more than half said that they had successfully stayed sober for a year. However, if one estimates that the vast majority of the remaining 29 percent did not stay sober, the success rate falls to approximately 35 percent. If one then assumes, according to standard protocols, that perhaps one quarter of the respondents did not tell Hazelden the truth, the success rate declines below one-third.

Dumping hundreds of millions of insurance dollars, as William Cope Moyers proposes, into AA-based treatment centers, many of which are far less capable than Hazelden, seems unlikely to put much of a dent in what remains a terrifying and costly disease. Yet treating addiction with drugs alone may not be as simple as some neuroscientists believe. The poor, uneducated addicts who cost society the most are also the least likely to take their medication: compliance rates for naltrexone, the antiaddiction drug that is most commonly prescribed today, are as low as 14 percent.

Nor are there any guarantees that neuroscience will actually be able to deliver a Prozac-like pill that cures addicts of their disease. Dopamine, which was recently identified as the so-called master molecule of addiction by Dr. Nora Volkow and her colleagues at the Brookhaven National Laboratory, is also the master molecule of pleasure. Without it, life would appear in even shades of gray. A drug that blocked dopamine surges, regardless of their cause, would block the naturally occurring highs of sex, or French cooking, or a summer afternoon in the park. What the new research on dopamine indicates, then, is that there will be no single cure for addiction. Unlike Prozac, which works on depression regardless of its cause, a drug that blocks cravings for crack, say, will not block cravings for other drugs, like alcohol or speed.

What the twelve-step treatment program may finally have in common with the new drugs being developed to end addiction is that neither will be able to deliver a cure. Addiction is a symptom, more urgent and dramatic, perhaps, of the constraints inherent in the human condition. The source of these constraints—our souls, ourselves, the chemistry in our brains—is hard to put a finger on.

IV.

The laboratory run by Dr. Marilyn Carroll at the University of Minnesota is only a few minutes by car from Fellowship Club. Dr. Carroll runs one of the preeminent addiction-behavior research programs in the country. "I personally don't think the medications are going to work on their own," she says. "The brain has ways of being unbelievably plastic, of getting around whatever roadblocks you try to put up."

The white-walled rooms of Dr. Carroll's basement lab are home, at the moment, to forty-eight rats and thirty-four monkeys, all of whom are addicted to alcohol, heroin, or crack cocaine. The animals are subjects in a variety of tests, some of which involve the promising D-1 antagonist SCH23390, which scientists hope will eliminate cravings for crack. Some of the monkeys watch television, to see if the competing stimulus will lower their desire for the drug. "Their favorite is *The Sound of Music*," Carroll says, "and they like watching *Oprah*, too. What they don't like, for some reason, are the nature shows."

Ten rhesus monkeys, or Macaca mulatta, live in one of the rooms. They poke their fingers out from between the wire-mesh cage fronts, make faces, and scream. Sticking out of the walls inside their cages are two stubby steel nozzles. The first is for water. The second is connected to a thin wire coil, like the inside of a cigarette lighter. Inside the coil is a rock of crack. In order to smoke the crack, the monkeys must push a lever an ever-increasing number of times, until a green light goes on above the pipe.

A room full of crack-smoking monkeys in cages is very different from a treatment unit at Hazelden. None of the monkeys tell personal stories. None take the Fifth Step, or surrender to the will of a higher power. At a low dose of SCH23390, a rhesus monkey named Lars will press the lever ten out of every ten times the drug is offered. At higher doses, however, his desire for crack radically diminishes: he will press the lever fewer than three times for every ten trials. Lucifer, another monkey, is doing even better: at high doses, his desire for crack declines to zero.

When we come to an eighteen-year-old monkey named Opus, however, Dr. Carroll rolls her eyes. "Out of twenty monkeys, you might have one or two that are exceptional, that are crazy about drugs," she explains. "We don't really know why." As she speaks, Opus pokes a finger through the wire at her, scratches at the number tattooed on his chest, and picks at the hair between his toes in a way that an addict of any species might find familiar.

According to his chart, Opus will press the lever a thousand and twenty-four times for a hit of crack in ten out of every ten trials. Low doses of SCH23390 have no effect on his desire for crack: he still presses the lever in ten out of every ten trials. On the highest possible dose, the number declines only slightly, to nine times out of ten that the drug is offered.

"He was our first monkey," Dr. Carroll says, looking at Opus and shaking her head like a disappointed but understanding parent. "We didn't know he'd be this way." The monkey looks back at Dr. Carroll, waggles his finger, and utters a guttural noise, whether in protest or to signal some more urgent desire, it is impossible to say. Maybe he is appealing to his higher power. Or perhaps his brain is wired in some unpredictable way. While we are standing there watching him, the monkey's eyes fade and go blank. Then he twists his head around and his face lights up again as he gazes up at the crack pipe inside his cage.

400,000 Salesmen Can't Be Wrong!

I.

"You want to be somebody so bad you can taste it, right?" says Greg Provenzano, staring out into the darkened vastness of the convention center in Columbus, Ohio. Provenzano is the president of ACN, the fastest-growing network-marketing company in America. Raising his hands above the crowd, he presses down lightly, once, with open palms, as if in benediction.

"Is quitting an option for you?" he asks.

"No!" the crowd roars.

"Are your dreams big enough?"

"Yes!"

"All you need is something to believe in," he says. "You have found that vehicle. You have found the vehicle called ACN."

Five thousand salesmen rise to their feet, applauding, stomping, chanting, cheering, and honking air horns. Cameras swoop in from the wings to beam back scenes of frenzied celebration to a forty-foot-high video screen above the stage, completing a high-energy feedback loop that threatens any moment now to blow the roof off the arena.

In the twenty-third row of white plastic folding chairs, a new recruit named Ed Kustanovich sits with a yellow legal pad on his lap and a ballpoint pen in his hand. He is a salesman by nature and a structural engineer by training, an energetic man in his late forties with owlish round glasses and wiry salt-and-pepper hair that stands up on his head like the bristles on a brush. During a break in the applause, he tells me that he joined the ACN network less than three months ago, at the invitation of his wife's second cousin. A moment later, he decides to tell me the rest of his life story. He speaks in heavily accented but complete sentences, which he accompanies with the vigorous circular gestures he might use to wash the windshield of his car.

"I come twenty years ago from Russia," he says. "I work hard from the very first day." He arrived in Providence, Rhode Island, where, he says, he got a job as a structural draftsman during the day and worked in a bakery on weekend nights until his English was good enough for him to gain his engineering license. Then he began working his way up to become a supervising engineer on large-scale construction projects, first in Providence and now in Los Angeles.

The chairs immediately to Ed's left are occupied by the members of his "upline," the chain of family members, friends, and friends of friends who introduced him to the company. ACN buys blocks of bandwidth and energy from wholesale suppliers, and then sells phone and electrical services to its customers at prices that may exceed those offered by more established providers. A significant proportion of the company's revenue, though, comes from the fee of $499 that prospective salesmen must pay to join. Each new salesman who, within thirty days, persuades eight people to sign over their long-distance or utilities accounts to ACN earns a bonus for whoever recruited him. In addition, for every new salesman that Ed recruits, he and the members of his upline will receive a bonus of between sixty and ninety dollars apiece. Prospective customers who refuse to sign over their accounts, or who ask too many questions, are known within the company as "rotten apples." The salesmen are encouraged to spend their time identifying crisp red apples and keeping their "personal belief systems" strong.

The salesmen in the convention center this morning have plenty of reason to believe in ACN. The company began with twenty sales representatives in 1992; it has now recruited more than four hundred thousand representatives worldwide. As a result of the recent, far-reaching efforts to deregulate the old-fashioned public power monopolies in California, ACN has also become one of the state's largest alternative providers of energy. California's experiment with open energy markets has contributed in recent months to disruptions of the power supply in the Silicon Valley, the interruption of traffic signals on busy streets in San Francisco, and rolling blackouts from Sacramento to Los Angeles. This January, Governor Gray Davis declared the state's effort at deregulation "a colossal and dangerous failure." For ACN, California's experiment with deregulation has led to the fastest increase in the size of any regional network since the company was born.

Seated immediately to Ed's left is David Halpern, who recruited him to ACN. Halpern is a friendly, bearded man who is Ed's wife's second cousin and the president of Crescent Jewelers, the largest retail jewelry chain on the West Coast. Next to him is Chris Bodig, a big man with soft brown eyes who works as a producer for a well-known sports channel. He was recruited by Joe Fortunato, his roommate at Yale, who used to write for *Living in Captivity*, a short-lived sitcom on Fox. Brian Sax, a crew-cut former engineer and captain of the Princeton track team, is the leader of Ed's upline. By working hard and following the ACN program, the salesmen are told, they can rise to the level of regional vice president, or RVP, in two to three years, travel to exotic vacation spots, receive a stress-free residual income that may place them in the top one half of one percent of money earners in the world, and enjoy many other wondrous benefits bestowed by what the speakers refer to, in shorthand, as "the Opportunity."

The convention speakers are vivid examples of how the capacity for belief can transform the lives of ordinary men and women; audience members are encouraged to identify with their rags-to-riches stories, in the same way that comic-book readers might identify with one of the Fantastic Four. Each speaker arrives onstage to a bouncy pop song chosen specially for him and an enthusiastic introduction that highlights his outstanding personal qualities, a ritual known inside ACN as "edification."

Montrel Jackson is a member of the Hall of Fame and the Circle of Champions. A trim black man in his midthirties, with a shaved head and a ready smile, he bounds onstage with the intensity and self-awareness of an old-time rhythm-and-blues performer. He grew up in Oakdale, Louisiana, where, he says, the people were poor because of their inherited attitudes toward money. " 'You know what? I don't want to be rich,' " he says, mimicking a sentiment he heard growing up. " 'I don't want to be rich,' " he repeats. " 'I just want to be *comfortable*.' " Suddenly, he grows serious. "Is it all right for your grandmother to walk while the minister rides by in his Cadillac?" Jackson thunders.

"No!" the audience roars back.

Next is Regional Vice President Debbie Davis, who looks like a down-home version of Christine Todd Whitman in a pale-pink business suit. She floats onstage to the tune of "Tupelo Honey" sung by Van Morrison: "She's as sweet as tupelo honey / She's an angel of the first degree."

"How many of you want to be set free?" she asks. One by one, the women in the crowd rise to their feet as Davis leads them in a chorus: "I will be set free! I will be an RVP!" The speakers continue their parade to the podium while Ed Kustanovich writes down sayings and statistics, and draws charts to illustrate the flow of money within the network, his engineer's mind overtaken by the frothy tide of optimism pouring from the stage. He is fully immersed in a looking-glass universe with its own separate language of achievement and success, designed to banish the thought that ACN might be a legal version of a pyramid scheme, rather than a driving force in the newly deregulated markets for telecommunications services, electricity, and gas. Those who have faith in the Opportunity, the speakers say, will succeed. Those who lack faith in the Opportunity will fail. As the day continues, Ed's eyes grow brighter.

Network marketing in America, as we know it, began with Amway, a company founded in 1959 by two lifelong friends from Michigan, Jay Van Andel and Rich DeVos. Beginning with one product, the Amway LOC Multipurpose Cleaner, Van Andel and DeVos took to the road in a touring bus, promoting an ever-expanding variety of Amway powders, soaps, and lotions. By the end of the sixties, the company had recruited more than a hundred thousand distributors, each of whom had paid for the privilege of selling the company's products. As profits from the network-marketing plan grew, the company's main production facility, in Ada, Michigan, was transformed into a mile-long city with a recycling facility, shuttle-bus service, a railroad station, and a private fleet of planes.

In the midseventies, the Federal Trade Commission prepared a case arguing that the company was actually a sophisticated pyramid scheme. When the case against Amway was dismissed, dozens of network-marketing companies sprang into existence, peddling things like water filters and calling cards through far-flung networks of representatives who are fed a steady diet of dreamlike inducements and hopeful scenarios which are limited only by the requirement that they avoid suggesting, either directly or through implication, any specific income, whether weekly, monthly or yearly, that the company's representatives can expect to earn.

The five men who founded ACN, collectively known as the Cofounders, came together in the fall of 1992 after working for other network-marketing companies that eventually disbanded or went broke. All of them are from Michigan, and none have college degrees or any previous professional expertise in telecommunications or utilities. But these men know from experience why people join companies like ACN. "They are dissatisfied with something in their lives," one of the founders, Tony Cupisz, explains backstage in Columbus. "They're dissatisfied with work, or with the glass ceiling, or by the feeling that they should have something better." Tony Cupisz and his brother Mike are twins, blonde and athletic-looking. Robert Stevanoski, the third Cofounder, bears a striking resemblance to Jon Voight's character in *The Deerhunter.* J. D. Williamson, who looks like a paunchy sheriff in an old Western, spends the least amount of time on stage.

Greg Provenzano, the company's president and fourth Cofounder, seems like a sober-minded suburban dad in a business suit, dependable and solid. He recorded the company's first recruitment tapes over preexisting recordings of a Woody the Woodpecker cartoon. As he talks about ACN, its great advantage becomes clear: the company has no physical connection to the services it provides. By eliminating the bother of a tangible, physical product, like water filters, hand lotion, vitamins, or soap, the five former sales representatives from Michigan have reduced the network-marketing business down to its essence—the hopeful, levitating faith of its members. They have summoned an empire out of thin air.

II.

When the speeches are over, thousands of ACN representatives spill out of the hall, talking and laughing and slapping each other on the shoulder and exchanging business cards on their way upstairs to the cocktail lounge of the Hyatt Hotel. It is time to build company spirit and trade stories with the thousands of other representatives who have come to Columbus from hundreds of towns and cities around the country. "I'm gonna do it, you know what I mean?" a large black woman in a leopard-print shirt tells a colleague from Mississippi. In a nearby corner, two white women from upstate New York are deep in discussion of "the stinkin' thinkin' " that stands in the way of realizing their dreams.

Striding confidently together through the crowd, Ed and his fellow Californians take the escalator upstairs to the Conventional Center Hyatt, where a party has already started in the lounge. Standing by the bar is James Maclin, an imposing black man whose enormous upper arms stretch the fabric of his electric-blue suit, and whose eyes radiate manic energy from behind a pair of huge glasses with the Gucci "G" emblazoned on the frames. He used to work in a steel mill in Cleveland; now he repairs electrical systems on private jets.

He has a story to tell me about his work, he says. One day, he walked into the cabin of a jet to do a repair and saw that the entire interior of the plane was white. The carpets were white. The walls were white. All the furniture, including the television set, was white. He sat inside that jet for half an hour, he says. The whiteness of the jet blew his mind.

"I want you to document this," he says. "I thought, I have to find a way to get me one of these jets." Two months later, he says, a friend, who was once a lineman for the Cleveland Browns, invited him to join ACN. When he strikes it rich, he says, the first thing he plans to buy is a white jet.

A little later in the evening, Ed Kustanovich and the members of his upline gather in room 839 of the Hyatt, sitting on the floor and on the bed and leaning up against the walls, to celebrate Brian Sax's elevation to the position of regional vice president. Poised on the edge of a piece of hotel room furniture, halfway between sitting and standing, Brian radiates the fragile, luminous energy that you might see in a runner after a race. The ACN motivation typology divides the company's representatives into four distinct groups, each of which is represented by a different totem-animal: Whales are motivated by helping others, Sharks by money, Urchins by facts, and

Dolphins by the promise of a good time. Brian is a whale. What he'd like now, he says, is for all the people here to share a few words about why they joined ACN.

"I didn't want to be the person who couldn't fly over Los Angeles at night," Chris Bodig answers. A big, easy man in his early thirties, he leads the life that most American men of his age might see in their dreams, producing an Emmy Award–winning sports show and sharing a house with a friend on the ocean in Hermosa Beach. Yet beneath the placid surface of his manner, there is clearly something unresolved, a glittering constellation of possibilities that will remain suspended forever in the hazy skies above Los Angeles at night.

Standing by the wall, Sam Friedberg, an engineer from MIT, prepares to speak next. He talks like an engineer and he looks like an engineer, with his receding hairline and heavy black glasses that fit like a pair of brackets around his crew-cut head. "It was something I couldn't logically refute," he says. There are people who don't make you feel good about your decision, he adds, looking down at the tan hotel room carpet, including members of his own family. "If I stop, and don't follow through," he says, as the forty people in the room nod their heads, "then everything they said will be right."

As the new members continue to speak, it appears that lack of sleep and the high emotional pitch of the proceedings have softened the barriers that often keep people from confessing their secrets to a roomful of strangers.

"The last person who invested with me lost his money," a middle-aged businessman with five kids offers. "The last person who worked for me lost his job."

"You get knocked around."

"Mediocrity becomes the way you survive."

With his back against the wall, Ed Kustanovich stares intently around the room. He appears fascinated and a little embarrassed, running his fingers through his wire-brush hair. Next to him is his first recruit, a long-haired commercial artist named John Gomez, who was a tenant in a house that Ed rented out. When his turn arrives, Ed steps toward the center of the room and tells the story of how he came to America twenty years ago without a penny to his name.

"God bless America!" Ed exclaims. "I work very hard. Made sacrifices for career. Twenty years later, working as hard as I can. Seems to me it is vicious circle. I make good income. I have good life. But you have to pay for it, all the time.

"I want team, nice people, friendship," he adds, stepping back toward the relative safety of the wall. His face is flushed, and there are traces of sweat on his forehead. He is happy that the moment is over. He is happy to let go of loneliness, anxiety, and striving, and to relax into the warm embrace of the group.

"This is how we used to do it in the old days," Jeff Carlisle says from the back of the room. The leader of Brian Sax's upline, he is a regional vice president, a member of the Hall of Fame, and one of the most celebrated money earners in the company—a blonde, well-tanned man in his midthirties with the winning smile and perfect teeth of a former child actor or a late-night pitchman selling blenders or real estate. "I just freaked out to a whole other level last Friday," he explains of his recent trip to Barcelona, where he met Cofounder Tony Cupisz for a vacation, and then met some people who invited him down to the Spanish resort of Marbella, where he partied all day and all night for a week.

"I came back," he continues, "and all I did was, I opened my mail and found three checks from ACN. I went to the bank and deposited my checks. Then I got on a flight and came here. How many of you would like to be in that situation, if all you had to do for your money was deposit it?"

Carlisle is a true professional, the Mario Andretti of high-pressure sales, shifting cleanly through the emotional gears from inducement to flattery, greed, personal obligation, and fear of loss while leaning casually forward into the room with one arm braced against the hotel room desk without betraying even the slightest hint of tension or strain.

"My job now is to get people to snap," he says. "You've got to snap."

In response, the barometric pressure in the room appears to drop, and the mood of the participants becomes darker and more revealing. "I used to put in a lot of effort and do well at everything I did," says Darryl Adams, a man in his early fifties who joined the network four months ago. As he continues to speak, his fear becomes palpable, a living, breathing presence in the room. "What if this turns out to be like everything else in my life?" he asks. "It would kill me," he adds.

"I've made a series of subtle errors in judgment," says John Crane, a fresh-faced MIT graduate in his midtwenties. Three weeks ago, he says, he left his job as an engineer at a manufacturing plant and moved from Michigan to Los Angeles to work full time for ACN. As he continues, it becomes clear that something has broken inside him, some fragile reflective surface like a mirror or a pane of glass. Deeper anxieties and fears come rushing to the surface. He starts to cry.

III.

The sales representatives have been warned not to approach the hotel's employees during the course of their stay. By the time they hit the departure gate at the airport the next afternoon, they can barely contain their enthusiasm as they buttonhole weary travelers in the check-in line with the familiar opening lines of the ACN pitch.

"If I told you of a great new way to make money off your telephone, gas, and electric bills, and the bills of your neighbors, would you be interested?" a fortysomething ACN representative named Don Rupp begins. The older blonde woman behind him in line doesn't return his smile.

"It's a way to spend more time with your family, or at the beach, or doing whatever it is that you want to do," Don persists. He seems weirdly alert.

"No, thank you," she says, smiling tightly as the proper mental template for responding to strangers in airports snaps into place. "But thank you very much for asking."

The woman behind the check-in counter has heard the pitch at least a dozen times. "If I told you about a way you could earn money off the telephone, gas, and electric bills of your neighbors, would you be interested?" someone asks. She continues punching numbers into her computer terminal until the boarding pass is printed out. She folds the ticket into its jacket and hands it across the counter before she politely declines.

Strapped into his seat in the back of the plane as it leaves for Los

Angeles, Don leans across the aisle and starts pitching his neighbor, a manufacturing representative, who promises to attend an upcoming meeting. Once the seat-belt sign goes off, the representatives spread the good news about the Opportunity to people in line for the bathroom and to members of the flight crew who are busy rolling beverage carts up and down the aisles. Ed Kustanovich is running through lists of friends, relatives, and business associates who might be interested in learning more about ACN, and whom he will contact on his cell phone the moment the plane touches down in Los Angeles.

Four days later, standing in the kitchen of his house in Simi Valley, Ed is still talking about the international convention in Columbus. "Any doubt I had in my mind, it walked away," he says. "I saw thousands and thousands of people. They wouldn't come all the way there to Columbus for nothing."

There are no rolling blackouts in Simi Valley. Ed's kitchen is stuffed full of new appliances, and the four bedrooms upstairs include a spacious master bedroom suite. The window behind his head frames a scene of palm fronds waving gently back and forth in the breeze above the heated swimming pool where Ed swims his laps in the morning. When I ask him what's wrong with his life here, he frowns.

"Real trouble in job when David approached me," he replies. "I think to myself, I cannot be slave. I've been slave before." If something bad happens on a job site, he says, he can be held liable under California state law. "There is lots of trouble sometimes with subcontractors. They make life sometimes miserable."

His wife, he adds, has a different answer. "She said, 'midlife crisis,' " he says. "Usually I have dinner, watch TV, am exhausted, fall asleep on sofa. Now sharp change." After Ed excuses himself to call the members of his team, I spend some time with his wife in the kitchen, where she is standing over a pot of borscht.

"If it sounds too good to be true, it usually is," she says. "Now I wait and see."

When I speak to Ed's son, Vlad, a graduate student in human genetics, he tells me that his father's impulse toward greater freedom led to the family's leaving Russia, but it has also led to his interest in various unprofitable ventures and get-rich-quick schemes, like manufacturing pendants and joining Amway. "I thought Amway was garbage," Vlad says. "But I think this is very different. You don't need to buy Amway lotion or Amway shampoo." Still, he worries. "I talked to my friend, who is also a scientist," he adds. "He said, 'Don't do this. It's a complete pyramid scheme. The majority of people don't make any money. They just end up working for the few people at the top who do.' "

Ed is pacing back and forth outside the sliding glass doors with a cellular telephone clamped to his ear. "Hello!" he says. "This is Ed Kustanovich. How is everything? How is family?" He is staring up at the sun-dappled palm leaves over his head. "Listen. Can you do me huge favor?" He begins reciting the lines of the standard ACN script for drumming up new customers. "Would you be interested in a great new opportunity to make money off your neighbors' utilities and telecommunications bills in your spare time? No?" Ed pauses for barely a moment. "Can you do me huge personal favor as part of my training? Would you at least try my services?"

A week after the international convention, Ed has succeeded in assembling a team of five new representatives, who have gathered together for the first time. The master bedroom has been outfitted for the occasion with folding chairs and refreshments—bottled soda, plates of cut-up vegetables, a bowl of potato chips. Ed's inclination would have been to lay out a more hospitable spread, in true Russian fashion, but ACN's policy limits refreshments to items that anyone in the room could afford to provide. The new members sit on chairs or on the carpet, taking notes on legal pads as David Halpern relates some important first lessons about the Opportunity.

"Don't get excited about getting new customers," he says with a friendly smile. "Your main role is to teach other people how to do the business." When they identify new prospects, it is important not to say too much. "Don't tell them anything about the business," he explains. "You pass them on to me."

It takes a moment or two for the message to sink in. Ed's friend Lyubov is the first to respond. She spends most of the meeting with her arms crossed over her chest. "Sounds so simple," she says.

"It *is* simple!" Ed says. "Now you understand what I'm doing, right? I have energy, and I give you energy!"

Next, David passes around some photocopied pages from "The Wave 3 Way to Building Your Downline," a popular network-marketing primer, and begins to paraphrase the text: "The government made the determination more than fifteen years ago that Amway was not an illegal marketing scheme. So it's a new era in network marketing right now."

In the wake of the Amway decision, the FTC did establish clear rules that govern the practice of network marketing. David Halpern is careful to observe these rules, which require network-marketing companies to sell an actual, definable product and prohibit them from charging exorbitant membership fees or making representatives carry expensive inventories.

"Your job is just to present them with the Opportunity," David explains. There are skeptics, he adds, who theorize that the number of clients that a network is likely to attract is limited, and that eventually the number of new representatives will decrease, profit margins will shrink, and then the entire network-marketing structure will collapse. The name of this theory, he says, is "saturation"—a bugaboo that haunts the recruitment efforts of every network-marketing company on the planet. Luckily, David explains, saturation is a fiction; the pool of prospective ACN clients is, in fact, endless. Everyone in the room looks relieved.

"Do not answer the question 'What are your rates?' " David instructs. "This is network marketing. You are relying on the relationship."

The chain of faith that holds ACN together is forged, link by link, from the families and friends of the company's representatives. When you look around the room, it is easy to see this process in action. Lyubov is here because she believes in Ed. Michael is married to Lyubov. Marguerite, the one American-born person in the group, is here because Ed's mother was friends with her mother in Israel, and because she dreams of having more time to herself and of living without debt. Vlad is here because he is Ed's son and wants to support his father.

"I'd like to take copies of those lists from you," David says. The combined efforts of the new members have already yielded two hundred new prospects for ACN. Under the heading "How I know them," Marguerite has given short descriptions of the people she plans to call, including "Dad's friends," "dentist," "Adrian's friend," "Jeff's ex-wife," and "sold me my car."

With the lists in hand, David Halpern reminds people to "edify" their upline representative. "Sam is a top-ten producer in our company," he says. He is edifying Sam Friedberg, the upline representative who will play the role of "expert" for many of the incoming calls that Ed and his team will generate. "He's an MIT grad, with a very successful career in engineering. And he's not just smart and successful. He's also a good guy, down to earth, likes people."

IV.

Sam Friedberg is a team coordinator, a position just below regional vice president in the ACN hierarchy; last month, he says, he earned more than fourteen thousand dollars. He spends his days in the living room of a modest one-bedroom apartment in Torrance, sitting in an overstuffed reclining chair and fielding three-way calls from prospective ACN representatives. He looks like an engineer from the fifties, with his close-cropped hair and heavy black glasses. Dressed in blue nylon sweatpants and a T-shirt, he surveys his living room, which he has furnished inexpensively with wall-to-wall carpeting, matching pine tables, and a seersucker couch. Arrayed on the living room shelves are a few spare personal touches, including a Go board, a chess set, a menorah, a wax dolphin, and a white plastic-covered photo album with "Sammy's Bar Mitzvah" inscribed in gold lettering on the spine. The phone rings twice. Sam clicks a button, then presses the big black cordless receiver to his ear.

"You're currently working?" Sam asks, staring up at the ceiling. "No? I think people don't do that enough." After thousands of calls, he has learned to hit the right notes without thinking, encouraging the caller to believe that he is talking to a high-level corporate executive whose busy schedule has not yet erased his basic human capacity for empathy and understanding. "That's not a way to live," he says. He talks about building a sales force whose leaders will be rewarded with a percentage of the company's earnings.

"On a more personal level," he continues, proceeding to the heart of his pitch, "we want to be in a position, in two or three years, to be at the beach with our families, traveling, or wherever we want to be, knowing that tens of thousands of people are turning on their lights, cooking on their stoves, and making telephone calls, and we're getting paid." He tilts his feet toward the ceiling, displaying a pair of white tube socks with gray heels. In a blue plastic tub by his feet is a stack of resumes that Sam has harvested from the Internet.

"OK. Mmmm-hmmm. Right." Sam is holding up one hand, and waving at the ceiling. "What's your schedule looking like next week?" The prospect is interested. There will be a meeting tomorrow in a nearby Courtyard by Marriott hotel, Sam explains, where he can meet the company's leadership. Later this week, there will be another meeting at a golf course called the Lakes.

In less than a minute, the phone rings again.

"Don told me you have a heck of a commute," he says. "What business are you in?" Sam nods. "I'm fairly familiar with that," he offers. "I used to work at the technical side of TRW." He launches into his pitch again, varying the phrasing and intonation to make it seem natural, and to keep his head in the game. He puts down the phone, and it rings again. The next call is from someone who met John Gomez on the plane back from Columbus.

"I guess you and John had the good fortune to meet on an airplane," Sam says. The opportunity that ACN offers, he explains, is "allowing people to retire and walk away from their jobs after working part time for only a few months." He invites the caller to a Sunday night meeting in Hermosa Beach. "Our goal is to capture 2 percent of the national market over the next two years—that's 2 percent of $650 billion," Sam explains. "And on a more personal level . . ."

The rest of the pitch takes less than a minute. Between calls, Sam tells me about his own introduction to the business, which came through a friend at TRW. When Sam first heard about ACN, he remembers, he thought it was a scam. Still, the job he had wasn't particularly appealing, either.

"We were all together in this big room with no dividers, no cubicles, just one big bay filled with desks," he recalls of his last project for TRW, which had something to do with satellites. As he describes the room, his shoulders retract slightly, pressing hard into the back of his chair. "The air was thick. It felt thick when you walked in. My association would be with, like, a big general-population jail cafeteria that you see in the movies." He was terrified of spending the rest of his life at TRW, he says, working his way up to become a midlevel manager toiling late into the night on secret projects for eighty thousand dollars a year.

"I remember my last performance evaluation," he continues. "There was a comment from one of my superiors, 'Sam would show up at ten and leave at six'—how the fuck did he say it?" Sam's face reddens slightly as he searches for the exact combination of words his superior used: " 'Which is not acceptable for someone assigned to work on a proposal.' It burned me up. First of all, I'm thinking, Who the fuck are you? Secondly, I'm thinking, You poor bastard, they've conditioned you to believe in all this. And, third, I'm thinking, If I get to be as good an employee as him, I'll be thinking that way, too."

A few weeks later, on August 3, 1998, Sam sent a round-robin e-mail to his colleagues to inform them of the reasons behind his decision to leave TRW.

"I plan to see if I can draw an income from playing poker in the L.A. area card rooms," the e-mail explained. "I think that the time is right for me to try this now. Smoking has been banned in the California card rooms since the beginning of the year (these card rooms are legal, safe, reputable businesses). I have money saved up, and have no large debts or dependants." Within a few months, however, he had discovered that playing poker at the Crystal Palace Card room in Compton at night was only marginally more satisfying than his work at TRW, and so he agreed to meet Brian Sax's roommate Ed Niu and another representative at a Chinese restaurant by the highway for lunch. Niu himself was a lapsed engineer, and by the end of the lunch Sam Friedberg was feeling more enthusiastic about the Opportunity than he had ever felt about anything before in his life. "I like being around people who all feel they're going somewhere," he explains. "It's like we're all breaking free together from societal norms and corporate jails.

"It is something where one's success does depend in large part on one's belief in the Opportunity," he goes on. "The more strongly you believe, the more likely you are to succeed." Because David Halpern has faith, he says, he is likely to become a regional vice president. As for Ed Kustanovich, he thinks it's too soon to tell. "I really like the guy," Sam says. "He's excited, he has a good attitude, he's coachable. If he can sustain that, he'll make it all the way." He pauses. "But most people can't."

V.

Driving from his home in the Valley to a meeting with a producer in Hollywood, Joe Fortunato makes a few calls, telling friends, friends of friends, and total strangers about the Opportunity. He is building his downline, trying to stay a rung above David Halpern and a couple of rungs above Ed Kustanovich. The calls he makes ten or fifteen times a day, he says, offer relief for his anxiety. At Yale, he recalls, he wrote papers about *Gilligan's Island* and dreamed of becoming the youngest president in the history of network television, even younger than his hero, Brandon Tartikoff. He is now thirty-three years old and self-employed. His last girlfriend came from a wealthy family, he says, and she broke up with him because he didn't have enough money. "My goal through ACN is to make a few hundred thousand, so I can do the things that will get me to ten million, and from ten million I can get to a hundred million," he says. He stops for a moment, and starts talking about the screenplay he's writing. It centers on a stockbroker named Billy who lives in New York and becomes a superhero whose exploits are chronicled in the *New York Post*.

He stops for a moment, and gazes out over the swimming pool at my hotel, then admires the view of the tree-lined streets and the freeway below as he waits for me to offer a suitable response. The story of Billy reminds me of the stories I used to write in my notebook during classes in junior high, and also of the boy I met outside the hotel the night before, who told me about his dream of distributing videotapes featuring himself playing his music in local clubs around Los Angeles. The people who would come to watch his music would also be included on the tapes, he explained, which would circulate widely and create a sense of community, which is important because there is no community among musicians in L.A. An engineer who once worked on an album by the heavy-metal band Slayer had already agreed to help with the songs. Having spent the past two weeks with ACN members, it took me more than five minutes to realize that his shirt was torn and that his eyeballs were rolling back in his head. I tell Joe Fortunato my story, and he shrugs.

"There's a lot of people interested in my movie," he says. "But that's Hollywood. You can never really tell if they are interested or not." What matters now, he says, is working hard, sticking to the ACN program, and keeping his "belief system" strong.

Jeff Carlisle's belief system is perhaps the strongest of any ACN representative in the state of California. A blond, well-tanned man in his midthirties, with the dazzling smile of a talk-show host, he is a regional vice president and one of the leading money earners in the company. His main function in the organization is to motivate others, by giving speeches and instructional seminars, and simply by being an example of the good things that can come to those who have faith. He has worked as a salesman since he was nineteen years old. Before coming to ACN, he was a real estate broker in Los Angeles. Before that, he sold sand.

When I meet Carlisle at a cafe in Manhattan Beach, he wants to talk about a glimpse of the high life he got while on vacation in the Spanish resort town of Marbella. He is dressed in a lightweight jacket and a pair of expensive-looking synthetic pants; his new Mercedes is parked a block away. "This guy I met was forty-four years old, he owns all the Living Room clubs, he owns thirty-five restaurants. His family owns the second-largest diamond mine in the world. 'Come to my house in Marbella, I spent fifteen million dollars for a party house,' he says."

The name of the house, he continues, was Villa Caesar. "There are gold pillars throughout, statues, just like the Caesars Palace hotel," he says, squinting a little. "There were thirteen bedrooms and two indoor pools. Each bedroom had a full-sized Jacuzzi next to the bed. I went down to the bay, and I counted forty-seven yachts over one hundred feet long."

Carlisle readily admits that his fascination with rich people has something to do with the experience of growing up poor in Iowa after his parents divorced. There he watched his single mother work three jobs, and drove to school in a rusted-out Chevy Vega. "I just felt very different," he remembers. "And not in a good way. I felt outside of the normal life that was available to everyone else, driving up to school in this shitty car, working after school, and not being able to have new clothes."

As he talks about these memories, it's clear that what makes Carlisle a great salesman is that he has such direct access to his emotions. The desire for money is the deepest thing in him, a salve for wounds that refuse to heal. When he started selling door-to-door in the summers, he says, he found that he could get anyone to like him within the space of ten or fifteen seconds. People loaned him their cars to use during his rounds. They gave him the keys to their houses so that he could take a beer from the fridge or swim laps in the pool.

"That's when I knew that there was something outside me," he remembers. "That I had triggered something out there in the universe that would give me whatever I wanted."

The Opportunity is founded on the hopeful premise that the company's network will continue to grow. Protecting that belief can be a demanding task for sales representatives, because it often collides with more traditional codes of behavior, especially toward one's family and friends. As involvement with the company deepens, so does the gap between the dreamworld of personal satisfaction and riches and the world of the representative's previous values, expectations, and friendships. The departure starts slowly, and it is often accompanied by shocks. Driving his Jeep to his job on a busy construction site in downtown Los Angeles, Ed Kustanovich makes calls from his cell phone, some in Russian and some in English, repeating the mantra again and again.

"If I told you about a way to earn money off the telephone bills, electric bills, and gas bills of your neighbors," he asks. Ed Kustanovich's faith in the company appears to be strong. But there's at least a hint of trouble, brought on by an e-mail he received from his best friend, Mike. The text of the e-mail is friendly and polite. It also provides an exceptionally clear description of how network marketing can feel to those on the receiving end.

"Dear Ed," the letter begins.

"I am sorry to disappoint you with my decision not to pursue ACN. I know you are disappointed in me. It is hard to say no when I know that you are so excited about ACN. I was considering signing up for the service so I could save some $'s on utility bills . . . but after carefully considering it, I realized I was reacting to hype, pressure and obligation! The main reason I showed up to the presentation was because of you, Ed—my friend. Because I value you as a friend I will be straightforward with you with my concerns about ACN. ACN relies on your ability to persuade and manipulate your friends and relatives. . . . You cannot help but expect people to sign up for the program, and if they don't, you are naturally disappointed. . . . Is the chance of eroding a relationship really worth it? I don't think so."

Describing the ACN representatives as "relentless and pushy," Mike also notes their refusal to provide before-and-after examples of utility bills or any other evidence of savings. "Ed, it was nice to see you and your wife," the letter concludes. "You seem to be much happier. I apologize if I have disappointed you in any way.

"Sincerely, Your friend—Mike."

VI.

The house in Hermosa Beach shared by Chris Bodig and David Halpern offers a wonderful view of the water and of the joggers, dog walkers, and Roller-bladers who crowd the boardwalk on weekend afternoons. On Sunday evenings, it is a favorite location for private business receptions, or PBRs, the group meetings at which new prospects are introduced to the Opportunity by Brian Sax and the other members of Ed's upline.

Standing in front of the large-screen television set in his living room, Chris Bodig edifies Brian Sax, who is looking even more confident than usual in a new suit and freshly crew-cut hair. "He's one of the most impressive people I've ever met in my life," Bodig says. He looks around the room at the dozen or so prospects. The mixture of people in the room suggests the range of those who are attracted to the Opportunity. There is a well-dressed black woman who works as a lawyer for a Hollywood studio; a man who recently moved to Los Angeles from Philadelphia; a middle-aged Asian man, whom I'll call Akira (he requested that his name not be used), who owns a recording studio in the Los Angeles area; a man who works at a garage; another man who makes baseball bats; and two Hispanic stock boys from the local grocery. As Brian begins his pitch, Ed and his wife sneak in the door and find a place by the couch.

Brian is especially forceful this evening; in a few days, he will be heading off to Las Vegas for a special meeting of the company's regional vice presidents. His shoulders squared like a corporal rallying his troops, he quotes statistics estimating the national energy market at $650 billion and tosses out questions to the crowd.

"Is it just me, or did we miss the boat on the Internet?" he asks. The founder of Amazon, Jeff Bezos, graduated several years ahead of Brian at Princeton. No matter what happens to Amazon, he says, Jeff Bezos and fifty of his associates are set for life. But, for those in the room this evening, what ACN offers is a second chance at success. "MCI stock has split ten to twelve times," he says. "Can you imagine what's going to happen with *our* stock? Where in corporate America can a person working for a company be in the position within a few years to out-earn the CEO of that company?"

"Nowhere!" The loudest voice in the room belongs to Ed. His wife looks shyly around the circle of faces, marveling at how many people are here.

Brian's presentation is followed by a short training session. Afterward, the representatives circulate through the room to answer any remaining questions that the prospects might have.

"A pyramid scheme is illegal," Ed Niu explains to a newcomer, David Herrera. "No one gets paid here unless you get customers."

"I would love to do it," Akira, the Asian man, tells Joe Fortunato as they stand together in a corner of the kitchen. "But I have to convince my wife to let me touch my savings."

Half an hour later, the two men are still locked in conversation.

"My name is important to me," Akira insists. "I want to know that my customers will be saving money."

"I don't tell people that," Fortunato parries. "My integrity is important to me, too." His face darkens. "If two hundred thousand people weren't happy with their bills, wouldn't they switch?" he asks. He is searching for a way out of the impasse that Akira has created with his polite but pointed questions. "Tell them, 'At least give me the credit that I know my business,'" he says.

Sensing a problem, Brian Sax walks over and puts his arm around Fortunato's shoulders as Ed Kustanovich lingers by a bucket of melting ice. "He's responsible for so much great leadership for our team," Brian offers, edifying his friend. But Akira refuses to budge.

"Is there any way to compare the actual rates?" he asks.

"Why do you need that information?" asks Ed Niu, who has come over from the other side of the room to help out. "I don't sell anybody on rates. And they're still with the service. We need volume of customers. Then we can start driving rates down."

"If I enroll, he makes a hundred and fifty dollars?" Akira asks. "I wish I could know a bit more in detail about what happens here. You can't pay out more than you take in." Behind his polite smile, and his occasional show of looking down at the kitchen tile, he clearly has some idea of how the system actually works. "Are you going to build a new power plant?" he presses, cocking his head expectantly to one side. "Because, with what the total profits were for the company last year, that's not going to do it."

"You're thinking like corporate America," Fortunato answers. But Akira has nothing against corporate America. He is a member of a group of four hundred of his countrymen who help each other in business by pooling their resources, he explains. He trusts them, and they trust him.

"How can I explain this to my friends?" he asks. "That eventually the rates might go down, but that in the meantime they are losing ten dollars a month?"

When the private business reception is over, I am driven back to my hotel by the man who has the distinction of being Brian Sax's first recruit as well as his best friend. His name is Quoc Tran, and he is a thin Vietnamese man who spends his days running distances of up to fifteen miles and watching war documentaries on the History Channel. His father was a South Vietnamese marine, he says, who died in a reeducation camp after the Americans left. His hatred of authority, he says, came from growing up in Vietnam during the war.

As we make our way up I-405 at night toward Los Angeles, Quoc remembers the night he left Vietnam on a boat with his three brothers and his mother. "I got very, very sick," he recalls, swinging the wheel over to the right. "I had an extreme fever. I was hallucinating. There was talk that I might be contagious. They would toss people over the side if they were contagious." He peers out over the dashboard, steering with one hand draped over the top of the wheel as he cuts across two lanes and heads for the nearest exit. "I had to move from the top level to the bottom level of the boat. It was so hot, I can't tell you. I would smell the urine and all that stuff. We were down in the very bottom pit."

Where Brian is organized and precise, Quoc's thoughts meander over circuitous pathways that tangle together like the fuzzy lines on an Etch-A-Sketch. "The condition was pretty deplorable, Dave," he says, of the refugee camp where he stayed in Hong Kong. "It was not sanitary." His mother wanted to go to France, but he insisted on America, "the freest goddamn country in the world." I urge him to turn left at the next light. He ignores my directions, and tells me about arriving in a small town in Indiana in 1980. He was amazed at how big the people were, and how clean and fresh everything seemed. "But there was a memory inside me that was still hurting," he says. "Everywhere you turned, there was another reminder of Vietnam. There was *Rambo,* and there were also the things that I remembered. There was a lot of anger in me," he says. "I thought to myself, How could a country so big, so powerful, lose the fucking war?"

When Brian first told him about ACN, he recalls, he thought he had found the answer he had been looking for. "It just turned on so bright in me, it was indescribable," he says. I look out the window and realize that we are lost in south-central Los Angeles. I encourage Quoc to turn the car around.

"The light was so bright inside me that I couldn't sleep for days," he continues as he pulls into a gas station, then heads back toward the lights of West Hollywood. "Because everything is energy, Dave. The company is about energy. I was pure energy. The energy was just unbelievable." The feeling lasted for about six months, Quoc says, after which he began to feel the presence of another force that was working against him. There was a time in his life, he continues, when he went into seclusion. He talked to angels. He looked deep into his soul. What he understood then was that there was no authority in the world that could ever govern his thoughts or his actions. ACN was just another kind of authority, he concluded, a way of controlling people's minds by exploiting their capacity for belief. What he wants for himself right now, he explains, is something much larger and brighter, and more difficult for outside forces to get at.

"I want to be a true democrat," he explains as he drops me off at my hotel. "I want to have what Thomas Jefferson had in his own mind."

VII.

Six weeks later, I get a phone call from Brian Sax, just back from the most recent ACN international convention, which was held in San Jose. "You wouldn't believe the energy," he says, and continues in the same vein for another few minutes, until he arrives at the point of the call.

"Guess who the most successful new member of the team is now," he says. "It's Ed! Ed's team has fourteen members. He's doing great. A lot of that is thanks to John." He asks me if I remember the long-haired artist who was Ed's first recruit. John Gomez cut his hair, Brian says, and has become one of the company's leading salesmen.

"And guess what Ed gave as the reason for his success," Brian says. When it came time for the team to share their stories in San Jose, he says, Ed stood up and talked about arriving in America, and then mentioned that someone—a writer from New York—had told him, not so long ago, that network-marketing companies often fail, and that he might have trouble succeeding as a salesman because of his accent. Ed was determined to prove that person wrong, he said. He would succeed. And now, thanks to ACN, and to all the people in the hotel room that evening, he had.

A Prince Among Thieves

As the sound of late-morning traffic on the Long Island Expressway fades into the heavily chlorinated silence of the backyard swimming pools off Exit 58, DJ and hip-hop producer Prince Paul is surveying his lawn. "It's a nice, wide-open place, relaxed and green, good oxygen," he says, describing the empty streets and tract-house mansions of Islandia, New York, with a sweep of his skinny arm. A slight man in his early thirties with a wispy hipster goatee and soft brown eyes, he comes at the world with the weird, off-kilter energy of a hyperactive fifth grader in the days before Ritalin was commonly prescribed. He has lived in the Long Island suburbs nearly all his life.

"I like to smoke my crack in private," he explains without a hint of a smile, bending down to pluck a blade of crabgrass. "My wife says I'm antisocial," he says, holding the blade up to the sun to see if perhaps it will grow. "I like to see people when I like to see them. My days go pretty much like this."

While most rap producers stick to a canon that has changed very little since the music began, Paul Huston has reinvented rap music three times in just over a decade. In 1989 he teamed with three friends from Amityville High who called themselves De La Soul. The group's debut album, *3 Feet High and Rising,* featured literate, almost scholarly rhymes and a wholly original sound—a mélange of hip-hop beats, blue-eyed-soul hooks, game-show patter, novelty records, and Berlitz language tapes, shot through with the unwound energy of four black teenagers sitting around in a Long Island basement and showing off for their friends. On his two most recent records, *A Prince Among Thieves* (conceived as a soundtrack to a nonexistent movie written, produced, and directed by Prince Paul) and last year's *So . . . How's Your Girl?* (produced with Dan "the Automator" Nakamura under the name Handsome Boy Modeling School), he took his musical intelligence and humor to the level of high art.

Prince Paul's creative success has come during a decade when humor, intelligence, formal innovation, and originality have very little place in rap music at all. As rap established itself in the 1990s as the most popular musical genre among young blacks and whites alike, what was once the most inventive music around became as derivative as the worst of '80s pop—the bass-heavy monotone for street-talking millionaire rappers who rhymed over slick, commercially processed beats about drug money, guns, private planes, iced-out platinum jewelry, and other subjects that varied little from record to record or year to year. The rappers, producers, and executives who made the records moved to suburbs like Alpine, New Jersey, or Islandia, where they could mow their lawns on the weekends, send their kids to nice schools, and otherwise realize the millennial edition of the American Dream. LL Cool J's house is two exits away. Pioneering DJ Grandmaster Flash lives a mile down the road, and Erick Sermon of EPMD (Erick and Parrish Making Dollars) lives in a pocket mansion at the end of Gooseberry Lane, with a custom-made radio-controlled wrought-iron gate in front and a full-length basketball court in back.

Prince Paul, for one, is definitely impressed by his neighbor's new house. "Erick's house is nice," he says, casting a secretive glance down the quiet cul-de-sac. "I'm not going to say all he has in there for the record," he continues, "because that would be wrong. All I can say is, he has a very nice basketball court. The Knicks could play on his court. Put it like that. And have sideline room to spare, and room for spectators and cheerleaders and professional stadium lighting. You could land an airplane there at night."

Prince Paul is different from his neighbors. He is an authentic oddball whose musical genius has allowed him a more or less tenuous career on the commercial margins of rap, with a following that he fairly describes as "Afrocentric women or men; a guy with dreadlocks, a beard that's grown far beyond handsome, and some really tattered clothing; a girl with an Erykah Badu hair wrap; some skateboarder white males between fifteen and twenty; white females who are into zany alternative stuff; smart college kids; and some Asian kids, too."

Where other rappers go for Gucci sunglasses and iced-out platinum chains, Prince Paul's version of material success revolves around the art of getting more for less. "Feel the fine Corinthian leather!" he says of his living room furniture. "It's *nice!* It's from Huffman Koos. LL Cool J bought his living room set there. He paid more than I did. The total?" he asks, flinging his skinny arms wide. "Sofa, love seat, the whole set was $2,000, which is really incredible for this kind of leather."

Standing in front of the sixty-inch color television set in his living room ("Remember when the Wiz was going out of business?"), he runs down a list of other bargain purchases, including wall-to-wall carpeting in the living room, a VCR, a boom box from Woolworth's, a display case for his DJ trophies, and a pair of matching table lamps, marked down from $149.99 to $49.99, then notes that all the clothes he is wearing today—from his stonewashed Polo jeans to a Levi's shirt made from some strange lime-green synthetic fabric—were given to him for free. "I also got a good deal with this refrigerator," he adds as we pass the kitchen counter, where a value pack of store-brand potato chips rests next to a four-pack of discount paper towels. "A $75 rebate on top of the already low, low, low discount price," he says.

When I ask Prince Paul to reflect on the deeper emotions he associates with discount shopping, he strokes his goatee for a moment, then responds, "The feeling? Elation! . . . It's the result of getting more for less." By now Prince Paul is fully inhabiting the character he has just invented—an exuberant host of a public-access discount-shopping show for budget-conscious B-boys. What he needs now is that one perfect line that will define his character and make him famous worldwide.

"I spend less. Less than your average B-boy," he crows. "The key is not how much you spend but how much you save."

"People want to call me corny," Prince Paul continues, his thin, intelligent features shifting from evangelical zeal to an expression that is almost serious. "But I'm not looking like a circus clown with baggy pants out to here, with some excessive *bling-bling* platinum jewelry on and a skeleton with fire on its head tattooed on my chest."

The records in Prince Paul's basement are arranged on wooden shelves according to a system that only Prince Paul understands. His collection includes albums by Mozart, the Chi-Lites, Hall and Oates, Steely Dan, Parliament-Funkadelic, Philip Glass, the Fifth Dimension, and William Shatner. The most important ones, records that contain critical beats or unknown hooks or especially rare or unusual sounds, are stored in anonymous white sleeves to protect their identities from unscrupulous rivals, burglars, or others who might find their way into Prince Paul's basement and reveal his secret musical formulas to the world.

Prince Paul's records are the sonic equivalents of the bits of found paper or plastic or candy bar wrappers that a suburban Picasso might use to make a collage from his fifth-grade class. They are archaeological evidence of the lifelong listening habits of the young music fan who wandered through his mother's house in his pajamas, tilting his transistor radio from side to side as he listened to the latest hits by the Treacherous 3 and the Furious Five on *Mr. Magic's Rap Attack* on WBLS. A photograph on his basement wall shows Prince Paul at the age of eleven, standing in front of his first-ever turntable, wearing a Spiderman shirt, Converse sneakers, and a fresh pair of Lee's and staring at a spinning record with the same hypnotic intensity that has informed his music ever since.

"You could look at an album cover for days when you were a little kid and just read lists of people, and it was a whole new world," Prince Paul remembers, slipping an old Parliament record off the shelf. "I remember seeing the logo of my man on the Mothership," he says, taking the album out of its sleeve and turning it over to display the logo. "And I was like, 'Oh wow.' Then I looked at the cover and read the credits and listened to the music, and it just kept on going and going, feeding that weird story that kept unfolding in your head. What did it mean?" In the moment, by the mixing board in his basement studio, the magic of those stories is still very much alive.

"You had so little information to go on," he remembers. "It wasn't until my older days that I realized, Oh, those guys were taking drugs.

But back then all you needed was a photo shoot, the liner notes, a little profanity here and there, a few sexual connotations. It was like, 'Oh, my God, that's so *forbidden*' "—his eyes go suddenly, alarmingly wide—" 'that's *bad.*' "

"Maybe it's because I'm older," Prince Paul remembers of the days when he rocked his first jams in the park in Amityville, Long Island, back before crack cocaine and random gun violence, when everything seemed colorful and exciting and a twelve-year-old kid from Long Island could hitch a ride with his friend's older brother to the Sunday afternoon jams in the South Bronx, where the competition was tougher and the DJs spun records behind their backs to move the crowd. "But it was just better. There was music all over the place," he says. "It was just a good feeling going out, man. You'd walk down the street and people would be playing Kurtis Blow's 'The Breaks' back in the day, or 'Christmas Rappin' or [Jimmy Spicer's] 'Superrhymes.' "

It was at a Sunday afternoon jam in Brooklyn that the fourteen-year-old DJ Paul was discovered by Daddy-O, an older rap pioneer ("He had on a leather jacket with spikes and braids down to the middle of his back, with purple beads—I thought he came to beat me up," Prince Paul explains) who made Paul the DJ for his group, Stetsasonic, and changed his name to Prince Paul. Stetsasonic's music wasn't bad, and the group became one of the more popular old-school rap acts of the '80s. Still just a teenager in high school, Prince Paul got to see the world.

"I remember the first tour we went on," he says with a grin. "Be sharing a room with somebody. They got some girl in their room"—Paul knocks on the wall—"Ah, so I can't get in. So I'd sit all night in the lobby with the girl's friend, asking, 'Oh wow, is clinical psychology really a good course?' And we'd both be bummed out. Then I'd finally get in my room, and there's semen on my bed. You know, it was like, 'Awww, I can't sleep in this.' So I'd sleep on the bus, on the bottom bunk, because that's the one they gave me, in the back, near the bathroom, where all the fumes come in." A few weeks later, he invited a groupie back to his room, just to talk, and she set his bathroom on fire, then smashed up the furniture.

Stories about Daddy-O and sex-crazed groupies made Prince

Paul (who spent his childhood playing practical jokes, making up outrageous lies, snapping on his brothers and his mother at home, missing the father who died when he was seven, and drawing concentric Spirograph circles on the inside part of his brain) the coolest kid at Amityville High. "I was *dressed,*" he explains. "Name belts. Colored Levi's. British Walkers. Playboy shirts. Le Tigres. I looked the role." Trugoy the Dove was a junior. Posdnuos was a sophomore. Maseo was a freshman. Together they formed De La Soul, recording tracks in Paul's basement, making the music that Prince Paul couldn't make with Stetsasonic. The giddy eccentricity of the sound Prince Paul pioneered was the perfect match for the oblique poetics and higher-consciousness message (*De La Soul / from the soul / black medallions / no gold*) of the group's two main lyricists, Posdnuos and Trugoy (now known as Dave).

As the members of De La Soul grew older and tried to sell more records, the group's relationship with their producer became strained. "I guess got tired of being my puppets," Prince Paul says. He pauses as if he can hear the little voice in his ear warning him that someone might be offended by what he has just said; then he grins, spreads his palms flat over the table and gleefully manipulates a set of imaginary strings with his hands.

Paul's next act, the Gravediggaz, was a ferocious parody of hardcore rap, which played well on college campuses and on a few urban radio stations, some of whose listeners seemed unaware of the group's ironic intent. *Psychoanalysis: What Is It?,* a record that Paul made by himself in 1997 for a small independent label, was even more ferocious in its attack on the mindless posturing and bootyclap songs that had taken over mainstream rap, and it attracted far fewer listeners. It was as if Prince Paul, at a low point in his career and in the middle of a painful and drawn-out custody battle for his son, wanted to make a record that would confirm he was alone in the world.

"I saw that record as the end of my career," he says. "No one would work with me. I had to beg my friends from high school to rhyme on my tracks. And then I came across this old psychoanalysis party record"—from the days when the hosts of a party would invite their friends over to sit in their living room in suits and dresses, serve canapés from Julia Child, and listen to funny records, the analyst helpfully notes—"and it was like, 'Oh, this is hilarious. This stuff is so crazy.' And I just wanted something to piece all my songs together so people didn't think it was just a whole bunch of garbage" —Prince Paul had previously used a game-show host and skits to tie De La Soul's 3 *Feet High and Rising* together, an idea that has been appropriated by Snoop Dogg, Wu-Tang Clan, and too many other rappers to count—"and then to really tie it together, I used my book from college, *Essentials of Psychology,* thumbed through it for some key words and put them as the titles to the songs." The result was one of the more arcane rap records ever made, a fixture on critics' top ten lists and the only rap record deemed worthy to be included in the Library of Congress's exhibition on the life and work of Sigmund Freud.

"It was just dumb," Prince Paul concludes with a sigh. "That record took no thought at all. I can't express that to you. It was just dumb, and I can't believe to this day the critical acclaim it received, or the number of people who just bashed it, either." The comedian Chris Rock loved *Psychoanalysis* and hired Prince Paul to produce his Grammy-winning comedy album, and Monica Lynch, the head of Tommy Boy Records, loved *Psychoanalysis* so much that she gave Prince Paul a long-term contract to make the kind of music he wanted—records like *A Prince Among Thieves,* the fake movie sound track, which is now being made into an actual movie, and the Handsome Boy Modeling School project. He is also producing acts for other labels and is peripherally involved with De La Soul's new project, a three-album work in progress. Prince Paul's next solo album, the details of which are sketchy, is due out sometime later this year.

PJ Huston is the person who understands Prince Paul best, because he is his father's son and they share the same blood and the same sense of humor and also because he is seven years old. He is waiting patiently upstairs in a white robe with a sash tied around his waist, waiting for his father to take him to karate. A few nights ago, he saw spiders upstairs. His father killed the spiders before PJ went to bed, but he was too afraid to sleep. "I was like, 'Man, what's wrong?'" Prince Paul remembers. "He said, 'Spiders.' I said, 'Man, you'll be all right. It's a small thing.' He was like, 'Yeah, right. You know what's going to happen. I'll wake up in the morning and a spider be chilling on my stomach.' Like this." Paul acts out the spider crawling slowly across his son's chest, then tells a few more stories about his son's fondness for practical jokes and his talent for painting pictures with words, talents that delight his father to no end.

A few minutes later, father and son are backing out of the garage in the Huston family's Cadillac truck with leather interior, purchased with only 700 miles on the odometer from an old man in Connecticut who wasn't comfortable driving so high off the ground. PJ Huston looks like his father. He has the same serious gaze and the same uneasy balance of giddiness and quiet abstraction. He is respectful to adults and patiently answers whatever questions you might ask.

"Do you like Barney?"

"Yes," PJ says, looking shyly at his father.

"Barney just does rip-offs," Prince Paul instructs as his son sits solemnly beside him. "He puts his own words to it. That's not uncommon, but he is blatant. Usually, a brother changes a few things, and you can't say that he's a biter. But Barney bites straight up. Barney's a biter." PJ smiles and nods. "But I guess he had nothing to lose. He was born disfigured."

Bringing Down the House

I.

The Loizeaux family's impact on the American landscape can be measured best by what is no longer here: the Cosmopolitan Hotel in Denver, the King Cotton Hotel in Memphis, the Northwest Bank in Minneapolis, an entire city block in Dallas, the Pruitt-Igoe housing projects in St. Louis, the Wayne Minor Houses in Kansas City, Missouri, the remains of the Alfred P. Murrah Federal Building in Oklahoma City, and the Hacienda Hotel, which vanished from the Las Vegas skyline on New Year's Eve before an audience of half a million delirious tourists and millions of television viewers across the country. The Loizeaux family has used its expertise to destroy weapons systems and missile sites throughout the former Eastern bloc states as well as burning oil rigs in the Gulf of Mexico and twenty-six earthquake-damaged buildings in Mexico City. In 1972, the Loizeaux took down a thirty-two-story skyscraper, the largest building ever demolished with explosives, in São Paulo, Brazil. They have imploded more than seven thousand structures in all, or an average of one structure every two days for the forty-five years that the family company, Controlled Demolition Incorporated, or CDI, has been in business.

Demolition is a particularly American act, a concise and visually compelling expression of the belief that history is transient, that a new beginning is always in the cards, that the glories of the past are only a prelude to a glorious and everlasting present. Although no one knows exactly how many buildings are demolished in America in any given year, estimates are that $2 billion to $3 billion worth of demolition contracts are bid on annually by six to seven hundred

firms. The overwhelming majority of these jobs—concrete stan-
chions, parking lots, five-story garages, tract houses, row houses,
apartment houses, highway overpasses, and worn-out shopping
malls—are accomplished over a period of weeks or months through
nonexplosive means: bulldozers, construction cranes, wrecking
balls, and jackhammers. The spectacular collapses of twenty-story
smokestacks and skyscrapers featured in the pages of *Demolition
Age,* the industry's stroke-book, published monthly, are accomplished by four major contractors: the Loizeaux family; Jim Redyke
of Tulsa, Oklahoma; Steve Pettigrew of Franklin, Tennessee; and
Eric Kelly and Anna Chong of Hayden Lake, Idaho. Of the four
companies, Controlled Demolition Incorporated is the most experienced and, not surprisingly, the best insured. Before striking out on
their own, both Redyke and Pettigrew were employed by CDI.

The Loizeaux family story can be read both as the heartwarming
tale of an ordinary family that does extraordinary things and as a
backwards-running history of the United States, written in dynamite
and detonating cord. The company was founded by "Daddy Jack"
Loizeaux, the seventh and youngest son of Alfred S. Loizeaux, chief
engineer for the Baltimore Gas and Electric Company, whose name
appears on the blueprints for the Southern Seafood building in Baltimore, which Jack's sons, Mark and Doug, and Mark's daughters,
Stacey and Adrienne, obliterated two years ago to make way for the
Baltimore Orioles' new baseball stadium at Camden Yards. Beginning with the tree stumps Jack Loizeaux dislodged with dynamite
during the 1930s, the family moved on to brick chimneys and coal
tipples, to low bridges cleared to make way for Dwight D. Eisen-
hower's interstate highway system, to worn-out steelyards and factories in Pennsylvania, to the blocks of low-rise slum housing cleared
in the name of urban renewal by presidents Johnson and Nixon, and,
more recently, to the high-rise projects built in their place.

Of all the many stops along the family's long march of destruction,
it is hard to imagine a better example of the particulars of their
method and the larger implications involved in their work than the
demolition of the Sands Hotel and Casino in Las Vegas. The Sands
opened on December 15, 1952, and closed its doors in July of last
year after a weekend stand by the comedian Gallagher, who enjoyed
a brief moment of fame in the eighties for an act in which he

smashed watermelons with a sledgehammer. In between, the casino welcomed Frank Sinatra, Joey Bishop, Sammy Davis Jr., Rotarians, and members of the Oklahoma State Bar Association, as well as hundreds of nameless men from New York, Newark, Los Angeles, Miami, Chicago, and Minneapolis who checked in with empty suitcases and checked out the next morning with thousands of dollars in cash skimmed off the top for their absentee bosses, who sold out in 1967, to Howard Hughes, under pressure from the FBI and the Justice Department. The Sands witnessed the rise and fall of strongarm men and billionaires, of LBJ and J. Edgar Hoover. It saw JFK in his underwear and the astronauts of Apollo 13 sunning themselves by the pool. The Sands was five decades of unwritten American history expressed in solid, structural form.

When, early last November, I met with Doug Loizeaux at CDI's Maryland headquarters, our conversation turned again and again to the family's plans to demolish the Sands on the Tuesday before Thanksgiving, until Doug made me an offer I couldn't refuse.

"The Sands should be fun," he said. "Why don't you come out to Vegas for a few weeks and help us with the job?"

II.

The Sands tower stands in the forward part of the casino lot, looming over Las Vegas Boulevard like a giant tube of lipstick, poker-chip balconies dotting its circumference and a narrow exterior staircase running like a seam up its right-hand side. In front of the tower stands the worn-out neon sun that lit up the Strip at night above the legend A PLACE IN THE SUN. The casino fixtures, from slot machines to gaming tables to the furnishing of the high-roller suites, were disposed of at a public auction held by the Robin brothers of San Francisco last August, and by mid-November the work of demolition is already far advanced. Wrecking cranes roam like prehistoric animals taking saw-toothed bites from the low-lying roof of the casino buildings adjacent to the eighteen-story tower. The original two-story stucco buildings of the hotel—the Santa Anita, Hialeah, Triple Crown, Belmont, and Arlington—are reduced to bare concrete palates where massive air-conditioning units and neat piles of switch boxes await the wreckers' trucks tomorrow. In the center of the hotel lot, a twisted heap of scrap metal erupts like a late-sixties public sculpture from the brackish waters of the Paradise Pool.

The Loizeaux brothers, Mark and Doug, will not arrive on-site until two days before the implosion. Until then, the preparatory work proceeds in stages. Floor by floor, the local contractor, LVI, clears each of the six "shot-floors" where the explosives will be placed—the ground, mezzanine, second, fifth, ninth, and twelfth floors of the Sands tower—with a jackhammer mounted on a Bobcat, a small, highly maneuverable, low-slung vehicle with a wire cab and a snub-nosed front that suggests an oversize children's toy. The destruction of the shot-floors is loud and dramatic: carpets are ripped up, mirrors shattered, walls punched out, until the hallways and hotel rooms where the tourists once unpacked their bags, dressed for dinner, and mourned their losses at the tables have been reduced to a rubble of concrete and plaster. The litter is plowed off the side of the tower by a Bobcat, and the floors are swept clean until only the structural elements remain: the bare concrete floor, the desert sun shining in through the empty windows. Concentric rows of cylindrical, three-foot-thick concrete columns ring the core of the elevator shaft like an arrangement of electrons around the nucleus of an atom.

Every building begins as a dream. Destroying a building, on the other hand, is a matter for realists rather than dreamers, a slow, almost biblical reckoning as the layers of wood veneer, smoked glass, and wallpaper—glued, screwed, tacked, and stapled onto the concrete walls—are stripped away. On the uncleared floors of the tower, the halls are lined with rows of cast-iron bathtubs, and the air is heavy with the sweetly tainted smell of rotting carpet and wet plaster. In the rooms themselves, the historical progression of the casino's decor is reversed as layers of wallpaper are scraped away: grandmotherly plaids give way to gaudy peacock reds and blues, and, finally, the original Casbah arches against a flat, tan background.

Overseeing the destruction of the wedge-shaped hotel rooms, home to generations of junketeering tourists, is CDI's on-site project manager, Jim Santoro, a cheerful forty-year-old. Before coming to work for CDI he ran a mental hospital in upstate New York, an activity that seems to have prepared him for dealing with the many different types of people one meets on construction sites worldwide. Jim's cheerfulness can also be explained by the flesh-colored hearing aid he wears over one ear, which allows him to survey the work undisturbed by the pounding drills. When he is finished inside he retires to the parking lot, where he sits in the front seat of his rental car and makes dozens of calls on his flip-top phone before breaking for lunch. He spends his afternoons driving around Las Vegas, submitting forms and plans to fourteen separate departments in seven regulatory agencies in order to obtain the five specific permits required before the Sands can come down.[1]

As each floor of the hotel tower is cleared, CDI's drilling crew moves into position. The crew is made up of six local day workers, black and Latino, in dusty blue coveralls. Working two to a drill, the workers bore holes 1.75 inches in diameter into the 131 shot-columns where the charges will be placed, as Thom Doud, Doug's handsome, black-haired nephew, shouts instructions, urging the workers forward like a high school quarterback in the closing minutes of a tight game. The paralyzingly loud drills they use, with their smooth-worn stocks and long, tapered noses, are picture-book examples of twentieth-century industrial design. The combination of the noise, the safety goggles pulled down over eyes, the earplugs stuck fast in ears, and the stark, monochromatic shade of the drilling floors creates an otherworldly landscape from which recognizable sensory cues have been erased. The work takes a tremendous physical toll, and by the end of the day the workers are tired and sore, their torsos covered with bruises and welts.

One of the first lessons of demolition work is that the blueprints and specifications drawn up by architects and engineers can never be trusted. In the case of the Sands, however, the problem arises not

1. The Street Occupancy Permit obtained from the Nevada Department of Transportation allows CDI to close down Las Vegas Boulevard on the night of the implosion. The Special Events Permit, signed by Clark County officials, licenses CDI to conduct operations that may create a public disturbance. The Blasting Permit from the Clark County Fire Department enables CDI to utilize explosives. The Air Quality Permit ensures that the blast will not adversely affect the air of Las Vegas. The Demolition Permit from the Clark County Building Department permits CDI to demolish the Sands.

from the usual causes of larceny, greed, and deceit but from the overscrupulous nature of the original contractor, who, no doubt frightened of the extralegal consequences that might result from the collapse of the Mob's favorite playground, packed the tower's concrete columns with tremendous concentrations of rebar, or reinforcing steel. The drilling proceeds much slower than expected as carbide drill bits that would normally retain their edge for weeks are worn within days to the smoothness of bone. The exterior staircase, fixed to the side of the tower with the same overzealous concentrations of rebar, presents a similar obstacle to a smooth demolition, and calls are made back to headquarters in Maryland to consult with CDI's engineers and to warn Mark and Doug that the Sands may not go down as easily as planned.

Once the drilling is done, the six-man covering crew—led by Mark's nineteen-year-old daughter, Adrienne—takes over, lugging precut rolls, six feet tall by eight feet wide, of chain-link fencing and thick black covering fabric up to the shot-floors to wrap the columns. Adrienne's presence on-site is something of a challenge, as the workmen gossip and speculate behind her back and mistranslate her instructions into Spanish. "How do you say, 'Bring the fabric up to the third floor'?" she asks a worker named Carlos, who smiles broadly, flexes his chest, and offers a different phrase, which Adrienne repeats. "Come up to my bedroom and screw me all night," she orders. After eight long hours of hauling the heavy rolls up three or four flights of stairs, the workers' discomfort with her has been transformed into a companionable respect, and so the laughter is gentle, if still loud.

The task of preparing the columns for the blast is simple and repetitive: each column is wrapped with a layer of the chain-link fencing and then with covering fabric, which is tied in place with steel wire. These materials will contain flying debris when the charges are set off. As the work progresses, each finished floor takes on the mysterious aspect of a modern Stonehenge, intended to measure the cycles of planting and harvest of the structural world.

III.

When not on the road or preparing for a job, the Loizeaux family lives and works together on a forty-five-acre compound in the pre-suburban horse country of Phoenix, Maryland, forested by well-spaced trees and graced by a picture-perfect babbling brook that lends the spread the overly peaceful feel of a Zen monastery. A 1940s brick manor house in the center of the property functions as CDI's corporate headquarters and is home on workdays to some seventeen employees, including secretaries, bookkeepers, an engineer, a drilling expert, two project managers, Mark and Doug Loizeaux, and Mark's oldest daughter, Stacey. The brothers and their families live on the property in rambling houses a hundred yards apart, which they have furnished over the years with stained glass, oak paneling, and other architectural features salvaged from the buildings they have demolished.

The first time I entered the manor house, I was greeted by a kitchen sink full of unwashed coffee mugs and then by an array of clocks above the desks of the secretaries displaying the current time in Minsk, London, Seoul, and the United States. The assignment board listed ongoing projects in red and blue Magic Marker: the Sands tower in Las Vegas; a seventeen-story office building in Norfolk, Virginia; the Lexington Terrace projects in Baltimore; the Clifton smokestack in Arizona; an oil rig in the North Sea; three cooling towers at a power station in Madras, India; SS-25 missile pads in Belarus. The preparation for each implosion—from getting the necessary permits to knocking out interior walls and drilling the holes where the explosives will be placed—can take anywhere from a few weeks to several months. The charge for a medium-size implosion, such as the Sands, ranges from $100,000 to $200,000. This is a surprisingly modest sum, but volume is high: at any one time, CDI is likely to have two or more teams preparing implosions across the country or around the world; the company's gross revenues last year amounted to roughly $12.5 million.

The CDI promotional literature presents the Loizeaux brothers as a pair of well-built men in their midforties with short-cropped hair and trimmed mustaches beneath matching white plastic hard hats, and so, meeting them for the first time, I was struck immediately by the fact that they look nothing alike. Doug, the younger brother, is taller and clean-shaven and moves with the lazy confidence of a high school athlete turned successful suburban businessman, a guy you would expect to find driving his sports car too fast or playing squash at the club when he ought to be at work. Mark, whose reddish hair is supplemented by a closecut beard, is more introspective. In the Hollywood action-hero version of the Loizeaux family story, Mark might foil a terrorist plot to blow up the White House on the eve of an important summit meeting with the Japanese, or he might be the terrorist. If you ignored the souvenir bricks and the lengths of steel cable as thick as your arm on the bookcase shelves, Mark's office could easily have passed for a *Better Homes and Gardens* illustration of how to give your workspace that gracious, lived-in feel while still retaining the formality necessary to the proper conduct of business. Doug's office, upstairs, has the wood-paneled walls, pitched ceiling, and outdoor terrace one might expect of a time-share rental at an upscale ski resort.

The morning I arrived, Doug was watching footage from CDI's recent Lexington Terrace implosion in Baltimore, in which five grimly functional red-brick housing blocks had been demolished to make way for low-rise, low-income housing. What interests Doug this morning are not the political uses to which his work is put, or even the technical aspects of the job, but the aesthetics of the event as seen through the lens: the long, slow sweep of the camera as the five brick buildings melt away from the skyline to reveal the city of Baltimore, clean and renewed against the horizon. As the buildings go down, one after another, a cloud of concrete dust billows toward the camera, leaching the color from the frame and flecking the lens with bits of paint and concrete. "That pan," Doug said, "was wonderful."

When he was younger, Doug wanted to make movies, an ambition reflected in the hundreds of CDI archive photographs of a younger, bearded, hard-hatted Doug with shoulder-length hair and a Super-8 camera in his hand, and responsible in part for the company's comprehensive library of still and motion-picture footage of nearly 7,000 structures in various stages of dynamic collapse. The most compelling of these appear in "The Art of Demolition," a four-minute montage accompanied by a synthesizer soundtrack that sounds like a cross between the theme from *Chariots of Fire* and the bass-heavy thump of a porno flick. "Look at those beautiful Palladian windows," Doug said, as the Cosmopolitan Hotel in Denver slid gracefully to the ground. Then we were treated to a particularly stunning sequence of a brick building in the final stages of collapse, filmed through the canyons of steel and glass that make up the modern, up-to-date city of Charlotte, North Carolina. "Mmmm," he said.

If the slow-motion disintegration of buildings under wave after wave of explosive charges has its own undeniably resonant aesthetic, whether seen as surrealist landscape or as sequences in the endless loop of televised collisions and explosions we consume like a drug, the CDI library serves a practical purpose as well. Films of past implosions allow the brothers to study the motion of falling buildings frame-by-frame and thereby learn from their experience: the Sands tower, for example, bears a structural resemblance to the core of the Landmark, the flying-saucer-like hotel and casino built by Howard Hughes that dominated the Vegas skyline like a prop left over from some ancient B movie until CDI cut the structure in half with explosives three years ago. The brothers' obsession with their craft has resulted in a symbiotic relationship with Hollywood—they frequently provide footage of collapses and custom-made explosions to augment the force of the make-believe. Doug's windswept footage of the implosion of the Traymore Hotel appears at the beginning of Louis Malle's *Atlantic City;* Joel Silver, the action-movie producer, employed CDI for special-effects work on *Demolition Man* and *Lethal Weapon III;* Tim Burton used footage of the Landmark implosion in his *Mars Attacks!*

Doug takes pleasure in the sense of directoral control that the work provides, a spectacular instant staged not merely for the camera but for the thousands who gather to mark the final moments of the buildings they have worked in, lived in, fought in, loved in, or simply walked past every day on their way to some other building. The emotion held in these moments is a mixture of sadness and hope and awe, a confirmation that the past is behind us, blown to pieces, while the future is waiting, wide open and new. "You hear people screaming, and it's such a venting of frustrations for so many people," Doug told me. "I used to think people came to see implosions the way you go to car races to see a crash, but it's not that. It's controlling something that they see as uncontrollable. And looking at something so large and seeing it reduced to nothing in a matter of seconds gives them a feeling of power. It's that scream—YESSSS!"

For television and print reporters, the implosion of a local landmark with high powered explosives is a gift from God, and the Loizeaux are proud of their ability to handle the press, to answer the standard questions—biggest building ever imploded, pounds of dynamite used per year—with understated, professional skill. The reassuring image the family projects is an important part of the work they do. The fact that CDI is a family company, with a grandfather, sons, and granddaughters all working together, tends to soften the fear that explosives demolition inspires, a fact that is hardly lost on Doug and Mark. Both brothers choose their words carefully, because their work demands precision and because the careful use of language is a necessary tool to help soften perceptions of what is essentially a destructive and risky occupation. The word "implosion," for example, was popularized by the family in the 1950s in an effort to put another comforting layer of distance between the work they do and the popular idea of an explosion as a violent, uncontrolled act. The family's attention to language has its advantages: CDI, unlike its competitors, is able to purchase upward of $300 million in liability insurance—enough to cover even the most unlikely disasters, from bricks in the head to heart attacks to the leveling of entire city blocks.

Apart from the obvious uses of the word "family" in their work, however, it is apparent that, like all families, the Loizeaux brothers see the family and its traditions from their own particular points of view. Doug keeps his family and the family business as far apart as possible: when asked what he does for a living at dinner parties, his usual answer is "contractor." Mark Loizeaux, on the other hand, was born to blow things up. Doug remembers his older brother as a boy floating paper boats down the stream in front of their house, then blowing them out of the water with charges fashioned from firecrackers. At ten Mark helped his father take down their first buildings with explosives, an apartment complex in Washington's Foggy Bottom neighborhood, where the State Department stands today. At twelve he designed and set off his first array of charges from start to finish, demolishing a 170-foot-tall bridge pier. At eighteen, after his father was hit by a car and injured, Mark left college and took over the company. His enthusiastic and single-minded absorption in his work is obvious; he combines an aesthete's appreciation of the way the buildings move once the charges go off with an engineer's ability to bring down a thirty-story tower weighing thousands of tons in a space the relative size of a shoebox without breaking so much as a pane of glass in neighboring skyscrapers. He actively encourages his two older daughters' involvement in the business, and takes his fourteen-year-old twins, Jason and Devon, on the road, with an eye toward educating them about the art of demolition and the proper handling of high-powered explosives.

"I think any craftsman is proud of what he makes or creates," Mark said, looking back on the family's three generations of demolition experience. "I can go into almost any major city in this country, or in the world, and drive by with one of my daughters or my son and say, 'Well, see that building there? I took down the structure that replaced the structure that my father took down, that this has now replaced, and that you'll be taking down someday.' " Mark enjoys demolition work's power to impress, the power to elicit feelings of fear and awe from thousands of spectators. He likes watching the pictures on TV. He likes making a plan in his head and seeing it expressed in the controlled collapse of thousands of tons of steel and concrete.

Mark's conversational manner is calm, logical, and direct, and so it took hours of conversation, over several days, to realize that the exterior Mark presents is very similar to that of a convinced Marxist or neurobiologist or horse player who believes that he has found the secret fix, the hidden lever that moves the world. He is a man whose entire being is energized by one big idea. Driving down the street with Jason, past the horse farms and the Christmas tree ranch and the herd of bison owned by a wealthy local dentist, they approach a radio tower, and Mark listens with pride as his son describes the array of RC-900 charges he would use to bring it down. Walking past Rockefeller Center to visit CDI's insurers, Mark passes the time by planning the precise sequence of charges he would need to alter the Manhattan skyline for good. "It's true, I admit it: it's human nature," he told me, his eyes lighting up with the reflected glory of the tens of thousands of explosions, real and imagined, inside his head. "The way a plastic surgeon looks at a woman with bags under her eyes, you know, and wonders."

My second night in Phoenix I met Mark Loizeaux and his family for dinner at a local restaurant, the kind of place you find in once-rural areas with names like "The Huntsman's Tavern" or "Hound and Horn," red-coated gentry riding to the hounds across the walls and local divorcees gathering in a knot at the bar on Thursday nights. Mark's wife, Sherry, has the blonde, blue-eyed look of a middle-aged Virginia high school prom queen. When she asked me sincerely if I believed in true love, there seemed to be no other choice than to say yes.

After a medium-rare steak and a couple of glasses of scotch, Mark's conversation strayed to what was obviously his own true love: explosives demolition. "I'll tell you the thing I've found really scary," he said. "More and more I look at structures and I think, 'If I were a terrorist, how would I take it down?' Oklahoma City really flipped some switches there," he added, a slight twitch having developed at the corners of his mouth. "I find myself realizing just how simple, how easy. It's like those silly things you walk through to get into airports. I walk right by that stuff. Do you realize that everything we have is just saturated with explosives? PETN, that powder they found traces of on TWA flight 800 because somebody hid explosives there when they were testing dogs months ago? Well, our bags are just steeped in that stuff. And I've never had a dog bark, wag its tail—'It's in there, boss.' Nothing." Having helped blow up buildings since he was eight, and having built up a profitable sideline in antiterrorist consulting over the past sixteen years, for private business and for the Army's Special Forces, Mark has solid, professional reasons for seeing the world as he does. But every good cop, as they say, is also part criminal.

"We could drop every bridge in the United States in a couple of days," Mark was saying, just thinking out loud, and then his eyes lit up as the idea took on its own special resonance inside his head. "I could drive a truck on the Verrazano Narrows Bridge and have a dirt bike on the back, drop that bridge, and I would get away. They would never stop me."

"How often does a thought like that occur to you?" I wondered aloud, as Mark took another sip from his scotch.

"Every time I cross a bridge."

One clue to the force of Mark's quasireligious obsession with the family's work became evident the next morning, as the brothers planned the demolition of an oil rig in the North Sea and laughed over the misfortunes of one of their competitors, who had just dropped the chimney of a high-rise apartment building across a commuter track, disrupting local rail service. As the brothers conferred, I had the chance to spend a few hours with their father, "Daddy Jack" Loizeaux. He looked remarkably spry for a man in his mideighties, showing up at the office in a gray track suit, having just won two hard-fought sets of tennis against a man twenty years his junior. He was happy to tell me about his life's work, which began on a sunny afternoon at the University of Georgia forestry school when he was introduced, in classic Mephistophelian fashion, to a Mr. Johnson of the Du Pont Corporation, who arrived on campus one afternoon to survey the Oconee River and resumed several weeks later with a truckload of dynamite. With a twist of the detonator, a shower of dirt exploded from the ground, the sky turned black, and the banks of the Oconee were straightened in seconds, an event that left the elder Loizeaux with a vivid and lasting impression of what he still refers to today as "the awesome power of explosives." Working as a forester in Baltimore, he soon turned to explosives as a method of removing stumps as Dutch elm blight killed off the stately trees by the thousands, until Mr. Johnson called again, directing his protégé to the Aberdeen Proving Ground, where the army needed someone to take down five tall brick chimneys. Young Jack solved the problem with *Popular Mechanics*–style ingenuity: he notched the bases of the chimneys as if they were trees and used explosive charges to lay them gently on their sides.

As Daddy Jack told his story, I found myself lulled into the same pleasant state of mind one experiences on a long drive when the only voice available over the radio is that of the announcer on the Christian station telling the miracle of the loaves and the fishes. The cause of this association is not hard to find. A deeply religious man, Jack Loizeaux raised Mark and Doug according to the precepts of the

Plymouth Brethren, a somber, Quakerish sect, and explosives demolition is for him a kind of parable in which the moral tenets of his
faith find their concrete, earthly expression. Before every blast, he
said, he would pray with his sons and "thank the good Lord for the
gravity."

Daddy Jack's ongoing ministry of destruction has taken him, he
told me, to the Naval Academy at Annapolis, to local high schools,
and, on one occasion in the 1980s, to the television studios of Jim
and Tammy Faye Bakker, whose literal-minded brand of evangelism
was not in sympathy with his own more sober beliefs. "He seemed to
have the impression that God had spoken to me from the heavens,
telling me to take down buildings," Daddy Jack related, cupping his
hand to his ear. "I told him it didn't happen that way at all."

He does, however, see the structural integrity of a building as a
physical metaphor for the soul, which can be undermined by bad
character and sinful actions. "I think about how long it took to plan
it, and to build it, and the expense," he said, of the moments before a
building comes down. "And then in a few seconds I can destroy it all.
And when I speak to young people, I tell them how important it is
when they build a character, a reputation, because whether it's sex or
drugs or their language, it's like taking the columns out of a structure. It gets weaker. And all of a sudden—bam! She's gone."

Jack Loizeaux is shrewd about his sons' vulnerabilities. Mark's sin
is the sin of pride and hard dealings. Doug's sin is the same as his
father's: he is soft. "Mark could be in Hollywood, or he could be an
attorney, one of the two," he said. "He can put up a real tough front.
But I've hugged him before we took down a building, and I can feel
him shaking inside. But nobody knows it. He'll walk around like he's
God. And Doug, I remember the first building he shot. He went into
the alley and vomited. He can get real upset."

As the sun sank behind the Maryland hills, Daddy Jack remembered the Mitsubishi turboprop plane he used to fly from job to job,
and the time the family was shot at with .22 rifles when they demolished the Pruitt-Igoe housing projects in St. Louis. He recalled
standing on an airport tarmac in the days before faxes and Federal
Express and handing the flight attendant a $20 bill to fly the plans of
a building from Baltimore to Los Angeles so that another engineer
could examine them: "If I had my way," he said, "I'd love to shoot

buildings before daybreak when nobody is around—no cameras, no nothing." The jobs he likes best, he said, are those on the water— just the crew and nature and God's gravity. "And then the charges go off—boom, boom, boom," he said, recalling the first pier he ever shot, "and we eliminate that pier with no fly at all. Now isn't that wonderful?"

IV.

Looking out over the desert mountains and the freeways from the top floor of the lipstick-shaped tower, with the fluorescent wallpaper peeling from the walls, the threadbare green carpet littered with broken glass, the secular forces behind the impending demise of the Sands Hotel and Casino are easy to spot. The Mirage Hotel across the street, into whose outstretched black arms the Sands tower would fit with many rooms to spare, was built by developer Steve Wynn in the late 1980s, the beginning of the exuberant wave of casino building that has made Las Vegas one of the fastest-growing cities in the world, a low-airfare-weekend-getaway paradise firmly grounded in current American themes of "family" values, shopping, and addictive-compulsive behavior. After the vulgar neon highs of the sixties and the shag-carpet lows of the seventies, Las Vegas is finally a city at ease with itself, a place where the red carpets are shampooed bright and early every morning as mothers push infants in strollers down marble walkways, pausing to wave hello through the glass partition at Siegfried & Roy's white tigers, continuing past the craps tables where Daddy is dropping next month's mortgage payment, before stopping stop in for a breather at the DKNY boutique. From the top of the Sands I count twelve origami-like construction cranes dipping their pointed beaks down to the city below, toward the waiting bounty of waitressing jobs and construction sites, video-poker machines in every 7-Eleven, and giant billboards looming above the downtown casinos, promising "Free brunch if you cash your paycheck here." Set to rise on the site where the Sands now stands is Sheldon Adelson's $2 billion Venetian, the latest in the wave of themepark casinos that began with the MGM Grand and the Luxor and now includes New York, New York, with its one-third-scale replicas of the Empire State Building and Statue of Liberty

crisscrossed by a giant Coney Island roller coaster. Soon to follow
are the Bellagio, a high rollers' version of the famous Italian villa,
and Paris, a neon version of the City of Lights, complete with its own
built-to-scale version of the Eiffel Tower.

The historic passage from the faded glories of the Sands to Sheldon Adelson's Venetian is a powerful testimony to the American belief in starting over; in lucky numbers, charms, and stars; and in our
expansive capacity for self delusion; and to the more general national transition from the smoke-filled back rooms where Las Vegas
was born to the hazy methadone smog of movies and television. The
pleasures of Las Vegas, old or new, however, hold little attraction for
CDI. Life on the road for the crew is a matter of passing through a
distant place at reasonable prices with the least possible resistance
or distraction. The crew usually stays together in hotels close to the
site with a bar downstairs and cable TV in the rooms. Sometimes the
accommodations are particularly awful, as they were in Seoul, where
Jim Santoro and Thom Doud shared an abandoned house and the
South Korean contract workers slept six to a room next door. By
those standards, the rooms at the Best Western on Paradise Road
are large and clean and even luxurious.

Because the work is so exhausting, and the schedule so tight, the
crew rarely ventures out of the Best Western. They meet in the
downstairs restaurant for drinks and dinner and light conversation
which revolves mainly around the requirements of the job, with sporadic excursions into the quality of the food, which is poor, and the
hairstyles of the women seated at the bar. Entertainment at the Best
Western involves video-poker machines in the lobby and nightly
performances by a bottle-blonde singer, perhaps twenty years old,
with the demure red lips and hairsprayed curls of an up-and-coming
Christian pop star. She has a bright and bouncy vocal style, as if
someone had implanted a microchip from an early Casio synthesizer
inside her brain, and her repertoire is composed of airbrushed standards, drained of whatever shards of human emotion might have
been embedded in the original versions: "The Tide Is High" by
Blondie, "Suspicious Minds" by Elvis Presley, "Hey Jude" by the
Beatles, "Bette Davis Eyes" by Kim Carnes, "Heart of Gold" by Neil
Young, several songs by Fleetwood Mac. Adrienne leaves early. The
others continue to drink at the bar, where Jim, who is friendly to a

fault, attracts more than his fair share of local wackos, who ask for a light and then go on for hours, laying it all out on the table—kids, divorce, retirement—until by nine or nine-thirty even Jim has had enough and retires to his room.

After a week or so of going to bed late and waking up at five-thirty in the morning, I feel the same desperate, free-floating detachment I detected in the chain-smokers at the bar, an emotion that manifests itself, a week into my stay, in a chance encounter in the parking lot with one face of the new Las Vegas—a former diver named Greg, who parks his beat-up VW microbus in the space immediately below my room on a Saturday night and plays loud, thrashing music, which, after twenty minutes or so, I decide would sound just as good at a lower volume. Greg is friendly, has long brown hair to his shoulders, and wears a black T-shirt advertising the Washington, D.C., punk band Minor Threat. He grew up in Galveston, Texas, where he learned to dive off oil rigs in the Gulf before getting into a jam with his foreman as well as with some "very heavy big-time people." The back of his van smells like an unwashed rug, and there is an army-green sleeping bag rolled up in the corner, along with the usual thrown-together mess of pots and pans and other equipment assembled by people who wake up one morning to take their show on the road and wind up somewhere like Las Vegas.

Greg offers me a soggy joint and explains that he has come to Las Vegas in the hopes of finding a job in a casino and making a fresh start. What he likes best about Las Vegas, however, is the desert, with the wide-open spaces and the cactus and the wildflowers that bloom after a storm, and as he talks about the desert, and then about the people he knew in Galveston—the speed dealers, a girlfriend named Linda, Linda's eight-year-old kid, Danny, a guy named Derrick, or Rick, and a number of other people who seem to have also existed in some shared nexus of amphetamines and oil rigs—I sense that his logic is skewed in a familiar, American way: he believes that what went wrong in Galveston was only bad luck and that by moving to Las Vegas, hundreds of miles from the nearest offshore oil rig, his luck will necessarily change for the better.

V.

The demolition site, when I arrive the next morning, is a hive of activity, with drills pounding and dust rising and massive dump trucks beeping and grinding as they back out onto the street, carting away their cargoes of historical rubble. Mark arrives on-site in the afternoon, hugs Adrienne, then retires to the front seat of his rented Buick Skylark, where he sits with his chin on the steering wheel for an hour or more in silence. Then he walks under a crane, up the stairs, and through the shot-floors, gazing over at the support columns, feeling the concrete like a sculptor running his fingers over a block of uncut marble. All of these actions are part of a ritual by which Mark hopes to cement what he describes as his "empathetic relation" with the tower: in forty-eight hours, the Sands will be gone.

The explosives arrive on-site just after 5:00 A.M. on Sunday. The driver, David Hoffman, meets us at the gate, a mild-looking man in his early thirties who sticks his head out the window of his 4 × 4 truck and shouts a friendly hello into the glare of the headlights. His stonewashed blue jean jacket features the words SANDERS CONSTRUCTION on a red and yellow emblem, and there is an exploding stick of dynamite emblazoned on his pocket. Behind his truck is a trailer that looks like a reinforced U-Haul. Inside the trailer are boxes containing detonating cord and blasting caps. The boxes resting on the open bed of the truck are filled with 880 pounds of dynamite, enough to blast a five-foot-deep crater into Las Vegas Boulevard and break all the windows of the surrounding casinos.

Unloading the explosives is an easy, unceremonious job. Because dynamite is more or less inert during transit, and detonators are volatile, the explosives must be stored separately. The inside of the trailer is lined with wood rather than metal, in order to prevent stray sparks from being struck while on the road. After a quick once-over, the crew unloads the dynamite from the back of Hoffman's truck, uncouples the truck from the trailer, and locks the detonators and the dynamite safely inside. Then everyone repairs to the Denny's, the next storefront over from the Sands, for an early-morning breakfast of bacon and eggs. After that, Hoffman drives off to spend the morning with his in-laws in Las Vegas, and the rest of the crew returns to the site, where we are joined by Doug and Stacey Loizeaux, who have flown out to lend a hand after imploding a seventeen-story office building in Norfolk, Virginia. The final stages of the job have begun.

The first order of business this morning—the test shot—will determine exactly how much dynamite will be needed to blow the heavily reinforced columns of the Sands apart; it is a step-by-step rehearsal for the larger and more complicated shot that is meant to reduce the tower to rubble on Tuesday morning. The dynamite itself looks much the same way it does in the Saturday-morning cartoons—familiar-looking foot-long sticks wrapped in waxed paper, a cheery red color lending them an unmistakably festive appeal. Mark breaks a stick in half with his hands to reveal a creamy, black-flecked substance the consistency of marzipan but surprisingly smooth and dry to the touch.[2]

Loading the column for the shot is fun to watch, a combination of the family's do-it-yourself inventiveness and the dangerous glamour of high-powered explosives. Mark pushes a silver detonator into the dynamite, then works the wired charge into the hole in the concrete with a sawed-off wooden mop handle until it hits the back of the column with a satisfying split. He follows the explosive with a brown paper sack filled with play sand, which will keep the charge from blowing harmlessly out of the hole, then wires the charges together with lengths of bright yellow detonating cord containing the highly explosive crystalline powder PETN. Two ground-floor columns are loaded and wired—one with a stick and a half of dynamite, the other with a single stick. The yellow detonating cord is then attached with electric wire to the blasting machine, a black transformer box like the ones kids use to launch model rockets after school.

The floor is cleared, Mark hands me the blasting machine, and on the count of five I flick the second and final silver switch, an act that is instantly rewarded by a rush of pure adrenaline to my brain and a boom that resonates in the center of my chest. "Check out the columns," Mark says, and as we tear open the covering fabric, which

2. Nitroglycerine, the explosive in dynamite, is also a powerful vasodilator. Among the occupational hazards involved in handling dynamite are the throbbing headaches that begin almost immediately as the nitro penetrates the skin and races through the bloodstream and into the brain.

has been only partially ripped open by the explosion, the pure pleasure I feel at the blast, stamped in cartoony Captain America colors, offering me the power to destroy my enemies with a pulverizing glance, is increased even further by the sight of the solid, three-foot-thick structural column reduced to a shattered mess of broken concrete and tangled steel. In the first column, where the lesser of the charges was placed, the concrete facing of the column has been blown away; inside, however, the inch-thick supporting rods and the helixes of rebar remain unbroken.

Working from the top of the tower down, Mark, Doug, and Stacey now slice open the covering fabric and pack the holes beneath—446 in all—with a stick and a half of dynamite each. The packed columns are then linked together with lengths of detonating cord and sequenced with delays—bright orange plastic tubes containing a dusting of the explosive powder RDX—allowing the brothers to time the detonations, floor by floor, and thus control the shifting weight of the tower as it comes down. As each shot-floor is wired, the Loizeaux family moves down to the floor below, leaving behind a spiderlike maze of yellow cord hanging down between the black, funeral-shrouded columns.

The worry now is that the steel reinforcing in the columns might be so solid that the tower will defy the force of the explosives and remain standing on the steel alone. Under Mark's direction, the crew pounds the tower's exterior walls with a jackhammer attached to the Bobcat, raising clouds of dust, knocking out concrete, and exposing rebar until the once-solid tower is transformed into a maze of black-wrapped columns, nests of wire, and ragged patches of clear blue sky. The crew then cuts through the rebar with acetyline torches, the thin blue flames licking through the steel with a surprising lack of resistance as showers of golden sparks cascade across the concrete floor.

The work continues all day Sunday and into Monday evening, with portable klieg lights illuminating the site like a movie set as the Sands tower is laced with explosives, transformed into a device for the controlled release of the massive amounts of kinetic energy that have been trapped inside its columns, floors, and walls for more than forty years. At eight in the evening, their hair gray from the dust, their faces exhausted, the workers break for dinner in the parking lot. They are too exhausted to speak. Seated on the long black rolls of covering fabric, they listen to music, rhythm and blues competing with Spanish rap. Cigarette coals stand out in the dark and cast a glow on the faces so that the scene resembles some temporary border encampment of campesinos resting for an hour or two until the coast has cleared and it is safe to go on. The air is heavy with concrete dust, and a pheromone mix of adrenaline and regret seems to emanate from the tower itself.

Mark Loizeaux puts a hand on my shoulder. His hard hat is dirty; there are purple bruises beneath his eyes. "Over the last few days we're been changing the way it thinks about gravity," he explains, gesturing up to the darkened tower. "We've been changing the way it thinks about itself. It doesn't have the sheer walls. It doesn't have the redundancy of the structural supports. It stood there for years, ready to take on seismic events, winds, elevators going up and down, people walking back and forth and partying on New Year's Eve . . ."

From where we are sitting, the exterior columns of the shot-floors, wrapped in black, look like armbands worn to honor the dead. Inside, more than 287 pounds of dynamite are ready, wired, and waiting to explode. "What's going to happen is, I'm going to use its very strength against it," Mark says, the familiar gleam returning to his eyes, his hands chopping away at the air in sequence with the planned detonation of the forty columns at the tower's base. "What I'm going to do is take the weight and hang it out there, and the tower is going to rotate right here, on the back of the elevator shaft, and pick the back columns right off the ground. They weren't meant to do that. And then it's going to go."

VI.

Dipping down through the neon-lit haze of Las Vegas Boulevard late Monday night, the helicopters hover in over the tower, shining shaky circles of light off the poker-chip balconies and down to the empty billboard below. All along Las Vegas Boulevard the Metro police are out in force, more than a hundred policemen in cars and on foot, circling the site, stopping traffic, massaging batons, manning barricades, and barking instructions as a football field away from the tower's base the late-night carnival crowd swells and surges forward, over 3,000 strong, insomniacs and thrill-seekers, curious tourists, gamblers and late shift waitresses, rowdy young men in Los Angeles Kings jerseys, college students on break, and tourists like Jimmy Dickson of Los Angeles, who got married in the Silver Bells wedding chapel thirty or forty years ago and spent his honeymoon night at the Sands. In the crowd tonight are hangers-on who remember the hotel in its prime: Sinatra strutting across the stage, his eyes alight with their icy, psychotic glitter; the Copa Girls kicking up their heels in white feather boas, wearing bowls of fruit on their heads, in metallic jumpsuits in honor of the astronauts, showing their stuff for the high rollers and the tourist couples, the husbands and wives of thirty and forty years ago.

The old-timers here are hard to miss. They hold themselves like movie-star gangsters from the thirties and forties, like Jimmy Cagney and George Raft, ready for action, their arms up near their chests and chins thrust forward. The way they walk is particular, too, standing way up on the balls of their feet and striding through the crowd with an exaggerated hip-swinging side-to-side roll like sailors on shore leave spoiling for a fight. There is Danny Roscoe, who looks like a retired rancher; John Getler, a bellhop, who learned never to take a suitcase from the hands of a guest; and Sonny Benqert, who brought Sinatra his hamburgers medium-rare. In their memories the faces from the hotel's history live on: the young JFK stands outside the Sands with Peter Lawford on a sunny afternoon in 1960, a pair of gold-rimmed aviator sunglasses in hand, having just spent his first stolen hours with Judith Campbell and intimately involved his future presidency with the Mob. Lyndon Johnson looks sleek and handsome in a three-piece linen suit, sharing a laugh with rumpled casino boss Jakie Freedman and several men in dark suits. They remember the new corporate style of Howard Hughes, when the casino started whittling away at the size of a whiskey shot—first to a single ounce, then to seven-eighths of an ounce—and the hotel's dreary final months, when the Sands lured walk-in slots players with $1 margaritas served in complimentary plastic mugs.

What the crowd will see tonight is, as always, the end of a dream. The men who built the Sands—Frank Costello, Vincente "Jimmy Blue Eyes" Alo, Meyer Lansky, Longy Zwillman, Joseph "Doc" Stacher, and the rest—were an all-star team of organized crime whose grander, unspoken ambitions of money, fame, and a place in the sun are present still in the tremendous concentrations of steel reinforcing the tower's structural columns. Freedman, the casino's original frontman, was a Jewish gambler from Texas who wore bolo ties and cashmere coats and ran the high-stakes Domain Privee in Houston. His application for a Nevada gaming license was turned down by the commissioners of Clark County, who reversed themselves several weeks later, whereupon the state agreed to forgo the standing request for net-worth statements on the grounds that the IRS might subpoena such documents for tax prosecutions against the licensees. Jack Entratter, who ran the Copa Room, had been sent out to the desert from his post as manager of the Copacabana in New York to book talent and to make sure that the suitcases of cash arrived on time. As opening day approached, Sands publicist Al Freeman grew more and more frantic, finally outdoing himself with a planted item in Frank Farell's "New York Day by Day" column in the *World-Telegram & Sun* announcing that the casino had "rigged a minor atomic burst for the opening in place of the usual ribbon cutting."

Despite the rain and mist that blanketed Las Vegas on December 15, 1952, the opening night of the Sands, the beginning of the dream that will end here tonight in less than an hour was all its sponsors could have hoped, with entertainment by Danny Thomas and a menu featuring asparagus and carrots from Holland, mushrooms and artichokes from France, curry and chutney from India, peas and onions from Belgium, candied chestnuts from Italy, and hearts of palm from Brazil. "Who's that at the gambling table next to you?" wrote Broadway columnist Earl Wilson, who, like the other junketeering East Coast reporters, had his train fare, food, and wagers paid for by the house. "Maybe a Texas oil man. Maybe a character from the underworld. It could even be Ursula Thiess, the German actress who's a friend of Robert Taylor and who does a nude swimming scene in the new picture, *Monsoon*." Opening-night action at the tables was fierce, fed by escalating reports of losses by the casino so massive that they made front-page news across the country. "Canny press release shouted banner heads of a $250,000 loss in the first eight hours," *Daily Variety* later reported, "but by the close of third shift . . . [the house] was off to the big-money races." The greatest scam America had ever seen was on, the dream of a place where the sun was always shining, everything was permitted, and no one batted an eye at the security guards pushing garbage cans filled with silver dollars all the way down Fremont Street to the downtown banks.

The further evolution of the timeless dream of transcendence is being unveiled tonight in a tinted-glass luxury suite at the Mirage Hotel before a mixed crowd of business-suited flacks and weary-eyed reporters. The Venetian, set to rise on the site where the Sands still stands, will be, according to one executive, "the largest hotel in the world." The new hotel will feature replicas of the Bridge of Sighs and the Lido beach, as well as gondolas and canals, a clock tower, "thirty of the world's finest restaurants," ten swimming pools, two casinos, 6,000 suites, and a 750,000-square-foot shopping mall, rendered in the accompanying drawings as a combination of Philip Johnson whorehouse-modern and the mock-classical public buildings bestowed by Mussolini upon Rome. "We're Las Vegas–izing the whole concept of Venice," explains Sheldon Adelson, whose unnaturally smooth, tight skin suggests that at any moment he might reach up beneath his chin, tear off his human face, and begin barking orders from his smooth-skinned masters who are hovering somewhere near Ursa Minor.

What Las Vegas is really about, however, is not gondolas or clock towers or luxury suites or new-style corporate gaucherie, but time, in its most precious, crystalline form: the time it takes to move walk-ins across the casino floor, or the time the average player will spend at the tables after gobbling down the $6.99 buffet. Time is what brings Sheldon Adelson and the Loizeaux together. In the eight and a half seconds it will take for the Sands to disappear from the face of the earth, Sheldon Adelson will gain eight or nine months that would otherwise be lost to the slow-motion work of wrecking balls and dump trucks, an intolerable pause in the sucker's ballet.

VII.

As the all-clear siren sounds above Las Vegas Boulevard, the cameras click and flash from the upper decks of the Harrah's parking garage to the right of the Sands, recording the final moments of the

eighteen-story tower about to vanish forever in a cloud of dust. Adrienne has rescued a family of pigeons from high in the tower, their
eardrums torn and bloodied by the noise of the drilling. She has
swathed them in covering fabric and laid them to rest in the backseat of her father's Buick. Now, with the shot only minutes away, she
and her crew put a precautionary black tarp over the windows of the
Denny's next door. As the news helicopters circle overhead and
shine their spotlights down on the lot below, Doug and Mark exchange a brotherly hug.

Crouched in the dirt a hundred yards away from the tower's base,
behind a massive air-conditioning unit, Adrienne is understandably
nervous. In a few minutes she will press the button on the blasting
machine, sending out an initial pulse of electricity lasting $^{25}/_{1000}$th of a
second. Too soon for the delay to be detected, the first flashes of
light will be seen at the base of the tower, initialing a sequence of explosions that, if Mark's calculations are correct, will rotate the structure off its axis at an angle of twenty-three degrees, just long enough
to rip the exterior staircase free from the tower. The upper floors of
the tower will then fold, as if connected to the floors below with a
hinge, and the tower will duck neatly under the falling staircase and
collapse in the open lot in front of us. "Resistance is 9.5," the walkie-
talkie crackles as Mark checks the electric charge in the wires
snaking out across the field to the tower's base. "That checks, Doug."
The walkie-talkie crackles again. "We're at two minutes now and
holding steady."

A silence has now fallen over the site, punctuated only by the occasional flashhulb, an expectant pause like the moment in an
Olympic stadium before a long jumper leaves his feet and hurtles
into the air. In this moment, you can feel the crowd's awareness of
the impending destruction of the tower in front of them expanding
into a larger consciousness of their own mortality: what if the building sends showers of concrete and steel up into the air and down
onto the thousands of spectators in the street below? "Let's have a
good, safe job," Mark says into his walkie-talkie. "You know," he reflects, his voice calm as he looks down at his daughter's hand on the
silver switch of the blasting machine, thinking back on the thousands of explosive flashes and the thousands of skyscrapers, bridges,
factories, hotels, prisons, apartment buildings, power stations,

drilling platforms, missile sites, and many other structures that he has seen give up the forms and purposes imposed on their materials by man and crumple back to the ground, "this is the first one of these I've done in a very long time where I haven't been 150 percent sure that the structure was actually going to come down."

Adrienne's thumb trembles on the switch as the countdown begins—"ten . . . nine . . . eight . . . seven"—the numbers following one another too loud and too fast in the continuing silence. "I think I'm going to throw up," she says. Mark is lost in thought, scanning the high arched windows on the tower's top floor for the initial tremor that will tell him whether the beams radiating out from the center of the roof like the spokes of a wheel have given way, whether the cantilever he has created by blowing out the two columns at the tower's base has failed as planned, and whether the tower will, in fact, come down. "One." Adrienne flicks the silver switch, and 25 milliseconds later the detonators go off: the explosive flashes light up the shot-floors with a quick succession of hard, thin bangs that echo like rifle reports among the nearby casinos.

A few thin wisps of smoke curl out from the floors where the flashes went off. Nothing more happens. The tower stands against the neon-blue sky as the frozen lattice of time spreads out over the casinos and the crowd like a sheet of ice. As the detonator smoke fades, you can hear the stunned collective intake of breath, a hiss of surprise and disappointment rising up from the crowd. The lights of the city come filtering back in, and the same thought occurs to everyone here: nothing ever goes as planned. While the seconds fall one after another like water dripping from a faucet, the spectators groan, as if at the same moment they had all let go of the dream that brought them together here at two in the morning, the dream of witnessing something out of the ordinary. They release their breath with a wordless "AAWWW."

Turning to Mark, I see his eyes flicker as his attention shifts to the staircase and another, louder, series of explosions splits the silence like a train rushing down a track. Floor by floor the sleeping charges awaken, sending dark gray spumes of debris sideways out of the cylindrical shell of the tower. The atmospheric pressure swells inside our eardrums. As the dynamite bursts through the black-shrouded columns, the concrete floors fold in on one another like playing cards, and the sum of the horizontal components of the downward pull jerks the staircase away from the tower.

Free from the exterior staircase, the tower buckles and melts away from the sky, undoing thirty years of static endurance in its slide toward the ground, and the rush of concrete and the crowd's screaming merge in a moment of transcendent violence as the tower bursts open. It is an awesome, hallucinatory sight. The solid crust of expectations built up over years and months, hours and minutes—bad checks, bad kids, busted transmissions, and thousands of other individual disappointments—shatters, too, and the cries of the crowd lift out into the haze above Las Vegas Boulevard. The spectators surge forward, holding nothing back, throwing themselves at the tower as it ducks under the falling exterior staircase with elephantine grace. Released from the stable form imposed on it by architects and engineers, 22,302 tons of steel and concrete go rushing headlong to the ground, in the precise sequence Mark imagined when he looked up at the tower only moments ago.

The impact of the event hangs suspended for an exhausted moment, broken only by the wailing of car alarms up and down the Strip. A cheer goes up and a dirty gray dust billows out from the place where the tower has settled, gaining in height and velocity as it rolls toward us. Gathering up the flashlight and the blasting machine in its worn leather case, we head for the parking lot, where Doug and Stacey stand before the cluster of lights, cameras, and fuzzy boom mikes, already answering questions from the television reporters about the force of the blast and the number of sticks of dynamite used and why the tower seemed to rotate and fall backward instead of straight down. Behind us the cloud approaches at surprising speed, as if to shield the crowd from this forbidden glimpse of the destructive capacity slumbering away in all things, an angel had descended from heaven, squatted down on the thirty-foot mountain of rubble, and begun beating its wings.

VIII.

Outside the fence, the Strip is alive with the aimless jangling excitement that you feel in a crowd outside a stadium after the big game, the lights too bright and the shouts too loud. In the alleyway on the other side of the wall, a white-haired man in a yellow plastic construction helmet, his brown tweed jacket festooned with security passes, stands with his eyes squeezed shut and an enormous pair of foam-rubber headphones clamped over his ears. He is grinning, delighted, stamping on the pavement faster and faster, as if the music inside his head had finally found an answer in the world outside.

"Do it again!" someone shouts. "I want you guys to blow up my house." The spell is broken. A passing film-student-type dressed in black rushes out of the crowd, a shock of dyed red hair flopping over one eye and his other eye doing speedfreak pinwheels in its socket. "What movie is this for? What's the name of the movie?" He can't get the idea out of his head: the collapse of an eighteen-story building only makes sense as a scene from movieland, where remarkable things happen all the time. "Hey, when is the movie coming out?" The workmen look modestly around and say nothing, transformed by the magic of the blast from working stiffs into rock stars. Their proximity to the explosion, the concrete dust in their hair and on their clothes, is sexy. A translucent blonde in a white synthetic fur places a kittenish hand on the arm of David Williams, one of the drillers, and begs for a brick. He is not exactly sure how to respond. "We're working now," he finally says. "I'll get you a brick after we're done."

At 2 A.M., as Adrienne's crew removes the covering from the Denny's window, another vision appears: the restaurant is packed with families, cabdrivers, and casino workers on break, and as the waitresses move from table to table, only a few of the diners look up at the window, glancing incuriously out at the workmen and the hole in the sky before returning to the GrandSlam breakfasts in front of them. Near the window, a large black man in a wide-brimmed hat and a full-length fur coat is sitting with three women, his left arm laid out over the red vinyl Denny's banquette as he counts out his money on top of the check: a hard night's work deserves its reward. As the workers roll up the cover in the alley, the crowd drifts off, some home to bed and some across the street to the Mirage in hopes of trading in their vision of the vanishing tower for a run of luck at the tables. On the site below, a graceful curve of masonry from the top of the tower has survived the fall nearly intact and sits atop a rounded hill of neatly fractured concrete as if placed there by design. The staircase is laid out over the rubble at a near-perfect forty-five-degree angle: the newspapers will note tomorrow that even the dust remained on-site.

"Come have a drink," offers Doug, a companionable arm around my shoulder. After months of auctions and wrecking balls, and after a single vivid instant of destruction, one last part of the Sands still stands: the Aqueduct, a horseshoe-shaped building decorated in mid-sixties California modern, where Sinatra used to stay in a luxury suite with a swimming pool and curved-glass doors. Tonight the third floor of the Aqueduct is home to Chuck Wilton, a white-haired seismologist who tested fallout shelters for the Federal Emergency Management Agency in the 1950s and has worked with Daddy Jack and his sons for years, measuring the impact of their blasts on the ground. He pours scotch into Styrofoam cups and hands them around, then pops a tape into the VCR.

"Perfect. Beautiful," Mark says as he watches the flashes of light and then, much faster than it seemed the first time, the answering roar of the explosives as the tower ducks under the staircase and the picture in Mark's head achieves its congruence with the picture on-screen. "Let's see that again," says Doug. The brothers were so busy watching the high arched windows for the first tremors of motion that neither of them really saw the tower come down. He stops the tape and rewinds. "Watch the front of the hotel." And as the tower falls, you can see hundreds of firefly camera flashes lighting up the facade of the Treasure Island casino across the street from the Sands in spontaneous tribute.

As the tension of the previous days and hours drains away, the brothers sip their scotch and the conversation wanders. The potbellied explosives handler from Vermont, with a heavy beard and quiet good manners, will be invited back to work with the family again. Doug talks about the great game of golf he has planned for tomorrow. Mark talks about the plans to blow up the Hacienda on New Year's Eve. Then it's on to the Clifton stack in Arizona, the power station in Madras, the missile pads in Belarus, and other used-up branches of the pitiless evolutionary process whose deeper ends remain hidden from our eyes but whose agents the Loizeaux surely are. Three weeks from now the rubble that was the Sands will be gone, and the illusion of a fresh start will vanish, too, as Sheldon

Adelson's dream of a Venice-in-the-desert assumes its inevitable earthly form. Tonight, however, walking through the parking lot, the lights of the Mirage shining through the empty place in the sky where the Sands once stood, it seems wrong to end on a sour note. The dust has lifted, a fresh breeze is blowing in from the desert mountains above Las Vegas, and, for the moment at least, anything is possible.

On Message

I.

The Briefing Room looks smaller and shabbier than it does on television. A bank of cameras is located in an enclosure to the left of the stage, which is littered with empty soda bottles and plastic trays from the Pentagon mess hall. In front of the podium is a portable soundboard where the network soundmen can jack in their mikes. The podium is made of a dull wood laminate, which has been treated to minimize glare. Behind the podium hangs the Pentagon seal, which is approximately the size and shape of a serving platter; it shows the Pentagon, in massive, reassuring detail, afloat on a silent, gray, military sea.

The secretary's briefing is scheduled at one this afternoon. Sometimes it is scheduled at nine. Or at noon. It doesn't matter. The time will keep shifting throughout the day. An hour before the October 8 briefing is scheduled to begin, only a few of the wooden chairs in the Briefing Room are occupied. The first two rows have already been reserved by those members of the press who maintain offices off the well-polished stretch of hallway known as the Corridor. Wandering behind the podium, I can read the affiliations of the reporters who have already reserved their seats in the front row: they work for *USA Today,* CBS, ABC, NBC, the AP, Reuters, CNN, AP Radio, ABC radio, and the Voice of America. Some are young; others are in their mid- to late fifties, in practical rubber-soled shoes that might save their feet the wear and tear of tramping back and forth to the Briefing Room, to the Press Office, and to occasional meetings with furtive sources. The details of the reporters' shoes, shirts, jackets, and ties are hardly particular enough to identify them as adepts of

any particular profession. They are reporters. They write in reporter's notebooks, gossip, and complain.[1]

The absence of even basic information about the war—such as
the disposition of American troops or the numbers of American
ships or planes in the general vicinity of Afghanistan—has reduced
most of the reporters to quoting the public statements of Defense
Secretary Donald Rumsfeld with very little additional comment at
all. Having served as secretary of defense during the Ford administration, Rumsfeld is entirely familiar with his role. His briefings are
wonderful theater, packed full of the lessons he has drawn from the
last forty years of official U.S. government interactions with the

---

[1]. I begin my morning by circumnavigating the Pentagon, exiting the Pentagon Metro stop into the parking lot, where the sidewalk has been closed to
pedestrian traffic, then walking up to the highway. The view of the burned-
out section of the building where the plane hit on September 11 has been cor-
doned off by a curtained fence, where a sign announces PHOTOGRAPHY
PROHIBITED. I make my way to the River Entrance checkpoint, which is
manned by military police in combat fatigues who carry assault rifles. Their ages
range from eighteen to twenty-one. They are up from Fort Bragg in North Carolina, they tell me, and they request that I don't use their names. One grew up in
Illinois. Another, a woman, is from out west; the other MPs refer to her forceful,
efficient, manner as "high speed." I learn other words as well. A "pogue" is a soldier with a low-ranking job and no special skills. They are happy to make friends
with a reporter, who is wearing a navy suit, and who might have some useful information about the war. After perhaps an hour or two of conversation, and
the gift of a few cigarettes from my bag, the MPs are kind enough to turn their
backs just long enough for me to cross over to the building entrance, where I
might hook up with someone with the right credentials, a network tech or a wire-
service photographer.

In addition to my daily copies of the *New York Times, Washington Times,* and
Washington Post, I carry a tape recorder, a notebook, two pens, a bottle of water,
and a paperback copy of *Moby-Dick,* which I hauled out of a packing box this
summer in honor of the hundred and fiftieth anniversary of the whale's birth and
started reading again in the hours after I saw the World Trade Center disinte-
grate outside my living room window. Here in Washington, I have been reading
Melville's novel with particular interest, ever since I arrived at the fifth page of
the first chapter, in which the narrator imagines the "grand programme of Providence" in which his voyage must play some small part:

Grand Contested Election for the Presidency of the United States
WHALING VOYAGE BY ONE ISHMAEL
BLOODY BATTLE IN AFGHANISTAN

press. In addition to the briefings, there are also daily "trial balloons," which allow public officials to gauge public opinion on vital questions or to outmaneuver their enemies in the ferocious bureaucratic wars that take place entirely out of earshot of the media. Reporters who wish to participate in these faceless games can gain tantalizing exclusives, which are duly prepared for print in the evening and then duly contradicted the next afternoon.

The briefing doesn't start for another twenty minutes. Yesterday morning the United States began its long-awaited bombing campaign in Afghanistan.

"Good afternoon," says Terry Mitchell, the Pentagon employee in charge of the Briefing Room. "It's that time of day when I give my cell phone speech." He is of medium height, with round, freshly shaven cheeks above which are mounted a handsome pair of silver-rimmed aviator lenses. "Turn them off," he says.

The camera lights are switched on, flooding the room with white, unnatural light. John McWethy of ABC is writing notes on a reporter's pad. He is a tall, handsome man in his early fifties, with thinning silver hair and the gentle, courteous manner of everybody's favorite history teacher in high school.

"Why are we saving the CBS chair?" McWethy wonders out loud. The joke is at the expense of his colleague David Martin, with whom he has shared the Pentagon beat for most of the last two decades. The joke gets a laugh from the CBS cameraman. McWethy caps his pen and slips his notebook inside the pocket of his blazer. The jokes, like the complaints and the gossip, are intended to relieve the relentless, mind-crowding tedium that comes from the absence of "ground truth," the reporters' term for hard, verifiable, firsthand information about the war.

By now, every chair in the Briefing Room is full, and at least twenty reporters are standing in the aisles, along with the usual crowd of photographers, who are always the last to arrive. They walk into the crowded room, take their cameras out of their bags, and play with the lenses, discreetly flexing one knee, then the other. Donald Rumsfeld walks in the door.

A fit and vigorous-looking man of sixty-nine, he strides confidently toward the podium, his body tilting forward, flanked by the Saxon-looking figure of Air Force General Richard B. Myers, the newly sworn-in chairman of the Joint Chiefs of Staff. Rumsfeld steps up to the podium. He sets his jaw. He is an organizer of men; he is a former navy fighter pilot, a congressman from Chicago, a bureaucratic infighter, a fierce partisan of the missile-defense shield, a deep thinker with a sharp sense of humor who enjoys the give-and-take with reporters and who is known to his intimates as "Rummy." General Myers stands a bit stiffly to the side, just behind the secretary's right shoulder.

The secretary of defense lowers his head slightly, then draws a single, carefully regulated breath.

Good afternoon. I have reported to the president, General Myers and I have, on a number of occasions over the past twenty-four hours, and today I'll make some general comments—

The autumnal gray weave of his jacket matches the color of the slackening flesh beneath his throat, which clashes with his silken moderate, late-nineties tie. He tightens the muscles above his jaw, striving for the effect usefully outlined in "Rumsfeld's Rules," a document he authored during the Reagan years and which is available on defenselink.mil, the Pentagon's official Web site. There are 154 of these rules in all, helpfully divided into eight subtitled sections. "Manage the interaction between the Pentagon and the White House," reads the third rule in the section entitled "For the Secretary of Defense." "Unless you establish a narrow channel for the flow of information and 'tasking' back and forth, the process can quickly become chaotic."

Today's rule is to manage the expectations of the press, in a style that will meet with the approval of the public and also of those segments of the elite that take their cues from the editorial boards of the *New York Times* and the *Washington Post*. Reporters know nothing. They put the lives of American soldiers in danger. Besides, this is not their war.

—and then General Myers will provide a little more detail, . . . and an early assessment of the battle damage.

As every head in the room nods along, the secretary settles deeper into the rhythm of his sentences, and the reporters do their best to assume the posture that their job requires, head bowed in ritual obeisance to whatever official-sounding statements are being made from the podium.

I want to stress that we're still in the early stages. . . . Today we'll be continuing to collect damage assessment and will be striking additional targets as appropriate. . . . The reports indicating that there were attacks on Kabul are incorrect.

The war, the secretary reports, is likely to be sustained for a period of years, not weeks or months.

This campaign will be waged much like the Cold War, in the sense that it will involve many fronts over a period of time and will require continuous pressure by a large number of countries around the globe.

This statement, or so it appears in the moment, might actually be news. The Cold War lasted for four decades; nearly 100,000 American soldiers died in hot wars in Korea and Vietnam. General Myers makes his remarks, and then the floor is opened to questions. As is customary, the first question is asked by the senior correspondent at the Pentagon, Charlie Aldinger, of Reuters. He calls out to the podium in a gentle voice, as though he were cooing to a baby.

General, the bomber aircraft . . . were cruise . . . first, were ships used today? And were bomber aircraft, both bombs and cruise missiles, used again today, as they were yesterday?

We will use some Tomahawk missiles today from ships. . . .

And Mr. Secretary, might I add, are U.S. and British forces attacking Taliban troop concentrations as well as air defense and airfields and other sites?

There have been some ground forces targeted.

The photographers have begun circulating through the room, in search of new and better angles. Moving in and around the mass of seated reporters, they get down on one knee and shoot, then shoot again. The camera shutters go off in succession with the sound that a playing card makes when laid face-up on a baize-covered table. The first flip is followed by several more flips, which trigger a waterfall of tertiary flips, until every photographer in the room has the shot. Then the room falls silent for a moment or two, until someone takes another picture. Working a press conference at the Pentagon is hard, physically demanding work. It takes stamina, sharp elbows, and a strong back. McWethy asks Rumsfeld about the 37,500 meals for the Afghans, the humanitarian MREs (meals ready to eat), dropped in a country where four million people are starving.

It is quite true that 37,000 rations in a day do not feed millions of human beings. On the other hand, if you were one of those starving people who got one of the rations, you'd be appreciative.

You've got to hand it to the secretary, I am thinking. Dropping rations while also dropping bombs might seem cynical rather than generous, or so the question was meant to suggest. In return, Rumsfeld gave an honest, hard-headed, realist answer: he even rounded down the number of MREs, from 37,500 to 37,000.

McWethy asks a follow-up, and then it's off to the races, with reporters shouting questions from every corner of the room:

Mr. Secretary, can you say whether the Northern Alliance is making any military gains on the ground?
. . . can you help us clarify something that you said the other day?
Can you tell us anything . . . ?
Have any Stingers been fired?

Standing high above the sea of upraised hands and waving pens, the secretary of defense is in complete and entire command of the deck. To say that the secretary is enjoying himself is wrong. Then again, it is true. He is clearly enjoying himself. It's like the famous five o'clock follies in Saigon, but in reverse: then, the press made fun of army spokesmen; now the secretary of defense is having his way with the press.

Will the NATO AWACS . . . ?
General Myers! General Myers!

When the secretary sees a familiar face, or hears the beginning of a question that he might like to answer, he points out into the crowd and the Briefing Room falls silent. When he doesn't want to answer a question, he responds with a selection drawn from an evolving menu of set phrases:

We don't discuss things of that type.
I wouldn't want to speculate on that.
Mr. Secretary, do you know how much this campaign is costing on a daily basis?
No.

Rumsfeld accompanies his spoken answers with a series of gestures that I have been diagramming in my little black notebook for a week and a half. When he wishes to emphasize a point during an answer, for example, he makes a fist and pounds, with the thumb laid flat across the platform of the other four fingers; at other times, he folds the bottom two fingers into his palm, then chops lightly at the air. When he says, *"It is clear to me,"* he supports the phrase by placing both hands on his chest, with his fingers spread apart. *"Terrorist networks"* evokes broad, sweeping, outward gestures of his open hand, suggesting that terrorist networks cannot be reduced to the whereabouts of a single man. He also has a special grimace, which is reserved for specific words attached to villains such as Saddam Hussein, who will be treated by the United States and its allies in such a way as to *"contain"*—he grimaces at the gruesome pictures that appear unbidden before his mind's eye—*"his appetites."*

The briefing is almost over, and I am still waiting for someone to question the secretary about what seems to me, at least, to have been the salient point of his opening remarks. Is this really another Cold War? Who exactly is the enemy?

The list of unasked questions that I am keeping in my head gets longer with every briefing. Today, as on previous days, for example, no one asks a single question about the root causes of the worst intelligence failure in American history. No one presses Rumsfeld to elaborate on the connection between the bin Laden networks and Iraq. No one questions our country's "alliance" with Saudi Arabia.

See you tomorrow! someone shouts.

Rumsfeld turns, and crinkles appear at the corners of his eyes. He is smiling. "See you tomorrow" is simply another part of the ritual, a friendly locker-room pat on the fanny. The secretary of defense alone will determine whether he shows up in the Briefing Room tomorrow or not. As he leaves, I occupy myself with the following thought: of the approximately one hundred reporters in the Pentagon Briefing Room this afternoon—from ABC, NBC, CBS, CNN, the *New York Times,* the *Washington Post,* and every other major news outlet in the country—not a single representative of the press, myself included, was possessed of the energy, or the foresight, or the leisure, to stand up on their hind legs and encourage the secretary to expand on his invocation of the signal military, political, and cultural event of the last fifty years:

The Cold War?

II.

The reporters file down the Corridor, past walls lined with framed reminders of the American victories on San Juan Hill, Iwo Jima, and the beaches of Normandy. ROOSEVELT DEAD, another headline announces. TRUMAN PROMISES TO RETAIN POLICIES. The clack of keyboards is already audible in the well-polished hallways. In the Briefing Room, the television reporters do their afternoon stand-ups; trash accumulates at the feet of their cameras. On the other side of the Corridor, close to the windows, is the breezy, light-filled office of CNN, followed by a cluster of three much smaller offices, inhabited by the correspondents for ABC, NBC, and CBS. In the press room, reporters type in their stories for *Time, Newsweek, U.S. News & World Report,* and twenty-odd newspapers, as well as Reuters, the AP, and Agence France-Presse. On the wall near the press room hangs a photo gallery of postwar secretaries of defense, from Forrestal to McNamara, Schlesinger, Brown, Weinberger, Cheney, Aspin, Perry, and Cohen. All of the portraits appear to have been snapped by the same photographer—a cold, distanced professional with a novelist's eye for the single, telling detail. There is McNamara's Brylcreemed hair; Schlesinger's professorial pipe; and Donald Rumsfeld's flinty smile. As I follow the progression of faces from the beginning of the Cold War to the present it is possible, perhaps, to notice a trend. It's not that the secretaries of defense got stupider. The job is different now. The men who administer the military aspects of that power are not philosophers or military strategists. They are corporate bureaucrats, the type one might expect to find at the top of General Motors or General Dynamics, running the largest industrial complex in the history of the world.

Pentagon spokeswoman Torie Clarke, a tall, blonde woman in her early forties, receives petitioners in her office at the end of the Corridor. There are more reporters in her office than chairs, and so the reporters wander, and chatter with the secretaries, and watch the bombing on CNN. The sun shines in, spreading lazy pools of light on the rug. Through a picture window I can see outside to the sunny perfection of an early fall afternoon in northern Virginia. The temperature is a spectacular seventy-one degrees, according to the weather map on CNN. Fluffy cartoon clouds are taped to the flat blue sky. Torie Clarke isn't here yet. She is meeting with the secretary upstairs.

Three captive reporters sit slumped in padded chairs near the door, looking up at those who stand. After five minutes, or sometimes ten, you can see the reporters break their pose and start shifting sullenly from foot to foot, like high school students in the principal's office. They lift their heads and raise their eyes, as if to indicate a yawning canopy of boredom overhead; they scuff their feet and stare down at the carpet. Efficient, uniformed secretaries type steadily away at their desks, sending lines of structured type across pages and pages of bonded government paper. Torie Clarke arrives, and she invites me into her inner office, where we sit together at a polished wooden table by a window. I am curious to know who decides to hold a briefing and when, and whether the statements that the secretary makes at the briefings are written out in advance, and by whom.

"We talk constantly with our counterparts and others at the White House, State, NSC, so that at the end of the day there are probably seven or eight people involved in the decision," she adds. These people, she says, include "Karen [Hughes at the White House], her deputy Dan Bartlett, [White House spokesman] Ari Fleischer, Richard Boucher over at State, Sean McCormack at NSC, Anna Perez at NSC." The "we" of her sentence, she explains, includes herself, Admiral Craig Quigley, and Larry Di Rita, who functions as the secretary's chief of staff.

The preparation of the secretary's opening statements, she says, varies from case to case. "Sometimes it's written," she says. "Sometimes he just writes notes based on conversations we've had leading up to it." More formal statements, she says, are written by some combination of the secretary, herself, one of the Pentagon's staff writers, and Di Rita, with occasional input from speechwriters and various government officials.

It is easy to see why Torie Clarke was chosen for her job. She is a highly structured, mentally organized person. From where she sits, Clarke believes that Americans will be able to understand a war they will not be able to see or hear, and for which conventional scorecards may not be available.

"I have a lot of faith that they can understand that this is a very different time, and a very different kind of war," she says with a hopeful, impatient glance out the door, anticipating her scheduled 4:45 phone call with General Tommy Franks, the commander of American forces in Central Asia, who is based down in Tampa.

The reporters, she believes, are getting the message. "Not the new ones who've all come flocking here in the last week or so," she explains, "[but] the ones who have covered this place for years, and are closest to what we are doing, to the military aspect of the war, have understood for quite some time that this is very different, and won't be covered and won't be seen in the same way that the Persian Gulf War was, or Kosovo, or Bosnia, or anything like that."

As she talks, she makes sure that her eyes never leave my face. "We've been very open about the fact that a lot of the military piece will be covert," she says. Torie Clarke has very pretty eyes.

"You're going to have to call General Franks in a minute," her secretary interrupts, before withdrawing from the doorway.

"I apologize," Clarke says. "I asked General Franks to hang out so I could call him." In my remaining few minutes I ask her to explain the object of the current bombing campaign in Afghanistan.

"It's not about one man or one network," she says. "It's not. It's about a lot more than Osama bin Laden. It's not about a country or a people or a religion." As usual, the aims of the war are defined in the negative. There are some reporters, Clarke adds, who complain about hearing the same message again and again and again from the Pentagon. "Well, I take that as a sign," she says.

"That you're 'on message'?" I ask.

"You know, 'on message' has taken on a certain connotation around here, in this town," she answers. "It happens to be what we're doing, and it happens to be the truth, and the fact that we're repeating it ad nauseam is a sign that we're sincere."

"Because everything we want to do, whether that's freezing people's bank accounts—" I begin.

"Right."

"—or military action—"

"Right."

"—is going to require the support—"

"Of course it will."

"—of other people, in other countries."

"The cooperation has been pretty extraordinary," she admits.

"So you believe the message is getting out, and support is there—"

"Oh, yeah."

"—and that the need to aggressively get that message out—"

"Oh yeah, without a—"

"—and everything is fine, and—"

The job will take years, not weeks or months. There is also, she says, the evidence of the secretary's recent swing through Saudi Arabia, Oman, Egypt, Turkey, and Uzbekistan.

"Without putting words in other people's mouths," she says, "we were all struck by the fact that most of the people with whom we met said exactly what we've been saying. Rumsfeld, he's a great listener," she concludes. "And person after person with whom he met said almost exactly those same things that we've been saying here."

III.

The day that the secretary of defense left for the Middle East and Central Asia, I spent a morning with John McWethy. One of the senior reporters on the Pentagon beat, McWethy, fifty-four, works out of a windowless cubicle that he shares with Barbara Starr, an ABC News producer who does radio. The office measures approximately eight feet by eight feet, the size of the cage at a parking garage, which it greatly resembles, with the addition of a dark institutional carpet that runs up the walls. Stuffed with books, papers, television monitors, and broadcast equipment, the office gives the two of them just enough room to work at their desks while sitting back to back. Fluorescent light pours into the room from a boxlike plastic fixture. It's government-issue light, the kind you might see inside a big-city courtroom in the middle of December. McWethy is talking on the phone to a producer in New York.

"They're not going to accept anybody but me on the plane," McWethy explains. Hunched over in his chair, he keeps quiet and still, like a kid who is praying for anything other than broccoli. McWethy has been covering the Pentagon and the State Department for ABC News for the last twenty-two years. Before that, he worked as a writer for *U.S. News & World Report,* covering the White House, where, as legend has it, ABC News president Roone Arledge saw him ask a question at a press conference, noted his handsome looks and intelligent bearing, and ordered someone to hire McWethy and put him on the air.

"We don't know what the itinerary is," he says. "We don't know shit."

A few more calls and McWethy has arranged for his camera equipment to be delivered to the airport; in forty-five minutes he will do his stand-up for the West Coast edition of *Good Morning America.* He gets to his office at five or six in the morning and stays until seven or eight at night.

"A lot of what happens will be absolutely invisible," he tells me. "I think it's going to make my job extremely difficult. It has already done so." What he has received from the Pentagon so far, he says, are "carefully sifted insights," compiled in accordance with a highly restrictive set of ground rules that "are tougher maybe than the rules in any conflict that we've been engaged in."

"He's so absolutely . . . I don't know how to say this," McWethy says, when I ask him about Rumsfeld. He pauses. "He has a passion for secrecy," he finally says, "and he is absolutely unforgiving and un-relenting on this issue." Not only has Rumsfeld threatened sources with legal prosecution, from the Briefing Room podium, on national television, he notes, but the Pentagon also refuses to confirm or deny much of the information that reporters do manage to find out, thus ensuring that the news that does reach the public is riddled with guesswork and error.

"You've already seen disinformation created by this policy," he says, referring to rumors of a deployment of F-15 fighter planes to the Middle East, which turned out to be false. Refusing to answer reporters' questions, he says, is hardly compelled by a desire to protect the lives of American troops.

"I think it's nonsense," he says flatly. In recent off-the-record meetings with the secretary, he adds, reporters aired their concerns about the effects of the department's policy for the second or third time this month. "I think he was delighted to hear the effect of his edicts," he says. "During the Gulf War, Cheney [then the secretary of defense] made his famous statement that 'the press has absolutely no capacity to police itself.' " In the talks that McWethy gives at the Naval Academy, he adds, he has noticed how often the cadets make reference to "the Vietnam effect," a phrase that implies, in so many words, that the press was responsible for losing that war.

"What they seem not to understand is that we were being lied to at the highest levels of government," McWethy continues. "This terrible breach of trust . . ."

The effect of this attitude on the psyches of even the most experienced reporters is easy to spot. In the middle of the afternoon, on the fourth day of the American bombing campaign in Afghanistan, David Martin, fifty-eight, the correspondent for CBS, is sitting alone in the dark. His office is larger than McWethy's, and it has a window: the sun is blocked out by a plastic shade. On the shelf above his head is a row of policy books with serious-sounding titles, including a book that he wrote in the eighties on terrorism. "It wasn't very exotic," he explains sadly. "There was the bombing of the Marine barracks in Lebanon, then the Libyans, you remember." Our conversation is interrupted by a knock on the door. The door opens, and in walks Dan Rather, the CBS anchorman.

"I'm sorry," Rather says. Since the attack on the World Trade Center, he has cut his hair short. It makes his face look wider. I stand up to give him my chair, as Martin points me, politely, toward the door. I exit into the waiting area, which is just big enough to accommodate a pair of filing cabinets plus the anchorman's three-person entourage from New York, which consists of a slick-looking white producer in a suit, an older black professional woman, and a young, pretty blonde who speaks with a pronounced British accent. The only flaw in her beauty that I can see is a slight, insect-bite-size swelling on her cheek.[2]

NBC correspondent Jim Miklaszewski passes by, swinging one leg ahead of him as he walks.

"Is he the real deal?" asks the CBS producer from New York. He is eager for the scoop on Rumsfeld, whom Rather will interview in half an hour.

"He's the real deal," Miklaszewski brightly assures him. "The trip I took with him last week was the best trip I've ever taken with a public official, by far."

The door to Martin's office opens. Everyone in the hall stands up. "I'm sorry to have disturbed your meeting," Rather offers, in a folksy Texas twang. "Thank you very much for your chair." He is a strange man, who is doing his best to meet the demands of a strange job at a very strange time. The anchorman waves and disappears down the hall. I ask David Martin to define the story that he will be reporting for CBS News over the coming weeks and months.

"As long as bin Laden is there, he is the story," Martin says. I ask him who his viewers are, and he tucks his head and offers me a weary smile.

"I've always imagined a person who is trying to eat dinner and to help his kids with their homework at the same time," he answers. "I do not have his full attention. And that's not patronizing. It's just a fact of how people live their lives. In this case, they're paying closer attention. They want to 'get' Osama bin Laden.

"I'm under no illusion that people necessarily want us to get the information that they need to be properly informed," he adds. "When the press is shut out, there is never any shortage of people applauding. 'Why do they need to know that?' "

---

2. Claire Fletcher, twenty-seven, is Dan Rather's personal assistant; she answers the anchorman's phone and handles his mail. She first noticed the sore beneath her mouth on October 1. On October 18, Fletcher was diagnosed with cutaneous anthrax.

It's no wonder that Martin seems depressed. The job he does now is no longer the same as the job he was hired to do. Like McWethy, Martin belongs to an older generation of reporters who imagined that television would provide them with a way to reach tens of millions of people with stories that shed real and necessary light on the actions of their government. By cutting news budgets year after year, and by eliminating investigative and foreign reporting in favor of the serial dramas of O. J. Simpson, Jon-Benet Ramsey, and Monica Lewinsky, the networks have succeeded in transforming "news" into yet another shabby subdivision of the Magic Kingdom. The networks now have little choice but to treat the war as a dramatic entertainment, rather than as an occasion for asking the questions that need to be asked.

IV.

Besides, being the Pentagon correspondent for one of the three major networks is no longer really where it's at. Around the country, and around the world, viewers interested in the latest installment of the Afghan campaign are likely to turn to CNN, the twenty-four-hour news channel, which has just pulled Bob Franken off of the Gary Condit scandal beat to report on the war. I talk instead to CNN's regular Pentagon team, Jamie McIntyre and Christopher Plante, whose sunny, capacious surroundings say all one needs to know about the relative importance of the networks and instant news: the total square footage of the CNN office is roughly equal to that of ABC, NBC, and CBS combined.

"The first 'N' stands for 'news,' " says Plante, gesturing toward the network logo with his thumb, "as opposed to the domestic entertainment networks down the hall." A news veteran in his early forties, he is CNN's senior producer at the Pentagon; he speaks in the sardonic, educated accent of Chicago's Lake Shore Drive. When I ask him about the secretary's evocation of the Cold War, he turns his head.

"How many Americans died during the Cold War?" he asks.

"A lot," I answer, after a pause.

Still, he says, there is very little information around that might be useful in determining what Rumsfeld's use of the phrase "Cold War" might portend. "We're covering an invisible war," he says.

Jamie McIntyre, forty-eight, applies his makeup in a small mirror above his desk. "The highlighter goes beneath my eyes," he explains. "A little foundation to even out my skin." He has been reporting from the Pentagon for almost nine years, he says; he applies the cosmetics with sure, even, professional strokes, while keeping up a friendly, *SportsCenter*-like banter. His next spot is in less than five minutes. The Briefing Room is empty, save for the techs.

"I'm still hearing domestic. I need to hear international," McIntyre says, holding his earpiece up to his ear. He does two or three spots an hour. As he prepares to speak, he holds a reporter's pad in his hand. The page in front of him is empty. When he notices me looking, he flips the pad over so I can see the next page, which is also blank, with the exception of a single pair of parentheses that have been written in with a red ballpoint pen. As the broadcast moves from Islamabad to Afghanistan then back to Atlanta, approaching the Pentagon, I notice that the space between the parentheses is empty. A trancelike expression settles over his features as he stares into the camera lens:

The reality is that it's just a small part of U.S. strategy, he begins, not so much an exit strategy but a strategy to never get fully in. Of course, Jamie McIntyre doesn't have the slightest conception of what U.S. strategy in Afghanistan might be; if a larger strategy does indeed exist, the reporters inside the Pentagon will be among the last people in the building to know. Still, his voice is a handsome instrument, conveying a familiar, soothing sense of authority.

"If you're on TV every hour for ten years," he says, once the camera light clicks off, "eventually you get the hang of it." He arrived at the Pentagon in 1992, he says, after Wolf Blitzer got promoted. He knew nothing about American military history, he says, or about the practical mechanics of fighting a war.

"My desire was to have a beat, any beat," he explains. "You don't need to be a lawyer to cover the Supreme Court."

Back at the CNN office, Chris Plante is shooting down a rumor that originated on debka.com, a Web site that offers hard reporting on troop movements, intelligence agencies, and the motivations for actions by foreign governments mixed with rumor-mongering by Israeli security sources. "Major portions of this story,"

he remarks, "will be impossible to verify and impossible to report."
Still, he adds, he is quite satisfied with the product that CNN is putting on the air.

"The guys down the hall do one show a night," he explains. "They
do one small package. They know what we have, because they're
watching us all day long. Our mission is to leave them with nothing
at the end of each and every day."

V.

There's plenty of nothing on tap at the Pentagon. As the sun sinks
below the highway, Charlie Aldinger is sitting in the press room,
talking to the Reuters Washington desk. "When in doubt, fudge," he
says. "You got that?" The rank of senior Pentagon correspondent is
not without its privileges; his cubicle adjoins a large window.

"The man was in a lot of trouble before the war came along," he
says, using his pointer finger to indicate the man upstairs. "He
staked it all on missile defense, then the tax cut eliminated the surplus." Back then, he says, Rumsfeld's relationship with the press was
poor.

"There was the sense that he didn't have time for the press and
that he didn't give a rat's ass about the press," he explains. His con-
clusion is simple:

"The war saved the man."

From the surrounding cubicles I hear the clack-clack-clack of
laptop keys, like ice cubes against the side of a glass.

In a rack by the door, I find an official Pentagon press release
dated September 10, 2001. "Secretary of Defense Donald H. Rumsfeld launched a battle against Pentagon bureaucracy today in a
speech opening the 2001 Acquisition and Logistics Excellence
Week," the text says, before proceeding to a quote from the secretary himself: "The battle against bureaucracy is a moral imperative
because the lives of Americans depend on it."

Clearly times have changed at the Pentagon. I corner Bradley
Graham of the *Washington Post,* who returned to the Pentagon last
week after finishing a book on missile defense. A balding, bearded
man with deep-set, intelligent eyes, he chooses words with great

care; his sentences are loaded with long, aphasic pauses, which he uses to further revise and correct his thoughts.

"There is a . . . deep fright about the release of even some basic information . . . which borders on . . . the irrational," he says. Academics at military war colleges, he tells me, have even been told not to talk to the press on historical subjects, such as the Soviet campaign in Afghanistan.

In search, nonetheless, of some historical perspective, I visit for a while with Raymond Cromley, whose honorary cubicle is situated in the Pentagon press room just to the right of the door. He is by far the oldest living reporter at the Pentagon. A wizened old man with lively eyes and a two-day growth of beard, Cromley wears a soup-stained navy sweater pulled down low over an oxford shirt, and a red tartan wool cap on his head for extra warmth. The front of his sweater reads CHAPS RALPH LAUREN.

Raymond Cromley is ninety-one years old. When I ask him to name the biggest change he has seen at the Pentagon, he shrugs. Then he offers a dry, one-word answer.

"Sloppiness," he says. When I ask for an example, he shrugs again.

"Why," he answers, as if the point were much too obvious to be anything more than a waste of his breath, "this thing right here."

In 1941, he tells me, he was the *Wall Street Journal*'s correspondent in Tokyo; after Pearl Harbor he spent six months in solitary confinement before he was repatriated to the United States, along with five of his fellow correspondents, in return for some Japanese spies.

"This was the intelligence section for Korea and Japan," he says, of the room where we are sitting now. His commander was General George C. Marshall. "He was head of everything, for some reason," he remembers. "He was a wonderful guy, don't get me wrong."

It was at Marshall's behest, he says, that he went to a cave in China to visit with Mao, who was interested in discussing American investment in his country after the war.

Then he shares a few stories about Einstein, whom he met while studying physics at CalTech.

"He was interested in people," he remembers, in a flat, uninflected tone that approximates the sound of good old-fashioned newspaper prose. "He loved to play this viola, this big bowed instrument. He was the lousiest player you've ever heard. Don't print that. He would sit in one of the common rooms at the college and play. Sometimes he played another instrument, with those strips of metal that you hit with a stick. What's that called?" he asks, describing the distant form of the instrument with his large, gnarled hands.

"Oh, yes," he says. "A xylophone."

The hour is getting late, so I ask him if he can sum up all that he has learned in a few simple sentences. He is happy to oblige.

"People of all countries are nice," he offers, gently. "There are some villains in every country. All the top commandments of every religion are the same."

Down the corridor, the Fox News guys are preparing for their seven o'clock hit.

"You tell Brad to get me a hotel room and I'll bring him a box of fucking energy bars!" a producer named Greg Headen barks excitedly into the phone. He is young and energetic, with crew-cut hair and the jockish, upbeat attitude of a recent Dartmouth graduate. I take a chair and examine his setup. A line of black-boxed videotapes marches west on a shelf across the far wall. They are the visuals, perhaps several miles' worth of Pentagon-approved operational footage of destroyers and aircraft carriers, bombers, fighters, and other weapons systems in action, produced in concert with the defense contractors who profit from their manufacture and who would love nothing more than to gain additional appropriations from Congress based on cool-looking footage. In the meantime, the footage stands in for the reality of a war that is impossible to see, hear, or touch.

"Khakis and white shirts," Headen says, enthusiastically repeating the wardrobe directions for his upcoming trip to Islamabad. "Jeans stand out. It means you're an American."

He joins me after his call is done. We sit for a while, and we talk about what it is like to work at the Pentagon.

"We just need a little something to go with," he explains. One month after the Pentagon building was attacked and the World Trade Center was leveled by terrorists, the threat that we are facing is larger than Osama bin Laden and the Taliban, and far less susceptible to crude force. Without the official briefings and footage, he says, the Fox reporters would have very little to put on the air. "So we're grateful for whatever they give us," he explains.[3]

VI.

It is now almost seven, and the television reporters have arrayed themselves in a semicircle around the perimeter of the Briefing Room. Cables snake across the floor and beneath the chairs, clinging to the gray synthetic surface with gummy-edged feelers of electrical tape. Soon the cameras will click on. Awaiting their evening stand-ups, the reporters seem to have lapsed into states of suspended animation, Jamie McIntyre by the podium, John McWethy by the far wall, and Mike Emmanuel of Fox by the bleachers. Then, one by one, they come to life:

There are reports of heavy U.S. bombing in Afghanistan, Mike Emmanuel begins.

3. A few weeks back, I happened to visit with a wise old man, a member of that particular breed that occupies a permanent place in the Washington hierarchy. It was a beautiful early fall afternoon, with the sun shining in the sky and the birds twittering away in the trees, and after I dropped the name of an old professor from college, I gained admittance to his office in an industrial park in northern Virginia. Since my interlocutor served as head of the Atomic Energy Commission, director of the CIA, secretary of defense, and secretary of energy, identifying the place where I visited him might, under present circumstances, constitute a breach of security. He asked after my old professor, whom I confessed to not having seen for years, and then we talked for three hours on a variety of subjects. Tall, with large, craggy features, he is one of the last active members of the generation that fought the Cold War.

"The Czechs were running camps, the Russians were running camps, to train terrorists," he remembered. It is his belief, however, that the problem always ran deeper than that.

"We tend to grandiose formulations about ourselves as the fount of democracy, human rights, free market values, what have you," he continued, shaking his plentiful white mane. The week before our meeting, he attended a meeting of the Defense Policy Review Board, an eighteen-member bipartisan body that advises the Pentagon on strategy, and whose membership includes, among others, Henry Kissinger, former CIA director R. James Woolsey, and former defense secretary Harold Brown. According to published reports, the meeting took place on September 19 and 20, and lasted for nineteen and a half hours. Both Donald Rumsfeld and his deputy, Paul Wolfowitz, were present. My interlocutor, the former secretary of defense, is still pissed off.

Well, Wolf, the U.S. is shifting its sights, Jamie McIntyre says, citing the arrival of the new, improved bunker-busting bombs.

Peter, the U.S. took another big step into Afghanistan's civil war today, John McWethy says. Every word of his report seems carefully chosen to further a perspective that is subtly different from that of the Pentagon. Afghanistan's civil war? A prophecy, perhaps. Then again, according to the badly corrupted logic of the corporate news cycle, it would be premature to wonder whether the Pentagon is telling the truth, or to detail the evident policy splits within the administration, which will determine the future course of the War on Terrorism, after the Taliban melts away into the mountains for winter.

The stand-ups are over. The room goes dark. "When you hear 'Pentagon insiders,' that's us," a tech explains. In a corner of the room, McWethy presses his earpiece in deeper, communing with Ted Koppel in New York. The private assessment he gives Koppel is more pointed than the report he delivered on the air.

"The Pakistanis have supported the Taliban, and they very definitely don't want the Northern Alliance running the country," he

---

"For the average aristocrat, as he looks about the manor, the serfs are all the same," he explains. "The U.S. is so powerful, and has been so protected, that it doesn't feel it necessary to probe what's in the minds of other people. We all know that they admire our way of life, and everything about it. We believe that everyone wants to be an American, and if they don't they're quite mad."

He recalls a story that was told to him once by a friend, who served as a lower-ranking officer in Vietnam. "He kept trying to inform his superiors that these villages, which were clearly marked as 'pacified' on a map," he says, "were honeycombed with VC sympathizers." He shrugs. "So he grabs a ten-year-old kid on the street, and the kid had a hand grenade under his shirt. Needless to say," he adds, "he did not get promoted." When I ask him what he would change if he could press a magic button, he leans back in his chair.

"I've learned over the years that so-called intelligence failures can almost always be attributed to the failure of a dominant political myth," he begins. "In the case of Vietnam, the myth was that we were so obviously a lovable people." I ask him, again, what he might change with a single push of his magic button.

"We need to understand that there are other cultures in the world, there are other societies, they have long histories that are quite relevant to the way they behave," he answered, taking special care to maintain the balance of his sentence. "There are many peoples in the world who don't like us very much, and we ought not succumb to the naïve belief that everyone wants to an American."

says. "There is no way that the United States can accurately measure what's going on in the country. None."

The gap between what the correspondents say in private and what they can say on the air is one of the most familiar features of the American corporate news business. The arrangement is fair to everyone—unless, of course, you are one of the 11.4 million viewers who watched tonight's broadcast of ABC News.

And on the Monday after we bombed Afghanistan, when the secretary of defense explained that the War on Terror would likely be as long and difficult as the Cold War, and would make use of strategies and tactics familiar from that very different and particular time, only one broadcast of the ten or so that I watched saw fit to highlight the day's biggest story: "American Secretary of Defense Donald Rumsfeld compared the campaign against terror to the Cold War," began the news on Deutsche Welle, the leading nightly broadcast in Berlin.

No one can say that Secretary of Defense Donald Rumsfeld has not been straight with the press. *"The cruise missiles and the bombers are not going to solve this problem,"* he says, speaking from a thirteen-inch monitor propped up on a chair in the Briefing Room, right around the spot where Jamie McIntyre was standing only a few minutes earlier. The secretary of defense has promised to tell reporters as little as possible and to prosecute leakers under federal law; he is followed by canned footage of F-15s in flight, which is followed in turn by footage of aid drops. I notice a crumpled handout by my feet. I pick it up.

Two USAF C-17s Globemaster III from Charleston AFB, SC, perform high-altitude humanitarian airdrops into Afghanastan [sic] using the TRIAD (Tri-wall Airdrop) system to deliver Humanitarian Daily Rations (HDR's) to fleeing refugees, I read. The text is a precise description of the footage I have just seen on television. I wonder, idly, when "fleeing refugees" might gain its own acronym. *This mission,* the handout continues, with pride, *was the first Combat Airdrop for the C-17 aircraft, the first operational test of the TRIAD system with the C-17, and the first high-altitude airdrop of its kind for the C-17.* The footage serves as a plausible facsimile of the war as defined by the Pentagon; it tells viewers nothing about the origins and nature of an enemy that Republicans and Democrats alike have been ignoring for the last ten years, out of deference to the demands of Big Oil and in the hope that a world of six billion people might wake up one morning, consider the odds, and start bowing to Bill Gates, Michael Jordan, and the Virgin Goddess of Democracy.

Somehow, it seems, the Pentagon has got the lessons of Vietnam exactly wrong. In a great democracy, a policy of honesty and openness with the public and the press is probably the only way to win the War on Terrorism. It is important for reporters to ask difficult, even unpardonable questions of people in authority, in order to keep themselves and the rest of us informed. We should all know the answers to the questions that are not being asked, or are not being asked often enough. Otherwise, it is difficult to imagine any other result to the present conflict than another long, expensive, frustrating, fruitless, and divisive war.

Buried Suns

I.

The Sedan Crater is perhaps the only place in the world where it is possible for a layman to comprehend the full force of a nuclear explosion. A wooden viewing platform stands above the hole like an abandoned lifeguard's tower, offering a quiet vantage point from which to contemplate the implications of a giant radioactive sand trap that seems to absorb sound the way a black hole swallows light. Three hundred and twenty feet deep and nearly a quarter of a mile wide, the Crater still radiates energy from the explosion of a 104-kiloton nuclear bomb on July 6, 1962. One of ninety-eight nuclear devices exploded that year, the Sedan "shot" was detonated 635 feet beneath the surface of the Nevada desert as part of a U.S. government program to investigate the feasibility of using nuclear weapons to excavate a deep-water harbor in Australia. In less than thirteen seconds, the earth was emptied of 6.5 million cubic yards of sand and rock, some of which was lofted up into the atmosphere to return as dust and rain, and the remainder of which was driven into the earth or simply vaporized.

The similarity between the cratered stretch of desert where I am standing and the moon was strong enough that the Apollo astronauts trained here and radioed back precise comparisons of the craters they found on the moon to the manmade craters of the test site.

"This is what I wanted you to see. You can never describe this to anybody," my guide says, as a unblinking green lizard skitters along the side of the crater, stops, and then skitters away under a bush.[1]

The paucity of visitors to this silent and instructive place can be explained by the fact that the Sedan Crater is locked deep within the Nevada Test Site, a 1,375-mile preserve the size of the state of Rhode Island, surrounded by fences and itself contained within an even larger secure archipelago of military bases where America's most advanced weapons are tested and stored. In the years since the Trinity test at Alamogordo, New Mexico, there have been a total of 1,054 acknowledged American tests, 928 of which took place here. Named after mountains, rivers, famous scientists, fish, birds, small mammals, automobiles, Indian tribes, trees, cheeses, wines, cocktails, fabrics, nautical terms, ghost towns, and games of chance and skill, the nomenclature of nuclear testing is an absurdist romp through the flora and fauna of the American continent and the many and varied tastes of its inhabitants, from Barracuda, Sardine, Pike, and Minnow to Marshmallow, Gumdrop, Gouda, Gruyere, Chevre, Asiago, Reblochon, Pile Driver, Discus Thrower, Double Play, Effendi, Akbar, Commodore, Knickerbocker, Harlem, Vito, Stanley, Noggin, Wineskin, Horehound, Diamond Dust, Seafoam, and Freezeout.

The Nevada Test Site is located in one of the world's largest stretches of desert, a prehistoric landscape of volcanic mountains

1. Five months after the Sedan Crater first bloomed, John F. Kennedy became the first and the only American president to visit the Nevada Test Site (NTS). At 1900 hours, the day before the president arrived, the Los Alamos National Laboratory shot Tendrac, a joint U.S.-UK test and shot number 299, at the NTS. Four days later, shots 300 and 301 were fired less than an hour and a half apart. Photos of the boyish-looking movie star president's visit show him arriving at the test site in heavy black-framed sunglasses and a neatly buttoned suit, and posing in front of the test stand for a nuclear-powered rocket that might fly Americans to the moon or to Mars.

Following his visit to the nuclear rocket program, the president rode through the test site in an open white Cadillac convertible in the company of Glenn Seaborg, chairman of the Atomic Energy Commission, and also the man who discovered the element plutonium. After touring the site, the president of the United States and the man who discovered the fateful element of mass destruction departed together in the presidential helicopter, which banked to the right and hovered briefly above the Sedan Crater before heading back to Las Vegas.

and dry lakebeds crisscrossed by thin ribbons of asphalt and build-ings laid out with the dry precision of an engineer's blueprint. The country's nuclear proving ground, on which the American nuclear telegraph fluttered seismic messages to the Soviet Union, was built by humble craftsmen who used recondite technologies to shape an archipelago of production plants and tens of thousands of bombs that might destroy all life on the planet.

The weapons that made American power possible were designed by teams of physicists and metallurgists and engineers at Los Alamos National Laboratory in Los Alamos, New Mexico, Lawrence Livermore National Laboratory in Livermore, California, and San-dia National Laboratories in Albuquerque. The secondary parts and components of the arsenal came from the Y-12 production plant lo-cated on the 35,000-acre Oak Ridge Reservation, about fifteen miles west of Knoxville, Tennessee. The plutonium and tritium that fueled the bomb came from reactors at the Savannah River Site in Aiken, South Carolina. The grapefruit-sized plutonium "pits" that powered the bombs were manufactured at Rocky Flats in Colorado. The fin-ished weapons were assembled at the Pantex plant near Amarillo, Texas. Eighty-five percent of the weapons in the current nuclear stockpile were designed by Los Alamos. The youngest warhead, the W-88, was introduced in 1991, and several of the key materials used in all nukes—including plutonium "pits" and tritium fuel—were last produced in the late 1980s. By 2014, the W-88 and every other weapon in the stockpile will have reached the end of its intended life, and by then the United States might not have a single weapons designer left with nuclear test experience.[2]

The first successful containment of an underground nuclear ex-plosion took place beneath the Nevada Test Site on September 19, 1957. When the test site miners drilled back into the cavity after the blast, they first hit a layer of black frothy rock. Further inside they found gunk filled with little beads of radioactive glass. Frozen inside

2. At present, the United States has approximately 24,000 intact plutonium pits, each of which could detonate in a blast a little smaller than the one at Hi-roshima. Of these, about 10,600 pits are inside active weapons. The rest are kept in sealed bunkers at the Pantex nuclear weapons assembly plant. For most of the Cold War, pits were made at the Rocky Flats plant in Colorado, which was shut down in 1989 after it was raided by the FBI for gross violations of environmental

the glass were pockets of gas that contained a perfect microcosm of the universe in which they had been formed.

In the microseconds after the bomb was detonated, an egglike cavity began to bloom beneath the desert floor, quickly reaching temperatures of over 100 million degrees Celsius. A few seconds after the shot, the temperature inside the cavity had cooled to between 800 and 1,000 degrees centigrade, which is close to the melting point of the rock, allowing a mantle of glass to start to form inside the cavity. Over the next few minutes, the temperature dropped again, and some of the glass fell to the bottom. By measuring the refraction of the light and the amount of water vapor dissolved in the glass, scientists found that they could estimate the size of the explosion with a very high degree of precision. Each kiloton of nuclear yield created approximately one kiloton of glass.

For those who spent their lives studying the containment of nuclear explosions, the forces that turned the sand into glass and kept the floor of the desert from blowing open would take on an arguably spiritual tone. While the Los Alamos Standard 5 Stemming Plan prescribed alternating layers of coarse and fine gravel and coal-tar epoxy plugs to keep a nuclear blast from erupting from the hole, even the most rational physicists and geologists who occupied themselves with the job of "caging the dragon" found themselves arguing like medieval theologians over the relative importance of "stress cages" and "block motion" and other invisible forces that widely became known as "the mystical magical membrane." The last American nuclear test was conducted on September 23, 1992. A laconic press release issued by the Department of Energy on that date stated simply, "An underground nuclear test was conducted at 8:04 A.M. (PDT) today at the U.S. Department of Energy's Nevada Test Site." Code-named Divider, it was the sixth American nuclear test that year.

---

law in the middle of a production run for the 450-kiloton W-88 warhead for the Trident II missile system. Since the raid on Rocky Flats, the United States has lacked the capacity to manufacture "certified" pits for its nuclear weapons. According to the National Nuclear Security Administration's most recent budget submission, the agency will spend $132 million next year to manufacture six pits at a temporary facility at Los Alamos National Laboratory, which is scheduled to deliver, sometime in 2007, at least one pit worthy of being deemed "certified."

Jim Magruder was running the Divider test from the Department of Energy's office in Las Vegas. A fit, taciturn man in his early sixties who looks like a retired astronaut and dresses like a real estate agent, he accompanies me on one of my first visits to the test site.

"I think once you shut a program down it's awfully hard to start it up," Magruder says in a flat Kentucky twang, as he gazes out at the crater through big, square, gold-rimmed glasses, "whether you have the personnel that used to do the work or not."

His companion, Larry Krenzien, dresses like an engineer, with a silver watch on his wrist and a practical, short-sleeved shirt. His voice is confident, easy, and deep, as befits a man who has worked on 400 or 500 nuclear tests during his lifetime, including Divider. He transferred permanently out to the test site in 1964, after working at Los Alamos and in the South Pacific during the atmospheric-testing program. Back when the air force would fly through the clouds after each test collecting debris, Krenzien was in charge of analyzing the radioactive samples from the clouds.

"I went out to Enewetak in '58 for two tests out there," he tells me. "Butternut, I think was one. Cactus was the other. They had steak every night, as many as you wanted. The beer was selling for five cents a can. It was pretty good living."

When I ask Krenzien about the glory years of exploding nuclear bombs at the Nevada Test Site, his face creases with pleasure.

"You'd go in on the arming party, and you would be the last people to leave," he remembers, as the lunar landscape slides by the green-tinted window of our van. "The test director, most of them at that time would come out for the arming party. Depending on who was doing the red shack work," he adds, referring to the firing shack that would be placed near the hole.

"Some people ask me how many have I worked on. Four hundred? Five hundred?" Krenzien asks with an easy laugh, as he folds his hands over his belly. "It was a fairly prestigious job, which I'd say most people never knew existed. I can remember that C-47 coming in with the device, and I would drive down in a regular flatbed truck and load it myself, get up there, put it in the building, lock the door, and go away," he recalls.

"Do you think you saw the last American nuclear test?" I ask Krenzien.

"I don't know if I want to answer that," Krenzien says, turning to Magruder. "We have inexperience on the test site and inexperience in the labs."

The desert outside our tinted windows is hot, dry, bright, and dotted with juniper and yucca plants. According to Krenzien, who is up on Indian lore, the Indians used the yucca plants to make sandals. They also made use of the seed bulbs of the plant, which they roasted and ate. The surrounding mountains are made of layers of welded volcanic ash. The dry lakebed we are driving through now is called Yucca Flats. To our right are two skeletal frame structures and a lone wall that looks like a remnant from a movie set, the remains of a Japanese village that was built in the middle of the desert. Made of local lumber, with plywood floors, the buildings were built to scale and were accurate copies of the structures they were intended to represent, with a lobby, living room, kitchen, and a "toko"—a raised alcove for hanging scrolls.

"There was a high tower called the BREN tower that had a nuclear reactor on top of it, and they could raise it and lower it at different elevations, to see the radiation doses that the Japanese got at Hiroshima," Krenzien explains.

We stop for lunch at a four-story square granary tower that stands in the desert over a 1,625-foot deep hole for Icecap, the next shot scheduled after Divider. Icecap was scheduled to go off a week after President Clinton stopped the testing program in 1993. Inside the tower is the 110-foot steel rack that would have housed the bomb and twelve experiments from the labs. The wind outside rattles the sections of the tower, making it necessary to shout to be heard.

"We were going to put in dry ice," Krenzien yells out, "and this was like a refrigerator to keep it cold. During the testing of some of the intercontinental ballistic missiles, they would encounter very cold temperatures in the outer atmospheres."

Behind the tower is the trailer park where the instruments for measuring the blast were kept. The Los Alamos data collection trailers are white and the Livermore trailers are silver. Inside the shock-mounted trailers were oscilloscopes, cameras, and other devices for collecting data from the explosions. The PINEX camera captured the flow of neutrons as the plutonium went critical. The SLIFER was a coaxial cable that acted as part of an oscillator circuit. As the cable was crushed by the blast, the frequency of the circuit changed, allowing scientists to estimate the size of the yield. The CORRTEX was a high-tech version of the SLIFER. Data from these experiments were fed into computer codes kept by the laboratories that built the bombs. The basic stellar evolution code used by the laboratories began with 700 lines of Fortran. It was later augmented by a variety of more complex codes including the UNEC (Underground Nuclear Explosion Code), and KRAK (the hydrofracture code), which modeled the effect of underground nuclear blasts.

"You could see a little ground motion on some of them," Krenzien shouts to me. "When Livermore was firing, and I didn't have to go to work, I would sit in my backyard and watch the swimming pool shake." He ducks his head into the collar of his jacket and shrugs his shoulders against the cold wind blowing across the desert.

Jim Magruder shows me how each instrument was hooked up to the rack for Icecap. "It was always the policy that we would return to testing," he says, "but we always needed one more thing. We were all convinced it was a temporary shutdown." As Magruder explains it, Hazel O'Leary—the first secretary of energy during the Clinton administration—"had her test, the grandma test. Whether it made sense to her grandma. And soon it became pretty obvious that we weren't going to resume nuclear testing anytime soon."

We get back in the van and drive past the rows of subsidence craters and abandoned shot towers that dot the desert landscape. Some shots never "cratered," Krenzien tells me. Sometimes they'd shoot a test two years later and a nearby hole would suddenly collapse.

The flat desert basin we are passing through now is the back lot of the atomic age, the movie-ranch setting for most of the civil-defense films of the 1950s that showed the effects of nuclear explosions on ordinary American towns and homes. For the Annie test on March 17, 1953, the men at the test site built a model of a small American town, with mannequins, school buses, cars, and fresh food flown in from San Francisco and Chicago. We stop the car at the remains of Priscilla, a 1957 test involving an underground parking garage filled with cars and a bank vault constructed by the Mosler Safe Company. The door of the safe was still intact. Sprouting from the ends of concrete columns are burnt ends of bent steel rebar that look like a book of matches someone lit all at once and then blew out. Ahead of me is a section of railway bridge built to European specifications that bears the faint but discernible imprint of a giant thumb. The shards of dull green glass at my feet are another indication that we are near ground zero of an atomic blast.

"You can tell the vintage of the tests by the letters," Krenzien points out once we are back in the van, heading for, or at least in search of, the final resting place of Divider. In his hand with the big silver wristwatch, he holds a map of over 900 buried nuclear explosions.

"I think we make a right here," Krenzien says, at the intersection of two rutted and weather-beaten roads with fewer than fifty yards separating the shot craters all around.

Magruder studies the map. "I still think that's it," he says.

"I remember it was a big, bare spot," Krenzien says. We get out of the van and study a cracked concrete pad from behind an uneven wire fence. It's the wrong hole; we keep driving. I ask Krenzien how he became test director for Los Alamos National Laboratory at the Nevada Test Site. He answers in a deep bass voice that has a little of the codeine-laced warmth of a Midwestern talkshow host on a lazy afternoon.

"There was a tunnel shot coming up, and I remember I was in the dorm," he says. "And there was a knock on the door, and the guy who was the test director on this tunnel shot stuck his head in and said, 'I'm not going to do this job anymore. You're it. Good-bye.' "

"There sure aren't many cables. It looks like an older one," says Magruder, buried in the map.

"That would not be it then," Krenzien responds. The man who helped run the last American nuclear test directs our driver to take the next right, then a left. As we pull down a rutted road, Krenzien sticks his head out the open window and we stop.

We step out of the van to see big strands of cable descending into an enormous, bowl-shaped depression in the sand surrounded by a plain wire fence.

"The trailers would have been sitting here," Magruder says, pointing to a spot beyond the sunken ground. "And these cables went to each individual trailer. And this line of posts down the center would have been the cables connected to the firing device."

"Looks like there were maybe seven trailers on it," Krenzien says. There is a dark patch in the middle of the crater and a ring of light sand around the edge. A nuclear blast, Krenzien explains, affects the soil "so that beautiful flowers come up in the spring."

I ask him again if he thinks that he shot the last American nuclear test. He considers the question for a moment, looking out over the pitted landscape he helped to create, and then he says, "I don't know that I can see us starting a test series ever again, as such."

The attempt to reconstitute a nuclear complex the nation spent a decade dismantling is not simply a matter of spending more money and building more bombs. The men who shaped the Nevada Test Site, who built imaginary cities and blew them up, who drilled holes in the mesas and the volcanic rock, who readied the devices and lowered them into the holes and triggered the explosions that announced America's resolve to its enemies, are mostly dead or retired. The mementos that hang on the walls of their modest homes in and around Las Vegas tell the story of how we faced the infinite and won a war that both sides decided that they could not afford to fight.

II.

WILLIAM GUS FLANGAS

Bill Flangas was the man in charge of drilling holes in the mesa. On the wall of his suburban ranch house is a photograph of himself as a wiry, tough-looking little sailor in 1945, on a bridge in the middle of Tokyo near Emperor Hirohito's palace. There are also pictures of four generations of Flangas men, who all appear to be cut from the same cloth, with extra fabric allotted for ears: there is Gus William Flangas, who begat William Gus Flangas, who begat Gus William, who begat William Gus.

The current William Gus Flangas was born in June of 1927, in Ely, Nevada, a copper town. Ely was one of the main towns in White Pine County, which also produced silver, gold, and molybdenum. The mining was done mainly in Ruth. When Flangas came home from Japan he became an engineer and went to work in the copper mines. As Flangas tells it, a man named Reynolds, who ran a mining concern that had been awarded the mining contract for the Nevada Test Site, "was hobnobbing with some Rotarians," looking for some mining engineers to take the nuclear program underground. "And that's where my name popped up."

With the support of his new boss, Mr. Reynolds, Flangas helped hire the first real miners at the test site from some local mines that were about to close down.

"Yeah, I was very fond of him," Flangas says of Mr. Reynolds, who was over six feet tall and started his company in El Paso in 1932. "He felt that if the customer was heading into a direction that he ought not to be, that you should have the courage to tell him that maybe this isn't right." Rummaging around, Flangas finds a copy of a Reynolds publication entitled *Our Little Red Book*.

"Time is the only natural resource which cannot be recovered in one form or another," he reads. "Because it is continuous, much of it is wasted, not realizing that the individual allotment of it is very limited indeed."[3]

One of Flangas's first jobs at the test site was to take a team of miners to the mesa and drill back toward Rainier, the first underground nuclear explosion. They drilled back hundreds of feet through the rock until they encountered a layer of glass. "Black, red, purple, all kinds of colors," he remembers. "When we entered the

3. Tests have been conducted in sixteen different tunnels in Rainier Mesa on the Nevada Test Site. The first test was conducted on August 10, 1957, when a zero-yield safety experiment named "Saturn" was detonated in C-Tunnel. By the early 1990s there was only one active tunnel in use by the Defense Nuclear Agency (DNA). The DNA evaluated the effects of nuclear weapons explosions, thermal radiation, blast, shock, X-rays, and gamma rays on military hardware, such as communication equipment, rocket nosecones, and satellites. The typical Horizontal Line of Sight (HLOS) test was primarily for radiation effects research. A large tunnel complex mined under the mesa contained the HLOS pipe, which is 1,500 to 1,800 feet long and tapers from up to thirty feet in diameter at the test chamber to several inches at the working point. Experiments were placed in the HLOS pipe test chambers. At zero time the nuclear device was fired, and radiation instantaneously flowed down the pipe. To prevent bomb debris and blast from reaching and damaging the experiments, three mechanisms were used: The first is the Fast Acting Closure—a 5-foot-thick plug of aluminum, lead, steel, and copper that was driven by 400 pounds of high explosives into a 20-inch section of the pipe in about one millisecond; the other two closures followed within 30 and 300 milliseconds, respectively.

cavity, there was just about an inch or more of plaster there, and it was very, very radioactive. And so we plastered that with lead." Fifteen months after the Rainier shot, the ground temperatures inside the cavity were upward of 160 degrees, and the ground was filled with radioactive water. The miners used dynamite to clear their way through hot, wet ground filled with steam from a buried nuclear explosion. Accompanying Flangas and the miners was a Livermore physicist named Gary Higgens.

"Oh, yeah, he was raised on a farm in Minnesota and he went all the way to become a PhD physicist," Flangas remembers. Higgens got along well with the miners. "They trusted him and he trusted them, and lo and behold that was one of the initial major breakthroughs in the underground testing."

When a group including Flangas became contaminated with tritium in 1959, it was Higgens who helped come up with the idea of isolating the contaminated men in a room and having them effect a full fluid exchange in their bodies by drinking full cases of beer.

"You know, if you want the maximum fluid in and the lowest retention—in other words, you want to be pouring it in on one end and a constant stream out the other end . . . ," Flangas explains. "I had one Latter-Day Saints guy there, my hoist man, and he refused. Which was okay, he was in his sixties then, and so he gave us a reference point. We just sat there, and we drank beer, and we drank beer, and we drank beer."

FRED HUCKABEE

Fred Huckabee has a mournful face like Huckleberry Hound or Lyndon B. Johnson, a fellow product of the Texas hill country. The license plates on the Buick Le Sabre in his driveway read HUCK. He keeps his house clean, with white placemats on the table at which he sits, sips water from a thirty-four-ounce plastic convenience-store cup, and watches golf on his big silver RCA color TV. He smiles when I ask him about the excitement of working with nuclear explosives. Hanging on the wall near the door is a medal graced by the American and Soviet flags and dated 1988. On the other side of the medal is a Russian inscription that reads "In memory of the visit" over the unmistakable image of a mushroom cloud.

Huck, as he is universally known, was born on a ranch in Bram-
field, Texas. After high school he went to work for Magnolia Petro-
leum and roughnecked on drill rigs in Midland and Odessa and up
through New Mexico. He graduated to become a driller with the
Great Western Drilling Company, then a rig superintendent, otherwise known as a tool pusher, a job that paid well enough for him to
marry a girl from Sonora and buy a twelve-foot-wide trailer. When
the Russians broke the moratorium on testing in 1961, John F.
Kennedy ordered the Nevada Test Site to swing back into action,
and Huck and his two closest friends from the oil field headed out to
Nevada with their rig.

"You could look off the mesa after dark," he recalls, "and it'd look
like a city down there of vehicles running around, you know, car
lights running around, drill rigs lit up and drilling holes, and it just
looked like a city down there."

Huck's memories of the site range from drilling back toward exploded bombs to the attempt to use nuclear explosives for commercial purposes in the mining and drilling industries.[4] But the most
memorable adventure of all, as far as Huck is concerned, was the
trip to Russia in 1988 and the visit to the Semi-palatinsk range, the
top-secret nuclear installation in Kazakhstan that was the Soviet
equivalent of the Nevada Test Site. It was dark by the time the
Americans arrived. They put on their overcoats and heavy gear and
walked out to the banks of the frozen Iratest River.

"They fed us a lot of tongue and mare's milk," Huck says. "That's a
mare of a horse, you know," he explains. "It had buttermilk, and I
liked that buttermilk, boy, but a bunch of 'em wouldn't even touch it.

4. In 1965, the Atomic Energy Commission encouraged the formation of the
CER Geonuclear Corporation, a joint venture of the Continental Oil Company,
EG&G, and REECo. The cost of a two-megaton nuclear device for private use
was set by the AEC at $2 million, a price that included arming and firing the
weapon but did not include the cost of preparing the site and digging the hole.
In December of 1967, in what was called Project Gasbuggy, the Geonuclear
Corporation exploded a nuclear device near Farmington, New Mexico. Gasbuggy was followed by Rulison, a shot done in concert with the Austral Oil Company out of Houston. A man named Les Donovan had the job of going from door
to door to inform families that three nuclear bombs would be going off in their
neighborhood on behalf of the Austral Oil Company, in order to stimulate the
flow of gas through the surrounding rock.

They didn't have salads or anything, and they'd feed us egg some-time, and with a tongue, with our breakfast. A lot of guys didn't like their food, but hell, I ate everything they had." In the evenings the Americans watched movies from home and made popcorn, which they shared with their Russian translators.

What Fred Huckabee learned was that the foe America had been fighting for forty years was using technology that was decades out of date. "They set up an army tent with little fireboxes inside, for heat, and it was a double-doored army tent, thirty by thirty or something like that, and instead of having projectors to give their presentations of how they tested and everything, they'd put a piece of paper up on a wire." When the Russians came to the Nevada Test Site, they were equally amazed by what they saw. Their American hosts took them to see Siegfried and Roy and then to a Smith's Food King off U.S. 95. The Russian delegates all bought children's pacifiers. One of the colonels bought a Timex watch, and Gorbachev's personal inter-preter bought a three-pound tin of Folger's coffee for his boss.

Relaxing in an easy chair, I ask Huck about the red shack, the small wooden building set up near the hole, from which the signals were sent to fire the device.

"Yeah, it was red," he confirmed. The device itself didn't spend any time in the red shack. "They'd bring it out when they were going to put it on the rack," he tells me. Working from the trailer park, the electricians laid out the diagnostic cable in a continuous line and wrapped it around the rack and around the pipe as it started down the hole. "That took maybe one day or possibly two days according to the depth," Huckabee explains, "and then they had to stem all that back and put cold epoxy plugs in and cement plugs and more stemming and more plugs and more stemming," he continues, re-ferring to the mixtures of materials used to ensure that radioactive gases did not erupt from the shaft. When the rack was ready, the de-vice was brought in on a pickup truck to the hole.

J. L. SMITH

J. L. Smith was the man responsible for preparing the shack from which the final shot was fired. In his late sixties, he lives in a neigh-borhood of low-built ranch houses near the Desert Mesa power plant, just around the corner from the Department of Energy in Las Vegas. Outside his house, a gray Cadillac is parked on the curb next to a desert-baked, baby-blue Chrysler white-top pickup. On the day I meet him, Smith is wearing a dirty Dallas Cowboys hat with a star on it, a white walrus mustache, and a big, warm smile.

"J. L.," he says, sticking out an ample palm. "That's initials only." He welcomes me into his low-ceilinged home, where pictures of angels and of Jesus and his disciples occupy the wall above the couch. The wall near the window is filled by a fifty-six-inch Magnavox TV.

Born in Mississippi in 1935, J. L. was raised on an eighty-acre farm and graduated from Betty May Jacks High School in Morton. His stepfather, whose name was J. D. Heald, liked to dress up like a cowboy and come out to Las Vegas every year for the rodeo. J. L. joined his brother in Las Vegas in 1955 and got a job building the first housing project in town. He joined Labor Local 872, which sent him over to the test site. As he sits beneath a picture of Jesus and tells his story, tears stream down his cheeks, though the expression on his face never changes. Allergies, he explains.

"Well, we would dig ditches and put in piping, build houses and blow 'em up," he says, when I ask him what he did at the test site. "We built a whole city one time, a whole city that had, like, the train station, the railroad, and there'd be railroad tracks and houses with people—dummies—sitting at the table like they were eating supper or something," he recalls. "They had fruit and stuff on the shelves, just like it was at your own home in the kitchen." The bric-a-brac in his living room includes old pictures of tumbledown cabins, a hand-painted statue of James Brown, a singing rabbit with a pair of antlers, and a fish that sings "Don't Worry, Be Happy." I am curious to learn more about the red shack, where the atom bombs were armed and fired.

The later shacks were made of metal, but the first ones were made of wood. They would be brought out to the hole on a flatbed truck. "Yeah, just a little shack," he says. "One room, and sometimes they had partitions in there," he explains. Once the marriage of the bomb and the rack was made, the scientists would open up the canister and arm the device.

I ask if he ever saw what was inside the bomb itself.

"Mm-hmm," he answers. "It looks like half of an egg, like a little egg-shaped thing, about that big around."

"Like the size of a softball?" I prompt him.

"Softball, about the size of a softball, about the size of half of a softball, something like that, like you cut the softball in half. It looked something like a foam, Styrofoam or something like that."[5]

"So there was something inside that made a lot of—"

"Made a lot of boom."

There were also hundreds of wires, he remembers, that suggested a wasp's nest. "They were small wires, you know. And it takes an hour, hour and a half, to get them all hooked up." As the men armed the bomb, they talked about neutral subjects. "They talked about what happened last night at the cafeteria and stuff like that. 'I saw a show last night,' that they had had a good shrimp dinner or lobster dinner or something like that, you know. Just usual, comfortable conversation."

ROMA B. WASHINGTON

Crane operator Roma B. Washington, who lowered the armed bombs down the holes at the test site, was in fact waiting for a bomb to be delivered to his crane when the American nuclear testing program ended in 1993. He is a choleric little man built like a cannonball. "We was delivering the last day in Greenwater. I was the man," he remembers. "I was up on the last one. I got all pumped up and everything. Then two hours later they told us, 'Hey, shut it down. Lock the building up, you got thirty minutes to get all your tools out,' and all that kind of stuff. I mean, it was trippy, like *The Twilight Zone* or something."

Washington's nut-brown skin flushes red beneath a gray wifebeater T-shirt. "I'd come home to a wife and everything, and I'd come home to a family, and I'd never mention nothing about I just set a bomb in a hole." He sighs heavily, putting his hand on his knee. "Because, you know, somehow or another, it's just a unrewarding

5. The pit is indeed the approximate size of a softball and is typically made of a hollow, round shell of Pu-239. Alloyed plutonium, like steel, can be cast, pressed, and machined into spheres.

job." He came to Las Vegas from Louisiana, got a job as a sauté chef, became a crane operator as part of an equal-opportunity effort in the unions, and was sent out to the test site. His specialty was putting the bomb to the rack, otherwise known as making the marriage.

"You swing the rack over, right over top of it, and then just lower it down. Then they marry it, with bolts and stuff, you know what I mean. Pick it up, take it to the tower, then they do that thing again, whatever they doing," he says, like an embarrassed dad laying out the specifics of a sex act to an underage son. "After they done what they do, and all the wires and all that," he continues, "you bring it out of the building, which was a very, a very technical move, and then you start lowering it in." Sometimes the process of lowering the rack down into the hole took three days. Sometimes it took eight. Washington's knee jumps up and down. "You lowered it down to a point, then you stopped and they did their little deal, then you'd slowly lower it down to another point, and they'd say, 'Stop.' "

I ask him how he shielded his mind from the knowledge of what he had at the end of his crane. He stares at me for a while before he answers.

"Some people, when they were to do that, it kind of worked on them. It kind of ate them up, you know? You could see them slowly deteriorate and all that. But it was all a mental thing with me, and I'm that way to this very day. My crane was kind of like a wife to me. I trusted her. I named every crane I ran."

"What were some of their names?" I ask.

"Well, that one was Gargantuous," he laughs, "that was Big Foot, and that was Lucille, Spirit of '76, Bertha, Piece of Shit, Miracle of 17 Hill."

"What was that one named for?"

"Well, that's another story," he says. "I had nothing to do with it."

The night before he lowered a bomb down the hole, he says, he always slept like a baby. I ask him about his feelings afterward.

"Well, what are you trying to say?" he asks, as his leg starts jumping again. "Do I go home and have a drink? Do I get drunk? Do I smoke a joint? Is that what you saying? You ain't as slick as you think you are," Washington declares. "Well, what if I said I came home and had sex with the old lady?"

I try to get back on his good side by suggesting that a little sex and whiskey seems like a reasonable enough response to the stress of operating a crane with a nuclear bomb attached to the end of it.

"I'm not going to tell you that I don't come home and have a beer, or I don't come home and have a shot of brandy, you know, after a day. I mean, I'm not what you'd call a stone drinker, but I like to have a sip every now and then."

I ask him again what it was like to help win the Cold War.

"I felt good about being a part of that history, the things that advanced America, advanced the world, you know what I mean? Now, as far as being something that's about blowing up a bunch of people, no, I wasn't proud of that, no."

III.

Sitting with the men of the Nevada Test Site during the afternoons and the evenings, I found it impossible not to feel that their work had shifted their angle on reality in a subtle but permanent way. Their literal, factual accounts of stemming procedures and postshot operations were often delivered with a deadpan humor that suggested a shared cosmic joke burbling just below the surface of whatever question was being answered. Having spent the better part of their lives working in a secret world pervaded by the daily aftertaste of inconceivable destructive power, the men of the test site had learned that the windows through which their friends and neighbors saw reality were cracked. In order to see what they had seen, or as much of it as would be shown me, I made arrangements to go down into the tunnels one afternoon and to get as close as I will likely ever come to the actuality of a nuclear explosion.

Just across the Mercury Highway from Divider is a green shot tower for Unicorn, a "subcritical" test that will happen sometime this year. A few hundred yards away from the Unicorn tower is the grave site of Ledoux, an underground nuclear test from 1990. Ledoux is now embedded in the Ula Complex, a tunnel system dug in the 1980s and 1990s to serve as a reusable home beneath the desert for low-yield nuclear tests.

I am met at the top of the shaft by Rafi, a cheery bearded man who works beneath the desert as the test-group director for Los Alamos. His full name is Ghazar Papazian, and he was born in

Egypt, he tells me, as I lace on a pair of miner's boots next to a sticker that reads, "If you ain't a miner, you ain't shit." When I ask him what America learned from setting off more than a thousand nuclear explosions on, or under, our own soil, he gives me a scientist's answer:

"What's odd about that data set is that for every nuclear test, the codes that run that nation, if you will, are calibrated to that specific test. So for system A, if it had six different tests, the density would change for each of those tests. Because to make the code work and give you the right answer, you had to turn knobs." We pass through a security gate and get ready to descend into the hole. "What we're trying to do with subcrits is to eliminate the knob turning and give the folks who do code development a single data point as far as what the density of plutonium is at a specific pressure."

Eventually, and with much patience from Rafi, two extraordinary ideas enter my brain: (a) that the entirety of 1,054 American nuclear tests has netted us less than a single second's worth of usable data, and (b) that we still know far less than we need to about the properties of plutonium. The rest of Rafi's job, as he explains it, is to comply with a recent White House directive to cut the time required to perform a critical nuclear test at the test site in half, "basically to bring up the long lead-time items from thirty-six months to eighteen months."

"Ready?" he asks, as the elevator door closes with an undersea clang.

A foghorn sounds, and we descend 963 feet to the bottom of the shaft. When the grinding noise of the elevator ceases, a gate opens onto an anteroom with a framed quotation from President Woodrow Wilson. "To the miner," it reads, "let me say that he stands where the farmer does; the work of the world waits on him."

Nearly 1,000 feet below the desert, smoking is definitely allowed. Near the miners' battered lockers are a host of big, old hotel ashtrays. "We overventilate the shaft," Rafi explains. Beyond him is a long gray hallway that looks like a bomb-shelter tunnel from the 1960s.

Rafi points toward the side of the shaft, where a sign reads: "Danger: High Contamination."

"That's the entrance into Ledoux," he says.

"What was Ledoux designed to test?" I ask.

"It was part of Star Wars," Rafi answers shortly.

I stand for a moment in silence in the tunnel and try to sense the energy of a dead sun.

"It doesn't compute in your mind," Rafi says, "the amount of power that's in your hand. You can hold it."

"You've held nuclear devices in your hands?" I ask.

"Sure. I've held test devices as we've put them into the experiment. I've held pits of TA-55 when they're produced," he says.[6]

"To do a nuclear detonation at minus forty is a challenge. How do you maintain the integrity of the cooling system so it will shoot three weeks after you've emplaced it 1,500 feet underground with layers of material over it," Rafi adds, with a wistful look around his tunnel.

"So when you walked into the tower, there was a can there—like a thermos bottle. In that thermos bottle you placed blocks of dry ice, and an automated system which was unique for that era manipulated fans and butterfly valves, and brought down the warm air from the device, sublimated the dry ice, and brought out the cold air. The requirement was to cool it down at one degree per hour and hold it at minus forty until you shot it," he continued. "We proved out that we could sustain it for thirty-odd days."

"Was that for submarines?" I wonder.

"Think of a system, any system, for example, that will sit on the wing of an aircraft, for example," Rafi explains. He follows my gaze up to the tunnel ceiling above our heads, which is held together by chicken wire and glue. "So, to show you how soft this stuff is," he says, reaching out his oversized hand to the wall and sending a cascade of sandy stuff down to the floor of the tunnel.

Continuing our walk, we pass by Kismet, a radioactive room that is sealed behind concrete and steel like an inadmissible thought. "It was basically a five-gallon drum of explosives and a commercial X-ray head," Rafi explains. Kismet was an ordinary dirty bomb of the type that any terrorist could explode in an American city. I peer through protective doors into a shattered room illuminated by a bare lightbulb. Rafi sometimes sends a mining-rescue team in to change the lightbulb.

---

6. Plutonium pits are coated with nickel or gold to contain alpha radiation, which is light enough to be stopped by rubber gloves or by a sheet of paper. They are slightly warm to the touch.

I ask him whether Kismet went smoothly. He shakes his head. "A miserable test," he says. "We lost all that data. People worked in bunkers. They worked in labs. They picked up some really nasty habits. The lesson learned was that if you're going to have a nuclear-readiness program based on an experimental program based on the Nevada Test Site, you can't just work in bunkers."

Right now, Rafi explains, one of the main focuses of the atomic-testing program is to examine the old plutonium pits, manufactured at the now-closed Rocky Flats plant outside of Denver, that make up the bulk of our nuclear arsenal and even to replace some of those pits with new ones made at Los Alamos. "The question is, how does it age? If you were to go and find a designer from the past, and said, 'Okay, you designed system XYZ, tell me what you thought the life span of that device was,' he'd tell you, 'Fifteen to twenty years.' We have systems in the stockpile today that are fifty years old. How do you gain confidence that a fifty-year-old pit will function as originally designed without having to test it?"

"How does the certification process work?" I ask him.

"Very complicated!" Rafi answers. "There's a guy in Los Alamos who oversees it. Certification is made by the director of the lab. He signs off a letter that goes to the secretary of energy, who sends it to the president. It says that this pit I am producing is equivalent to the pit that was produced at Rocky."

In the background a voice echoes through the tunnels from a distant loudspeaker—"Five, four, three, two, one. One, two, three, four, five"—and for a split second I wonder if a bomb isn't about to go off.

Rafi stays calm. We walk through the tunnels until we come upon a cluster of miners and other refugees from the glory days of the test site.

"This is Chuck Eaton. He's the miner in charge," Rafi says, introducing me to a burly man with an incredibly deep bass voice. I ask Chuck how long he's been down here. "I've been underground since '72," he says. "I did construction mining, development mines, sinking shafts, until I came here." The old days, he tells me, bear very little resemblance to what I am seeing now.

"There were tunnels, and pipe shots, and it was a whole different ball game than this." When I ask him what impressed him the most about his work, he shakes his head, smiles, and answers without hesitation: "Well, setting off a nuclear bomb."

IV.

Sitting at the counter in a darkened sports bar, safe from the flat Las Vegas sunlight, Nick Aquilina takes another sip of his Diet Coke and says something nice to the waitress. This is a place he likes to come to in the afternoons, he says. A handsome man in his sixties, he has the face of a wise old janitor at a local high school who lets the kids sleep in his office and finds them jobs raking leaves. He wears his white sideburns neatly trimmed, and his thick salt-and-pepper hair is fixed with pomade. The gold watch on his wrist attests to decades of faithful service to the testing program, and the golf ball embroidered on his chest testifies to his current love of leisure. "There's never a bad day at the test site," he says breezily.

On September 11, 2001, Nick Aquilina was with Troy Wade in Washington. The two men had been called to Washington by the agency in charge of the country's nuclear weapons, he tells me. They were meeting at the L'Enfant Plaza Hotel, which is right up the street from the Department of Energy, where a number of the veterans of the testing program were discussing, in very general terms, how the country's nuclear bureaucracy should be organized and what it might take to restart the country's nuclear-testing program, when an airplane hit the Pentagon, less than a mile away.

"Bob Kuckuck was there. Don Pearman was there, and Troy and I," he says, naming several luminaries of the test program and the labs. When the men at the meeting stepped outside, they could see smoke coming from the Pentagon.

That night, three of the old-timers—Aquilina, Wade, and Kuckuck—met for dinner at an Italian restaurant. Together, the three men had helped to develop and test nearly every weapon in the American nuclear arsenal.

"I think we were mostly talking about what was going to happen the next day," Aquilina remembers. "We were concerned. Was this the first in a series of things? Was something going to happen the next day? And how can we respond to something like this? Who do you respond to?"

After employing 120,000 men to drill about a million feet worth of holes in the desert, or roughly the distance from New York to Washington, and to blow up more than a thousand nuclear bombs, the test site and its work were over and done with. The secret that bound the men of the test site together was the knowledge that both the United States and the Soviet Union were rational actors and that neither one had actually intended to use nuclear weapons. The warheads were poker chips, and the test site was the baize-covered table on which America bluffed the Soviets into folding. But the Islamic zealots who attacked the World Trade Center and the Pentagon with bombs fashioned out of passenger planes do not have a military–industrial complex that can be bluffed with nuclear weapons. The familiar strategic equation of American global supremacy was reversed: no longer the masters of the plutonium age, we are now its potential victims, living in fear of the day the terrorists gain possession of an atomic weapon detached from one of the dissolving state structures left over from the Cold War.[7]

7. Still, there is nothing wrong with sitting back for a moment and admiring the view of the world that America's nuclear weapons testing and production complex helped to make possible. Wandering through the acres of shops inside the Venetian Hotel and Casino after one of my visits to the test site, I was jolted from my reveries about the deeper meaning of the bomb by excited shouts of "It's him! It's him!" As a line of uniformed men came sprinting toward me, I found myself looking into the painted face of the rock star Michael Jackson, who was dressed in a black waiter's costume and a white shirt and was accompanied by an Indian girl and two young children, who are wearing masks, and may be his true sons. A ton of heavy flesh-colored makeup gave his features the appearance of a soft claylike mask. Flashbulbs erupt as Michael Jackson reaches out to the crowd, as the uniformed hotel security men form a line to hold back the throng.

"Ohmigod!"

"It's him!"

"It's Michael Jackson!"

Down the green tile corridor, past the indoor canal where the gondoliers sing comes the echoing cry of the crowd, a well-heeled scrum of two hundred vacationers and their agitated offspring. Looking frightened and pale, Michael Jackson enters the Ca'd'Oro to buy some beaded handbags as the security guards hold back the throng. After the excitement ends, I visit briefly with the head magician in charge at Houdini's, whose name is Geoffrey Hansen, and who used to play Mandrake the Magician on television.

"He said, 'Show me some magic,' " Mandrake relates, before he shows me the trick he showed Michael Jackson—a silver half-dollar with the face of Robert

V.

The element plutonium, a heavy metal, was first formed in the blowoff from supernovae that exploded after the Big Bang and made all the elements in our sun and its planets. Plutonium was dis-

---

F. Kennedy that turns into a Chinese coin when tapped twice with the edge of a playing card.

A little while later, still pondering the mysteries of celebrity magic, I enter the Venetian Hotel's museum, a far-flung arm of the Guggenheim located just off the casino floor. A poster outside advertises treasures from the Hermitage Museum in St. Petersburg, Russia—renamed Leningrad by the rulers of the former Soviet Union. Inside, I stop in front of Paul Cezanne's *Autoportrait a la Casquette,* which shows the artist in his greatcoat, heavy beard, black-peaked cap, with old woman's eyes. Over his left shoulder the artist has painted pure brick-shaped splotches of color, predicting the direction of the next century of art. In *Nature Morte Avec Rideau et Pichet Fleuri,* two bowls of taut-skinned peaches sit on either side of a flowered pitcher, like a set of scales. The brownish drapery behind the table has been pulled back to reveal the solid blackness beyond.

At this moment I realize that the museum is entirely empty and I am alone with fifty of the greatest paintings in the world, hidden away from Western eyes for the better part of the twentieth century—the penultimate spoils of the Cold War on display in an empty museum in Las Vegas. In the next room is a painting by Chagall entitled *The Soldier Drinks,* which shows the soldier with one crazy red eye, and one eye of harlequin blue, with his hat hovering above his shiny bald head and his index finger pointed like a gun at a tiny cup beneath a samovar that takes the shape of a bear. The painting that holds me the longest, though, is by Amadeo Modigliani, a spiritual sensualist. The title of the painting is *La Sweater Jaune,* which is known in English as *Jeanne Heburtine with Yellow Sweater.* Jeanne Heburtine, the painter's mistress, is an African fertility fetish with olive skin and a yellow wool thrift-shop sweater and an oval face. The Siamese slant of her empty blue eyes is underlined by the feline way that she folds her hands on her lap.

In the last of the four rooms in the exhibit, I stop in front of an exquisite Kandinsky, which from one angle looks like an exploded cubist Russian Easter egg, and from another direction looks like a Princess with a veil and a white fur collar being pulled on a sleigh through snowy St. Petersburg. As I stand and contemplate the painting for a third time, I realize that I am no longer alone. I have been joined by two plump girls with lovely ripe olive skin and matching suede jackets, who have stopped in front of a Franz Marc painting called *Gelbe Kuh.* We stand there together and admire the painting in silence. "How beautiful," one of the girls exclaims, struck by the dream of solid, healthy flesh in motion, as the golden cow jumps over the moon.

covered by mankind on February 23, 1941, when Glenn Seaborg, then a young Berkeley PhD in chemistry, isolated a minute quantity of what he and his colleagues at first called element 94.[8] The first one-gram shipment of plutonium arrived at Los Alamos in February of 1944. Much of Los Alamos National Laboratory's energy since that date has been spent in the attempt to engineer plutonium into a stable form. "After more than fifty years of plutonium research at Los Alamos, we might be expected to understand the strange properties of this metal," wrote George Chapline and James L. Smith in "An Update: Plutonium and Quantum Criticality," one of several dozen recent publications on the subject by Los Alamos scientists. "Instead, we are still stumped."

Nearly twice as heavy as gold, plutonium is silvery, radioactive, and toxic. The pure metal first delivered to Los Alamos showed wildly differing densities, and the molten state was so reactive that it corroded nearly every container it encountered. Happier as a liquid than as a solid, plutonium has seven distinct crystallographic phases and the highly democratic ability to combine with nearly every other element on the periodic table. It can change its density by 25 percent in response to minor changes in its environment. It can be as brittle as glass or as malleable as aluminum. Chips of plutonium can spontaneously ignite at temperatures of 150 to 200 degrees Celsius. When crushed by an explosive charge, plutonium's density increases, which decreases the distance between its nuclei, causing the metal to release enough energy to vaporize a city.

Jay Norman, former director of the weapons testing program at Los Alamos and the current deputy manager of testing and operations for the National Nuclear Security Administration, meets with me one afternoon in Las Vegas to explain how a nuclear bomb is designed and tested. A pleasant-looking, soft-spoken man with sharp features, he wears clear, rimless eyeglasses, and his hair stands on end like a mad scientist in a comic book. His white linen jacket is

8. Seaborg named the new element "Plutonium" after the planet Pluto, which had been discovered just eleven years earlier. Plutonium-239, a variant of the element Seaborg discovered, proved more likely to fission than uranium, making it the perfect fuel for a nuclear bomb. Seaborg chose the letters "Pu" for the new element as a childish joke. All of the plutonium presently on Earth is manmade.

perfectly starched, and his grape-colored cotton shirt balloons gently over his belly.

"Now anybody can think of things: well, let's just capture a little star and put it in a little box and all will be well," Norman explains, with a professorial nod. "Once somebody shows how you do a fresco, then everybody can do a fresco. The guy who invented the fresco technique is somebody else entirely."

Although Norman is not allowed to talk about the weapons he makes, the way a nuclear bomb works is not all that difficult to explain. A modern thermonuclear weapon consists of three operative elements: a primary, a secondary, and a radiation case that encloses the parts. The plutonium pit is surrounded by high explosives. This is the primary. Detonating the mantle of high explosives surrounding the plutonium squeezes the primary into a supercritical configuration. The energy from the primary is then trapped and forced to surround the secondary part of the device, which is a highly combustible radioactive substance such as uranium. Enormous pressures are created, and the secondary implodes, releasing nuclear yield.[9]

The goal of most of the nuclear weapons designs of the last four decades or so consists in getting bigger yields with less weight by refining existing designs and materials. As a result, the nuclear package or "gadget" that weighed 10,000 pounds at the Trinity test now weighs 250 pounds and can fit inside a suitcase.

In the early phases of a design for a new weapon, Norman explains, Los Alamos and Livermore would compete to develop a winning design that would meet the specifications handed down by the Defense Department and the Department of Energy. "Livermore

9. John Coster-Mullen, an amateur photographer who took some physics classes in high school and now works as a truck driver in Milwaukee, was able to put together remarkably accurate models of the Fat Man bomb that was dropped on Nagasaki. Coster-Mullen made his estimates available in his self-published book *Atom Bombs: The Top Secret Inside Story of Little Boy and Fat Man,* which is available over the Web. The technical specifications for the more sophisticated devices in the American nuclear arsenal are available in *Swords of Armageddon,* an eight-volume CD-ROM set begun by an obsessive civilian named Chuck Hansen, who died on March 23, 2003, after compiling the most extensive catalog of the American nuclear arsenal that has ever been made available to the public.

might say, 'Well, I think it ought to look like this and this,' and Los
Alamos would say, 'Well, let's do this and this,' and each lab would go
out and test their proposed configuration, and each lab would learn
something," Norman says, in his equitable manner, pinching his
cheek between his soft white cheek and his manicured thumb.

"About a year beforehand, we would fire up the field effort," Norman explains: A half-dozen or more field operations would normally
be under way at the test site at any one time. Six to nine months before the scheduled test, the design of the device would be frozen.
Three months before, the test rack that would hold the various
measuring instruments would be delivered to the site.

"The device itself was being designed and the piece fabricated
from various parts of the complex to be delivered four to six weeks
before the event, and so that was kind of the general timing of
things," he explains. The lab's X-division weapons designers would
show up at the test site a few days before the test, Norman concludes, "to see the device and just kind of give it the ole eyeball."

"Without trivializing it or making it too mundane," Norman says,
"there are a lot of similarities in the stockpile, like a Ford sedan, and
a Chevy sedan, a—"

"Chrysler?" I suggest.

"There you go, a Chrysler," Norman says.

"No Lexus or Mercedes?" I ask. Norman cocks his head and gives
me a strange look.

"A Lexus is just a more expensive car," he says tentatively.

"So we have plenty of Lexuses," I conclude.

"I think you know that in 1989 the last order for a new nuclear
weapon was canceled, and that the last nuclear test was Divider,
which was three years later, in 1992," he says. "But there were always questions about would this be better than that, and would this,
and so . . ." His voice trails off.

One morning, I decide to skip the test site and drive six hours
through the desert to visit John Stewart, the man who set off the last
American nuclear bomb. In his cowboy boots, blue jeans, black belt,
salmon-pink shirt, Stewart looks like a prosperous weekend rancher.
A copy of the Book of Mormon sits on his glass-topped coffee table
in his ranch house on a dead-end street in St. George, Utah. While

Stewart's faith in Mormonism is real, his true religion is the Nevada
Test Site. He was born in 1935 in Loa, Utah, and went to work at
Hanford after college producing plutonium. One summer, he col-
lected fallout samples from Sedan.

"Now when Sedan went off that whole earth just came up in a big
bubble and just burst and came out, course through all that fallout
debris around the crater and a dusty dirty cloud that went off, and it
was pretty spectacular," he remembers, sitting squarely in the middle of his comfortable couch. "We went all over the West, up
through Utah, and collected vegetation and rabbits, and we'd fish of
course and do other things as we went along." As he talks about the
work he did at the test site, he gains strength and conviction; it is
possible to see this man swell into a majestic and powerful figure in-
carnating his mad ancestors as he talks of the glory of "the system"
that he saw out in the desert. I ask him to tell me about the last
American nuclear test.

"Okay, the day before we, as you learned from Jim Magruder,
we'd go through a whole series of briefings. Early on we'd look at the
package itself, the laboratories would do a briefing that tells us, okay,
basically—to the test community, the panel members, you know, the
EPA and the weather service—tells us basically what the test is," he
explains, settling down into an easy rhythm as he reviews the familiar procedures that he went though hundreds of times over the
course of his career. "And then we would look at the security plans to
make sure that was still in effect and look at the potential protestors
and off-site intrusions. Worry about the ranges. Just review the
whole process to make sure that we were ready to go ahead and do
the final dry run and do the final arming," he remembers.

The device was armed in the field with a briefcase. "It's just a normal briefcase with the computer system in there," Stewart explained. "You'd have to have two knowledgeables to make sure
somebody didn't go crazy," he says. Back in the control rooms, the
test director would arm the device from a switch that sent a signal to
a computer to begin the countdown. "Also, during all this process
you're pulling all excess equipment away from ground zero," Stewart adds. His job as test controller in the final minutes was to sit and
make sure everything proceeded according to plan. "The thing I
found was that you actually get calmer as you go through that

process. You just force yourself to concentrate on what's happening," Stewart explained.

I ask him if he ever dreamt the night before a test about stuff like the bomb not going off, or an explosion that would leave a huge crater in the desert. "No, I'd dream about golf and I'd, you know, get my golf ball on my tee and stuff like that," he answered. "Do you ever have those dreams?" he asked me. Looking out into the sloping green lawn outside his window, he shook his head with finality. "I never did dream about the test," he said. We shake hands and I get back in my rented car, and wave good-bye.

On the drive back from St. George, Utah, to Las Vegas, the landscape is beautiful and otherwordly. It is a landscape that has swallowed a thousand suns and remains unchanged. I turn up the stereo and listen to Neil Young sing about Pocahontas and the Civil War as the highway median rail bisects the desert speeding past in the rearview mirror and millions of years vanish among the mesas. The sun sets, the desert gets darker, and soon the mirror goes black. Perhaps the true meaning of the Nevada Test Site is how quickly it disappears into the desert. The nuclear dread that forced its way into the sinews of human civilization around the world is swallowed up by a desert that exists in geological time. As Neil Young sings his keening songs that dissolve at the end into the grainy blackness, I am thinking that three years from now, or a decade from now, an American president will set off another bomb in the desert, to ensure the security of the nuclear stockpile or demonstrate the nation's resolve. How would Americans respond if we could no longer destroy the world 10,000 times over? Around another bend, I look up from the highway and see the city of Las Vegas spread out before me in a field of electrified light.

VI.

The Atomic Test Site Museum, a mile and a half from the Vegas Strip, is today the center of a shadow world populated by the men who once lived with the madman's knowledge of total destruction out in the desert. The museum's founding spirit is Troy Wade, who was with Nick Aquilina in Washington on September 11. Hawkishly handsome, at seventy-one, Wade dresses like a jazz piano player, in a black turtleneck and elegant gold chains that dangle from his wrists. He grew up in Cripple Creek, Colorado. His mother went to Juilliard and taught high school. His father played C-melody saxophone in a band. Wade began his career at the test-site mining tunnels, then ran Livermore's explosives-assembly facility, and finally wound up as assistant secretary of energy in the second Reagan administration, responsible for overseeing the secret world of the bomb.

The walls of Wade's office in the Frank H. Rogers Science and Technology Building are bare except for an aerial view of the Pentagon and an aerial view of the test site. "Are you familiar with the Sedan Crater?" he asks me, pointing up to a large crater in the middle of the upper quadrant of the test-site photograph. "Well, the very first nuclear weapon that was totally my responsibility—that I put together with these two hands—was Sedan, which is not a bad way to start in the business." After some pleasant conversation, he graciously agrees to walk me through the half-finished halls of the museum.

"So, when we open, this is the Wackenhut Guard Station," he says. "You're going to buy your ticket here. It's going to be about eight or ten bucks. The message we have to tell people here," he continues, "is: Why in the world did the United States get into this business? So in ninety seconds you're going to learn about what was happening in Nazi Germany, a little bit about what was going on in the Soviet Union, the Einstein letter to Roosevelt that sort of said, 'If we don't do this, somebody else is going to.'" The next exhibit concerns the history of atmospheric testing at the Nevada Test Site, which began at 5:45 A.M. on January 27, 1951, when a one-kiloton bomb named Able was detonated above Frenchman Flat.

"That is the entrance to the underground-test area," he says, as we pass into the next exhibit hall. "This is what it's going to look like—it's all covered in rock." He pauses by a one-fifth-scale model of a bomb rack like the one I saw out at the test site. The next room contains a big grain silo, on the side of which is painted the word "Sioux" with an arrow through it. "There will be a little theater in the round in here that will tell the story of the experimental farm, including the fistulated steers, where they were measuring the uptake of radionuclides into the food."

The museum will also house the McGuffin Collection of Piute

Shoshone Indian artifacts collected on the test site by Don McGuffin, who gave it to Charlie Neeld at Livermore, who, when he was dying of cancer, gave it to Troy Wade. After some negotiations, the tribal elders of the Shoshone Nation agreed to keep the collection together and allow it to be displayed at the museum.

We discuss the fact that all these hundreds of tests out in the desert gave us less than a minute of data, and his eyes glimmer. "It's actually less than a second," he tells me. "It's a fraction of a second. It was millionths of a second." I ponder the smallness of the knowledge gained against the size of the mushroom clouds this man witnessed.

"Let me tell you," he says, "the specter of seeing this mushroom cloud. . . . You can actually see the shock wave coming across the desert at you, and when it hits you, you feel the thermal effects and you feel the shock, and it'll knock you right flat on your butt. I became a better American and a better patriot and a better God-fearing man because I did see them."

VII.

During the day, the ghosts of the American nuclear-testing program tend to stop by the museum. They drop off stacks of faded company newsletters or shoeboxes full of patches and certificates attesting to the role they played in making the desert bloom. One such ghost is seventy-four-year-old Ernie Williams, a white-haired, blue-eyed Nebraskan who looks a little like Johnny Carson. He is dressed like a prosperous alfalfa farmer, in a white shirt with silver snaps and a silver key ring fastened to his belt that holds the keys to the atomic kingdom. In his spare time, he works here at the museum as a security guard. By his own estimation, he saw about eighty atmospheric tests before the program went underground. He enlisted in the air force in 1951, after graduating from high school. Assigned to Lackland Air Force Base, he scored high on an aptitude test and was sent to school to study the assembly and disassembly of nuclear weapons. After leaving the air force, he took a job with the Atomic Energy Commission and was sent to Enewetak Atoll in the Marshall Islands, where he soon became acquainted with Dr. Edward Teller, the father of the hydrogen bomb.

"Dr. Teller was the type of an individual, if you were the janitor, you thought you were talking to another janitor," he says. "He never came across to you as 'I am the father, I am the physicist.' " While waiting for the bomb to go off, the men played rounds of penny-ante poker that Edward Teller inevitably won. "You'd just say, 'Oh, I'll throw my cards in,' and then he'd turn his cards up and he wouldn't have anything," he recalls. "But that's the nature of playing cards."

It was only after Williams went to work at the Nevada Test Site that he saw a vision of the apocalypse he had been assembling with his hands. In the desert there were rows of trenches, with fifteen to twenty soldiers in each trench waiting for the bomb to go off at 4:30 in the morning. The trenches were about five feet deep and eighteen to twenty inches wide. The desert was pitch black. Jeeps and trucks with Army markings were parked at varying distances from the shot tower, and dogs and pigs were staked at varying distances from ground zero.

"You'd hear the countdown: 'One minute. Put your goggles on.' Everybody got their goggles on, and then you would hear, 'Fifteen seconds.' And the next one would be 'Ten seconds,' and then you would hear, 'Nine, eight, seven, six, five, four, three, two, one, zero.' And when zero hit, you know, a bright light, extreme bright light— even with the 4.2 density goggles on, it's extremely white. The mountain range around when it goes off is just like daylight, just like the sun's shining."

The soldiers were understandably jumpy under these conditions, and Williams recalls that officers were present "to direct and say, 'Look, you know, it's okay. It's not a problem.' " Once the shock wave had passed, the troops were marched out of the trenches over the radioactive ground toward ground zero.[10]

While serving as the proving ground for nuclear war, the Nevada Test Site was also its sound stage, the source of photographs of weird protoplasmic blobs erupting from the desert, those civil-defense

10. Getting American troops used to the idea of marching through radioactive blast zones was an important part of the atmospheric program. At the Desert Rock I test, in November 1951, more than 600 men would be interviewed by psychologists from the Human Resources Research Organization, a new government contractor. Worried that "inclination to panic in the face of AW [atomic warfare] and RW [radiological warfare] may prove high," the Joint Panel on the

films depicting the effects of a nuclear blast on the average American family, and many of the spectacular atmospheric blasts shown every fifteen minutes in the Atomic Test Site Museum's surround-sound theater.

The source of many of these images, and the technology that captured them, is a company called EG&G, the MGM of the Cold War. The partnership that would become EG&G began in 1931 with the invention of the stroboscopic flash, the first timed flash unit for photographers, by an MIT instructor named Harold "Doc" Edgerton and Kenneth Germeshausen, his assistant. Their flash timing system would prove to be a key element in the design of the electrical detonating system for the bomb.

One afternoon, while I am watching films of mushroom clouds at the museum, I meet Pete Zavattaro, the former head of EG&G. In his white polo shirt with navy piping and tan chinos, his white beard and white mustache, he looks like a former record-company chairman who has turned late in life to charitable works. As we speak, Zavattaro flips through a book of EG&G photographs of the atmospheric shots taken with RAPATRONIC cameras that eventually achieved exposure times of less than a millionth of a second. By the time of the Divider test, Zavattaro says, the dream of the photographers was almost in reach.

"To be able to actually see this radiation flow in three dimensions was the ultimate goal," he says, a little sadly, "and we were getting closer and closer."

I sympathize with Zavattaro's longing to capture the ultimate knowledge that lies at the core of the nuclear explosions he recorded over decades at the test site. Nanosecond by nanosecond, expanding in real time, a picture of creation might yet emerge. It is hard not to see the quest for the ur-moment as a secular equivalent to the yearning of the prophets to see the face of God.

Toward the end of my stay at the museum, I spend some time

Medical Aspects of Atomic Warfare proposed to increase research efforts, in the scientific study of panic and its results by exposing "as many men as possible" to nuclear tests. During Operation Jangle, teams of soldiers were ordered to walk over ground zero for one hour to test the effectiveness of protective clothing, while others rode tanks through contaminated areas to check the shielding effects of the armor.

down by the guard station with Layton O'Neill, a little man with happy, nutty eyes and thinning hair. As far as he is concerned, fears of radiation and atom bombs are so much nonsense. He is seventy-seven years old and has the energy of a mountain goat. His security-guard badge is fastened to his blue shirt, which he wears with a black string tie and a decorative clasp in the shape of the state of Nevada. When I ask him for the secret of his bountiful energy, he credits the small doses of radiation he absorbed during his days at the test site. He believes that "small amounts of radiation are beneficial to humans," referring me to the research of a man he calls "Dr. Lucky."

As much as anyone, Layton O'Neill is responsible for the effort to preserve the history of the Nevada Test Site. He tells me he comes from a nuclear family. "I have a brother who was making plutonium up at Hanford," he explains, in his excitable way. "I had another brother in California building guidance systems for submarines and missiles." His own job was to track the edges of the radioactive cloud produced during the atmospheric tests by driving along the roads in a car, without the benefit of protective clothing.

"We found it by a meter sticking out the window," he says, his eyes blazing. "And then we found the 'hotline'—the hottest, highest reading of the cloud—and they wanted to know where that was. And then the other edge—turn around and go back through it again. The sunglasses I had were brown sunglasses, and I could see the cloud when other guys couldn't see it."

O'Neill runs his hand through his thinning hair. "I didn't wear a hat in those days, and our hair would be radioactive," he says. "Sometimes you'd have dust on your clothes that they could detect. They'd clean us off, decon us. Yeah, it was beautiful."

Because it is a Friday afternoon, and the hour is late, and there is no one else here, he takes out a clear canister to show me his greatest treasure, a shard of melted brown sludge that formed at 5:30 A.M. on July 16, 1945.

"That's white sand that's been turned into green glass by the heat," he explains. I look curiously at the sludge, which is known as Trinitite—the material formed in the first nuclear blast at Alamogordo, New Mexico. Inside the glass are tiny air bubbles dating back to the exact moment when the atomic world was born. O'Neill holds the glass up to the light.

"It's reading ten to fifteen MR per hour, as I recall," he says.

I ask him what else he has.

"I stole a nut," he says. "And a camera lens." At that moment O'Neill's wife, Melva, whom he met twenty years earlier when the United States conducted a nuclear shot in a salt dome in Carlsbad, New Mexico, enters the room and overhears the last part of our conversation.

"Don't tell him that," she says.

"Well," he says gently, "it's not radioactive anymore."

Being Paul McCartney

I spent last Saturday afternoon at my new girlfriend's apartment in Brooklyn, where I stretched out on a sunny spot on the living room rug and listened to *The Beatles 1,* the latest Beatles rerelease featuring twenty-seven number-one hits that did more to define love and sex for the baby-boom generation than Jesus Christ and Alex Comfort combined. Every song on *The Beatles 1* presents a slightly different take on love, beginning with "Love Me Do" and ending with "The Long and Winding Road," a late-period Paul McCartney song that is equally appropriate for weddings and funerals. *The Beatles 1* was the best-selling record in America last week. I was curious to see whether the emotions in the music would make sense to me again, now that I was in my thirties and maybe but not yet definitively falling in love.

My new girlfriend and I are getting to know each other better. We are at the stage in our relationship where I am beginning to relax into the promise of a new kind of happiness that appears to be as clear and blue as the sky in the ads for Zoloft and Wellbutrin. I offer her my coat when she is cold, and ask her deep, probing questions about her parents and her favorite Beatles songs in the same easy, deceptively casual voice that I might use to ask whether it is snowing in Boston or sunny in L.A. Her answers are seldom if ever obvious. She approaches my questions like a trick shot artist prowling a pool hall. When she banks a particularly difficult shot, she ducks her head, and allows herself a private, inner-directed smile.

My original plan for the afternoon was to get high so that I could fully inhabit Paul McCartney's bass lines. My girlfriend lives in Brooklyn Heights, and my Ziploc baggie of high-grade pot is sitting in an earthenware jar on a bookshelf in my apartment back in Manhattan. I turn up the bass, and relax into the supersaturated stereo sound which expands with that same surge of pleasurable anticipation of the future that my girlfriend and I are secretly imagining together as we drink our tea and talk about the songs. Her favorite Beatles hit is "Ticket to Ride."

Most people who take the Beatles seriously as art, especially men, go through the necessary phase of seeing the band as a collection of mediocre personalities and semitalented musicians who were blessed with the opportunity to serve as extensions of the reigning genius of John Lennon—an understanding that is not in any way diminished by Lennon's awful solo releases culminating in *Double Fantasy*, a record that must be blamed in its entirety on Yoko Ono. Having bought into the received narratives of the Beatles experts since the age of twelve or maybe even nine, I can make the case for Lennon's greatness with barely any effort at all. He inhabited the full range of masculine emotions that have always been attractive to men and women alike but have little place in current popular music outside the precincts of rap and a few aging punk bands. He was smart, angry, funny, vulnerable, jealous, and controlling. He radiated sex. He met groupies backstage in the Hamburg clubs and pulled down their panties and fucked them standing up against the wall. As for McCartney, he was something else entirely: he was a one-man band, and easily the best bass player of his generation outside of Memphis and maybe Detroit. He was the sentimental, middle-class man who loved Magritte, Cocteau, and his wife Linda, and translated Lennon's angry intelligence into well-crafted pop songs. One imagines McCartney setting Lennon's angry, associative rants to music, and then taking Linda out to dinner somewhere smart in Chelsea. Paul and Linda collected antiques. They drank fine wines. She made jam and grew organic vegetables. He let her play synthesizer on some but not all of his solo albums.

My new girlfriend likes my identification with John Lennon. She likes that I am wearing a T-shirt and jeans, and that I am sprawled out on the floor in the sun.

I have no strong feelings about "Ticket to Ride" despite the fact that I've heard the song approximately a hundred or more times in the course of a lifetime. "Ticket to Ride" is a Lennon song. It sounds different this time, because it is my new girlfriend's favorite song.

What I am hearing now is an oddly ambivalent and baffled example of Lennon's inability to reconcile his desperate need for love with his destructive need for control over the object of his desire. The girl that is driving him mad is going away. Good riddance, Lennon sneers. There is ice in his voice. Her emotions are shallow. She's hurt him badly. He coils himself up behind the microphone in the recording booth. He jabs a finger at the men behind the glass. "Don't know why she's riding so high / She ought to think twice, she ought to do right by me." But in his heart, he admires the strength that allows her to throw off the weight of his emotional demands and his anger and his need for control and walk out the door. The final longing chorus of "My baby don't care" is the highest praise that the singer can offer. The girl he loves is nobody's fool. She knows that John Lennon is an asshole.

"It's her song," my new girlfriend says from her place on the couch. "Not his." She talks some more about how the girl owns the song. She thinks that Lennon's anger and his longing are sexy. The sun is moving slowly across the rug. The afternoon is almost over. In an hour, I will take the subway home.

"Maybe McCartney's emotions were just as honest as Lennon's," she suggests. "He just wasn't as angry. And he loved his wife." I met Paul McCartney backstage at a concert once, I tell her. He was wearing cowboy boots with two-inch heels, and he was shorter than I am, a small, well-formed man with the pleasant, unpretentious manner of a master carpenter who makes superbly finished dining room tables out of maple and oak. I used to listen to John Lennon on the radio when he stopped by WNEW to talk about the music he loved so much. He was angry, he was a great artist, he tried not to be angry, he married Yoko Ono because she wrote the word "yes" in very small letters on the ceiling of an art gallery in London. Then he wrote "The Ballad of John and Yoko," became a heroin addict, and then became some weird sexless Moonie, curled up into a ball in his bed in the Dakota for years on end.

The night John Lennon died, I left school early and stood outside the Dakota. Everyone around me was holding candles and crying. I cried too. John Lennon was dead. Paul McCartney was still alive. Twenty years later, it seems easy to say that Lennon and McCartney were two different but equal types of man.

I expect my new girlfriend to be pleased with my answer. We have spent the last two days straight together. Sitting next to each other on the couch feels almost familiar. I like the way the sunlight comes slanting in through the bay window in her living room, and highlights the reddish tints in her hair. I am getting in touch with my inner Paul McCartney, I tell her. She smiles. But she is not dumb.

"You don't have to be Paul McCartney if you don't want to," she says.

Sleeping on Roads

My brother Henry dropped by my apartment the other day unannounced, about a week after I returned to New York from Los Angeles. I was drifting through a pleasant afternoon, listening to Neil Halstead's new album, *Sleeping on Roads*. Best known as the lead singer for Mojave 3, Halstead writes modest, literate, addictive songs warmed by mellow, late-night guitars.

Henry and I are not related by blood. Henry's father married my mother when I was eleven and Henry was fourteen years old, making us the eldest of an eventual total of six children. We grew up in a lower-middle-income housing project in Brooklyn, under the occasional supervision of our smart and high-spirited, if emotionally operatic, parents. Linda and John, as they insist on being called, work in the caring professions and are very concerned with issues of the moment, which makes them easy targets for the wizards of direct mail.

Our families came together during the Hostage Crisis autumn of 1979. By the time Henry left for college in 1983, he had established himself as the family's reigning authority on various subjects including the art of M.C. Escher, chess, army surplus pants, Patricia Hearst, Gerald Ford, the Manson family, and the complete works of Hunter S. Thompson and the Ramones, which Henry gathered together under the ideological umbrella of Punk Rock, along with the Mekons and his trademark cartoons of smiley faces with the eyes X-ed out, with captions like "Mr. Happy Commits Suicide."

Now thirty-six, with fine-boned features, olive skin, and thinning hair, Henry was standing in my doorway, wearing a dirty fisherman's sweater and a gray surplus overcoat. He held his hand up in greeting. Then he stepped into my peaceful, white-walled room, and thudded down on my uncomfortable midcentury Modern red couch.

"I'm happy you came over," I said.

"It was sunny and I wanted to get outside," he answered. He didn't ask if I was busy. I'd been dissecting the floral patterns in the rug when Henry buzzed from downstairs. I'd also been enjoying the pale winter light, which seems to sharpen the outlines of objects while emptying them of substance and weight.

My brother takes medication, which makes it easier for him to deal with people. During the week, he holds down a job in an architect's office; the meticulous line drawings of imaginary office buildings that he turns out appear to represent his desired level of contact with reality. The purpose of his life, he told once me, is to tread lightly on the earth and not to be too much of a burden to others. At night, he takes walks around our neighborhood; he is constantly amazed at the things that other people decide to throw out. The last time I visited his apartment, in a city-sponsored facility near the East River, he showed me a tattered red couch and a pair of battered wooden chairs that he had picked up off the street near where we grew up.

"They're from the elementary school," he told me. The incessant motion of tiny bottoms had polished the seats to a dull, unhealthy-looking sheen; the gray gun-metal legs of the chairs reminded me of the institution where my brother spent what was supposed to be his last year of college.

I made Henry some coffee, and then started the Neil Halstead album over from the beginning. It is not the type of music that he taught us to like. The guitars on *Sleeping on Roads* are warm and soft, and the lyrics portray a familiar gallery of lovers, drifters, and victims in a voice that privileges tenderness over anger and resignation over bite:

> *Music for your head*
> *Lovers for your pain*
> *Drugs for when you're lonely*
> *Polish for your nails.*

The lyrics reminded me of Mojave 3's *Excuses for Travelers*, released in 2000, which was my favorite album of the year, a warm bath of late-seventies guitars and lonely-depressive songs that I imagine were written by a person who spends his winters inside an old stone farmhouse, puttering around his kitchen, getting high a lot, and writing letters to his friends, a collection of tender-hearted isolates—something like me and my brother Henry.

Sitting on the couch, Henry took a few sips of his coffee, lit a cigarette, and listened intently to the first few songs of *Sleeping on Roads,* flicking his ash into his cup. He liked "Driving with Burt," a song I associate with the pleasurable emotion of arriving at John F. Kennedy International Airport at five in the morning and finding a cab, and also "Martha's Mantra," a lullaby about a girl who loves and gets lost. I stood up from my chair to get an ashtray. The next song, "I Dream I Saw Soldiers," is filled with intimations of a future that never arrived, backed by pretty Topanga Canyon guitars.

> *I climbed out the window*
> *And stared at the stars*
> *But the moment I wanted*
> *Was already past.*

"It's a Volvo ad," my brother said when the song was over. He was still sitting on my couch, wrapped in his raincoat. He dropped some more ash on my carpet, ignoring the ashtray that I had thoughtfully provided along with the coffee and a wedge of cheese.

"It's such a human song," I said. "It's a lot like Nick Drake."

"Nick Drake lived with his parents and then he killed himself," Henry said. "Then they made his music into a Volvo ad." *A Volkswagen ad,* I thought.

It occurred to me that in the last few years, my brother's life had become more stable; the medication has helped. He holds down his job and maintains steady contact with family members, which our mother insists on portraying as a very, very encouraging sign.

"It's about living with disappointment," I said, pressing bravely onward. "It's not about pity, or feeling sorry for yourself."

"I didn't say that," Henry said. "I said that the emotions are too easy. It's music for the architects in my office, or the people who style their hair." He mashed out his cigarette in the ashtray and stood up. I handed him the copy of *Pet Sounds* I'd bought him for his birthday.

"Everybody's favorite genius," he said, bestowing a brotherly grin on the picture of Brian Wilson with a llama. Then he glanced at my copy of the Neil Halstead album and shrugged. I was hurt, of course. Since my life is easier than Henry's, I would choose Neil Halstead's companionable, melancholy lyrics over Brian Wilson's unspeakably sad and gorgeous harmonies on any given day of the week. That is the difference between being sick and being well.

"You know it's their twenty-third wedding anniversary on Sunday," I reminded my brother. For a moment I saw him struggle with the thought of the occasion, as he imagined the scene around the table.

"I'll stop by and have coffee," he said, "and pay a visit to the dog."

Life Is Full of Important Choices

I.

An afternoon trip to the post office is part of my normal round of errands, proof of my success in becoming a respectable person, a proper citizen of my native borough of Brooklyn. I have a wife, an apartment, pleasurable work. I visit my local post office this afternoon on the principle that it is good to stand in line with your neighbors, and because my wife reminded me this morning to buy more stamps. My assigned task is to mail another stack of the thank-you notes that we owe from our wedding, the aftershocks of which continue to send tremors along the major fault lines of my psyche. Reflected in the wall of black glass behind the counter toward which the line is moving, my suntanned features are split by the mile-long stare of a person who has spent a summer afternoon parked on a bench, looking out over the bright harbor in the shadow of the Brooklyn Bridge. Over my shoulder I carry a brown leather bag that I bought on vacation with my wife in Rome, in the hope that it might distinguish me from the other neighborhood characters who tote tattered shopping bags filled with books and periodicals along the Promenade.

I am more than just another passing shade seeking comfort in the arms of the U.S. Postal Service. Having survived the long ocean voyage of my late adolescence, I am storming the beaches of adulthood, a new arrival in these parts with a silver wedding ring and decent manners and very little else to show for myself, aside from the fact that I am dog-tired. I identify with my fellow Americans who make themselves up from scratch and then balance like acrobats on a tightrope, suspended between the imagined and the real. I have done most of my own personal self-inventing in libraries, where I sat at long wooden tables and read books, or doodled, or colored in the margins of a sheet of graph paper, or listened to "God Save the Queen" by the Smiths on my Walkman, and absorbed page after page of varied rhythms and words and common phrases that I have mysteriously transmuted into the stuff of a distantly viable literary selfhood. Us library-goers have many things in common. We belong to that particular social group who matured late or not at all, wore glasses, wore black, claimed allergies to wheat, didn't wear deodorant, read Ursula Le Guin and Alexander Pope, and avoided the hard truths of our unpopular condition while we glutted ourselves on stories and fables about heroes who were loaded up with all the big disadvantages and weighty contradictions you could imagine but nevertheless managed to slay their dragons and come out on top.

In my head, I am writing the adventures of a gentleman in the coin-operated-machine business who wears a Kangol cap and dark-gray sunglasses, a character based in part on a real person, an old Jewish gangster whom my wife refuses to allow into our house because he spent time in jail and has abandoned his wife and is living in sin in Union City, New Jersey, with a nice Brazilian lady who loans money to other Brazilians. We live in a floor-through apartment on a tree-lined block, around the corner from a movie theater and only nine blocks from the middle-income housing complex where my sister and I used to drop water bombs on the heads of our neighbors. There are so many people doing nothing in my neighborhood during the day that the schedule I keep has started to seem almost normal. I wake just before noon and walk to the river before I sit down to work. Brooklyn became especially dear to me after my parents relocated us to New Jersey, condemning my adolescent self to spend many late nights on the floor of Port Authority bus terminal along with low-flying pigeons and the floridly homeless. I am very glad to be back in Brooklyn, the city whose streets are etched close to my heart like a secret tattoo.

Having witnessed the yuppie real estate surge of the last few years, Court Street still lives up to its name. The signs above my head read "Bad Apple Bail Bonds" and "Checks Cashed." Young men in black velvet yarmulkes and Ghanaian street peddlers service rumpled jurors, judges, attorneys, perps, and clerks. A Hispanic dad in a purple "Brooklyn Family Court" baseball jersey holds the hand of his young daughter as they make their way together to a matinee at the corner movie theater, a thirteen-theater ziggurat with expensive popcorn and stadium seating that is the product of one of the borough's more intricate real estate scams.

Ahead of me now in line is the enormous black dude in a bright-green hooded tracksuit who lumbered past me on his way to the check-cashing spot earlier this morning. He's six feet tall plus several inches and must easily weigh two hundred and seventy or even eighty-plus pounds, with a big, round baby face swaddled in the folds of his green velour hood. Behind me is a black woman in her fifties maybe, with a white kerchief wrapped around her head to accentuate her thin face and fine features, the most notable of which are her eyes, two liquid pools of sadness; she has been touched by one of those sad stories that you can read about in the papers. Addiction. A shooting. Jail.

Stepping up to the counter now is a young black man, thin, in a space-age Knicks hat, clean white sneakers, and a dark maroon-dyed denim jacket of extraordinary stiffness which gives the impression that the denim has been waxed. Someone looks after him. He is not alone.

I, too, have been lucky enough to feel lifted up out of the common muck. I am grateful for the love of a gray-eyed American beauty who joined her life to my own, a decision that led me to very seriously consider the idea that a sentient higher being might in fact be watching over us. I still have some dry cleaning to pick up, and various other errands to run on Atlantic Avenue—a perfect excuse to check in with my wife.

"You're my favorite person in the whole wide world," I banter. "I love you with my whole heart."

"Oooo," my wife might answer, her lips pressed tightly together like a child who seeks to conceal the evidence of having eaten an entire chocolate cake. "That's nice."

The mosque next door to our apartment serves an immigrant population of shopworkers and cabdrivers, many of whom came from Yemen. Now, whenever someone asks me how I feel about living next to a mosque, I make the same joke again. It's the safest place in Brooklyn. I leave old clothes on the stoop, and give my pocket change to the women in black robes who beg for money to feed their families, and eat lamb with the Imam at Eid. They teach me some Arabic, which I will use when I travel to the West Bank and Gaza. I teach them some English. In short, we are neighbors. We share secrets. Every so often, violating the strict promise I made to my wife, I buy a pack of cigarettes from the devout Muslim man at the corner newsstand, where the charity boxes show pictures of fuzzy-looking mosques in Mecca and Jerusalem. Neither one of us is allowed to smoke. The Pakistani man who owns the laundromat down the block is a more secular type, and sometimes we watch tapes of ancient cricket matches together. He explains the finer points of the game in tune with the spin cycle, and asks after my wife, whose clothes he has washed since before I met her. I sometimes wear an orange T-shirt with navy Arabic script that reads "al-Kufr," which means "the Infidel."

On the corner, men in African robes sell copies of *The Poky Little Puppy* and *The Little Red Hen* for one dollar—a bargain at the price—alongside pirated CDs of the latest Hollywood movies laid out on woolen blankets. I know where the bootlegs are made and how they are shipped. In a pinch, I can trace your pirated DVD copy of *The Godfather II* back to the People's Army 101st Regiment Factory No. 5, "Great Uplifting Joy in Service," located fifteen minutes outside Shanghai.

II.

Let me tell you a bit about the girl I fell in love with. Her favorite sight in the world is the moon. Her second-favorite sight is the unspooled lengths of cassette tape that wind themselves around the branches of trees, a weird phenomenon of nature in Manhattan and Brooklyn that I had never noticed before Virginia pointed it out to me on our second date. How the black magnetic tape gets tangled there is a deep urban mystery. Virginia estimates that tape can be found in the branches of one out of every seven trees in New York City. She first noticed this indisputable phenomenon while helping a friend, an artist who was engaged in a project to recover the lost voices on the tapes—answering-machine messages, dictated letters, rap songs, interviews with minor and major celebrities, and so forth.

The omnipresence of music and conversation preserved in this windblown form lifted Virginia's gentle spirit into a gleeful private dance. I admired how she could dwell in her loneliness without apology.

In addition to having pioneering instincts and a native sense of mischief, my wife is a big fan of reality television shows. She watches television all day. She is a television critic, which seems to me a very urban-modern occupation, like trendspotting or pharmaceutical research, jobs that young people of an equivalent age and social status might also perform in Frankfurt and Tokyo. In the course of her day, she also visits women's health sites on the Internet and orders perfume. She records her favorite shows on TiVo and views them at her leisure, fast-forwarding through the ads that promote our way of life to our Arabic-speaking neighbors next door.

Watching television, my wife sits on the sofa with a child's soft woolen blanket protecting her legs from the air-conditioned chill. I have forgotten to take my morning fiber pills, and I want a jacket to protect me from the breeze outdoors.

"Don't forget your umbrella," my wife teases me, her soft-bellied husband. Above her head is a giant American flag made of red, white, and blue feathers, which I bought in a junk store on Sixth Avenue in Manhattan, near my old bachelor's apartment. We go regularly to the gym and watch our diets in the hope that, someday soon, we might delight our neighbors by conceiving a child.

My life when I met Virginia was similar in some ways to my life now in Brooklyn. A free man in the nineties, I believed in the slogans of our technological age. Everything was connected to everything else. In the mornings, I used to put on my shirt and head for the kitchen, where I would pour milk into a blue ceramic bowl. Frosted Flakes are crisp and sweet, a condition that lasts for approximately a minute and a half before they dissolve into a soggy mush. The milk is the onward flow of life which proceeds independent of the mind that seeks to ensnare us in desire. I ate a bowl of Frosted Flakes for breakfast every morning since I was nine years old. I loved the smiling tiger with the orange and black stripes. "Tony the Tiger says 'they're gre-e-e-a-a-a-t!' " I would say, as my mom smiled, ignoring the sugar-sweetened cereal's near-total absence of nutritional value. She had a movie-star laugh to go with her movie-star looks, a high sound like sleigh bells over snow. Lying on her bed, she would clip pictures of famous actresses from the movie magazines she bought in Prairie Du Chein and then hang them up in the bathroom. When she caught me looking, she would catch me on the bed, then tickle my stomach and play with my hair.

I find it hard to escape the sense of a significant break or fracture that separates the person I was during my childhood and late adolescence, which extended until I was almost thirty years old, from the person I am today. My most conspicuous item of clothing during that period was a supersoft navy sweatshirt with gray ribbing on the cuffs. The zippered hood was lined with a waffle-patterned material. I bought it at my favorite store, located near my apartment, where goofy synthesizer loops floated above a spacey, bone-snapping beat. What I loved best about this store was the way it turned urban dislocation into a consumer experience in which aloneness carried with it no reciprocal obligations other than to pay for the merchandise you selected. The weaving of soft, chiming guitars sent a pleasant emptiness echoing through the cement-floored showroom, where all the salesmen had the jaded, inward-looking faces of discotheque veterans, unmoved by their proximity to so much expensive stock.

My favorite record was a bootleg recording that had faithfully captured the sonic imprint of an evening performance at a soccer palace in Milan by the rock star Kurt Cobain, who I named "Denny-Blaine," a nickname meant to mock the fancy Seattle neighborhood where he bought a million-dollar house and settled down into an uneasy domesticity with his wife, Courtney Love. An expressive vocalist, Kurt could touch five different emotions in every note. His mainstays were screaming anger, whispered fear, loneliness, exhaustion, a narcissistic desire to be enfolded in an overpowering maternal love. The sound of his guitar was like a frayed autumn sweater, or a fallen leaf that had crumbled around the edges. I admired the guitarist's ability to invent a catchy melodic line and then repeatedly find and sustain inventive angles of departure without the chord progressions ever becoming too mathematically predictable, and without losing the fragile thread that holds a three-minute-and-twenty-eight-second pop song together. He blew his head off above his garage, because he couldn't find God, or because his stomach hurt too much, or because his brain was wired wrong.

The sense of abandonment I am trying to describe took many forms that I tried my best to classify according to a taxonomy that seemed entirely new at the time. Most of my friends went on antidepressant medication that promised to alter their personalities for the better. Anxiety disorders were treated with Paxil. Those who didn't take the drugs suffered alone. The most extreme period of dislocation I experienced was when I returned to New York after being engaged to a girl in Miami who didn't want to leave her family. We were old friends, and I had been living rent-free in her New York apartment before we started going out. When we split up, she dyed her hair platinum blonde and bought a new car. I found a new girlfriend. One night, while we were lying in bed together, she told me a story about a tragedy that struck her high school in Oregon.

"It was a really cool place, with a long dirt road leading up through a mountain," she remembered in her bored adolescent voice, preserved like a precious rock concert T-shirt across nearly two decades of experience with the rough perils of the adult universe. Father Daniel, the head of the school, was a gentle man who wore robes and smiled on the kids. He was six feet seven inches tall.

"I used to walk around in my bare feet because it felt good to feel the grass between my toes and because I wanted attention," she remembered. "He used to tell me not to go barefoot."

God was in the grass and the trees. Every class in the school had its own traditions. The tradition for the sophomores was to climb Mount Hood. The trip was led by a teacher named Brother William, who was older than Father Daniel. It was likely that Brother William was too old to survive on the mountain in the middle of a blizzard.

"Seven students and two teachers were stuck on the mountain. No one could rescue them. At the school the parents were drinking coffee and crying," she said. "All they could do was to sit and wait." Only two of the seven students and one of the teachers made it down the mountain.

"They dug a cave in the snow," she continued, pulling the blanket around her bare skinny shoulders. "After Father Daniel was gone, there was no one left to tell me to put on my shoes."

A plea for love and attention, her story was also an entirely sober analysis of a larger spiritual crisis that denied any possibility of a cure. To make myself feel better, and to give my life some sense of purpose, especially on the weekends, I developed a rooting interest in the New York Yankees. If being a Yankees fan was like rooting for the Microsoft Corporation, I found a welcome solidarity in the subway rides out to the Bronx and in sitting in the stands, cheering and booing the players, and exchanging rude remarks. Win or lose, Yankee Stadium was the only place I knew where people seemed happier when they came out than when they went in. I enjoyed the skill of the players and the five-dollar beer.

"What is happening?" Virginia repeated as we stared at the picture on the television screen of the towers falling, one after the other. We went to the hardware store and bought white paper masks so we could safely breathe, and then we went down to the Promenade, where my father used to take me to look at the cargo ships. We stood in the crowd of onlookers and watched the black cloud cross over the river. Walking back, with the paper masks still over our faces, we noticed a tangle of cassette tape caught in the branches of a tree. Flecks of ash stuck to the windowsill outside her bedroom.

III.

A few weeks later, we went to a party to celebrate the birth of someone's second child. The apartment was eighteen hundred square feet of McMansion cantilevered above a rainswept stretch of city traffic. The older child, a pretty little girl named Agnes, ran around the apartment crowned with a tiara. She discovered a giant blue inflatable ball and nudged it to the center of the room, and rolled back and forth with yogic glee.

"That's Mommy's exercise ball!" exclaimed a guest.

"Sigh-ball!" Agnes said. The child's tiara had fallen on the floor. She had her father's broad face and her mother's blue eyes, and a head of brown curls. She picked up the crown in her hands and toddled up to Virginia, my wife. The person to my right was talking about President Bush. The firemen who ran into the towers were brave. The attacks were the President's fault. A young couple spoke of leaving for their house in the country, where they'd be safe from a future radiological attack.

"You roll back and forth," the little girl stoutly insisted.

"Who does that?" Virginia asked.

"Mommy does that." The child folded her hands over her stomach, and looked curiously up at Virginia again.

"In the bedroom there's a egg with a sweater," the child said.

"A pink egg?" Virginia asked.

"You're not allowed to touch it," the child solemnly warned. She smoothed the front of her yellow French print dress, and looked curiously up at the moonfaced giant above her.

"You look like a duck," she declared.

"I look like a duck?" Virginia asked.

The little girl laughed again, her blue eyes sparkling with mischief. "The egg is in Mommy's bedroom," she said.

At home that night, under the sink, I discovered Virginia's secret stash of tranquilizers—Valium, Vicodan, Xanax—and a tube of triple-codeine aspirin she'd brought back from London, each pill individually vacuum-sealed in a plastic and cellophane packet bearing mute witness to an internationally recognized brand of sadness. Next to the tranquilizers was an unopened pregnancy test that she had bought three years before. "If it is positive, a donut forms."

Virginia was reading a book in the bath. She had reached some definite conclusions about the book's former owner, Martha Avery, whose penciled-in name had faded decades ago to a moth-wing gray. The daughter, most likely, of a New England divine, she had worked for many years running a women's crisis center before retiring to her family home in Putney, Vermont, where she read *Six Essays* by Ralph Waldo Emerson.

"She had this peculiar idea," my future wife suggested, lifting one long leg out of the water and propping it up on the edge of the tub. "The descriptions of the stars in the *Odyssey* were also the record of actual Mycenaean voyages, so you could tell exactly where the Argonauts had gone. The Mycenaeans were a seafaring people, they navigated by the stars, and so it made sense that they might preserve the record of their journeys by telling stories that people would remember. The stars are the same. The only thing that's changed at night in over three thousand years is the brightness of the cities," she argued. "It's still the same moon."

IV.

For the three months after the fall of the towers, I rode the subway anticipating a sarin gas attack or an abandoned knapsack containing a bomb. Near my apartment in lower Manhattan, the fluttering posters peeled off the walls and the telephone poles, and the family members still stood like characters from a science fiction novel, handing out posters of loved ones in badly xeroxed prom-night photographs. "The blue sky, no clouds to be seen, the sun radiating warmth and light, a splendid background to an act of hate and evil," one writer said of that day, in a pamphlet that is now part of my collection of neighborhood ephemera. After the planes hit the towers, the author's mind had abruptly switched gears.

"What is the signal, how do I interpret it?" he wondered.

"I bring you physical results, not promises," promised Dr. Rev. O. Dibia, an African healer whose writings were also widely distributed. "E.g., I can transfer a human blindness onto a goat."

I was called to jury duty in a downtown courtroom, where two jury-selection workers traded off reading names from a list in a flat, genderless tone designed to penetrate the crowded space with maximum force. Listening to the names recited in alphabetical order in the oxygen-depleted atmosphere by the alternating voices of the municipal workers, one female and the other male, had a lulling effect on the would-be jurors. The list was a ritual invocation of duty, offered by our appointed celebrants of the civic mass. After every name was called, the congregants proclaimed their preferences: "morning," "afternoon," or "excused." I answered "excused." I would do my jury service another time, I decided.

Outside on the courthouse steps, policemen stood in their winter coats and hard-brimmed caps next to the blue-painted barriers, moving pedestrian traffic up and down the steps. I called Virginia on my cell phone.

"Did you ever see the movie *Ikiru*?" I asked her. "It's the one that ends with the lonely old man sitting on the swing in the playground with the snow falling all around him. The one and only interesting thing about his life is that he built this playground, and now he's swinging back and forth in the dark, and then he dies."

"It's snowing outside," she answered. "Why don't you come over?"

V.

Every Friday, the male worshippers at the mosque next door touch their heads to the sidewalk, wearing cheap parkas and long woolen overcoats in the winter. The principle behind their action is submission to a higher power. Some kneel on cheap, brightly woven prayer carpets. Others prostrate themselves on a bare piece of cardboard. Through a series of physical and mental operations performed at the same time of day, every day, for the rest of their lives, they hope to further the sense of an immutable order, a thirteen-hundred-year-old structuring of perception that might be interposed between the one who perceives and the formless chaos of existence. There is no God except Allah.

What had collapsed along with the towers was the illusion of continuity between one set of certainties and another. Hearing our neighbors' call to return to God, Virginia and I lit the Sabbath candles together, and said our blessings over the wine. We would have something in common with Ralph Waldo Emerson, my wife and I agreed, as well as with our Muslim neighbors. The fact that we were no longer lonely did not mean that other people approved of our choices. We would not eat pork. Friends expressed their discomfort with the idea that two educated people would choose to celebrate the deadly fiction of a Supreme Being. Virginia's mother called to tell us that Jesus Christ offered the only pathway to salvation. Car bombs exploded in Tel Aviv.

Still, no one could dispute how beautiful Brooklyn was less than one year later, the summer after the towers fell. It was as if the ashes from the tower had fertilized our neighborhood. The local population of stoop-sitters, myself included, were the recipients of an unexpected bounty. Gardens flourished. Boutiques and restaurants bloomed. Funereal ash clogged our air-conditioner filters, which we cleaned in the bathtub. We washed the last traces of ash down the drain, and then we scrubbed the drain and the inside of the tub with disinfectant, and then we were done.

Marginal Notes

No one becomes a reader except in answer to some baffling inner necessity, of the kind that leads people to turn cartwheels outside the 7-Eleven, jump headlong through a plate-glass window, join the circus, or buy a low-end foreign car when the nearest appropriate auto-repair shop is fifty miles away. With these dramatic examples fresh in your mind, you'll probably require only a small amount of additional convincing that my little theory—based on years of painful experience—is true. Reading requires a loner's temperament, a high tolerance for silence, and an unhealthy preference for the company of people who are imaginary or dead.

It also requires patience, or what my high-school gym teacher, whose name I remember as Randy Fisk, or Fist—a bantamweight Irishman with a ginger mustache who exhibited a suspicious delight in watching his fourteen-year-old charges vault a padded "horse"— used to call "good old-fashioned stick-to-it-iveness." His opinion was that readers were pale, unnatural freaks with a built-in resistance to normal physical exercise. And because, like so many freaks, I have a desperate desire to appear normal, it pains me to admit that Mr. Fist, or Fisk, was right. Readers are freaks. There is no point in denying it.

The comparison between readers and writers on this score is instructive. While writers have historically made a point of displaying themselves as unusually sensitive, troubled souls (see Verlaine, Rimbaud, Thomas Wolfe, Plath, Burroughs, Ginsberg, et al.; note that most of the truly crazy ones are poets), it is also my theory that their dramatic sufferings are very often the product of too much ambition. Too much actual, organic suffering in one's biography can make it impossible to sustain the energy and egotism necessary for a successful literary career. A career of reading, on the other hand, allows for more prolonged and spectacular forms of disturbance. It is no accident, at least, that most readers I know were unhappy children. They spent months in the hospital; endured long periods of friend-lessness or bereavement; watched loved ones die of cancer; had par-ents who were crazy or divorced; spent formative years in a foreign country; suffered from early exposure to "fantasy" or "adventure" novels for boys or "mystery" or "romance" novels for girls; or lived through some overwhelming experience of dislocating weirdness, such as growing up on an army base, or on a farm, or in a cult.

My own reasons for bookishness are less dramatic. There were the stresses of a home where my unhappy parents fought all the time, inculcating in me a very natural desire to escape from reality. But the greatest injury I suffered was the absence of a television set, which cut me off from the comforting stream of voices, pictures, characters, and stories in which my peers ritually immersed them-selves every day after school. Assigned the role of Gilligan from *Gilligan's Island*, I remember standing on our asphalt playground in Brooklyn without the slightest idea of what to say or how to behave. After school, I went home and read books. It was less boring than staring up at the ceiling or listening to my parents fight.

By the age of fifteen, I was a full-time reader. I hid books under my desk. I read in the library after school. Reading was an escape from the crushing pressures of adolescence, such as speaking out loud in class or making direct eye contact with my peers in the halls. Books were a promise that I might at least learn to impersonate someone normal. I loved *The Great Gatsby*. If Gatsby himself was blurry and suspicious, Nick Carraway was the kind of friend I would have liked to have. Hemingway was good, particularly the early sto-ries (how to talk to hoboes and boxers). Flaubert was great, particu-larly *Sentimental Education* (Madame Bovary reminded me of my mother). Edith Wharton had a wonderful eye for details but there was something disturbing about her take on humanity. Reading her books was like watching a brilliant hostess in her drawing room mak-ing witty observations to dullards and bores. Henry James was worse. Virginia Woolf was a very great writer. Still, it didn't escape my attention that Septimus Smith threw himself out a window, and that Leonard Bast, my favorite character from Woolf's great predecessor, E. M. Forster, was crushed to death beneath a shelf of books. Woolf and Forster were terrible snobs. Of the "modern" American writers, John Updike was like Flaubert, except he used his terrific skill to convince the reader that he actually liked Rabbit Angstrom, whereas the Updike I imagined (namely, me) would have hated him. What a jerk. Philip Roth hit too close to home.

Of all of the famous writers I read, J. D. Salinger most actively courted my adolescent longings and fantasies, particularly when it came to the dreamlike specificity of his Manhattan interiors. In *Franny and Zooey,* the author speaks through Buddy Glass, a writer who admired *The Great Gatsby,* "which was my 'Tom Sawyer' when I was twelve," and whose main business, as far as I could make out, was sitting around dispensing cracker-barrel wisdom like a deadbeat old-timer at the track. Still, Buddy was always happy to share the insider details I craved, namely the cool wall hangings, reading habits, vocal inflections, and bathroom-medicine-cabinet contents of the precocious, sensitive, unhappy children who lived on the Upper East Side of Manhattan. (My family lived in Brooklyn, then moved to New Jersey when I was nine. The mental Post-it I attached to *Franny and Zooey* reads something like "Notes on the Inner Lives of People with Cluttered Apartments in the East Seventies.") It was encouraging to know that my yearnings for a guide through the darkness of this world were answered by the tender proclivities (which now seem stranger but no less affecting) of the famous author of *The Catcher in the Rye,* a novel that played on self-pitying adolescent instincts without offering even a smidgen of useful wisdom in return, except, perhaps, for preppies. Seymour Glass would have hated it. It is no accident, I believe, that both John Hinckley Jr. and Mark David Chapman were carrying copies of Salinger's little red book when they shot Ronald Reagan and John Lennon, respectively.

Between the ages of fourteen and twenty-four I read *Franny and Zooey* from cover to cover at least five times. I underlined passages and made cryptic notations in the margins, hoping to become an acceptable character free from the bipolar alternation of uncontrolled aggression and sad passivity that I saw in my parents' marriage and was only beginning to recognize in myself.

• • •

By relating this horrifying mishmash of biographical details in a jaded, older-person voice, I hardly mean to suggest that my reading was not worthwhile. Nor do I intend to explain away, through an act of knowing posthumous revelation, the failings of my fourteen-year-old self, who deserves tons of sympathy and understanding, but whom I have little interest, should the opportunity somehow present itself, in ever meeting again. (His unhappiness, his eagerness to please, and his frantic desire to escape from his family give me the creeps). What bothers me about him has nothing to do with his aesthetic sense. It is his lack of any real capacity to enter sympathetically into the minds of other people. I read books in order to learn how to be the *right* kind of character in the *right* kind of novel. The authors of these novels were not people like my parents or me, who were anxious from morning through most of the afternoon, and at night were very often *scared to death.*

Franny and Zooey was my *Stover at Yale.* The wisdom that Salinger was interested in dispensing was more difficult than the simple stick-to-it-iveness of Dink Stover (a step up from "striver") or my high school gym teacher, Mr. Fisk, or Fist. I never felt much identity with such well-balanced characters anyway. I didn't know anyone who went to Yale. Dink Stover (a hero-athlete, admired by his peers) or F. Scott Fitzgerald was too far a reach. In *Franny and Zooey,* the Dink Stover character, waiting on the train platform in Princeton to receive Franny Glass, was called Lane Coutell. "Lane Coutell, in a Burberry raincoat that apparently had a wool liner buttoned into it, was one of the six or seven boys out on the open platform. Or, rather, he was and he wasn't one of them." In the paperback *Franny* I owned at fourteen, and have read ever since, I underlined "he was and he wasn't one of them" twice in blue ink. (Did the Princeton men of 1984—the year of the Talking Heads' best album—still meet "dates" on train platforms wearing Burberry raincoats? I believed the answer was yes.)

There was no getting around the fact that I was bad at sports and had trouble looking directly at other people in the halls, and J. D. Salinger knew it. He knew that his readers feared and resented the Lane Coutells of this world with the profound self-hatred that only adolescents can muster. And unlike Fitzgerald, or Hemingway, or the author of *Stover at Yale,* Salinger was on our side. "I've *missed* you," Franny tells Lane. The words are no sooner out of Franny's mouth, the author eagerly informs us, "than she realized that she didn't mean them at all."

It wasn't Lane we were supposed to like. It was Franny. Lane is a self-important snob, a charm-boy, a gym-class standout who uses words like "testicularity" and then pretends that he said something else. Franny isn't fooled. And as she cuts him up, "with equal parts of self-disapproval and malice," Salinger is careful to keep the reader on her side by assuring us that her disdain is self-conscious and specific, and would never be extended to us. You don't have to hate yourself, I felt like telling my beloved disconsolate Franny. Lane is an *asshole.*

Franny was blameless, brave, and falling apart. Also selfless and knowing. "I'm just sick of ego, ego, ego," she says. "My own and everybody else's." I underlined that line with a vengeance. "I'm afraid I *will* compete," one page later, was even better, rating both a five-pointed star *and* an exclamation mark in blue. The underlined passages are obvious attempts to engage the sympathies of adolescent loners by telling a familiar story (Dink Stover at Yale) from the more original and appealing reverse angle (Franny, who thinks he's a jerk). I was charmed. The specter of testicularity was ridiculed and banished. Despite her emotional condition, and the difference in our ages, I might even have considered asking Franny out on a date.

The centerpiece of the next section of the book is Buddy's letter to his younger brother Zooey. I confess that my fourteen- and even my twenty-year-old selves were never very interested in this letter. The writing was looser, stammering, written by a stand-up comic with sweaty palms and a brand-new routine. I didn't care that much about Buddy Glass. I wanted to know more about Franny. I was disturbed by Salinger's desire to shift the ground of his story, to break through the conventional demands of rewriting *Stover at Yale* or early Fitzgerald from a sly, sardonic angle and infuse the voice with a more self-conscious humor that underlined the vulnerability of his narrator—a person of adult years and experience who was willing to admit, in public, that he "burst into tears at the first harsh or remonstrative word." I knew that line was a joke. (I wrote "joke" in blue ink

in the margin.) Still, it was the kind of joke that made me nervous.
Entering into a pact of sympathetic understanding with such a person was unwise.

On my second reading, at age seventeen or eighteen, I found
Buddy's sense of humor more sympathetic. I liked "if my Muses
failed to provide for me, I'd go grind lenses somewhere, like Booker
T. Washington." I was proud of myself for getting why the linkage of
Buddy Glass and the author of *Up from Slavery* was funny. ("Unexpected," I wrote, in pedantic red ink. "*Not* Benjamin Franklin.") I
also appreciated the description of Les Glass, later on in the book, as
"an inveterate and wistful admirer of the wall décor at Sardi's theatrical restaurant." I underlined the phrase "theatrical restaurant,"
because it was the addition of those two words to "Sardi's" that made
the joke work.

Funny or not, Buddy Glass—from the perspective of age fourteen and age seventeen or eighteen, and even age twenty—was
never as interesting as his dead brother Seymour, who left behind a
deceptively simple three-line koan whose meaning tantalized and
captivated me for ten years without ever quite becoming clear: "The
little girl on the plane / Who turned her doll's head around / To look
at me." Because Seymour Glass plays only a ghostly Jamesian role in
Franny and Zooey, it seems wrong to go into my idealization of him
here. Why did Seymour kill himself? Was the beauty of the little
girl's gesture—is she trying to be *polite,* does she really think the doll
is a *person*—not enough? Was it a protest against what the girl
would become when she grew up? Or did the charming gesture contain the seeds of the adult corruption that would later destroy her
soul? None of these questions can be answered within the text of
Franny and Zooey.

Zachary Martin Glass, or Zooey, was my favorite character in the
book. He is Seymour and Buddy's Zen teachings, he is the rebellion
against those teachings, he is funny and handsome, he is an actor,
and he even bears a passing resemblance to Lane Coutell. (Both are
objects of adolescent male identification. The demographics are different, that's all.) He is the recipient of his brother Buddy's practical
advice: "*Act,* Zachary Martin Glass, when and where you want to,
since you feel you must, but do it *with all your might.*" If Buddy
Glass made me uneasy, Zooey was a perfect stand-in. He is an air-

brushed version of Buddy, a character any adolescent misfit would be happy to have as a friend. Someone in the family was normal. At the same time, my feelings for Zooey contained a hard, uncomfortable kernel of self-hatred that never quite dissolved, no matter how many times I read the book.

But this piece of dishonesty was more than made up for by my favorite scene in the book, the bathroom scene between Zooey and his mother, Bessie Glass. Bessie is a classic. (Les Glass tap-dances his way into the text only twice, in a memory of a long-ago birthday party and as a semighostly presence who proffers a tangerine to his daughter.) She is a "svelte twilight soubrette . . . photographed . . . in her old housecoat." The sentence that follows a few pages later is worthy of Balzac, a real beauty. The subject is Bessie's housecoat:

> With its many occultish-looking folds, it also served as the repository for the paraphernalia of a very heavy cigarette smoker and an amateur handyman; two oversized pockets had been added at the hips, and they usually contained two or three packs of cigarettes, several match folders, a screwdriver, a claw-end hammer, a Boy Scout knife that had once belonged to one of her sons, and an enamel faucet handle or two, plus an assortment of screws, nails, hinges, and ball-bearing casters— all of which tended to make Mrs. Glass chink faintly as she moved about in her large apartment.

Slovenly, patched together, proceeding according to a purely comic logic, if by any logic at all, and stopping just short of the darker comedy of Beckett, Bessie's old housecoat is the best description of domestic memory that I know. Perhaps the ability to find meaning in that memory is ultimately what saves us. Zooey is exasperated. Bessie is a dope. Still, Salinger is willing to give Bessie and her housecoat their due.

The love scene between Bessie Glass and her son is the answer to the love scene between Franny and Lane in Princeton, and to the lousy television script that Zooey reads in the bath. "This is supposed to be a family of all adults," Bessie says. She knows that Franny is hurt and she hurts because she can't fix it. And just when the scene might get too sentimental, Buddy steps in to let us know that the eyes that used to announce the tragedy of her two dead sons now tear up at the solemn announcement that some remote Hollywood starlet's marriage is on the rocks.

"Why the hell doesn't he kill himself and be done with it?" Zooey wonders of the absent Buddy. (That Buddy Glass is putting this sentence in Zooey's mouth didn't hit me until two readings later, in my junior year of college, an additional complexity that I noted in blue.) I trusted Zooey because he was angry. "I'm a twenty-five-year-old freak and she's a twenty-year-old freak, and both those bastards are responsible."

That was where I stopped underlining. I never marked the last line of the scene, when Zooey makes fun of his mother's pitch-perfect exit ("In the old radio days, when you were all little and all, you all used to be so—smart and happy and—just *lovely*. Morning, noon, and night."), but softly, so that "his voice wouldn't really reach her down the hall."

It did not occur to me until after I had graduated from college that Salinger was entirely serious about the last third of the book, or that *Franny and Zooey* was intended as something other than a novel. I had always wondered about the little books that Franny carried in her purse, *The Way of a Pilgrim* and *The Pilgrim Continues His Way*. Her interest in the religious practice of a thirty-three-year-old Russian peasant with a withered arm who repeats the prayer "Lord Jesus Christ, have mercy on me" until it enters the rhythm of his heart always seemed to me like a precious symptom to which the author had devoted perhaps a little too much attention. *Franny and Zooey* and *The Way of a Pilgrim* were similar, if not the same book. They were answers to the question of how to live, I realized.

The question interested me because I was twenty-three years old and living in my parents' basement in West Orange, New Jersey, along with the family dog, an unwashed poodle. Before that, I had been living in Manhattan, in a five-room apartment on East Fourteenth Street between Second and Third Avenues that I shared with five people between the ages of twenty-four and thirty-two. I paid $320 a month for a room with three doors and no windows. It was hot in the winter. The summer was worse. People wandered in and out. The building next door was a residence for the deaf, and at night its tenants would bring their Dominican boyfriends to our stairwell, lean up against the wall, spread their legs, open their mouths, and roll their eyes toward heaven without making a sound. Everyone I knew wore leather jackets and took drugs. Two of my roommates were heroin addicts. I was afraid to put a needle into my arm. Over time, I became afraid of the way I was living.

When I moved back home, I stopped taking drugs, which made me angrier than I had been before. I was also scared. In the book, Bessie Glass wanted to send Franny to an analyst, like Philly Byrnes.

"Philly *Byrnes*," Zooey answered. "Philly Byrnes is a poor little impotent sweaty guy past *forty* who's been sleeping for years with a rosary and a copy of *Variety* under his pillow." That wasn't me either. If there was someone out there with "any crazy, mysterious *grati-tude* for his insight and intelligence," it wasn't any psychiatrist I knew. And it wasn't J. D. Salinger either. I was looking for answers, and the notes I made toward the end of the book at age twenty-four quiver with sardonic disappointment. " 'Nancy Drew and the Hid-den Staircase' lay on top of 'Fear and Trembling.' " That seemed like a better description of the weakness of *Franny and Zooey* than any-thing I could invent on my own. I noticed that Franny is described as "a first-class beauty," and I found the description cheap. I marked Zooey's line to Franny, "How in *hell* are you going to recognize a le-gitimate holy man when you see one if you don't even know a cup of consecrated chicken soup when it's right in front of your nose?" In the margin I suggested that Starbucks could use this motto on a new line of greeting cards. Those were the last words I wrote in my copy of *Franny and Zooey*. The affair had gone cold.

Reading the book again, I was amazed by how many perfect mo-ments there are, by how rich and funny and wise it is, and by the fact that the entire book is only two hundred pages long. I still love the bathroom scene the best. But I also love the end of the book, partic-ularly the moment when Franny announces that she wants to talk to Seymour, the moment of pure emotion that the book has been building toward for almost the entire two hundred pages, and that Salinger, Buddy, and Zooey answer by looking out the window and seeing a little girl in a red tam, with her dachshund wandering on the sidewalk nearby. It's not Seymour exactly. It's the little girl from the airplane, or someone like her, a vision of sustaining innocence that will carry us through the harder part of the lesson, Like Seymour's Fat Lady, for whose sake Zooey Glass polished his shoes every night before appearing on the radio. She had thick legs, very veiny, and her radio was always going full blast. She had cancer.

"There isn't anyone out there who isn't Seymour's Fat Lady," Zooey says. The Fat Lady is Christ. Or forgiveness. There was a time when this sentence didn't convince me to put a check mark or a star in the margin. There may be higher peaks of wisdom to climb yet. I closed the book, then I opened it again, got out my fancy new pen, and added a black check mark. I am still grateful for this book. That is what I mean to say.

The Light Stuff

"Starting one, clear one!" Jon Conrad called out. As the portside propeller of the *Spirit of America*, the Goodyear Tire and Rubber Company's newest blimp, whirred to life, Conrad, who had recently been named Goodyear's one and only pilot-in-training, sat to the left of his instructor, John Crayton. After Crayton gave him a nod, the young pilot looked through the cabin windshield and signaled to the ground crew. He held up two fingers and made a rotary motion, then started the second prop. After pausing for several seconds, he spread one palm wide and punched the air with his other hand, communicating his readiness for takeoff. The *Spirit of America* rolled across the wide green airfield, bounced once, then sailed serenely up into the fading blue sky above Carson, California.

Conrad was dressed in a white short-sleeved pilot's shirt and a Stars and Stripes tie. His right hand rested on a large wooden wheel, which he moved gently back and forth to adjust the altitude of the ship. The cockpit of the airship, where Conrad has been polishing his skills for the last three months, Wednesday through Sunday (blimp pilots have Mondays and Tuesdays off), would be familiar at once to any fan of the illustrations in old science-fiction novels—it's a fanciful vision of the future as imagined by Jules Verne. Shaped like a deluxe ski gondola, seating six, with windows in front and on the sides, the cabin offers spectacular 270-degree views of the freeways below and the surrounding hills. The pilot sits in a high-backed chair, resting his right hand on a large wooden ship's wheel, which he moves gently back and forth, adjusting the altitude of the ship like a man maneuvering a wheelchair into a comfortable spot. The ship's direction is controlled by two pedals, one on the right and one on the left, which Conrad works like an organist, using constant, minute flexings of toe, heel and calf to counter the shifting air currents while maintaining an easy, unhurried bearing.

A thirty-three-year-old native of Scottsbluff, Nebraska, Conrad is an even-tempered, pleasant fellow whose conversation is punctuated by exclamations like "I'm as chipper as a blue jay." He is well over six feet tall and has 20/400 eyesight (a debility that would disqualify him from becoming a pilot in the air force). He resembles a grown-up version of the cheerful lad in overalls who appears on cans of Dutch Boy paint. Before landing the opportunity to fly Goodyear's newest blimp, he put up steel-frame houses in the 40-degrees-below winters in Nebraska, and logged over three thousand hours as a pilot for the Met Life blimps, Snoopy One and Snoopy Two. In the three months since accepting Goodyear's offer and moving to Hermosa Beach, California, he has yet to ask a woman out on a date. As the Goodyear Rubber and Tire Company's only blimp pilot-in-training, he spends his evenings floating a thousand feet above the 405 freeway between Los Angeles and San Diego.[1]

There are three Goodyear blimps currently operating in the United States: one is based in Carson, California; one in Pompano Beach, Florida; and the third at the company's headquarters, in Akron, Ohio. Each blimp has four pilots. Conrad's mentor, John Crayton, is known as the PIC of the *Spirit of America;* those initials stand for "pilot in charge." He is a courtly, old-school gentleman with a walrus mustache and an easy manner, whose twin mantras are "Get lower" and "Get slower." As Conrad curved the blimp northward, Crayton said, "I have a basic theory of blimp pilots. It's all about getting used to where the buttons are, and learning patience."

After takeoff, Conrad settled into the normal cruising pace of thirty-five miles an hour; at that speed, even the lightest single-engine airplane would fall out of the sky. Blimps are so placid that they are the only aircraft certified for flight without seat belts. Cartoonish and otherworldly in flight, blimps are also quite noisy, espe-

---

1. The derivation of the word "blimp" is unclear. One common explanation is that it was coined in 1915 by Lieutenant A. D. Cunningham, of the British navy. During an inspection at a landing strip in Capel, England, legend has it, the lieutenant playfully poked one airship's balloon with his thumb; an amusing sound was produced when the bag's fabric snapped back into shape, and Cunningham responded with a verbal imitation: "Blimp!"

cially when both propellers are running at full throttle. Every Goodyear pilot I met except Conrad is partially deaf.

Conrad radioed the control tower, which is in Torrance. "I'd like to climb to twenty-five hundred feet, because of some clouds up here," he said, tilting the elevator flaps at the rear of the airship. The blimp ascended smoothly. To the west, the sun hung on the edge of the Pacific Ocean.

At 4:55 P.M., the sun set, and the sky along the coastline turned pink. Dark clouds hung low on the horizon. "The sunset's really loaded up with reds, golds, and pinks," Crayton said. The two pilots stopped talking for several minutes and gazed out at the subtly shifting skyscape. The clouds developed a mellow tinge; the sky darkened, and the sandy-orange underside of nearby clouds became firelight bronze. Watching the sun set over the Pacific while floating in a Goodyear blimp is like being suspended inside the world's biggest lava lamp. Rolling the wheel forward on its axis, he causes the elevator flaps at the rear of the airship to tilt upward, which alters the flow of the air over the control surfaces, encouraging the blimp to climb another few hundred feet. A pair of white toggles on the panel above Conrad's head controls the inflation of the ballonets, or airbags. The rubberized envelope of the blimp contains a central helium balloon along with fore and aft ballonets that help control the ship's pitch. Since air is heavier than helium, pumping air into the fore ballonet will cause the nose of the blimp to dip; air in the tail will cause the nose to rise. A red toggle on the right allows for the emergency dumping of fuel. Blue and yellow toggles control the vents for the blimp's 202,500 cubic feet of helium, which are located on either side of the airship, inside the letter "Y" in "Goodyear"; helium is only vented in emergencies, when the blimp gets too light.

As Conrad calmly navigated the skies, his goal of securing a seat in the clouds felt tantalizingly within reach. Two weeks from now, on January 15, Don Ploskunak, Goodyear's chief pilot, would arrive from Akron to check out Conrad's skills. If he failed the written or the oral portion of the daylong exam, or made a serious mistake during the three-hour flight test, he would be out of a job. If Conrad passed, he could look forward to a trip to San Diego, where he would help cover the Super Bowl, Goodyear's biggest television event of the year.

"This airship is bigger and more stable than the ships I used to fly," Conrad said admiringly. "You have more power behind you. It's more like flying a truck—a big semi."

For decades, Goodyear's large silver blimps (which are now painted an odd combination of silver, navy, and yellow) ruled the skies unchallenged. Since the nineties, though, the company has had to compete for television exposure with the Lightship Group, which flies blimps for MetLife, Saturn, and Sanyo, and has put an end to Goodyear's dominance of big-time sporting events like the World Series and the Super Bowl. Even so, within the tiny airship subculture—there are fewer blimp pilots than there are astronauts—flying for Goodyear remains the most coveted job on the planet. It's been so long since Goodyear hired a new pilot in California, in fact, that the tailor who made Jon Conrad's uniforms left him alone in the fitting room for an hour while he tried to confirm that the new pilot wasn't an impostor.

Conrad eased the blimp higher into the twilit sky, then turned eastward, in the general direction of the Orange County Auto Show. "I'm learning from the masters," he said, gesturing toward Crayton, who is fifty-seven. He explained that he had also been tutored by two expert pilots, Tom Matus, who is sixty-five, and Charlie Russell, who is fifty-six. Between them, these men had ninety-one years of experience flying Goodyear blimps. Conrad noted that the pilots had different styles: Matus flies tail-heavy; Russell excels at landings; and Crayton likes a little extra weight in the nose.

Conrad radioed the ground crew. "Can you give me the surface temperature?" he asked.

"Seventy-three," came the response.

Conrad was thinking ahead to the landing. The air had cooled off, he reported, but not too much. The blimp's weight gain was probably not excessive, which meant that he wouldn't need to burn off any extra fuel.

"Can you give me a bag count for E.Q.?" he asks. E.Q. stands for equilibrium, the point at which the weight of the craft, equipment, and crew will be exactly equal to the weight of the surrounding air— namely, zero.

"Thirty-nine for E.Q.," comes back the voice from the ground-crew chief, Tony Sanico. Before takeoff, the ground crew placed 39 pounds of ballast, in the form of lead-filled "shot bags," inside the blimp's cabin. Knowing the bag count and the surface temperature will help Conrad calculate how much fuel he has to burn to bring the ship back at the proper weight for landing. Three hundred pounds heavy is a preferable weight; the ship will be sinking, but not too fast. More than eight hundred pounds heavy can be dangerous to the airship and to the crew members who will have to catch her.

"This is the Goodyear blimp," Conrad radios in to the control tower in Torrance. "I'd like to climb to 2,500 feet because of some clouds up here."

Floating on invisible currents of air by the droning engines, the ship provides a comforting sense of bouyancy and stability—the ship floats upwards like a balloon while also suggesting that there is something solid below, as if you are floating on water. People who are afraid of flying often enjoy the experience of blimp flight. The ideal wind speed for flying an airship is a steady ten miles per hour. Too little wind over the rudder will deprive the pilot of control over the ship.

"It's a thinking man's craft," Conrad suggests, as he eases the blimp eastward, in the general direction of the Orange County Auto Show. "You can make a wrong calculation about how heavy or how light you want to go out, and it will burn ya."

From morning to night, nothing about the ship stays constant. From early morning on, the blimp gains superheat—a measure of the difference between the temperature helium inside the rubberized envelope of the blimp and the external temperature (helium heats up faster than air); with every added degree of superheat, the blimp gets twenty-five pounds lighter. Even a slight momentary shift in the wind can make the blimp impossible to land. One sunny, breezy morning, I saw John Crayton scatter his crew across the grass five times before he finally put the airship on the ground.

The low clouds have at last cleared up. "We're going to descend back down to fifteen hundred," Conrad radios in. Even in ideal conditions, the process of landing is awkward: Two long ropes hang down from the blimp's nose like a Fu Manchu mustache, allowing the crewmen to tug it down out of the sky.

Accustomed to slowness, nearly all the pilots I meet have one area of their lives in which they like to go fast. John Crayton enjoys downhill skiing. He also likes pie. "That key lime pie is good stuff," he notes sadly, patting his gut. In his three months on the job, Conrad has already developed a modest pilot's paunch, which he did not have before coming to work for Goodyear.

With plenty of flight time left to kill, Crayton gladly reminiscences about the experience of traveling with Goodyear airships on long summer trips, which used to last from May through August, up the California coastline to San Francisco and up to Portland for that city's famous Rose Festival, then over to Seattle for the Sea Fair. "When I joined in 1971, airships had a mystique about them," he remembers. "People would come out in droves to see the blimp. There wasn't the high security and the fences." Since then, the crowds have thinned out—though on their last trip through Wichita Falls, Crayton says, the blimp drew quite a crowd.

"An airship pilot is a patient person," Crayton repeats. "You get there when you get there. That may take you two hours, or it might take you five."

Sometime after the skies went dark, Crayton raised his hand. It was time for the "weigh off," in which Conrad would perform a maneuver to determine the blimp's current weight. "Now, you want to take off the aerodynamics and slow it down as much as possible, till it's standing still, and then see how fast it falls," Conrad explained. The rule of thumb is that a rate of descent of a hundred feet per minute means that the blimp is a hundred pounds heavier than E.Q. The blimp sank two hundred and fifty feet within the space of a minute, indicating that the ship was close to the ideal weight for landing.

The *Spirit of America* began its descent into Carson. The brightly lit Arco refinery in Carson was visible to our right. Directly below us, a diamond appeared on the landing field. The top of the diamond was white; the other points were flashing red.

"The object here is for Jon to fly into the diamond," Crayton explained, as the crewmen waved their lights back and forth below. Conrad cut the motor and glided toward the ground as if he were guiding a boat into a dock. The crewmen grabbed the ropes and pulled the airship down out of the sky. The vehicle rolled thirty yards, then stopped on its landing wheel.

John Crayton was pleased with his student. "Jon has some good, old-fashioned Midwestern characteristics," he said later, sitting in a trailerlike office that Goodyear had constructed next to the landing field. "He's meticulous. He's thorough."

Inside the office, Conrad gathered up a stack of flight manuals and prepared to head home. "I'm brushing up on blimp theory, blimp regulations, weather," he confided. "I feel pretty confident with weather—but you never know." He was nervous about the differences between the Snoopy blimps and the Goodyear airship. "I was used to one ballonet, and this has two," he said. Although this flight had gone well, he was still having difficulty keeping the ship in trim, and sometimes suffered from the wobbles during landings. "I hope that doesn't hurt me," he said, in his usual calm, unhurried tone.

Jon Conrad grew up next to a country airport outside Scottsbluff. When he was five years old, he used to stand by the airport fence with his dog, Laddie, and watch the planes take off; later, he would sneak onto the runways, lie on his back, and watch them land. "I always wanted to fly a crop duster, because they looked like they were having fun," he told me. Too shy to talk to the pilots, Conrad would sit in the airport waiting area and read *Rotor & Wing*. When he was about ten, he went on a summer trip out West with his family. His father took him on a helicopter ride into the Grand Canyon.

"The pilot had a beard, cool flying shades on, his headset on—every kid wanted to have one of those headsets," he recalled. "We were flying over the trees, which looked like a lawn, and then my stomach dropped as the land below us disappeared into the Grand Canyon. It was the most amazing thing I'd ever seen."

When Conrad was nineteen, he enrolled at Emery Aviation College, in Greeley, Colorado, to become a certified helicopter pilot. Upon graduating and returning to Scottsbluff, he—like the overwhelming majority of commercial flight-school graduates—was unable to find a job. A wealthy local couple had just bought a helicopter, and they hired him to fly it. When the arrangement ended, four years later, Conrad lost the cabin that he'd been living in, and his girlfriend broke up with him. Of the hundred and fifty resumes that he subsequently sent out, he received only three responses. His first job offer involved working for someone who didn't speak English; another came from a man in South Dakota who needed someone to fuel his airplanes. The third response offered him a job flying the MetLife blimps.

"I knew the blimp had engines, we were going to travel, and these guys were going to pay for my hotel rooms—and also there was free golf, because MetLife covers golf," Conrad said. "That was all I knew about blimps." The pilot who interviewed Conrad was Marty Chandler, who hired him over the phone, and told him to report to Mesa, Arizona, immediately.

Conrad arrived at Falcon Field in Mesa at 9 A.M. on a Wednesday to see the oblong craft floating on its nose above the mast to which it was tethered—a result of thermal currents in the desert air. "I'm thinking, Oh, my God, what did I get myself into?" Conrad recalled with a chuckle. "I asked whether that happened often, and the guy on watch told me, 'Oh, yeah. Out here it happens all the time.'" He spent his first flight struggling to control the pitch of the ship as it bucked up and down on the heat currents. "To be honest with you, I was a little green, but I didn't puke," he said.

A week into his apprenticeship, Conrad flew from Arizona to California through Banning Pass, up past the Hollywood sign, and then over the Pacific Ocean—a sight comparable, he said, to the view of the Grand Canyon from a helicopter. After he had been on the job for two years, a MetLife cameraman requested him for a golfing event, the first time he had been singled out for his blimping skills. Around this time, Conrad said, he began to believe that he had found his vocation—and he decided that he wanted to fly the Goodyear blimp.

"I felt like we were Shasta and they were Coca-Cola," he said. "If we wanted to know something about blimps, we had to call Goodyear. We couldn't call the manufacturer of our blimp, because they didn't know." One of the MetLife cameramen had worked at Goodyear. "He told us that we weren't good enough to fly for Goodyear," Conrad recalled. "He beat that into us quite often—that they could do amazing things with airships."

When Snoopy One spent the night at the same airfield as the Goodyear blimp in Chicago, the Goodyear crew wasn't particularly friendly. "They weren't snobbish, but they certainly suggested that they'd been around a lot longer than I had," Conrad said, with his habitual shrug.

Conrad started making occasional calls to the Goodyear airship operations headquarters in Akron, asking for technical advice from Jim Maloney, a legend even among the pilots at Goodyear. "He was extremely cordial," Conrad told me. "And every time after that I talked to him he was very helpful, too."

Maloney's father, whose name was also Jim Maloney, had flown an airship for Howard Hughes before becoming a pilot at Goodyear; most stock photographs of the singular flight of the *Spruce Goose,* the tycoon's flying wooden boat, show the shadow of the elder Maloney's blimp passing overhead. The young Jim Maloney was on board, and he was enchanted. Aware of the rigors of an airshipman's life, Maloney Sr. proceeded to block every application that his son made to fly for Goodyear, from the age of sixteen on—through college, through graduate school in electrical engineering at the University of Southern California, and throughout a successful career as a university professor and an engineer. After his father died, in 1976, the younger Maloney's application was finally accepted.

Conrad idolized men like Maloney, and was eager to become a member of their fraternity. If he did, Conrad promised, he would never leave. "I could see myself doing this every day for the rest of my life," he said happily, "and then I could retire to Nebraska, and buy myself a nice farm."

In 1925, Goodyear launched a promotional blimp called the *Pilgrim.* The company soon had a fleet of six ships, each of which appeared over the skies of America's major cities and fairgrounds. The fleet was the brainchild of P. W. Litchfield, the industrial genius who built Goodyear into the foremost tire company in the world. An MIT graduate who grew up in Boston, Litchfield appears in photographs as a tall, dignified lord of science, resplendent in gray wool suits and rimless glasses. After joining the company in 1900, Litchfield developed and promoted many of Goodyear's most successful products, including the air-filled truck tire, the airplane tire, and the standard all-weather tire tread.

It was P. W. Litchfield's unshakable conviction that blimps could serve as practical "land yachts" for the residents of inland states like Ohio.[2] His commercial interest in airships began in 1910, when, as a young Goodyear executive, he traveled to the North British Rubber Company factory in Edinburgh, Scotland, and witnessed the operation of a machine that spread rubber over fabric. He bought the machine, which was built to produce tires, and had it shipped home to Akron. Back in Ohio, he became acquainted with the publicist Walter Wellman, an airship enthusiast and later a correspondent for the *Washington Record-Herald*. With its new Scottish machine, Goodyear agreed to produce the fabric for a 258-foot hydrogen-filled airship, called the *Akron,* for Wellman and his partner, Melvin Vaniman, who intended to pilot the ship across the Atlantic Ocean. The *Akron* left Atlantic City, New Jersey, on July 2, 1912, and promptly exploded, killing Vaniman and his crew.

Litchfield was not deterred. During World War I, Goodyear manufactured about a hundred airships for the military; it also sent aloft eight hundred observation balloons, most of which blew up under enemy fire. In 1919, a Goodyear blimp took off on a demonstration of the craft's peacetime potential. It erupted into flames and crashed into the roof of a bank in Chicago, killing thirteen people, including two reporters who had gone along to record the flight. A mechanic, Henry Wacker, fell to the street and miraculously survived, thereby giving his name to Chicago's most famous thoroughfare, Wacker Drive.

In the nineteen-twenties, most of the American blimp industry switched from hydrogen to helium, a much less flammable gas which makes up 30 percent of the mass of the visible universe but is difficult to obtain in bulk quantities. In the twenties, nearly all of the world's available supply of helium was in underground deposits within four hundred miles of Amarillo, Texas. The Helium Act of 1925 gave the U.S. government a virtual worldwide monopoly on the production of the gas, which it sold to Goodyear and denied to

2. Motorized balloons were not Litchfield's invention. On September 24, 1852, Henri Giffard flew a 145-foot-long blimp with a three-horsepower engine from Paris to Trappes, seventeen miles away. In the midnineteenth century, a German pilot named Ferdinand Graf von Zeppelin embarked on a decades-long quest to build ever bigger airships with rigid hulls. His famous aircraft would later bomb London during World War I.

the company's German competitors. (Thirty-two billion cubic feet of the gas is now stored in an underground reservoir in Texas called the Bush Dome.)

In 1926, P. W. Litchfield became the president of Goodyear; soon afterward, he christened the *Pilgrim*, and began a campaign to convince Americans that blimps were the future of air travel. On September 29, 1931, a Goodyear pilot, Frank Trotter, flew an airship close enough to the spire on the Empire State Building to toss the morning papers onto the roof. The next day, Trotter returned in his airship to pick up the mail.

Trotter's two daring flights above Manhattan were the closest that America ever got to realizing Litchfield's extraordinary vision. A series of deadly airship disasters, beginning with the crash of the *Shenandoah* in 1925 and culminating with the fiery explosion of the hydrogen-filled Hindenburg in 1937, marked the end of America's casual romance with airships.

Even after Litchfield retired as Goodyear's president, in 1940, he clung to his belief that airships might have an important role to play in shaping the future of mankind. In his memoirs, he wrote, "Two or three reconnaissance airships, able to patrol the ocean from Alaska to Panama, might have prevented the tragedy of Pearl Harbor." The Goodyear blimp fleet survived as the sole incarnation of Litchfield's dream, diminishing slowly over the years until blimps more or less disappeared from the skies.

In 1958, a Madison Avenue executive named Bob Lane moved to Akron and took a job as Goodyear's vice-president of public relations. When he arrived in Ohio, Litchfield's fleet of six blimps had been reduced to a single, aging ship, the *Mayflower*, which flew over the beaches of Miami advertising Coppertone lotion for two hundred dollars a day. Lane discovered that the Goodyear management regarded the blimp as a weird relic of Litchfield's reign.

"They didn't realize what they had," Lane recalled. "It was like having the only sign in Times Square!" In his first few weeks on the job, Lane convinced Goodyear's board of directors that the blimp was a unique corporate icon, a floating, inflatable billboard whose lumbering vulnerability could inspire wonder and yearning in children and grownups alike. He obtained permission to send the *Mayflower* on a six-month tour of the East Coast. Lane's hunch was right: people lined up in the streets to see the blimp, and contacted Goodyear asking for rides.

Two years later, Frank Chirkinian, a short, energetic sports director for CBS, proposed placing a camera on board a blimp to broadcast aerial images of a football game. "I had done the Orange Bowl game in '59," he recalled. "I was impressed with the shot they had taken from an airplane flying overhead, and I thought, Well, geez . . . Goodyear has a blimp."

Chirkinian's favorite cameraman for risky assignments was Herman Lang, a CBS regular who had endured a series of escalating torments at the hands of the director, including being placed on top of a 700-foot radio tower at the Cotton Bowl and in a 150-foot crane suspended over Miami Harbor. "He always volunteered for the worst possible job, just as long as he could stay on the crew," Chirkinian remembered. "He wasn't a great cameraman by any stretch of the imagination. But he was eager."

The place for Herman Lang, Chirkinian decided, was inside the Goodyear blimp, taking shots of the Orange Bowl. He called Mickey Wittman, the *Mayflower*'s publicist. "I asked him, 'Is there enough room in the gondola?' and he said yes," Chirkinian told me. "Then I asked him, 'Have you any idea what it would cost?' and he said, 'Well, we wouldn't charge you anything, as long as you took a shot of the blimp.'"

A historic bargain had been struck that would shape the future of televised sports. A camera mounted in a blimp could help establish the physical location of an event before or following commercials, or be used to photograph formerly inaccessible places, like the back end of a golf course; the slow movement of the blimp guaranteed crisp aerial shots, and the vehicle could easily be positioned for the perfect angle on the game. All Goodyear asked for in return was "pops," occasional ground shots of the blimp accompanied by a few kind words about Goodyear tires, embedded in broadcasts of the World Series, the Super Bowl, the Final Four, and other major sporting events. The blimp reportedly gains Goodyear twenty million dollars' worth of free television exposure per year, against estimated operating costs of seven million dollars.

Although Chirkinian is grateful for what Goodyear contributed to televised sports coverage, he has never been a fan of blimps. "There's something about that big fat cow up there that does not look at all stable to me," he said. "I'm reminded of the tragedy of the dirigible in New Jersey." When I pointed out that the Hindenburg was filled with hydrogen instead of helium, he shook his head with vigor. "That image is burned in my mind forever," he said. "You can espouse all the safety factors you want, but there's something about that blimp that just bothers me."

Entranced by the sight of Jon Conrad practicing his takeoffs and landings on a Sunday afternoon, one visitor after another pulled off the 405 freeway and made his way to the Carson airfield. Whenever Conrad landed the blimp, the spectators responded with oohs and aahs. A few of them went inside Goodyear's blimp operations office, a low structure on the northern edge of the airfield, to inquire about rides. Jim Wood, a Goodyear publicist, typically handles such requests. The good news is that there's no charge, he tells them. The bad news, he adds, is that blimp rides are reserved for Goodyear's corporate customers.

The walls of the trailer's modest reception area are hung with photographs, cartoons, and other mementos testifying to the blimp's place in American life. Hanging above battered, comfortable couches are framed photographs of celebrities. There are shots of Ronald Reagan, Johnny Cash, various Rose Parade princesses, Johnny Depp, and the white-helmeted daredevil Gary Gabelich, who set a world land-speed record by driving his Blue Flame race car 622.407 miles an hour on the Utah salt flats using Goodyear tires. There is a photograph signed by the entertainer Jester Hairston with his catchphrase, "Rolly On, Amen."

Outside, the ground crew was preparing Conrad for another takeoff. John Seiuli and Sean Siatuu are two big Samoans who anchor the ropes on the blimp. Seiuli said that his neighbors were always excited to see the blimp, and often asked him for rides. He told me that he had been up in the blimp only once. "At first I was nervous," he recalled. "Then it wasn't so bad."

"It's the gentle giant of the sky," Siatuu said.

"He told me, 'You're going to have dreams about it,'" he continues, nodding to his brother-in-law. "I dreamed that some of my family from San Diego happened to stop by, but we had to walk through a trailer park to get to it."

"I dreamed it was parked in my backyard and all our neighbors were coming over and asking for rides," John Seiuli says, before adding, "I think everyone on the crew has the dream where it flies away."

Jeff Robinson, the crew chief, said that he thought Jon Conrad would make a good pilot. "He's relaxed and kicked-back," he said. "I think he'll do real well." He added with a laugh, "I've been here for twenty-three years, and he's the first new pilot I've seen, so who really knows?"

As a pilot-in-training, Conrad was not yet allowed to ferry passengers. Instead, he had spent much of the day's training session wearing "foggles," dark sunglasses with lenses that have been severely sandblasted, save for a small rectangular cutout. The lenses, which made Conrad look like the villain in a cheap sci-fi movie, allowed him to see the instrument panel but not the windshield. By restricting his view in this way, the foggles would help teach Conrad to land the blimp in heavy fog or other conditions that impede a pilot's vision.

Three men to a rope, the crew walked the ship away from the blimp mast, a thirty-foot pole in the center of the airfield. As the blimp bounced softly down the runway, the crew heaved it into the air. The maneuver, known as an "upship takeoff," provided Conrad with an additional angle of lift.

With Crayton at his side, Conrad circled the landing field. Using instruments as his sole guide, he swooped low over the field and then headed back up into the sky. At a height of a thousand feet, Crayton unexpectedly told him to take the blimp up another two thousand feet, above the afternoon cloud cover. At three thousand feet, the blimp was buffeted by an upward gust of wind. Conrad shook his head, annoyed. The blimp wobbled.

"You know you have a big wind up here," Crayton chided. "You know you have to be more aggressive."

Conrad's other problem was that the blimp was at least three hundred pounds too light, thanks to the superheat added by the ascent above the clouds; direct sunlight can make the blimp lighter in a hurry. As Conrad tried to bring the ship down low over the Links of

Victoria Golf Course, which is adjacent to the airfield, the extra lift queered his approach. The blimp was so light that it felt as if Conrad were trying to force a cork underwater. The assistant crew chief, Tony Sanico, waved him off. Conrad had botched the landing. Crayton told him to start over.

Conrad retracted the blimp's landing wheel and headed into the clouds again. He circled over the 405 freeway, then returned for his second attempt. He floated momentarily over the high-voltage wires to the west of the airfield, then brought the ship down low enough for the crew to catch it. But this time he hit the ground roughly, forcing the crew to let go of the dangling ropes. Once more, Conrad retracted the wheel and pushed forward on the throttle. On his third try, the crew caught the airship's ropes, then tugged the reluctant craft toward the mast, securing it by its nose.

"I thought we were going to stay below the clouds," Conrad explained, after climbing wearily from the cabin. For the first time in two weeks, he looked exhausted. As he walked back down the runway, his brow was glazed with sweat.

"I should have taken off heavier than I did," he said. "I got a good workout today. I'm not a real ball of fire right now. I'm spent."

As usual, John Crayton's advice was short and to the point. "During the transition to instrument flight you were a little sloppy with your tracking," he said. "You recovered nicely. You came to your decision point. Your timing was right." Crayton paused. "Did you come back in the correct weight configuration?" he asked.

"No," Conrad said glumly.

"He's much better than when he started," Crayton said, after his student had gone off to study. He had a few doubts, however. "He hasn't quite got the smoothness yet," he said. "He still makes mistakes."

The crewmen who work with the Goodyear blimp do not think of it as an inanimate object. Forever expanding and contracting, the blimp comes to resemble a living thing. The "A-watch," which begins at eleven at night and ends at seven in the morning, is when the blimp's true personality is said to emerge. Fabian Furriel, who had been on A-watch for the past four nights, has served on the blimp crew for the past sixteen years.

Furriel is famous among the other crew members for his peculi-arities, which include the practice of wearing his Goodyear summer uniform of shorts and a short-sleeved shirt year-round, rain or shine, even in the snow. If you ask him whether he's cold, he answers back, "Define cold." Then he stares straight at you, in a not-unfriendly way, just intent on hearing your answer. "Define wet," he will sud-denly say. "Define happy." No matter what kind of definition you give, he will explain to you why your answer is wrong. Leaving the office just after 11 P.M., Furriel walked down the field toward the air-ship, whose ghostly creaks and clanks echoed through the heavy fog. Under his arm, he carried the *Spirit of America*'s immaculate log-book, which will minutely chart the craft's vital signs, hour by hour, for the next ten years or so, until its demise.

"I do a walk around the mast, check the cables, the mast junction box," Furriel said, describing how he typically began his evening routine. The blimp's envelope, he said, weighs 3,772 pounds, is made from 2,400 square yards of fabric, and comes in a box that's about the size of a small van.

As the blimp slowly tracked around the mast, a rainy pitter-patter on the asphalt seemed to get heavier as the airship moved toward the patch of grass where we were standing. The blimp sheds water at night, and in the morning can often be found surrounded by a pud-dle of water.

For the next eight hours, Furriel stayed in constant motion while giving me a series of lectures on the operation of his favorite craft, the one thing in his life that he had ever mastered, he said.

"That yellow box, that's the handrail junction box," he said. "That gives us the main power from the mast." He resumed going down the checklist in the logbook.

"You've got the pressure switch box, the blower cable, the dome light, the rectifier—that's a fancy word for a hanging battery charger," he said, barely drawing a breath as he grabbed the railing of the blimp car and swung into the cabin. "I make sure the wheel lock is installed, and the gas blower is working. That's a fan that blows air into the forward ballonet. If we have a storm and need to maintain pressure, we have the gas blower on continuously. As the outside temperature cools down, the helium cools down, and that creates a void. The void has to be filled. I like to use the analogy that the ballonets act like a pair of lungs."

Hooked up to cables, boxes, and switches, and shedding water at a furious rate, the airship at night resembled a sick whale on life support. Hanging out of the pilot's side window was a pressure switch box, which was connected to four plastic tubes that took readings from different areas of the ship: the forward ballonet, the aft ballonet, the bottom of the helium-filled portion of the bag, and the center of the leviathan's belly.

"Each hour, we take a set of readings," Furriel said. "The outside temperature. The temperature of the helium. Wind velocity. Amount of fuel aboard. The pressure settings." At midnight, the air temperature was 51°F, the helium was at 46°F, and the wind velocity ranged from zero to five knots. The ship was carrying a 126 gallons of fuel. The pressure was currently at 1.5 inches, Furriel explained, which meant that if a person somehow climbed on top of the blimp and jumped up and down, it would feel very much like a moon walk at an amusement park. Adjusting the switches inside the car, Furriel ran the gas blower for a couple of minutes to pump a little more air into the fore ballonet. The *Spirit of America* flew best slightly nose-heavy, he said.

"Life? Define a life," Furriel said, when I asked him how standing A-watch had affected his life. "I started Wednesday night, and I'll do this till Tuesday morning. I go to church. On Tuesday night, there's a men's study group."

He often dreamed about airships, he told me. "Blimpmares, that's what I call them," he said. "Most of the dreams I have are fatal to the airship." His dreams had included collisions in which propeller planes and helicopters tore through the blimp. He recalled that in 1990 a twenty-eight-year-old man named John Moyer crashed a radio-controlled plane with a four-foot wingspan into the Goodyear *Columbia,* ripping a foot-long gash in the envelope. The airship was forced to make an emergency landing at the Carson airfield.

Standing in the back of the blimp cabin, Furriel stuck his head up into a giant Plexiglas bubble. A catenary curtain, which draped over the balloon and held it tightly in place, was visible as a dark scalloped swath of fabric at the top of the bag. Cables suspended from the curtain connected it to the top of the car.

At around one o'clock, Furriel climbed outside and polished the underside of the car as it slowly drifted and bounced around the mast. By 3 A.M., the air temperature had reached 49°F, and the blimp was hovering three feet off the ground. Inside the main envelope, the helium purity level was at 98.9 percent, meaning that very little air had leaked. It costs about twenty thousand dollars to fill a blimp with helium, Furriel said. By 4 A.M., the blimp was hovering eight feet above the ground; the helium, trapped inside the insulating balloon enclosure, was now substantially warmer than the chill outside air. Furriel hauled the blimp back down and added weight by tossing four bags of lead shot into the cabin. Although he had been up with the blimp for five nights in a row, he did not complain of feeling tired. "Sooner or later, the airship takes over your life," Furriel admitted. At 5 A.M., Fabian throws another two bags into the ship, then sticks his head up into the astrodome. The superheat reading is now at zero.

"In a rainstorm, can you build superheat?" he questions, delving once more into the mysteries of his chosen craft. "It's the radiant heat that builds up," he triumphantly explains. "I was with the blimp once in the middle of a snowstorm and it was building superheat," he says, gesturing into the fog. "That doesn't show up in your Fahrenheit reading. But it's there."

Having just completed the written portion of his Goodyear pilot's exam, Jon Conrad was being grilled on his answers by his examiners, Don Ploskunak and John Crayton. The men sat around a brown Formica table inside the office. Conrad was wearing his American-flag tie. Ploskunak, a tall man who resembles a Texas football coach, was wearing a green polo shirt and dark sunglasses.

"Do you know how shot bags are put together?" Ploskunak asked.

"Yes, a crew member showed me," Conrad answered.

Ploskunak looked down at Conrad's answer sheet, and he read the young pilot's answer about the ideal pressure for the *Spirit of America*'s helium balloon. "You wrote, 'Pressure should be between one and two inches,'" he said. "We prefer to come in at two inches." It wasn't clear whether Ploskunak thought the difference was significant.

"You wrote down that the maximum rate of descent is one thousand feet per minute," Ploskunak continued. "Fourteen hundred is the figure we use."

Conrad protested that the figure given in the pilot's handbook was one thousand feet. Ploskunak checked the handbook. "We tested it out at fourteen hundred," he said sternly. "But the book does show one thousand." He looked down at Conrad's answer sheet again.

"Why do we hook up the rip line to the rip handle when the ship is on the mast?" Ploskunak asked.

"That way, the ship will deflate if it comes unmoored," Conrad answered.

"That way, your blimp doesn't take the mast with it and land in a cornfield somewhere in Missouri," Ploskunak teased. When Conrad was interviewing for the Goodyear job, he admitted that once, while he was piloting for MetLife, the Snoopy One had flown off its mast, traveled a hundred miles, and crashed into a barn filled with coffin linings in rural Missouri.

As the questioning continued, the scene became reminiscent of a graduate student taking general exams in a proudly esoteric subject, like Aramaic grammar. Ploskunak and Conrad discussed the fine points of superheat and volleyed opinions about landing techniques. After an hour, the three pilots broke for lunch.

"He's got that real laid-back, lighter-than-air attitude," Ploskunak told me. "He's probably ready to fly."

In the afternoon, Conrad headed outside to board the *Spirit of America* with Ploskunak and Crayton. For his flying exam, he was told, he would have to do some figure eights above the local stadium, then bring the airship home.

"Okay, gang, this is Jon's big day," Crayton said, addressing the crew. The test was to last from one until four. Conrad was in the pilot's chair, with Ploskunak to his right; Crayton sat behind Conrad, offering a comforting presence. Conrad started the propellers, and the crew jerked the airship fifteen feet into the air. As the crew watched, Conrad gunned the engines, and the ship angled upward about thirty degrees and crept up into the sky with elephantine grace.

Hanging for a moment above the field, Conrad paused to retrim the ship. The nose was awkwardly high.

"If you don't do such a steep climb, you won't have to retrim," Ploskunak advised.

Conrad climbed to 2,600 feet. Flying over the Home Depot Center, a new soccer stadium, he expertly simulated some TV-event maneuvers, making left-hand box-pattern turns around the stadium. Then he performed figure eights.

"Ballonet blowers on, props forward, mixture's rich, slow my speed down," Conrad reported. Ploskunak took occasional notes and issued terse instructions.

"Turn left," he said.

"The nose feels like it doesn't have enough air in it, so I'm going to put some air into the nose," Conrad said, as he readied the craft for his first landing.

"You don't want to put too much air in the nose," Ploskunak cautioned. "You don't want to plow into the ground."

"This is my favorite part," Conrad said calmly, as the ship approached some high-voltage wires near the airfield. Coming in low amid very light winds, a pilot has comparatively little control over his craft. "I don't have anything to work with," Conrad said. For a moment, the airship hung in the air above the power lines. The cockpit was silent as the blimp made its landing approach. The ground crew broke into a trot and grabbed for the ropes, as the ship floated slowly back to earth. The landing was perfect. Crayton shook Conrad's hand.

Later, Crayton gathered the crew around the mast and made a little speech. "We welcome you to a fraternity of pilots that's seventy-seven years old," he said to Conrad, handing him a box with his silver pilot's wings—a winged Goodyear blimp. "And one more thing we have here as part of the process," he added, stepping neatly out of the way so that the crew could dump two buckets of water over Conrad's head. Conrad smiled, and then went inside to the pilot's lounge, dripping wet, to call his parents, Jack and Norma Conrad, back in Scottsbluff.

"Well, I got my wings, finally," he said.

"Well, I thought your test was tomorrow!" Jack Conrad joked. "Congratulations on that."

Conrad was already thinking about his first solo flight as a Goodyear pilot. "I can't wait to get down to San Diego and flash these babies," he said, pointing to his new wings. "As far as being a blimp pilot goes, it doesn't get any better than the Super Bowl."

Two days before the biggest sporting event of the year, the *Spirit of America* hovered four feet off the ground at Brown Field in San Diego as, nearby, platoons of Navy SEALS drift slowly down to earth from gray C-130 transport planes in preparation for the invasion of Iraq. The SEALS have attracted the eye of Demetrius Hammond, the quiet man who climbs the mast to attach and reattach the blimp. Hammond, who grew up in Compton, joined the Army Rangers at eighteen and saw action in Grenada, Panama, Iraq, Haiti, Bosnia, and Kosovo. "I still jump every six months just to keep in shape," Demetrius explains.

Docked nearby were some of the blimps owned by the Lightship Group. The Sportsbook.com blimp was a third the size of the *Spirit of America* and came equipped with a flame-themed paint job that would have been at home on a souped-up Camaro. Jon Conrad ambled around the field, drinking a Coke. On Sunday, he'd be flying the Goodyear blimp solo back to Carson. His crew chief from his Lightship days, Ben Archer, works across the field on the Sanyo blimp. He stops by for a visit, offering his friend a hug before stepping back to check out his new wings.

"How do you like the new boys?" Conrad asks, nodding his head toward Sanyo's A-150.

Archer grimaces. "They like to go off the mast heavy, about 250 down," he says.

The Lightship crew chief looks around the airfield at the fifteen-member traveling crew, the semi and the bus with the Goodyear logo. Conrad takes his old crew chief to see the mobile riggers shop inside the semi.

"How many mechanics do you have?" Archer asks.

"Three with us," Conrad answers.

"How many technicians?"

"Four."

"How much does all this cost?"

"A lot," Conrad says proudly.

All week long, the *Spirit of America* had been taking exclusive aerial shots for various pregame shows on ESPN. The live footage was captured by a large Gyron camera, a giant black-and-white eyeball that hung out of the blimp cabin's left door, clamped between a heavy pair of brackets. Javier Estrella, a Goodyear cameraman, beamed back dreamy, brooding shots of the city's glittering esplanade and its sports arena, QUALCOMM Stadium.

Estrella would be returning to the sky that afternoon with Tom Matus, the oldest, most experienced pilot on the crew. Before takeoff, Matus stood beside the *Spirit of America* holding an empty bottle of Wisk laundry detergent. It was his "wickie bottle," he explained—the vessel into which he relieved his bladder while flying.

A natural charmer, Matus has the genial, boasting manner of an ex-athlete who is popular at local bars. He likes to describe himself as "the handsomest pilot." He has been flying the Goodyear blimp since 1968—before Conrad was born. An admirer of astronauts, Matus is proud to have taken Buzz Aldrin on a blimp ride. Above his desk in Carson, he keeps a signed picture from the legendary test pilot Chuck Yeager, inscribed to "The man with the 'Light Stuff.' "

Matus, who is one of the best storytellers on the crew, promptly filled me in on the origins of wickie bottles, which go back to an extra-innings Dodgers game in the nineteen-seventies. "We lost a shot in the fourteenth inning and the director was furious," he recalled. "Fourteen innings—a man's got to take a leak." He told me that he had kept the same wickie bottle for years. "When I retire," he added, "I'm going to nail that thing to a nice piece of walnut."

Matus was taking the blimp out for its final flight before Super Bowl Sunday. Bidding goodbye, he climbed into the cabin, then signalled to the ground crew for a rolling takeoff. He started low, with the crew running alongside the blimp, and lifted off, heading over the runway. The airship angled sharply upward—too sharply. The blimp was suddenly out of control. Its tail wheel smacked into the ground with the sound of tearing metal. The ship bounced once more and headed back up into the sky. Below, the crew stopped in their tracks. Carved into the grass near the runway was a twenty-foot-long scar.

Crayton watched the accident from the ground. "He dinged the tail wheel," he said, in a worried voice.

The Goodyear blimp hung in the air like a wounded bird. The airship's rudder wasn't working properly, Matus reported by radio. With a broken rudder, the craft would be difficult to land. When the *Spirit of America* made contact with the ground, it bounced awkwardly.

Using the wind to push the ship sideways, the crew backed the blimp onto the mast. Steve Dien and Mike Spurlin, two mechanics, shined their flashlights on the underside of the aircraft. In addition to the dinged tail wheel, the tri-pulley for the starboard-side control cables had flipped over and needed to be flipped back into place. Matus walked across the field alone, his shoulders slumped in his Goodyear flight jacket, his wickie bottle by his side.

"The sun will shine tomorrow," he said. "It will be a better day."

On Saturday morning, however, things looked even worse for the Goodyear crew. Dien, the chief mechanic, told everyone the story of what had happened during A-watch. At 1 A.M., Dien found that a pulley controlling the upper rudder had come loose. He also discovered that a rivet had been sheared off the blimp's frame. At seven in the morning, Dien called Crayton, who called Jeff Sassano, the ponytailed chief rigger, to report that there were "major problems with the airship."

At 10 A.M., the crew reported to the field, but winds were high, making it impossible to do repairs. The bump on the runway couldn't have come at a worse time. To skip flying today not only meant the loss of another chunk of free airtime for Goodyear; it also meant leaving the skies to Saturn and Sanyo. Crayton shook his head. Later in the afternoon, he hoped, the wind would die down and repairs could proceed.

At six o'clock, the crew reassembled on the field. There was no wind. Four hours later, the field was dark and the men were still working. Goodyear's most experienced pilot had crippled the airship on the eve of the Super Bowl.

When dawn broke on Sunday morning, the *Spirit of America* was ready to fly. Overnight, Crayton reported, the crew had fixed mechanical problems, including the loose pulley, that usually took a few days of hangar time to resolve.

The *Spirit of America*'s readiness for flight was particularly good news this morning. Owing to security concerns about terrorism, the federal government had ordered the airspace closed within a seven-mile radius of QUALCOMM Stadium from eleven o'clock on Sunday until the end of the game. The Goodyear blimp would be able to make some game-day appearances before heading back to Carson. Demetrius Hammond sings an old Army Ranger song as he marches across the dew-laden field at 6 A.M. with his climbing harness slung over his shoulder. The rest of the crew soon gathers by the mast.

"I want to thank all you guys again," announces Steve Dien. In under three hours, he says, the crew fixed a problem that would usually take a day or two to solve.

"Today is going to be a heavy off-wind rolling takeoff, which means that you're going to pull the ship and align it with the runway, and keep tension on the lines," John Crayton announces, after praising the men for their work of last night.

At 6:30 A.M., Crayton climbed into the cockpit of his airship and took off in the direction of Qualcomm Stadium, followed closely by the Saturn and Sanyo. At 10:55 A.M., with the temperature climbing, a trio of blimps floated back over the horizon. Goodyear was again in the lead. Charlie Russell, another pilot, was waiting with Jon Conrad on the ground. "Most people couldn't live this way," Russell said, yawning.

"Your wind is out of the southeast, very, very light as of now," Conrad advised Crayton via radio. Conrad's former teacher steered the airship toward the landing field, as the crewmen tried to tug it down to earth. The blimp hovered thirty feet above the ground, and then started to float back into the sky.

"Let it go, let it go!" the ground chief called out as several crewmen fell onto the grass. Crayton's next three tries didn't go any better. Thanks to the superheat, the ship was now at least five hundred pounds light. On Crayton's fifth pass, the crew wrestled the ship to the ground and loaded on another eight hundred pounds of ballast.

It was Jon Conrad's turn to fly. The flight home to Carson might take three hours, he joked, putting on his pilot's shades. Then again, it might take five.

"I need a good upship, guys," Conrad said. He checked the instrument panel and the toggles, and then gave the ground crew a big thumbs up. The crew gathered around and tossed the great rubber blimp into the air. It bounced once and headed up into the sky, with its nose at an elegant angle of twenty-six degrees. Leveling off at fourteen hundred feet, Conrad headed west; on the ground was Celine Dion's jet, which had ferried the singer to San Diego to sing "God Bless America."

The no-fly zone was now in effect. At 11:32 A.M. on Super Bowl Sunday, the skies over San Diego were empty. For the moment, the Goodyear blimp was the only craft in the sky. And Jon Conrad was the only pilot.

The long reflection of the afternoon sun slanting off the Pacific suggested the inspiration for countless California rock-album covers of the seventies. "The Goodyear ten-alpha is up and green—excellent job on the ground," Conrad said. He slowly steered the blimp toward the sea. At a thousand feet, you could see the waves breaking three hundred feet offshore. A plume of what looked like white smoke rushed to the water's surface, leaving a lacy filigree in its wake.

"Crayton was planning on coming back at E.Q., and he came back five hundred pounds light, and he's been doing this for thirty-one years," Conrad said when I asked him what he'd learned in his first full week as a Goodyear pilot. "That's the nature of airships. Just when you think you've got it figured out, you don't."

Conrad's legs bobbed up and down as he talked. "As a kid, I used to love watching Disney on Sunday night—a world that was just happy and peaceful—even for an hour," he said. "Well, that's exactly what it feels like up here."

Flying over the Pacific is the equivalent of highway driving; the even temperature of the ocean means there are no thermal currents to navigate, allowing the blimp to quickly pick up speed. At five hundred feet above the water, and with the wind at our back, our speed increased from twenty to thirty-four knots as the ship sailed over the flat, dark ocean, past Dana Point to Laguna Beach. The visual excitement was above us, in the clouds—the cotton-ball-like stratocumulus and, even higher, the wispy altocirrus, and the two enormous conelike cloud towers off to our right. A powerful convective lift drew moisture thousands of feet straight up into the air.

"If we saw that in the Midwest, that would tell you there might be some activity by the afternoon," Conrad explained. The skies over

Carson were clear. Shifting the engines into neutral, Conrad assumed a look of peaceful concentration as he let the ship drift gently downward over the Links of Victoria Golf Course. It took about a minute to descend seventy-five feet; the ship's landing weight was perfect.

The Carson airfield came into view. Four hours after leaving San Diego, the blimp had arrived only minutes after the ground crew's truck, which had broken down twice along the way. Below, the exhausted crew members gathered around the mast, eager for an easy landing so that they could go home, see their families, and watch the Super Bowl on TV. Conrad pulled down on the right forward damper toggle to put a little more weight in the nose. He paused when I asked him for the time.

"I stopped wearing a watch once I began my association with airships," he said. "It was either that or find a new job."

A Fistful of Peanuts

I.

The real-life process of electing a president of the United States can be understood as a single-player game like Pac-Man, the old Reagan-era arcade favorite in which a smiley face devours a trail of luminescent yellow dots—each dot in this case representing a bundle of $3 million or $4 million assembled by a team of fund-raisers in a hotel banquet hall near an airport. The circuit of fund-raising events having been set up in advance by the president's finance team, the goal is for the bundlers to pack the rooms with $2,000 donors while the candidate gobbles up enough campaign-funding dots to placate the pollsters and the phone-bank gods and to keep the image makers happy while avoiding Inky, Pinky, Blinky, and Clyde. George Bush's total of 130,000,000 in 2004 campaign dollars was more than the combined Pac-Man scores for Howard Dean, John Kerry, John Edwards, Wesley Clark, and the rest of the president's Democratic opponents. Individuals who write checks, out of conviction or for sport, are largely irrelevant to the campaigns. We are only pixels—fractions of a dot.

The Houston Galleria is a perfect place for the president to run up his score. It's the best shopping mall south of Los Angeles. Actually, the Galleria is four malls in one. The old Galleria, Houston's original luxury indoor shopping mall, has a year-round ice-skating rink, so you can shop and skate in the middle of July, when the temperature climbs over a hundred degrees and the humidity is so bad that the outdoor parking offered at inferior area malls can be hazardous to your breathing. In addition to the ice-skating rink and multilevel indoor parking, the Galleria features more than 2.4 million square feet of retail space and more than 350 fine retail establishments, including Neiman Marcus, Macy's, Tiffany & Co., The Sharper Image, Ralph Lauren Collection, Lord & Taylor, Houston's only Nordstrom outlet, Church's English Shoes, Gucci, Louis Vuitton for luggage, Jacadi Paris for nursery clothes, Baccarat for crystal, and a jewel-like Prada boutique nestled inside the cashmere-soft womb of Saks Fifth Avenue.

With the new wing that opened in March 2003, the Houston Galleria became the fifth-largest mall in the nation, a temple to America's thriving addiction to shopping. The new wing employs nine types of stone and several more of wood, suspended glass balconies, plush leather seating, skylights, a Starbucks, three premium office towers, and two Westin hotels—the Westin Oaks and the Westin Galleria—which are popular destinations for luxury-brand shoppers from Mexico City as well as for wealthy Houstonians, nearly 700 of whom have gathered this afternoon in the Galleria banquet room to pay tribute to the forty-third president of the United States, George W. Bush. Houston is a city that belongs more to the president's father, George H. W. Bush, the forty-first president, who represented Houston's seventh congressional district between 1967 and 1971. After losing the 1992 election to Bill Clinton, Bush 41 retired to Houston, where the local airport was renamed in his honor.

"On the boats and on the planes, they're coming to America!" Neil Diamond's stentorian voice rings out.

"Today? Today! Today!"

"Oh, wow," a pretty girl in a party dress exclaims. The music is turned up so loud that most of the Sunday-afternoon crowd has no choice but to drink pretty heavily in preparation for the president's arrival, still more than an hour away. In the middle of the windowless function room, which suggests a cross between a casino floor and a concrete bunker, are three round tables decorated with an electric-lit Lone Star boot set in the middle of the canapes. The vegetable platter on each table includes a selection of freezer-burnt carrots and cauliflower, while the cheese plate offers supermarket-sliced sticks of smoked gouda and cheddar. Deep-fried items that look like egg rolls appear on closer inspection to be quesadillas; the breaded heart-attack chicken fingers are unaccompanied by dip or sauce. The high, round cocktail tables scattered around the room boast finger bowls filled with peanuts and pretzels, to alleviate the rigors of the open bar. Altogether, a dedicated scavenger working these tables might be able to put together the equivalent of the in-flight meal on a commuter flight to Phoenix. Barely any of the food has been touched.

Chad Sweet is a perfect candidate to be raising money for George Bush in Houston. A handsome, dark-haired young banker who works for Goldman Sachs, Chad looks like a grown-up version of one of the rich preppy characters on Fox's nighttime teen drama *The O.C.* One thing that makes Chad a likely fund-raiser for George Bush is that his boss at Goldman, Peter Coneway, was a big Bush fund-raiser in 2000. Just when I am thinking that Chad Sweet's name is too good to be true, a pretty girl in the party dress introduces herself as Chad's sister. A friendly, peaceful-seeming young woman, she is wearing a maternal but sexy halter dress; she supports the war in Iraq, she says, "regardless if there were any weapons of mass destruction or not." What matters, Chad's sister explains, is that the president did something. He acted, and acted decisively, in defense of America's children, and Sunday afternoons at the mall.

By the nearest pretzel table, I meet two young lawyers, Jesse and David, who work for a powerful Houston firm that represents clients in the oil and gas business. I tell them that I am in town to write a movie about baseball, which is more or less true.

"You should try to go to a game here in Houston then," Jesse says. "The stadium is great."

"There's a retractable roof," David adds. "It's kind of cool. It can retract in five to seven minutes."

Jesse calls out to his friend Patrick Hughes, a tall, dark-haired attorney in his midthirties, who walks over and shakes everyone's hand.

"I'm glad I'm not the only one who wrote a check," Patrick says. "It seems like everyone I talk to says, 'Hell, no, I didn't write a check.' "

"I didn't have a choice," Jesse says. "There's a lot of muscle in my office."

"I'm really getting tired of it," David says. Jesse and David don't give their last names, because the senior partner in their law firm is a major donor to the Bush reelection campaign who yearns to represent the United States as an ambassador to a foreign country. ("I think any country will do," David says.) In keeping with customary practice in recent Republican and Democratic administrations, nearly two dozen of Bush's biggest contributors, many of them only casual acquaintances of the candidate himself, received the keys to U.S. ambassadors' mansions in foreign countries in return for their prowess in assembling big bundles of cash; Robert Jordan, senior partner in the Houston-based law firm of Baker Botts, is the current U.S. ambassador to Saudi Arabia.[1] Fund-raisers pledge to meet target amounts and are assigned a tracking number, which appears on every check they bring in to the campaign. Those seeking the campaign's highest fund-raising designation, that of "Ranger," must come up with the equivalent of a hundred personal checks for $2,000 made out to "Bush-Cheney '04." Those who bring in $100,000 worth of checks are "Pioneers." There are performance incentives along the way. Those who raised at least $50,000 for the Bush campaign's kickoff dinner in Manhattan on June 23, 2003, were treated to a special off-the-record "leadership luncheon" with Karl Rove, the president's chief political strategist. By recruiting his sister, her husband, and another eight friends, coworkers, and business contacts to buy ten $2,000 tickets to this afternoon's event, Chad Sweet has earned himself a photograph with the president and the First Lady in a smaller ballroom upstairs, where he is marking time right now along with the other fifty or so bundlers whose big-

1. Our quadrennial fund-raising rituals must take place in crappy banquet halls because of three decades' worth of "reform laws" that prohibit any individual from donating more than $2,000 to the political candidate of his or her choice. The result is a system in which ambassadorial hopefuls like Robert Jordan must round up bushels of checks from friends, relatives, vendors, contractors, and young attorneys who hope to make partner. In the 2000 presidential campaign, nearly 60 percent of the money that George W. Bush received came from 59,279 donations of what was then the maximum legal amount of $1,000—more than triple the number of maximum donations compiled by any competitor. Proof of the easier availability of $2,000 checks to the Bush campaign in 2004 is the fact that fund-raisers no longer receive credit for donations gathered by those they recruited, as they would in any decent incentive-based network marketing system, like Amway; they get credit only for checks that they hoover up themselves.

money contributions are represented in the ballroom below in human form.

"It's not like it was back in the eighties," explains Patrick Hughes, who works for Haynes and Boone, a Dallas-based firm with what is reputed to be the largest white-collar-defense practice in Texas. "There's been some oil and gas fallout," he adds, when I ask for signs of economic damage from the terrorist attacks, recession, and war. "Oil traders, every twenty years they go bankrupt." A fan of George Bush, he is accustomed to his lowly status as a pixel, a serf on the campaign-finance farm. "This is more than I expected," he says, when I complain about the paucity of my $2,000-a-plate spread. "I'm going to get myself a piece of that chicken."

Mixing with the plebes by the bar is Joe B. Allen III, the politically wired former senior partner of the Houston super law firm Vinson and Elkins. He left the firm after the Enron debacle. A Bush Pioneer in the last election, he is standing with a spidery, desiccated-looking lobbyist in a blue-and-white seersucker suit, a Dust Bowl vision of Uncle Sam.

"This isn't exactly our second rodeo," Allen confirms. Vinson and Elkins provided more money for George Bush during the last election cycle than any other corporate entity in Texas. "There are very few people in Houston you can point to and say these are the Bush people," he confides, over the blare of "Living in America," the James Brown number. "The key people are mostly in Midland and Dallas."

A Vinson and Elkins secretary is lurking nearby, dressed all in pink. "I do love Laura Bush," she confirms, when I ask her if she enjoys dressing like the First Lady. Together we scan a small knot of ladies in pink silk suits and Hermes scarves, representatives of a spooky subterranean world where everyone loves George W. Bush, or is eager at least to score points with the boss. The secretary is understandably reluctant to give me her name. She works for partner Thomas Marinis, another lawyer for Enron.

The next donor I meet is more forthcoming. Willie Carl of Beeville, Texas, is a pleasant, moonfaced man who proudly claims to be the owner of two ranches in addition to a hunting spread and an office building downtown.

"Well, good for you!" he exclaims with real pleasure, when I tell him that I'm from New York. When I mention the summer humidity in Houston, he claps a friendly hand on my shoulder. "We have air-conditioning," he explains.

A History Channel buff, he also enjoys watching programs about current events. "I'm a Tony Blair fan," he says. "Did you get to hear that Tony Blair speech on Fox? I thought he was Patrick Henry—'Give me liberty or give me death!'" Willie Carl chuckles. "I've had two British friends, they're both dead, one died of cancer and the other flew a plane into the ground," he says in a speculative voice, as if wondering what conclusions a man in late middle age might rightfully draw about the transience of all flesh. When I ask about the absence of Stetson hats in the room, he gives me a doubtful glance.

"I've got an uncle here, he might have on his Stetson," he says. "He was probably the last guy in Houston to take off his open-road hat." He looks mournfully out at the trickle of well-dressed men and women who are now joining the crowd by the bar. "You remember LBJ's hat? Well, that's the same one. The open-road hat. There's a lot of different Stetson hats and they all have different names. I wear my Stetson when I go check on the ranch, where we have exactly two cows, which is about all the cows that you really want."

All in all, he says, George W. Bush has done America proud in the years since he was elected president.

"This kid, he's a real person. I'd give him my last dollar so he could be president for the next four years," he says. When I ask him why he isn't upstairs with the president and the First Lady right now, he sighs, loud enough to make me feel bad for asking.

"I've had all I need," Willie Carl says, with maybe a touch of defiance, tucking his thumbs in his hand-tooled black leather belt. "Enough to pay for my $2,000 egg roll and live in a million-and-a-half-dollar house, paid for, and enjoy my 3,000-acre rice farm. I just don't have any money, that's all."

II.

"Well, gang, we are doing well in Texas," says the tall, silver-haired man at the podium, Fred Meyer. His sunburnt skin glowing against his white shirt, dark suit, and blue tie, Meyer stands with an easy, aw-shucks manner before a patriotic backdrop in which the flags of the United States of America and the Lone Star Republic of Texas are given equal billing.

"In the 2000 election, it was Texas that led the nation in financial contributions to the GWB campaign," Meyer says with an easy grin. "Ladies and gentlemen, we're going to do it again in 2004."

A former captain of the Purdue Boilermakers' marching band, where he played the piccolo, Meyer is a natural master of ceremonies. His ecumenical demeanor hides the true face of one of America's most terrifyingly successful political fund-raisers, the man who transformed the Texas Republican Party from the sleepy, relatively impoverished back-office operation it was in 1988, when he took it over, to the triumphant financial and electoral juggernaut it is today, with Republicans in all twenty-nine statewide offices, including two senators, the governor and lieutenant governor, and speakers of the house and the senate. As chairman of George W. Bush's Victory 2000 campaign, Meyer directed Republican fund-raising throughout the fifty states, then he served as fund-raiser in chief for the presidential inaugural. Over the last six weeks, Meyer explains, the Bush-Cheney '04 campaign has raised more than half of the total raised during the entire eighteen months of the 2000 campaign. To Meyer's right, a sign-language interpreter spells out the symbol for financial contributions with a wide gesture of her hands, indicating the size of the Bush campaign's recent haul.

"Your money goes first and your heart goes afterward," Meyer says, in a soothing voice. "But they're both together once your money's in the till."

Having explained the facts of life to any doubting hearts in the audience, the former state party chair now goes on the offensive, attacking "the media, trial lawyers, and various extremist groups that are constantly harassing the president and the programs that the majority of the American people support." Then he nods benignly, looking out over the audience of secretaries, lawyers, contractors, subcontractors, and big-money fund-raisers, still glowing from their $20,000 photo ops with the president and the First Lady.

"Our president has integrity beyond question," he intones. "Our president does what is best for all Americans. Our president will stay the course, and he has the courage to do that. And he will again demonstrate to this country the great, strong leader that he is."

The big-money donors in the crowd this afternoon have reason to applaud. To date, 43 of the 538 known Pioneers from the 2000 campaign have been rewarded with federal appointments, including ambassadorships to France, Spain, Switzerland, the Netherlands, Portugal, New Zealand, and more than a dozen other countries, as well as positions with various government boards and commissions. Two of the 2000 Pioneers have made it into the president's Cabinet: Labor Secretary Elaine L. Chao and former governor Tom Ridge of Pennsylvania, director of Homeland Security. Still, it would be wrong to characterize the sponsors of tonight's event as being interested merely in accumulating fancy letterhead and foreign vacation homes at taxpayer expense. They are here after bigger game. John W. Johnson of Permian Mud Service, Inc., is interested in tax laws and the regulatory structure that governs the energy business. Pat Oxford works for Bracewell and Patterson, a large Texas law firm that represents banks. Stephen Payne, a lobbyist, has plenty of clients who are interested in contracts with Halliburton or its local subsidiary, the construction firm of Kellogg, Brown and Root—lifelong backers of the last Texan president, Lyndon B. Johnson, and the recent recipient of U.S. Army contracts for services in Iraq worth a potential $7 billion. Tom Loeffler, head of the law firm of Loeffler, Jonas and Tuggey, another sponsor of today's event, knows the ins and outs of such arrangements better than anyone else in the room. As the congressman serving George W. Bush's hometown of Midland, Texas, he made friends with the president early on, sharing his interest in hunting, football, baseball, and politics. As a lobbyist, he came to represent Tom Hicks, who made George W. Bush rich by buying his shares in the Texas Rangers baseball team, a transaction that allowed Mr. Bush to run for governor. Loeffler has represented the Monsanto Company, the American Gaming Association, and the Nuclear Energy Institute, a corporate umbrella group whose members profit greatly from the Bush administration's energy policies.

That the presidential photo-op crowd has come downstairs to mingle is a clear signal that the president himself will soon be on his way. As bundlers and small-time donors alike crowd the stage, I find myself next to a tall, blond, fit-looking man named Steve Papermaster, who was just upstairs with the president and who says he spent "plenty of time" at the governor's mansion in Austin.

"We love the Bushes," says Papermaster's pretty blonde wife, Kathy. "They're incredibly warm, wonderful, gracious people. I don't think that being in Washington has changed them one bit."

Once mentioned as a possible cabinet member in Bush's administration, Papermaster never made it to Washington. Instead, as the head of Agillion, Papermaster became one of the most visible symbols of the late 1990s' tech-stock madness in Austin, spending $3 million on a 30-second advertising spot to promote his Internet company during the 2000 Super Bowl. According to a recent lawsuit filed against Agillion and Papermaster, the company succeeded in attracting only "a few dozen" customers for its services; revenues were so inconsequential, the lawsuit states, "that management never recorded a single dollar in revenue in their internal bookkeeping." Nevertheless, Papermaster spent half a million dollars to take Agillion's employees on a trip to Cabo San Lucas, Mexico, where he donned a sombrero and addressed his staff through a wireless microphone while cantering his horse along the beach. In 2001, Agillion bought another Super Bowl ad. Six months later the company filed for bankruptcy.

If Steve Papermaster is in the market for lessons about how to spend his shareholders' money, he could do worse than to look to Michael Dell, one of the sponsors of this afternoon's event. After contributing $250,000 to the Republican National Committee in 2002, Dell received a seat on the President's Export Council, as well as a $500 million contract to provide computers to the Pentagon—a two-thousand fold return on the Austin tech entrepreneur's initial investment—for less than one-tenth the cost of one of Papermaster's Super Bowl ads. Equally instructive is the story of Rich Kinder, the former president of Enron. Healthy and tan, he stands near his wife in a privileged corner by the stage, having suffered no apparent damage from his former employer's implosion; he left the company in 1996 with a $200 Swiss army watch on his wrist and a $30 million severance package. He also took Ken Lay's personal secretary, a woman named Nancy McNeil. After divorcing his wife Anne and marrying McNeil, Kinder started buying up Enron's tangible assets, parlaying his golden parachute into three companies with a combined market capitalization of $13.5 billion.

To the high-society gossips in the crowd, this afternoon's successful fund-raiser for the president is the second leg of a social trifecta that began with Nancy Kinder's successful fund-raising ball for the Houston Museum of Fine Arts last year and will conclude with the completion of the $12 million house the Kinders are building on Houston's Lazy Lane. Those with more earthy interests will note that Rich's company, Kinder Morgan, is the largest publicly traded oil—and gas-pipeline limited partnership in the United States. With 25,000 miles of pipeline and 80 terminals, Kinder Morgan moves 2 million barrels of gasoline and other petroleum products per day, and up to 7.8 billion cubic feet per day of natural gas. In a June 11, 2003, conference call with analysts and investors, Kinder laid out the current state of his business.

"The Texas pipelines have been experiencing pretty good load; that's of course a lot of hot weather in Texas," Kinder explained. "And our Rocky Mountain pipelines have been running pretty full, too."

Earlier that day, Kinder Morgan announced that it would increase its dividend 167 percent, from $.60 to $1.60 per year. The increase in the dividend made sound business sense, Kinder assured David Fleischer, an analyst at Goldman Sachs, thanks to the current occupant of the White House, who would continue to serve for the next four and a half years.

"We would expect continuous increases in the dividend on a going-forward basis," Kinder informed his fellow corporate contributor to the president's reelection campaign. "Assuming that this tax regime is in effect, and it will be, I'm sure, through 2008."

After a short intermission, Fred Meyer returns to the stage, accompanied by white-haired Houston banker Ben Love, the former chairman of Texas Commerce Bancshares (now part of J. P. Morgan Chase), and the state's governor, Rick Perry.

"It's my great honor to introduce our great friend, a strong leader, a great Texan. He's led America with a strong hand and a clear vision," Meyer says, gesturing broadly at the man to his right. Having raised $4 million the previous evening in Dallas, then spending the night on his ranch in Crawford, the president of the United States looks calm and relaxed in a dark navy suit. He's a healthy athlete at the top of his game, standing in a patch of empty space in front of the American flag. His wife, Laura, stands beside him. "He's shown

the world his commitment to—to values, and freedom," the fund-
raiser offers. "Ladies and gentlemen, the president of the United
States."

III.

"First let me say, it's great to see so many familiar faces," George
Bush begins, nodding at the crowd. "A couple of them scolded me
when I was a kid." Nodding his head like a schoolboy at the applause, he continues with the traditional invocation. "A lot of the
people in this room worked hard to see to it that I became the governor, and I want to thank you all for your continued friendship and
your support," he says, allowing a little down-home Texas grit to fil-
ter into his voice. "I want to thank you for your loyalty to our country,
and I want to thank you for comin' tonight."

Editorialists don't like the president. His blunt talk, the way he
stands with his legs apart, his very political DNA inspire a fevered
hatred in the one third of the electorate that can be counted on to
vote Democratic, a hatred that in turn inspires a reflexive support of
the president in the reliably Republican third of the electorate. Like
Bill Clinton before him, his aim is to capitalize on the hatred of his
foes and the support of his friends in order to win over the remaining third of the electorate to the proposition that he is a reasonable-
enough man who is doing his best to keep America strong and safe.
With the hatred of the left assured, and no shortage of threat warnings on the evening news, he operates in a gravity-free zone, discard-
ing his previously stated political positions whenever the mood
strikes him, or he sees the potential for gaining another few thousand votes. Gone is the president's dislike of nation-building and foreign adventures, his opposition to affirmative action, his preference
for balanced budgets, his opposition to increased immigration, and
other keystones of his carefully focus-grouped persona from the
2000 campaign. Freed from the laws of political gravity, the president can decapitate unfriendly regimes, occupy foreign countries,
rewrite the tax code, and plan to send astronauts to the moon and
Mars while turning a $200 billion surplus into a $500 billion deficit
and thereby buying the favor of the uncommitted middle at zero risk
to his political base.

Bush makes an after-dinner joke about a recent encounter with a pair of mating elephants in Botswana. "Learned a lot more about our party's mascot," he says. As he speaks, it is possible to hear the father's clipped, East Coast Yankee accent beneath the son's Dust Bowl drawl. The president gets a laugh.

"We're going to need your help at a grassroots level," he says, rehearsing the lines of the stump speech he will deliver another ten dozen times before the election next fall. "We're going to need you to talk to your neighbors and to send out the flyers and put up the SIGNS and turn out the VOTE."

He tunes up the Texas in his voice another notch. "And I'm gettin' ready," he says, flexing his shoulders to an appreciative laugh. "And I'm loosenin' up." The crowd laughs again. "It's a funny time for politics," the president reflects. "Right now, I'm focused on the PEOPLE's business in Washington, D.C."

By hitting the word "people" a bit too hard, the president has thrown himself off his rhythm. He looks mad. "We will continue to work hard to earn the confidence of all Americans by keeping this nation secure, and strong, and prosperous, and free," he recites, with a scowl. Her head tilted to the side, Laura Bush focuses her attention on a point somewhere out there in middle space. She has complemented her pink suit this afternoon with a silver necklace.

"I'm glad Laura is here tonight," her husband says, with an appreciative nod. "I love her a lot, and I hope she loves me a lot for dragging her out of Texas." The crowd hollers at the phony gallantry, but one look at Laura Bush's face during such moments is enough to convince even the most hardened observer of political spouses that her husband is serious—the First Lady couldn't care less about health-care policy or haute-couture dresses. Laura Bush hides in plain sight, projecting a steady beam of approval that doesn't disguise the fact that she would rather not be up here on the stage. What the First Couple have in common isn't politics but rather the fact that they grew up in Midland, where their early lives were marked by death and by the excessive consumption of liquor. George W. Bush lost his sister and grew up to become an alcoholic. Laura Bush killed a high school friend in a head-on collision. Now she's the First Lady and he's the president—a pair of privileged people who suffered and then cleaned up their act, a born-again Tom and Daisy Buchanan who have learned that they are no better than the lowest wretch.

The president is duly grateful. He praises Rick Perry, the tall, boyish-looking Republican standing to the president's right, as "the right guy to be governor of Texas," because he "watches the people's money very closely," and he thanks Nancy Kinder for "puttin' on this party tonight," as well as everyone else who worked so hard. Then the president turns to his left, searching out a familiar face in the crowd.

"I want to thank my friend Tom DeLay for being here," the president says, acknowledging the old Republican dragon from Sugarland, Texas. A sallow-faced former pest exterminator known as "the Hammer," DeLay is the majority leader of the U.S. House of Representatives. His latest contribution to the national debate is something called STOMP—the Strategic Task Force for the Organization and Mobilization of People, a group of specialized volunteers who, according to the congressman's Web site, will be deployed across the country in time for next fall's elections.

"Congressman DeLay is a leader . . . ," Bush says, his voice trailing off. What more is there to say? Tom DeLay is a nasty piece of work, the type of friend who is best kept under wraps.

"Lieutenant Governor David Dewhurst is here," Bush says, adding insult to injury by ungratefully lumping the majority leader in with a procession of state and local officials, including the speaker of the Texas House of Representatives and Joe Nixon, a patsy for the health-care industry who was named one of the worst legislators in the state in the July 2003 issue of *Texas Monthly*.

"I came to this office to solve problems," he announces, "not to pass them on to future presidents and future generations."

Invigorated by the declarative strength of his lines, the president stands up straight behind the podium. "Terrorists declared war on the United States of America, and war is what they got," he pronounces. "We have captured or killed many key leaders of Al-Qaeda. And the rest of them know we're on their trail. . . . Those regimes chose defiance," he says, manfully resisting the urge to squint, "and those regimes ARE NO MORE."

The president nods his head in self-assent, then presses on. At the words "morale was beginning to suffer," the sign-language lady makes a sad, sinking motion with her hands.

"Fifty million people . . . once lived under tyranny. Today they live in freedom," the president proclaims, in a measured voice, leading up to the clincher. "We acted."

He leans back a bit from the podium, satisfied. In two words, he has summed up an entire political philosophy. He is the anti-Hamlet. His role is to act.

"We have twice led the United States Congress to pass historic tax relief for the American people," he says, falling back into his folksy accent. "It is not the government's money. It is the people's money. We're returning the money to the people—help 'em raise their families." His next line needs no folksy accent to go over with the crowd: "We're reducing taxes on dividends and capital gains to encourage investment." If the president's 2,600-word stump speech has earned him a record $2,700 per word over the last twenty-four hours, these are no doubt the most profitable words of the day.

"We are challenging the soft bigotry of low expectations," he says. The applause-getting line from his last campaign lands with a thud. He squints out at the crowd. Clearly no one out there gives a hoot about dismantling affirmative action anymore. "The days of acute thinking are over," he promises. Or did he say "excuse making"? Waving his hands, he summons forth "new markets for America's entrepreneurs and farmers and ranchers." Then he essays a fib so large that not even the friendliest hometown audience can possibly believe him.

"We passed a budget agreement that is helping to maintain spending discipline in Washington, D.C.," he says, bouncing on his heels for extra emphasis. The crowd is silent. Even some of the less acute thinkers in the room are aware that the budget is fundamentally out of whack. The Bush administration enacted a 6 percent increase in nonmilitary, non-homeland-defense-related government spending in 2002 and an almost 5 percent increase in 2003. By 2008 the country will be another $1.9 trillion in hock, whether we are still in Afghanistan and Iraq or not.

"Our country has had no finer vice president than Dick Cheney," the president says. The applause for the former Halliburton chief is just barely respectable, as many of the people in the audience study their shoes. No one in this room wants to end up like Dick Cheney, a pasty-faced heart-attack man locked away in a bunker somewhere.

"Mother may have a different thought," Bush says, after a pause, completing the punch line to the joke. Relieved, the audience gives the president his biggest laugh of the day.

"On the continent of Africa, America is now bringing the healing power of medicine to millions of men, women, and children now suffering with AIDS," he assures his friends. Shazam! It's happened again, right there on the stage. In a flash, just like Bill Clinton, the man who defeated his father, then balanced the budget, slashed welfare, and used U.S. government jets to fly business executives to China, Bush has used the opening supplied by the anger of his political enemies to morph into the opposite of the man who ran for office, busting the budget, adopting a starry-eyed program of nation-building, and saving African children from AIDS. At moments like this, when the president hits his rhetorical stride, it is interesting to contemplate the conceivable limits on his actions. A moment later the answer becomes apparent. The man can say and do whatever he wants.

"We need to cut down on the frivolous lawsuits that increase the cost of medicine," Bush offers. Pursing his lips as he lashes out against lawyers "fishing for rich settlements," the president of the United States seems weirdly angry. Putting his hand to his brow, it takes the president a moment or two to calm down. "We must be less dependent on foreign sources of energy," he suggests. It's not a bad suggestion. Then again, the Zamboni driver on the Galleria skating rink upstairs might lose his job. In the "ownership society" of the future, the president promises, every American will be "empowered" to own his or her own home, health-care plan, and personal-retirement account. What Americans must understand, the president explains, is that we alone are responsible for the decisions that we make in life.

"Absolutely," someone calls out. Encouraged by the response, Bush warms to his theme.

"It is you who is responsible for lovin' your child!

"If you're concerned about the quality of the education in the community in which you live, you're responsible for doin' somethin' about it!

"If you're a CEO in America, you have the responsibility to tell the truth to your shareholders and your employees!"

The president's voice drops like Elvis Presley's in the talking parts of "Love Me Tender." "In responsibility society, each of us . . . ," he says, turning all heavy-lipped and pouty, "responsible for lovin' our neighbor . . . jus' like we'd like to be loved ourselves."

The message is clear: in the new America, there will be no more government sugar tit to suck on—except, of course, for the fortunate few in the audience. A young couple near the Papermasters are making out. The girl—brown-skinned with high cheekbones, bare-shouldered in a black dress with embroidered tulips—is kissing her boyfriend, a blond, bleary-eyed preppy in a white shirt and navy linen suit, as the president praises "the vibrancy of many of the faith-based organizations and neighborhood healers that are concerned about saving lives." Although the phrase "neighborhood healers" might be unfamiliar to the well-heeled crowd at the Westin, it will surely resonate later this year with those of the president's supporters who believe in snake handlers and voodoo charms, as well as with the increasing number of Americans who lack affordable health care.

"All the tests of the last two and a half years have come to the right nation," the president says, his head up and chest thrust forward in a pigeon-toed stance, like a runner crossing the finish line.

"Abroad, we seek to lift whole nations by spreading freedom. At home, we seek to lift up lives by spreading opportunity to every corner of America," the president says. The crucial element of his pitch is the word "we." George Bush and America are a single character, ready for action.

"May God bless America," the president says.

IV.

For those not wealthy or powerful enough to merit a photograph with the president upstairs, there is always the rope line after his speech. The art of the rope-line campaign photo op requires the balance of a halfback to make it through the scrum, as well as the participation of a willing accomplice whose shutter-finger reflex is fast enough to capture the grinning donor in the two- or three-second window before the president moves on to shake the next hand. As President Bush walks the rope line, donors hurl themselves forward, grabbing for a golden handshake with the Man. "Stop pushing, stop pushing," someone says. Grinning broadly, his hair plastered across his forehead, an Indian gentleman leans over the rope at a 45-degree angle as a coworker photographs the president clasping his forearm. "Good work," the Indian man says, as he shakes the president's hand.

Halfway down the rope line, the president whips out his Sharpie. Like everything else that happens at these events, the move has been choreographed in advance by the president's handlers. In the time it takes to pose a single photograph, he can sign three or four items, suitable for framing.

Emerging from the hectic scene, those who succeeded are naturally elated. "I did feel his animal magnetism, yes," says the secretary from Vinson and Elkins. A younger black man in the crowd is also pleased. "I'm a homebuilder. I'm trying to do a little modeling and acting on the side," he explains, as we compare our experiences shaking hands with the president. From what I could tell, in the second and a half that I shook his hand, the president is a man in peak physical condition. He has an athlete's grip. I found his handshake firm and dry, with a well-timed squeeze at the end. It's a terrific handshake, the homebuilder agrees. A middle-aged ethnic Chinese man named Morgan Lin pops out of the pile; he has brought with him a delegation from Sugarland. "I supported him as governor," he says of the president. "No better man than him."

"Look here," I say, showing him the back of my invitation to the event, on which the president has signed his name with bona fide celebrity flair.

I find Chad Sweet in a quiet corner away from the bar. "9/11 changed everything," he says. "I was pretty active, but a moderate Democrat. Socially, I felt stronger on the Democratic side. I was prochoice. Republicans, for the most part, they're fiscally more sound, and national-security-wise, you can't beat the Republican Party." And yet there are things about the Republicans that puzzle him still. "Historically, the Republican Party is the party of Abraham

Lincoln," Chad says. "I don't think we need Kevlar-coated bullets or automatic weapons, I'm in favor of safety locks, but people ought to be able to own a gun."

Ideologically, what Chad Sweet has in common with his new-found friends in the Republican Party is that nothing he says makes any sense. But politics isn't about coherence anymore. That the version of George W. Bush that exercises power today with the support of a clear majority of the American people is so radically different from the candidate who was rejected by a majority of the American electorate three years earlier has a number of obvious causes—the bombing of the World Trade Center, the evil of the radical Muslim fanatics who attacked us, the belligerence of the president's advisers, the inept diplomacy of Colin Powell, and the president's skill at the political game. But the bottom line, as always, is us. Americans are dreamers. The pursuit of moderation and humility has never really been the American way, and, as Bush learned in 2000, it makes a poor slogan at election time. We are in no mood to stop driving SUVs or to give up skating at the mall in July. Chad Sweet sticks out his hand. The banquet room is almost empty. It is time to say good-bye.

V.

Upstairs, by the skating rink, local kids in Ecko Unlimited and Phat Farm gear are watching the Zamboni circle the ice. Skating at the Polar Ice concession costs $6 if you bring your own skates, $9 if you don't. The electric bills here must be incredible. I peek into the nearby Abercrombie & Fitch, a riot of gravel-ground authentic vintage camouflage fatigues with jump straps hanging out everywhere. It's military chic, the dreadlocked clerk explains. Beneath the Starbucks is a music store called FYE, which means "For Your Entertainment." There are racks and racks of CDs by the Byrds, the Butthole Surfers, Da Brat, DJ Screw, Del Tha Funkee Homosapien, and hundreds of other artists—a fact worth mentioning only because I'd never heard of FYE before I set foot in the Galleria. I ask Susan, a pretty, blonde-haired clerk who is walking the aisles, how many FYE outlets there are in America.

"I couldn't even tell you," she says, her blue eyes glazing over at having to contemplate something so vast: "I can't tell you how many there are in Texas." Behind her is a cutout of a G.I. in combat fatigues standing next to a cutout of George W. Bush. I ask her if she knew that the president was here at the Galleria today. She shakes her head no. I show her the president's signature on the back of my invitation to the $2,000-a-plate event. She stares curiously at the back of the card.

"What does it say?"

The question catches me off guard. I look more closely at the president's signature. It comes in three distinct parts, I notice—a bold "G," the last half of the letter "W," which looks a bit like a "U," and the last two letters of Bush.

"It says 'Gush,' " I say. "Or 'Guze.' "

"G'Us," she says, peering over my shoulder. "It says 'Gus.' "

"You're right," I tell her, examining my presidential souvenir in the unblinking twilight of the Galleria mall. "It's Gus."

The Blind Man and the Elephant

I. A Layman's History of Sports for the Blind

What better way could there be to spend a cold and rainy afternoon than in a closed rehearsal space at Wayne State University in Detroit, jamming on some of the best-loved songs of the sixties and seventies in preparation for the one day every year that unites Americans of every race, religion, and creed while the rest of the world is watching soccer? The horrible sleeting rain, and the cold, and the gray skies, can hardly dampen the mood inside where an all-star cast of performers and musicians including India Arie and John Legend blow through a rehersal for tomorrow's pregame performance, and then jam on Coltrane's "Giant Steps." Wearing a nubby African-themed muumuu, his hair in neat braids that an adept of celebrity hair culture might recognize as extensions, the genius at the piano bench is now forty years older and well over a hundred pounds heavier than when he was stealing the show from Smokey Robinson, Marvin Gaye, and the Supremes. Shaking his head from side to side, and flashing his famous smile to all four corners of the room, he pounds out ecstatic and surprising changes with his left hand, which is the repository of not one brilliant career in American music but three. The first career, enjoyed between the ages of twelve and twenty-one, was as the blind boy with the harmonica who became one of the most popular recording artists in Motown history. The second career, which followed the star's creative emancipation from Motown at the age of twenty-one and his discovery of the synthesizer, included such classic jams as "Superstition" and "Sir Duke," and concluded with a brilliant and strange biotic orchestration, "Journey Through the Secret Life of Plants." In the 1980s he

made a third career as a theme-song wizard and a singer of saccha-
rine duets with the likes of Sir Paul McCartney. Oh, what would it be
like to inhabit, if only for a fleeting moment, the magical, ever-
expanding three-dimensional headspace of this mischievous individual, now fifty-five years old, who delights in being able to play
every instrument in the studio better than the hired hands who have
been known to walk off the stage out of sheer exasperation at having
to compete with the master-blaster, whose dominion extends not
only over the piano and the harmonica but also over the drums, the
bass guitar, and the funky, nasty, dirty, stinking Clavinet?

It is hard to imagine a more appropriate choice than Steveland
Hardaway Judkins Morris, better known as Stevie Wonder, or just
plain Stevie, to provide the pregame musical entertainment at
Super Bowl XL, the latest and most profitable incarnation of the
biggest big event in American history. What better choice to enter-
tain the restless continental abstraction that threatens to engulf the
planet than a prolifically funky New Age adept who founded his gigantic career on the principle of oneness under a groove? The NFL's
invitation arrived less than a month ago under public pressure from
the people of Detroit, who were mad because the league was planning to host the biggest party in the city's history and not invite any
of the city's world-famous black musicians to play. A compromise
was reached: Stevie Wonder would play the pregame show and introduce a medley of Motown hits, while the Strolling Bones, of London, England, and Montserrat and various other offshore tax havens
that shelter their global touring income, would take center stage at
halftime.

The last time Stevie Wonder opened for the Rolling Stones was in
1972, when Detroit's greatest-ever musical genius was barely
twenty-one years old, newly emancipated from Motown, and with
all the hit records of the 1970s still in front of him. More than three
decades later, the Stones are still the biggest band on the planet, and
Stevie Wonder would still be an opening act in his hometown.

As the musicians carry their instruments offstage, Stevie stays behind, talking on a cell phone, occasionally sweeping his head from
side to side to give the crowd of distant relatives and well-wishers at
the foot of the stage the impression that they are being seen. It is no
secret that Stevie believes that his blindness is a gift from God. The

world the musician inhabits might be interpreted as one in which the experiences of depth, distance, size, color, and proportion normally provided by the visual cortex have been remastered into a unified cathedral of sound. By suggesting that he can see, Stevie stakes his claim to the completed version of humanity that sighted people unthinkingly reserve for themselves. He enjoys playing little pranks that put sighted visitors at their ease, commenting on the color of their shoes or neckties and otherwise suggesting that he is not, in fact, blind, a suggestion he often reinforces by slipping words like "watch" and "see" into casual conversation.[1]

All of Stevie Wonder's children can see. Aisha Morris, best known as the wailing infant celebrated in "Isn't She Lovely?" a favorite of doting dads and wedding band singers the world over, will sing onstage with her father tomorrow along with her siblings Keita, Mumtaz, Chad, Kwame, Sophia, and Kailand, and Aisha's son, Miles. Stevie walks over to the piano bench, picks out a chord for one of his sons, and discusses some family business. "I wanted them to come and see Detroit, and meet some of the people that I know here," he explains, once his children have scattered. "I wanted them to see snow. I prayed for snow. You don't have snow in Los Angeles, unless you head up into the mountains."

Detroit is where Stevie Wonder made his name. "I have so many amazing memories," he says, tilting his head toward me and leaning forward in order to create a more intimate space between us. "I remember as a little boy one incident that is always amazing to me, tied to Detroit and Wonder Bread. There was a thing," Stevie says, using his all-purpose word for a song, a riff, a happening, or an ad on TV, "a commercial that said, 'Wonder Bread, when you squeeze the package, it says 'fresher.' '" Delighted, he imitates the commercial announcer's high-pitched voice again. "Fresher!"

Stevie Wonder's stories are loose and open constructs that allow

1. In 1999, Stevie Wonder briefly made headlines for his interest in a surgical procedure that would have fit him with an intraocular retinal prosthesis, but the operation never panned out. Seeing Stevie's children gathered around the piano reminds me of a line with which Lulu Hardaway, Stevie's mother, reportedly dismissed a girl who threatened to bring a paternity suit against her son when he was still a teenager: "If that baby comes out black, blind, and playing the harmonica, then I'll believe you."

the singer to convey the enduring capacity for amazement suggested by his name. As he speaks, I realize there is also something about the secondary manifestations of his blindness, the exaggerated way he lets his head flop from side to side, that suggests he has recently arrived from a distant planet, a playful, gigantic black baby who has absorbed all terrestrial sounds and language in a single gulp.

"I wanted to get that Wonder Bread, and my mother wouldn't get it," he remembers, establishing the key of the story. As he remembers the past, the register of his voice ascends to a high childish tenor. "I said, 'I want dat Wonda bread!' Because I wanted to hear it say 'fresher!' " he explains, imitating the sound of air escaping from a plastic bag. "So I had my mother drive all through every single grocery store, all over Detroit, to find the one that would say 'fresher!' 'Here's one, squeeze it, see what it says!' 'Fwhoosh.' " Wonder's face falls at the sound he just made. "Fifteen or twenty minutes into the thing she figured it out. So she said, 'Here, squeeze this one.' And then she said, 'Fresher!' " Wonder laughs. The saving power of imagination can make anything real. At the age of twelve, he recorded a number-one single. When his voice changed, his record sales went flat, and he was shipped off to the Michigan School for the Blind.

"When I heard 'For Once in My Life' when I was eighteen, I had another interpretation," he says, executing a smooth quarter-turn on the piano bench to face the instrument. His hands poised above the keys, he gives a little head shake.

"For once in my life! I have someone to hold meeee!" he brays, as his hands hit the keys and he pounds out a few bars of the white man's version of the standard.

"Which is beautiful," he says, deadpan. "Tony Bennett did a great job of it." Shaking his head from side to side, he then parodies himself, playing a jumpy stride piano and singing in a high staccato tenor.

"For! Once! In! Mah! Life!"

No one makes fun of Stevie better than Stevie. "I think that kind of sound, the timbre, is a sound that goes all the way back to Africa. You mix that with church, with gospel, with listening to different pop artists," he explains, when I ask him about the emergence of his distinctive vocal style. "Also, I think it's important to be in character when you sing a song. That's what we call reading a song. If I'm singing a song like this," he says, putting his fingers back on the keyboard and picking out the same melody he has played twice before, lifelessly intoning the words, "that's nothing. It's bullshit."

At age sixty-two, the great blind singer may no longer be interested in the ecstatic highs and the heartbreak and the all-night songwriting jags that fueled his greatest work of the 1970s. His performances have become rarer, and it's been over twenty years since he recorded anything that could reasonably be called a hit song. At the same time, he is recognizably the same artist who melded jazz, electronic music, soul, funk, and pop to create a new kind of American music. Where most of his peers need teams of backup singers and musicians to sustain the bare illusion that they can still hit the high notes and the low notes, Stevie Wonder's skills as a musician are undiminished by time and his voice has never sounded better. I joke with him about why he never released an album of funky Clavinet riffs like the one at the beginning of "Superstition."

"There is such thing as a groove. You can get into a groove. You heard some of the rehearsal, right?" he says. "We were just jamming on 'Giant Steps.' Something as great as John Coltrane, improvisation is endless," he says, spreading out his broad, strong fingers and attacking the left side of the keyboard until it yields an impossibly funky sound.

"You have a bass line like that, and you're playing on top of it, and you just feel it, then it just goes on and on," he says, as he continues to play, his whole body filled with an enviable alertness. "I listened to Parliament, to Funkadelic. I listened to Sly Stone. I listened to some rock artists that came. I listened to James Jamerson, the bass player for the Funk Brothers," speaking of the legendary backbone of Motown's house band. One of the greatest bass players ever, Jamerson played on more number-one hits than the Beatles; he got paid $10 a song and then drank himself to death after Motown moved to Los Angeles.

I ask Wonder about his song "He's Misstra Know It All," from his album *Innervisions*.

"It can be for a man or for a woman," Stevie explains. "Miss-tra. Though the song is basically in the 'he' form. It's about a person who thinks they know everything, you can't tell them nothing, they're out of control."

"Did you have anyone in particular in mind when you wrote the song?"

"One time I smoked some grass, and I said, 'Oh, shit. Am I talking about myself?' " Stevie laughs. Where Michael Jackson mutilated his face and skin, Stevie Wonder was blessed by nature with a disability that made him better able to understand and live with the deeper fictions that support our national life. Color-blind from birth, he is the boy genius with the full-dress orchestra inside his head and unlimited access to the the best instruments and best musicians and the biggest recording studios in the world. He is the Temptations, the Four Tops, Marvin Gaye, the Supremes, James Jamerson, Ray Charles, Earl Hines, Sly Stone, and the Beatles rolled up into one. He is the pregame show at this year's Super Bowl.

Now that Stevie Wonder has stopped playing the piano and is taking a few moments to give some final instructions to his kids, this seems like as good a time as any to haul out my own pet theory about sports in America, which is that each of our major team sports gains its narrative interest by mirroring the evolving contradictions in our national psyche. Baseball, played in a green pastoral setting enclosed in the built-up space of a city, subjected farm-boys from Oklahoma and Kansas (now Puerto Rico and the Dominican Republic) to the exacting discipline of base paths, rules, uniforms, and set positions. As visceral entertainment, rather than as an exercise in gentle nostalgia, baseball ceased being adequate to the emotional needs of most Americans once the demographic balance of the country shifted from country to city to suburbs after World War II. Basketball, with its delicate balance of the freewheeling individual and the team, became a vital American sport in the sixties and seventies, when it provided post-urban-riot America with the satisfaction of watching young black men in shorts and T-shirts playing together with whites, and being disciplined by middle-aged men in suits, a pleasure that was fatally reversed by the rise of highlight shows on ESPN that specialized in the no-look pass and the dunk. Football, the national sport of the moment, marries the fading industrial assembly-line work ethic with the modern craft of remote-control warfare waged from glassed-in booths where grainy reconnaissance photographs are analyzed on the fly. It is no accident, then, that the cost of a 30-second spot during this week's Super Bowl is $2.5 million, up from last year's record of $2.4 million, which was almost seven times the cost of a 30-second spot in the 2004 World Series, when the Red Sox finally won.[2]

Sitting on his piano bench, on a rainy gray afternoon before the biggest Super Bowl in history, Stevie Wonder can only feel one piece of the elephant at a time and try his best to extrapolate the whole.

"Technology is the same everywhere, so the sound does get homogenized. What I do find with Detroit more than any other city is that there was such a melting pot here, so you have the sounds of the people that originally came from all these countries in Europe, who came from the slave trade, and you can hear these influences in the instruments and the grooves." He garbles some made-up stuff, a funny rap that I recognize from his album *Innervisions*.

"That was because I used to mock the sounds that I heard on the radio. I was just making up some stuff. 'I'm from Beirut. I speak, uh, very fluent Spanish. Iraq. Iran.' It was funny to me. As a little boy, I could hear on one station, WJLB, I could hear polka hour, and then you would hear maybe some Italian music, and then some Spanish announcer, then you might hear some Greek thing happening, then some R and B might go down. I knew that my skin was black. I couldn't understand why there was a difference. It was like a joke to me. Because I felt, that thing within me told me, that God made everyone. Growing up as a little boy, I had music that I liked, and it

2. The NFL is well aware of its vital and lucrative place in the content-provider universe. The league recently announced that it will broadcast a package of eight games next season on the league's own cable channel, allowing the league to keep all broadcast revenues for itself while controlling all aspects of the broadcast, and continuing to further its reach through the NFL's proprietary Web, cell-phone, and satellite radio–based networks: NFL.com, NFL Mobile, and NFL Radio. At a press briefing during Super Bowl week, the NFL's commissioner, Paul Tagliabue, unfolded the league's imperial vision of football's crowning event. "The Super Bowl now takes on a magnitude that almost defies the imagination, and it is due to many things, among them the passion of the fans, how the game completes each season of terrific competition and crowns the champion," Tagliabue intoned, adding that the $600 ticket price for the Super Bowl "is actually pretty restrained and conservative."

was from different people, different cultures, different languages, I just thought it was all wonderful music, great stuff."

On the other hand it's quite hard for blind people to understand football, he explains, since most of the action makes sense only when seen from above.

"I used to be a crazy wrestling fan back in Detroit, listening to the British announcer on CKRW—this is way back in the days of Dick the Bruiser and Leaping Larry Chene and all that stuff," the singer remembers with pleasure. "You'd wrestle around your mother's house and break furniture and all that crazy stuff. Body-slam! You're throwing your brother across the room, you hear the sound of a lamp, the lamp breaks. It was exciting, you know what I mean?"

I ask him what team he wants to win, and he smiles and playfully shakes his head.

"You know my team. If you think real hard about it, you'll know my team." he says, almost singing the words. "I believe my team is going to win."

II. Marvin and Smokey

Detroit, when Stevie Wonder grew up there, was home to nearly 2 million people; today, the city's population is 950,000, one quarter of whom live at or below the federal poverty line. On "Black Monday," the week before the Super Bowl, the city's unemployment rate of 14.5 percent received a significant boost when Ford Motors cut nearly 30,000 jobs. It was in this atmosphere of headlong decline that Detroit's mayor, Kwame Kilpatrick, decided to tear down the old headquarters of Motown Records to make room for another fifty parking spaces for the Super Bowl. This being Detroit, no one bothered to save the contents of the building, which included Marvin Gaye's desk and the Motown studio production logs.

Wandering in the shadow of Ford Field on the evening before the game, I find myself in the vestibule of the Music Hall, a second-rate theater from the 1920s with the original details still pretty much intact and posters advertising a recent performance by Chaka Khan. In the foyer near the coatroom, "Tracks of My Tears" is being rehearsed by a pickup string section, overseen by an older black man in a woolen overcoat.

"You're not coming in together," he warns the two violinists in the back row, who keep messing up. Smokey Robinson will be playing the Fox Theater tonight, in a concert organized by Don Barden, a black casino magnate. I hang around for most of the afternoon and early evening in a windowless room in the basement of the theater where the performers wait for Smokey to arrive. I spend most of my time here with Marvin Tarplin, a skinny guitarist in a black tuxedo, whose square glasses give him a perpetually wondering look. The only touch of glamour in his entire getup is a gold ring that he wears on his right hand.

"It cost about sixty or seventy dollars," he says, when I admire the ring, which is shaped like a gold nugget. "My daughter was buying some jewelry so I decided to get it." He grew up on the West Side of Detroit as a big country-and-western music fan, he says. "I used to listen to Casey Dark's jamboree on the radio in Detroit back in the midfifties," he says. "I sent off for this mail-order guitar that was advertised on the show, I think it cost $29.95."

He started off playing guitar for his friends Mary and Florence, who sang with a third friend from another high school and called themselves the Primettes. When Smokey Robinson heard the Primettes sing, he signed the band to Motown and renamed them the Supremes. Then he stole Marvin Tarplin away to play guitar and write music for the Miracles.

Smokey Robinson's favorite guitarist is more of a baseball fan than a football fan, he says. In his spare time, he also likes to play the slots at the casinos where Smokey plays most of his gigs. What he loves most of all is music. I ask him about "Tracks of My Tears," one of the greatest love songs to come out of Detroit. "I wrote that," he says. His method was simple.

"I'd sit in my room and put something on tape," he explains. "If Smokey liked it, then he'd write some lyrics, and we'd have a song."

As show time approaches, Tarplin begins to get antsy. "I've never been in a place where they didn't have a can of soda for the performers," he complains. "I always take a soda with me onstage." I feel bad that the man who wrote so many great songs doesn't get a soda.

"What flavor do you want?" I ask him.

"7-Up."

The soda machine in the corner of the room is out of 7-Up. There's Coke, Diet Coke, Lipton Iced Tea, and grape soda.

"Grape," he answers, happily.

I ask him about the song "Going to a Go-Go."

"I wrote that too," he says. Marvin Tarplin wrote the music for nearly every one of Smokey Robinson's famous hits. "I stole plenty," he explains. "What I'd do is take the figure in a song and then turn it around." "Tracks of My Tears," he explains, is simply an inverted version of Harry Belafonte's "Banana Boat Song"; Stevie Wonder then stole the song again to write "Tears of a Clown," which he gave to Smokey Robinson as a Christmas present. When I ask Marvin Tarplin if he ever stole anything from the Rolling Stones, he smiles.

"Why, 'Going to a Go-Go,' the song you just mentioned," he answers proudly. "That's from the Rolling Stones' 'Off the Hook,' 1965. I was a big fan of Keith Richards, and of Brian Jones. Pretty much all the British groups."

When I ask him if he met Jimi Hendrix, he nods. "Sure," he says. "He played with the Isley Brothers. Oh yes, he stood out. He was a star even before he became a star."

The door to the greenroom opens, and Smokey Robinson walks in, wearing a floor-length black mink coat. Diamond earrings glitter from his earlobes, and a Louis Vuitton clutch dangles from one hand.

"I heard he got called Smokey as a kid because he liked westerns like *Gunsmoke*," I ask Tarplin.

"He liked love stories," Tarplin replies, skipping a beat. "He used to go to the movies and cry."

"Did you know any other guys in Detroit who did that?" I ask.

"No," he answers, picking up his old guitar and playing a few notes. "Just Smokey."

III. The Man in the Glass Booth

Jerry Anderson sits high above the empty expanse of Ford Field in the glass catbird seat of NFL Control, watching George Toma, the NFL's storied groundskeeper, inspect the artificial grass.

"George has been involved in every Super Bowl," Anderson explains, leaning back in his chair and folding his hands over his belly.

"Because this is an artificial turf, there are probably three to four coats of paint on there," he explains, in his mellow voice. "When we're on a natural turf, in order to get that intensity and depth of color, there will be around seven or eight coats of paint on that field. It's a work of art, what they do."

An architect by training, Anderson worked in San Francisco before he joined the NFL to renovate the press boxes for Super Bowl XXIX. In his spare time, he has also run most major world sporting events that have been held in the United States during the past decade, including the 1994 World Cup soccer tournament, the 1996 Summer Olympics in Atlanta, and the 2002 Winter Olympics in Salt Lake City.

Over the years, Anderson says, the Super Bowl's operational blueprint has become so complicated that it is impossible to educate all the people you need on-site in one month's time. To supplement his own staff, he now imports stadium managers from all over America to run the big event. "That guy who just walked by was the general manager of the Superdome," he says. "Lost his house, everything."

Anderson's company, HOK Sport Venue Event, arrives on-site the day after New Year's. In the following weeks, the stadium is buttoned up inside eleven miles of fencing and laced with 60,000 feet of electrical cables for lighting, cameras, and telecommunications.

The long, narrow glass booth at the top of the rafters, where we are sitting now, is the nerve center of the biggest show in America. The booth is portable and is moved from location to location every year. NFL officials sit at two tiers of long desks with a panoramic view of the stadium. On the wall behind us are blueprints of Ford Field with the Super Bowl XL logo.

"This is the brain of higher functional stuff," Anderson explains. "You've got stadium management up here, you've got NFL security up here, you've got the officials. The theory behind this is that anything that needs—let's call it higher-level guidance—comes to this booth."[3]

3. The men in the glass booth are Mike Pereira, the NFL vice president in charge of officiating; Greg Aiello, the chief league spokesman and a twenty-seven-year veteran of the NFL; Glen Adamo, a former producer with NBC Sports who is now the league's vice president in charge of broadcasting; senior director of broadcasting Dick Maxwell; Frank Supovitz, the senior vice presi-

Anderson's walkie-talkie goes off and he excuses himself to take a call from his number-two logistics guy, Todd Barnes.

"Todd, it's Jerry," he begins. "It's two o'clock. Over at Tiger's garage. You need to get the garage open. You're going to walk through the mags."

As Anderson lays out the method for testing the magnometers that will scan for metal objects at the security checkpoints, he takes an obvious pleasure in working the exhaustively detailed master plan that he and his team have designed for the big event. When his call is done, I ask Anderson when the Super Bowl got so complicated.

"I think the show elements, the pregame show and halftime show, turned in Super Bowl XXVIII at the Rose Bowl," he answers. "That was the Michael Jackson show. And it became a single performer's single presence on the field, and it was a fantastic show."

This year's halftime show will involve 680 feet of stages that have been broken down into fifty-five separate numbered pieces, lined up inside the Comerica Park stadium next door. All the stage pieces along with 2,000 cast members will have to enter and exit the field through a single tunnel, which will also be shared by the performers and staging for the pregame show and the postgame ceremony and by the Steelers and the Seahawks. When I ask Anderson what the proper number of tunnels would be for an event of this size, he answers "four."

"Actually, when you talk about turning points, 9/11 was perhaps the greatest turning point in big-event history," he adds. According to Anderson, each person who enters the stadium tomorrow will go through a security process that will require a total of approximately 12,000 man-hours to get the fans into the dome.

"Somewhere around eleven o'clock we'll take a moment, catch our breath, and then we'll deploy to our positions, get our people inside the tunnel," Jerry Anderson says when I ask him to describe what his morning will be like tomorrow. "Somewhere around one o'clock we'll be ready to go live."

---

dent of NFL Events; Mut Ahlerich, who runs the NFL's security operation; Jerry Anderson; Paul Ridgeway, the head of Ridgeway International, which oversees transportation; and Dr. Til Jolly, who oversees the NFL's medical teams on site.

IV. God Almighty Does Not Love Everyone

The Marriott Courtyard Downtown hotel is located directly across the street from the General Motors Renaissance Center, a gigantic riot-proof construction that includes the headquarters of General Motors and also another Marriott hotel, where the NFL has taken up residence. The traffic circle outside my hotel, ten blocks from the stadium, is a popular place for Pittsburgh Steelers fans, who stand outside in the cold and the rain with signs advertising their desire for tickets. "I need tickets," declares a man named Don Lewis from Youngstown, Ohio. The price of a ticket is $2,000 and climbing.

"Sports is my life, and I'm close enough to the Super Bowl to go," he explains. His two children, Andrew, fifteen, and Danielle, twenty-one, stand near the valet-parking booth and strike up conversations with strangers. If they don't find three tickets, they will watch the game on the television in their room at the Best Western in Woodhaven. I head across to the Renaissance Center ballroom for the annual reporters' brunch.

Of 3,200 credentialed members of the media, 800 are invited to the pregame brunch, which is paid for by the league and where the spread is enough to bring tears to the eyes of even the most battle-hardened reporter. To see a group of 800 reporters together in the flesh is like seeing a convocation of bedraggled dads who have lost all of their worldly possessions in a hurricane or a flood and have been generously outfitted in a hodgepodge of cast-off fleece jackets, scratchy V-neck sweaters, and pleated chinos. Game-day lanyards hanging from their necks, they enter the ballroom on the fourth floor of the Renaissance Center, where they are greeted by a fantasy that any red-blooded American boy would recognize as his own. Standing at the entrance to the ballroom is a pair of four-foot-high ice sculptures depicting the team logos of the Seahawks and the Steelers, which are replicated in smaller sizes on every table in the room. As the NFL pregame show blares from giant-screen televisions above their heads, the reporters head for the buffet tables, where they are greeted by silver trays of lemon almond bars, Mackinac Island fudge, chocolate-dipped strawberries, and rugelach, and a birthday cake that says "Super Bowl XL." There is chocolate-chip cheesecake, key lime cheesecake, Oreo cheesecake, New York cheesecake, and three other kinds of cheesecake. There is also a large selection of more traditional morning heart-attack fare, including French toast, cheese blintzes, and magic pepper bacon. The salutary crunch of bodies hitting the turf echoes through the room.

"In order for it to be meaningful, he has to win it all," the announcer intones. NFL employees also attend the breakfast with their families, some of whom seem nonplussed by the sight of so many ill-dressed men with heaping plates of food, like a living tableau of Okies fleeing the Dust Bowl.

"This is a bloodthirsty defense," the announcer's voice proclaims to another series of lip-smacking hits, accentuated with the orgasmic reverb effect that is the NFL Films trademark, and which has been turned up so high this morning that it seems like every bone in the players' bodies is being broken. The reporters keep chewing.

Up in the luxuriously outfitted media room, the NFL has provided a buffet of quotes to match the generous spread in the ballroom.

"It's a great plane," says offensive tackle Walter Jones on Monday about the team plane provided by Microsoft billionaire Paul Allen. "It's comfortable and has everything that you want; satellite radio and television. We get to catch all the games. The whole entire plane is first class."

"I don't view football in that way—as a violent barbaric sport," objects Steelers safety Troy Polamalu. "To me it's a very spiritual sport, especially for a man and the challenges a man faces within the game of football. . . ."[4]

The NFL has also provided buses to take reporters to the game, where they will enter the stadium through a special gate, an arrangement that will spare them the experience of standing outside in the cold. I wait in line outside with Jim and Buck Degenheart, a father and son from Pittsburgh, who are here with their friend Mike Shea, a little red-faced fireplug of a man who stands just under five feet

4. Cheat sheets and pool reports in hand, reporters are free to enjoy the much-heralded delights of Windsor, Ontario, across the river, where Cuban cigars are legal and "100 Percent All-Nude Canadian Girls" can be found at Cheetah's. A *Detroit News* report revealed that the girls at Aphrodite's, an "exotic massage parlor," had been working double shifts without a day off for the past week. It comes as a shock to realize that the local economy is so bad that

tall, wearing a black-and-gold Steelers jersey emblazoned with the number "69" and the nickname "Spanky." When the Steelers lose, he says, all of Pittsburgh feels depressed.

"On Monday the town is just dead," he says, shaking his head. "I typically don't read the paper. By Tuesday, maybe Wednesday, I start to read it again."

I ask Jim Degenheart if the Steelers' season will be a total waste if the team doesn't win the Super Bowl.

"Absolutely," he says.

"Dear God," Spanky says, confronted by the apparition of a purple-haired female Seahawks fan. Most Seahawks fans are in their thirties and forties, and appear to have stopped off at the Super Bowl for a few hours on their way to someplace else. Seattle is the home of Microsoft and Starbucks, of polar fleece clothing, of Paul Allen's private island, Bill Gates's $50 million mansion, and other wonders of the world. Both Kurt Cobain and Jimi Hendrix came from Seattle. The steel industry of Pittsburgh, whose corporate symbol is emblazoned on the Steelers' helmets, died over twenty years ago. After doing the cultural math, I determine that it would be impolite for the Seahawks to win today's game.

We turn the corner and come face-to-face with a man holding a well-worn copy of the Holy Bible.

"I am hoping that somebody gets saved and goes to heaven," he explains when I ask him why he has come to Detroit. His name is Ron Komer.

"God Almighty Does Not Love Everyone," reads another sign. Among the people that God does not love, the sign explains, are

---

even the girlie bars have fled to Canada. Even worse than the image of clean-cut Canadians muscling American sleaze operators out of business is the contempt with which they treated their desperate clients from across the river. "It looked like some of them were very disoriented, like they'd never seen nude women before," jeered Peter Barthind, manager of the Studio 4 strip club, one of Windsor's finest. Whether as the result of the massive breakfast or late-night visits to strip clubs, it is true that a visitor to the media lounge five hours before the game will find no fewer than five middle-aged reporters, their name tags on prominent display, in varying states of drooling unconsciousness only a stone's throw from the pool table and a refrigerator filled with free sodas.

"Sodomites, the Wicked, Fornicators, and Some Children." The man holding the sign is dressed in a filthy green parka.

"We think of a person as a child of God or a child of the devil," explains the man in the green parka, whose name is Larry Kraft.

When I return to the line, Mike Shea is eager to know which children won't go to heaven. When I finish the answer, he nods.

"That's what I thought," he says. "The kids with the horns."

Forty-five minutes later we have reached the mag lines, which are defended by a series of cattle gates laid out in a parking lot. Bodies flicker back and forth as a friendly announcer's voice repeats the same message at two-minute intervals.

"Today we are using enhanced security checks to ensure your safety," the voice begins, before launching into a long description of the safety measures that will protect football fans from being blown into a million pieces by a shoe bomber or a tanker truck that has been wired to explode.

V. Ladies and Gentlemen, Stevie Wonder!

Having spent a quiet evening with family and friends, Stevie Wonder arrives at the dome at 3 P.M. and goes straight to the partitioned locker room with lockers on two walls where he will spend the next three hours. A caterer's table on one side of the room is supplied with sodas, alcohol, and crab cakes. For the concert, Stevie will wear a blazer with a sweater underneath and his braids pulled back tight from his oversized melon. When he was a blind boy growing up in Detroit, every singer he knew sang songs about love.

"I think in the time when those songs were done there was hope," Stevie Wonder says, when I ask him why so many great love songs came out of a cold industrial city. "Because the reality is that we all laugh the same, we all cry the same, we all eat the same, we all sleep the same, we all breathe the same, we talk in the same ways, even though we speak different languages. We are all products of the same greatness."

Before showtime, he gathers his family, the musicians, the choir singers, and the production crew together and prays. Then Brian LaRoda, Ron Taylor, and LaTanya Marble escort Stevie down the tunnel and onto the stage, as 68,000 people cheer. The singer can feel them as waves of sound, palpable emanations of the great rustling abstraction that is the American mass audience.

"Ladies and gentleman, a Detroit-born artist who has become one of the most beloved and enduring performers in musical history, Stevie Wonder!"

"Aisha, sing it, all the family sing!" Stevie chants, flashing his famous smile and swirling his braids.

Aisha sings "Uptight," the song with the bass line by James Jamerson of the Funk Brothers.

No football hero or smooth Don Juan / Got empty pockets, you see I'm a poor man's son.

Aisha's serviceable voice is no match for her father's. The medley flips to a version of "Dancin' in the Streets," fronted by India Arie, and to John Legend's version of "Ma Cherie Amour." As he launches into "Living for the City," Stevie Wonder shakes his head until it seems like his braids will come undone.

His father works some days for fourteen hours / And you can bet he barely makes a dollar.

The audience greets the music with a roar. Maybe they take the lyric as a tribute to the working-class virtues of the players, many of whom were raised by parents who worked menial jobs. Or maybe as a tribute to the virtues of Americans willing to pay $600 a ticket to watch a football game in Detroit.

"*When you believe in things that you don't understand, then you suffer*," Stevie explains, to the funky wah-wah chorus of the next song. "*Superstition ain't the way.*"

"Now is truly a time to love," Stevie says, in the closing seconds of the twelve-minute slot he has been allotted to represent Motown. "Let us come together before we're annihilated. Peace."

His announcement is followed by a second or so of dead air on the television set backstage, until the announcer rouses himself.

"We can see that Motown is definitely ready for some football."

VI. America Loves Jessica Simpson, America Loves the Muppets

Standing by the mouth of the tunnel, Stevie Wonder can feel the breeze as the players run by onto the field, the Seahawks first, to a Wyndham Hill–sounding theme, and the Steelers to sweeping lights and a steamy beat.

"In the event of an emergency situation, this is the game plan," a voice announces before laying out a mind-numbingly detailed series of evacuation instructions for each section of stadium accompanied by multiple schematic drawings whose complexity suggests that many thousands of people will be trampled to death in the event of an emergency. In the crowd near the field, I find Kristan Miller, vice president of brand marketing for Pizza Hut, whose Super Bowl ads starring the company's new Cheesy Bites Pizza have already aired at least nine times in the run-up to the game. Miller grew up in Turlock, California, where none of her four brothers played football. "I did cheerleading," she confesses. "So I was involved that way, on the sidelines."

Pizza Hut, Miller says, which owns a 15 percent share of the highly fragmented pizza market, is the market leader, followed by Domino's and Papa John's. Pizza Hut's corporate branding strategy focuses on the idea of family. Miller's job is to manage and promote the Pizza Hut brand.

"Pizza is eaten in groups, particularly families," Miller explains, as the crowd beyond the luxury-box area starts to roar. "And yet each family member is busy with different activities. Time together around the dinner table is precious time. For some families, it can be aspirational, meaning that they want to come together but they may not come together as often as they'd like," she says.

Jessica Simpson was a natural choice as the face of the brand, Miller says. In some of the ads, the part of Jessica Simpson will be played by Miss Piggy of the Muppets.

"Americans love Jessica Simpson. Americans love the Muppets. Americans love pizza. So it's a good combination," Miller explains.

"Ladies and Gentlemen, the colors of the United States of America," the stadium announcer intones, requesting a moment of silence for Rosa Parks and Coretta Scott King. Miller folds her hands on her lap and assumes an appropriately abstracted expression. The stadium announcer then invites the 68,000 fans at Ford Field to "join two cities that have long been vital to America's musical soul," as Dr. John and Aaron Neville of the hurricane-ravaged city of New Orleans take on Detroit's own Aretha Franklin in the singing of our national anthem.

If Aaron Neville's weird, high tenor is hardly appropriate for the song or the venue, there is also the memory of Thursday's press conference, at which a reporter thought to ask the singer about the reconstruction of his hometown. "It's a hole surrounded by water, and nobody's fixing that," Aaron Neville explained. "People go back and see their homes, have heart attacks, and die."

Aaron Neville is a bummer. Besides, nothing the man does in the next thirty seconds can match the sight of Aretha Franklin in the flesh. Rolls of fat begin just below her eyeballs and cascade down in waves to her chin, then to her neck, and down to her enormous bosom. A 300-pound mountain of congealed hurt, the Queen of Soul is clad in a black-and-white frosted fake fur coat that looks like it is made out of some kind of cheap insulating material of the kind that you spray on with a hose. When she opens her mouth, though, it is also clear that Aretha can still sing, even if she does look like an extra from the original *Star Wars*. On the television monitor above my head, the camera cuts to Condoleezza Rice, the secretary of state, whose warlike scowl belies the fact that she is enjoying herself, sitting in the commissioner's box with her sometime escort, NFL executive Gene Washington.

"I really consider myself a student of the game. I find the strategy and tactics absolutely fascinating," Rice said recently, explaining why being commissioner of the National Football League might be an appropriate next step on her otherworldly adventure.

"Military history has swung back and forth between advantage to the offense and advantage to the defense. When the offense has the advantage, then a new technology will come along that will temporarily give the defense the advantage and vice versa. Football has that kind of pattern, too."[5]

---

5. As the announcer mentions Rosa Parks and Coretta Scott King, I flash back to an incredibly weird scene that I encountered two nights earlier at the NFL

VII. In the Moog

Stevie Wonder sits in the windowless locker room, on a leather-covered chair at the end of the rows of lockers, away from the television but still close enough to hear the game as friends and family sprawl on the love seat in front of the television, in easy chairs and folding chairs around the room, watching Pittsburgh cornerback Ike Taylor get burned by Seattle receiver Darrell Jackson. Seattle can't score. Pittsburgh can't score either. The new Gillette Fusion Razor promises "the comfort of five blades, the precision of one." A can of Diet Pepsi goes into a recording studio with Sean "Diddy" Combs and has a bottle-popping orgasm. It was great to stand on the field and feel the air move as the players ran by. What he is looking forward to now is hearing the Rolling Stones play "Satisfaction," which is the Stones' greatest song.

"I don't have any personal ill feelings about the Stones," Wonder said, his voice trailing off, out of frustration, because Stevie is not

---

party at the Henry Ford Museum in Dearborn. Built by the famous crackpot after whom Ford Field is named, the Henry Ford Museum is a monument to the mind of a man whose racist obsessions and fulminations against an "international Jewish conspiracy" were matched by his unquenchable desire to collect ancient steam engines, guns, turbines, and airplanes. The museum's collection includes a mustard green Montgomery City Lines bus that has been faithfully restored right down to the original license plates. In the back of the bus I find a group of five middle-aged white executives in business suits sitting with cocktail glasses in hand. In the front of the bus, where Rosa Parks sat down and refused to move, are two large black men in expensive suits and a black woman dressed in rags. I recognize one of the men as Doug Williams, the first black quarterback to play in the Super Bowl. Starting for the Redskins in Super Bowl XXII, Williams threw four touchdown passes in a single quarter, putting to rest the idea that black men couldn't play quarterback in the NFL. Sitting nearby is Meeia Martin, who lives on Cass Avenue in Detroit. Martin is a big believer in history, a stance, she tells me, that comes directly out of her daily experience portraying a slave on Henry Ford's model plantation. "A lot of people are aware that there was slavery, but they are not sure of what that means," she explains. "Slaves were property. They were not people. They didn't eat the best. Families were broken up. They wore whatever they were given by their masters. In the fields, sometimes people would fall out, just keel over while they were working." Her mistress is portrayed by another historical presenter named Larissa Fleishman. "She's wonderful as a person," Martin assures me. "She doesn't do no whips or anything like that."

about anger; Stevie is about love. "I'm good with them. I love Detroit. I'm a music lover."

What frustrates Stevie Wonder the most is that people don't listen. They want to buy the myth about someone who overcame great
obstacles and rose to the top, a story that is sometimes true and
sometimes not, but has nothing to do with the music. We talk for a
while about Marvin Gaye, who played the drums on Stevie Wonder's
first record and opened the way for Stevie's own journey of personal
expression on records like *Talking Book* and *Innervisions* with his
classic soul record "What's Going On?" which Gaye released in 1971
after finally convincing Berry Gordy that it would be a hit.

"I don't want to focus all day on the fact that Marvin Gaye was
shot by his father," Stevie Wonder says. "That was a horrible thing.
Or his drug problem. I want to focus on the fact that this man did
some incredible music in his life. How many people sang 'Heard It
Through the Grapevine' at different parties, or talked about 'What's
Going On?' or got down to 'Let's Get It On.' "

However, the record that truly changed Stevie Wonder's style in
the seventies, that introduced him to a whole new way of hearing
and making music, was nothing that you might expect, even though
it offers a fair account of how the free-floating weirdness of American life will always escape any attempts to make us seem like a normal country rather than a furious human-wave assault on the
farthest shores of reality.

"I heard *Switched-On Bach* by La Carlos, and that was my entrance into really hearing the Moog synthesizer," Wonder playfully
explains, leaning into my field of vision to underline his point. "Bob
Moog's invention of the Moog synthesizer opened up so many doors
in the minds of us musicians."

The Moog was invented by Dr. Robert A. Moog, a 1952 graduate
of the Bronx High School of Science, who started selling do-it-
yourself Theremin kits to fund his studies in electrical engineering at
Columbia and physics at Cornell.[6] Starting with his Theremin kits,
Moog began to experiment with additional circuitry that could be

6. An electronic instrument invented by a Russian physicist named Lev
Termen in 1919, the Theremin was taken up after the Bolshevik Revolution
by Lenin, who learned how to play the instrument and commissioned 600
Theremins for distribution throughout the Soviet Union.

used to create instrument-like sounds, and soon added a keyboard. In 1968 a composer and musician named Walter Carlos released *Switched-On Bach,* an album consisting of work by the seventeenth-century German composer played entirely on a Moog synthesizer.[7] Carlos, who studied physics and music at Columbia and Brown, used some of the proceeds of the album to undergo gender reassignment therapy and took the name Wendy Carlos, before going on to write the sound track for "A Clockwork Orange" and other artistically and commercially successful works of electronic music.

Bouyed by the success of Carlos's album, Moog introduced the all-in-one Minimoog Model D, a forty-four-key version of Moog's custom modular synths that featured three oscillators with six selectable waveshapes, an oscillator mixer, a pitch wheel and a modulation wheel. That same year, in 1971, Stevie Wonder fulfilled a threat he had been making for several years to the executives at Motown with the memorable words, "I'm twenty-one now. I'm not going to do what you say anymore." Taking a million dollars that had been held in trust for him by Motown, Wonder checked into a hotel room on the Upper West Side of Manhattan, took over a state of the art recording studio called Electric Ladyland that the guitarist Jimi Hendrix had built for his personal use in the months before his death, and became entranced with *Switched-On Bach.*

"And then I met Malcolm Cecil and Bob Margouleff," Wonder continues, "and they were with Tonto's Expanding Head Band, so that was my second time seeing the synthesizer, with a much larger setup." Tonto was an acronym for "The Original New Timbrai Orchestra," the world's first and largest multitimbral polyphonic analog synthesizer, which by the time it was finished measured over nine feet long and may have included two Moog Series 3 synths, four Oberheim SEMs, two ARP 2600s, and an array of other electronic gear calculated to blow the mind of even the most devoted seventies gearhead. Arriving at Cecil's studio in a pistachio jumpsuit with a copy of the Tonto's Original Expanding Head Band record "Zero

7. Produced in Carlos's studio on West End Avenue in Manhattan, the album, which showed a corpulent man in a periwinkle frock coat standing next to a Moog keyboard, was introduced on the *Today Show* by Hugh Downs and won three Grammys.

Time" under his arm, Wonder demanded to see the instrument that had produced such a stunning range of electronic sounds. Beginning with "Music of My Mind," Wonder, Tonto, Cecil, and Margouleff would combine to make some of the greatest soul records in American history.

As it happens, the creative height of Wonder's career also coincided with the Rolling Stones' 1972 concert tour. The Stones were legendary aficionados of black American music, having begun their careers by trying and failing to play note-for-note versions of blues songs by Muddy Waters and Howlin' Wolf.

"When I came to New York, we were performing at Madison Square, and that's when I wrote 'Superstition,' " Wonder remembers. "I opened for them then. And that was cool." When pressed for a memory of that tour, Wonder breaks into his familiar mischievous smile.

"There was one where I was in New York and we were trying to get in to do the show, and the guy at the door says, 'No one can come in here except Mick Jaaagaah,' " the musician says, his grin getting wider. " 'Only Mick Jaaagaah can come in here.' So I said, 'Wait a minute. Hold on, sir. I'm Mick Jagger.' And he said, 'Oh, you are?' And he said, 'Well, why didn't you say so?' And I said, 'I'm sorry.' So he let me in."

VIII. Big Pussy

Halfway up the downward-sloping tunnel in the dark stands a little man in his early sixties who seems plugged into a direct source of vibrating cosmic energy that would overtax the circuits of a man half his age. Looking down the tunnel, he tosses a clear plastic bottle of water from hand to hand, like a high-wire juggler rehearsing his routine. He is the Mick. His insalubrious partner, Keith Richards, plays Thanatos to Jagger's strutting, bantamweight Eros. The roadies in the tunnel are awestruck.

"Did you check out Richards?" the man to my right gasps after the spectral guitarist passes. "He could barely stand."

Talking my way past three different layers of security guards in red and navy blazers, I am finally stopped at the mouth of the tunnel by a monstrous woman with a silver brush-cut and dressed all in black, who is surrounded by a retinue of ladies in their late thirties with English accents.

"Where are your credentials?" she asks. She studies my face with interest as I twitch and mutter something about Jerry Anderson and the halftime show. The fog clears, and I read the name tag on the front of her jacket.

"Where are your credentials?" I ask her. Her face turns red with suppressed laughter as she turns to let her retinue in on the joke. She is Shelley Lazar, VIP ticket director for the Rolling Stones and longtime vice president in charge of artist relations for the concert promoter Bill Graham.

"Me no credentials," she howls. "Got big pussy." Big pussy indeed. But this isn't some American Express commercial shoot in Toronto. It's the Super Bowl. Shelley Lazar is just another kibbitzer here. When the guy in the navy blazer goes to talk to the network guys, I walk past him into the mouth of the tunnel, where the carts are awaiting their cue.

The stage for this year's show is approximately 6,000 square feet and will be assembled from numbered pieces that will be carried onto the field on twenty-eight wheeled carts, each of which was custom-made weeks ahead of time and weighs anywhere from 1,000 to 3,500 pounds. The carts will descend through the tunnel onto the field to be docked next to one another to form the Rolling Stones' famous outthrust tongue. The time allotted for this to happen is six minutes.

The guy behind me in line has an electronic device marked "Petzl" strapped to the center of his forehead. It's a tiny flashlight that will allow him to see under the stage. "Only forty-eight seconds left, people," the guy at the head of the line announces. Twenty seconds later the white sheet that has been covering the mouth of the tunnel flies off, and I am standing in the bright white light of a hospital delivery room as Seattle's 54-yard field goal attempt flies wide to the right.

The Seahawks trudge past us down 7–3, accompanied by chants of "You suck! You suck!" Helmets off, they walk uphill into the tunnel, followed by the officials, a cadre of zebra-striped men in their fifties with perfect abs, whose purpose is to prohibit excessive celebration on the field, penalize false starts, and watch the clock.

"Get outta the way!" someone screams from the depths of the tunnel. The cry is followed by a low rumble of breaking ice. Cartloads of speakers rush past me onto the field, followed by a catapult-like boom and a pair of heavy cameras.

"Let's go! Let's go!" the lead driver of cart number 4 shouts.

"Go Go Go Go Go Go Go Go!"

Ten to twelve volunteers push each cart down the tunnel and onto the field, followed by blasts of cold winter air. "We have two thousand kids coming out of that tunnel. Don't let anyone out of there!" a man in a gray striped suit orders.

"Go, baby! Whoooo!" the man on top of cart number 28 urges, like a driver in a sled race. With fewer carts left in the tunnel, the remaining carts can really pick up speed before hitting the field.

"Hey, Detroit!" the team pushing cart number 28 cries out. They are followed by a wintry howl from the open tunnel doors, and then the distant pitter-patter of the 4,000-footed beast. A moment later, the sound explodes into full color, led by a coterie of adults who seem entirely out of their minds.

"Hurry up! Hurry up! We've got to get to work!" a middle-aged man with a Boy Scout–leader mustache screams. He is followed by 2,000 screaming teens and tweens in spangled pink sweatshirts, jiggle-happy Britney Spears tank tops, and Federline scruff, locker-room-slut sweatpants, dorky athletic gear, fashionable low-rider jeans that button around the waist exposing flabby acres of belly fat. A skinny kid in giant bug-eye sunglasses prances by with a filmy Velvet Goldmine scarf around his neck. Fed a diet of sodas and energy bars for the past five hours, the kids celebrate their freedom by tripping over their platform shoes and nearly collapsing with the wonder and excitement of their big moment under the lights. Jumping up and down and screaming at the top of their lungs, the kids are herded by their adult masters to the center of the field, where the Rolling Stones' gigantic tongue logo licks at the frothing caffeinated mass of teens who wave their hands in the air in tribute to their skeletal elders, who are not twice but actually four or five times their age.

Prancing at the edge of the stage in a cutoff black T-shirt, Jagger wiggles his ass and shows off his size 28 waist, while Richards lugs his guitar around the rim of the stage. Every four or five steps he turns to show the sacred object to the crowd, like a priest celebrating mass in a Brazilian soccer stadium. About two-thirds of the way around the tongue, he cracks a smile: being a member of the Rolling Stones is a license to print money. The Stones finish off their brief set with "Satisfaction." All that is audible from the field is the echo of the bass bouncing off the steel-and-concrete facing of the dome's interior.

"Move, move, move!" the wranglers urge their teenage charges, who run off the field applauding themselves. After going all out for the cameras, it makes sense that the kids are in somewhat worse shape than before. The more agile kids leave the field first, leaving behind a crowd of nearly a thousand lumbering, out-of-breath fatties, heaving and panting and sweating and red-faced as they huff and puff their way past the goal line, where a minor traffic jam has formed. Everything that issued forth under the bright lights twenty minutes earlier must now be sucked back inside the vaginal opening of the dome. With one minute and twenty-three seconds left, the Rolling Stones' tongue is sucked up inside the tunnel, followed by two cartloads of fallen silks. The music is over. It's time to play football.[8]

IX. Safe

As the third quarter of the game begins, Leon Oster is on his break. A handsome young black man in a bright yellow Super Bowl XL

---

8. Near the entrance to the tunnel, which is now empty, I find Duke Fakir, the last original member of the Four Tops.

"They were probably the greatest five-man group ever," he says of his hometown rivals, the Temptations. "They had a little more soul. The Four Tops were more of a crossover group. We danced, but we were more impromptu. The Temps were one of the best moving, dancing, choreographed groups in the world."

I ask Duke to explain the mystery of my two favorite Four Tops songs, "Reach Out" and "Standing in the Shadows of Love," which are really the same song, but contain exactly opposite emotions.

" 'Reach Out' is a great hope song," Fakir says. "It's a song to the woman, or a great folk song, like an Exodus song. It's a song of hope addressed to the loved one. It has widespread and universal meaning. 'Standing in the Shadows of Love' is a song about the feeling of being alone once a love has ended. There's a fleece vest provided by his employer, SAFE, he is one of the 3,000 private security guards at the Super Bowl. He has no prior experience as a security guard. "I just started working for the Super Bowl," he explains. A job with SAFE pays $8.75 an hour. Once the game is over, he hopes that a spot in an apprenticeship program will open up so that he can learn a trade.

"I have epilepsy," he says. "So I've been going through that. Back and forth on disability and so on."

As a plumber for the city of Detroit, he explains, you can get an easy job working for the city and operate your own business on the side.

We stand and watch the game for a while. Pittsburgh is ahead 14–3. On the field, the Seahawks intercept another bad Steelers pass and score a touchdown. The score is now 14–9.

I make my way up to a skybox on the second tier of the dome. Here, no one pays much attention to what happens on the field. Everybody watches the game on television. The cost of a sixteen-seat luxury box at the Super Bowl is $67,200, which doesn't include

---

darkness there. Both songs were written for us by Holland, Dozier and Holland. I call them the greatest tailors of music that there ever was. They would make you a suit that fit."

I ask Duke why this cold, gray, dirty, decaying city inspired so many artists, from Stevie Wonder to the Temptations to the Four Tops, to write so many love songs.

"Detroit is a hard-working city, a hard-working town, manufacturing, school-teachers, maybe a few professionals. In a climate like that there is always singing, because hope comes from music. During the hard struggles of the American people and the black people, in the cotton fields, in the factories, they always sang about love, and the future, and a time when they could feel at ease. Most of us started singing in church. You had soulful feelings, and you would take this along with your hopes and your dreams. You would hope and wish that all of these good things would happen. 'I need to get out of this place.' 'I wish for one true love.'

"Later on, Marvin Gaye started asking some different questions, like why are we rioting, and why are our brothers dying in Vietnam. He saw something that was not as apple pie and American as some of the songs we were singing for Motown. When the riots happened here in Detroit in 1967, I was really hurt. That was the neighborhood that I grew up in. But music means a lot to the people who live here. Detroit was furious when the NFL decided to have the Rolling Stones play halftime and not to honor Motown."

catering, booze, and tips. Add those in, and the cost of a seat in box C-4, which belongs to the Big Boy restaurant chain, probably costs five grand per person. I am here to meet Jim Taylor, a personable forty-nine-year-old Canadian who is the general manager of Cadillac, the official car of this year's Super Bowl.

"P. Diddy is in the next suite over. He wanted four Escalades for the Super Bowl," Taylor says, ticking off the names of famous rappers on his fingers like a pretty girl talking about all the important men she has dated. "Fat Joe calls me. Nelly calls me." I wonder if Taylor worries that Diddy and Nelly might have a negative impact on the Cadillac brand.

"They want it, they get it," he explains. "But you can't force it." What he means is that every marketer in America would kill to have Diddy or Nelly wearing their clothes or driving their cars. After all, black people are the most imitated Americans on the planet. Louis Armstrong was black. Charlie Parker was black. Chuck Berry is black. Martin Luther King was black. Michael Jordan is black. Oprah is black.

"It's a little bit of the paradox of this whole market," Taylor says. "Doctors, well-off housewives, they want to be seen in the cars that the rap stars are driving. If we sat down five years ago and you told me we'd be selling cars this way, I would have said that you were nuts."

I ask Taylor what he makes of the long-term future of the American auto business.

"There is no doubt we're at one of the lowest points in our history," he says. "No one looks at the cars coming out of Detroit and says, 'I've got to have that vehicle.' We've got to replace the current fleet with cars that people actually want to buy."

X. The Moons of Jupiter

The noise inside the dome is audible as distant static as the closing minutes of the game tick off the clock. In a room just off the tunnel, the NFL has set out fourteen podiums where reporters harvest quotations from exhausted athletes for the front pages of tomorrow's editions. Nearby, a brand-new Cadillac Escalade is being readied for Super Bowl MVP Hines Ward.

"Good job!" a thin speed-freak-looking tunnel rat in a black death's-head T-shirt and dark blue jeans yells out. "Good job!"

When I look up, I see the Seahawks trudging up the tunnel in single file, helmets off, heads bowed. After a second or two of silence, the assembled stagehands and security guards applaud the losers. They, too, were part of the day's entertainment. As the Seahawks enter their dressing room, Pete Abitante of the NFL calls off the podium numbers where the athletes will appear.

"Parker to eight, Farrior to ten," Abitante announces, as his coworker Randall Liu writes the names and podium numbers in blue magic marker on a large white board. James Farrior, a linebacker for the Steelers, used to play for the hapless New York Jets. It feels good to win the Super Bowl.

"Oh, yeah, man," he says, looking elated. "Best feeling in the world."

From the distant gleam in his eyes, it appears that Farrior may be orbiting the third moon of Jupiter. Still, the Pavlovian reflex triggered by the sight of so many reporters is too strong for him to ignore.

"We had a lot of tough losses in the past," Farrior is saying. "But that's all erased. We're the world champs."

"Jerome Bettis will be at podium fourteen," Abitante announces. Inside of a minute, the entire press corps is gathered around the massive, sweating running back who is known as "the Bus." His eyes are wide.

"I'm still in a place here," he apologizes. "That was amazing. You play your whole career . . ." He stops talking for a minute and allows the fullness of the moment to wash over him, swallow him up, and then spit him back onto the shore. He blinks, then begins reciting clichés like a well-oiled machine.

"It is an ending. It's been an incredible ride. Mission accomplished," he finally announces. "With that I will bid farewell."

"Is that official, Jerome?" a reporter asks, in the same officious tones that reporters use at the Pentagon to inquire about the latest news from Iraq.

"It's official like the referee's whistle," Bettis says. "I'm the luckiest football player who ever played."

Suddenly, Bettis's eyes go wide again as he spots his teammate

Willie Parker across the room. He raises up his massive head and trumpets like an elephant.

"Hey boy, you a champion! You a world champion!" Bettis proclaims. Then he turns back to the reporters for one final round of clichés.

"We knew they were a very good football team, but destiny is what you create."

The air inside the Steelers' locker room is blue with cigar smoke. Ben Roethlisberger, the winning quarterback, sits in front of his locker with head bowed, thanking Providence for having delivered a victory despite the fact that he played his worst game of the year. Lithe blacks in bathrobes roam the locker room, bumping fists with mountainous whites with purpled legs and tiny jockstraps.

"Top of the world!" yells Ike Taylor, who got burned repeatedly during the first half. Now he is smoking a cigar.

"Did what we supposed to do, dawg!" a rookie in a white bathrobe answers.

In the center of the room, Steelers owner Dan Rooney acts the part of the NFL's elder statesman by answering the same questions over and over again. A dried-up little Irishman with white hair and frighteningly large ears, Rooney also owns a dog track in Florida. His hard blue eyes give him the appearance of a Jesuit priest or a bookie.

"How does it feel?" asks a six-foot-tall woman in high heels, with a camera crew at the ready.

"Feels great. Really does," Rooney answers, having combined the answers to the original question and the inevitable follow-up question in a single preemptive four-word response. I ask him how the league has changed since his father bought the Steelers.

"It's very different. You've got the media. You've got television. You've got all these people," Rooney says. "The players are different. They're pretty good, though. I will say that."

More than half the players are filming themselves with camcorders, holding the machines at arm's length and starring in their own TV shows.

"You a real playa, dawg!" one of the younger Steelers yells into the lens of his camcorder.

Backup safety Mike Logan sits in front of his locker with his two young sons, Mikai and Trey.

"Say 'world champs,' " he prompts Trey.

"World champs," the little boy squeaks.

"Say 'best in the world.' "

"Best in the world!"

Having played for ten years in the NFL, Logan knows enough to savor the moment. A month later, he will be released by the Steelers for what are described as "salary cap reasons," so that a younger, less expensive player can take his place.

The Seahawks' locker room is nearly empty.

"It breaks your heart. I'm not going to say it doesn't," says Lofa Tatupu, the Seahawks' rookie linebacker out of USC. There is something uncomfortable about standing with someone who just lost the biggest game of his life before an audience of over 300 million people; what if losing is contagious? I ask Tatupu why there are so many great Samoan players in the NFL.

"Name another one," he says, staring at me as though I might unzip myself and reveal the Martian beneath my skin.

"Troy Polamalu," I answer.

"I'm not letting you get off so easy," he says. "Name another."

"Samoans are everywhere," I parry.

"We're a special culture," he says, relenting. "Samoans are athletic, skilled, and strong. Actually, I'm only half-Samoan."

As I exit the locker room, the postgame routine echoes through the empty tunnel.

"We have the greatest fan base in the country," a disembodied voice repeats. "We thank God for this victory. It feels great. We are the champions of the world."

Only Love Can Break Your Heart

I.

The belief in our native good luck is a vital part of the American birthright, a celebration of the democratic virtue of chance over more aristocratic virtues like manners and talent. Luck's banquet has furnished us with a rich continent and amber waves of grain, the Anglo-Saxon system of law and government, a population of hard-working, can-do people from other countries, the strange forbearance of the savages we penned on reservations to eat bad meat and get drunk, the brains of the Jews, the music of the blacks, George Washington, Thomas Jefferson, Alexander Hamilton, Abraham Lincoln, Walt Whitman, Herman Melville, Edgar Allan Poe, Louis Armstrong, Charlie Parker, Elvis Presley, Thomas Edison, the Wright brothers, the Roosevelts, the Chinese coolies who built the railroads, the soldiers who won the wars in Europe and the Pacific, the astronauts who flew to the moon and back, Warren Buffet, and the smart boys in California who invented the microchip, the home computer, the Internet, and Google. Our God-given birthright includes the gifts of putting our hard-earned money in the stock market, and placing bets at the track based on the fact that the crop-eared nag in the third race has the same first name as our great-great-grandmother Annie. A winning bet is an affirmation of our personal election by the all-knowing, all-seeing God who makes the last first and the first last and rewards the faithful every Sunday with Hail Mary passes that are caught in the end zone.

Devoid of what suspect glamour attaches itself to football and horse racing, dog betting is organized gambling in its most atavistic and least promising form. Those who truly believe that a better life lies right around the corner buy lottery tickets or head for Las Vegas. The dog track is where America's belief in good luck goes to die.

Although greyhound racing is currently legal in eighteen states, including Alabama, Arizona, Arkansas, Colorado, Connecticut, Iowa, Kansas, Massachusetts, New Hampshire, Oregon, and Rhode Island, close to one third of America's forty-eight dog tracks are located in Florida. Foremost among these, in terms of both renown and sheer longevity, is the Derby Lane Greyhound Park, a quarter-mile of fine-grained sand backed by waving palm trees in the city of St. Petersburg. The track's main grandstand resembles an oversize bowl-o-rama flanked on either side by orange-painted valet-parking stands of early sixties space-age design, which are connected by a concrete overhang to two admissions gates, one for regular customers and the other for Derby Lane clubhouse members. In front of the grandstand is an oversize parking lot in which pickup trucks and aging Toyota Corollas are greatly outnumbered by pigeons waddling through the puddles left over from last night's rains.

In the glory days of Florida dog racing, which began in 1931 when betting on the dogs was legalized and ended in 1988 when the Florida State Lottery was introduced, dog-track owners held what amounted to a monopoly on legal gambling in much of the state, a monopoly they preserved through the ingenious device of a sin tax, revenues from which were divided equally among Florida's sixty-seven counties. If the arrangement was a generous one for track owners and legislators alike, it was also the product of a culture in which gambling was understood to be a vice. When that understanding vanished with the arrival of scratch-off games, Powerball jackpots, Indian-reservation casinos, riverboats, and other ever-multiplying forms of legalized betting in the 1980s, so, too, did the revenues and influence upon which the dog-racing industry had come to depend.[1] In response, Florida dog-track owners have increased the percentage they skim off the top of the betting pool—known in the trade as "the take-out"—to as much as 30 percent. This

---

1. The sin tax, unfortunately, remained, and the state continues to collect at a rate of 7.6 percent, or more than three times what it collects from wagers on horses. This year Florida will receive an estimated $44 million in revenue from its dog tracks, down from more than $70.6 million only four years earlier.

extraordinary percentage, approximately twenty times that extracted from slot machines in Las Vegas, makes winning money at the track impossible for all but the luckiest bettors.

Dog racing at Derby Lane is an oddly formal affair that proceeds every evening according to a ritual altered only slightly since the 1930s. On the stretch of sand between the starting box and the finish line, eight racing dogs stand at attention. They are held on leashes by their lead-outs, local high school students dressed up for the occasion in a uniform of black pants, white shirt, and a tie. An eleven-piece orchestra, the High Stakes Derby Lane Band, sits at the ready in a washed-out lemon-meringue bandstand.

An hour before the races begin, the dogs are brought from their kennels to the paddock behind the finish line to be weighed. Their weights, which range from fifty pounds for the lightest females to eighty pounds for the heaviest males, are recorded in black Magic Marker on a board listing the dogs entered in each race. The dogs are then led down a sloping track into the basement, where they are locked in the dark to howl and whine. Half an hour before race time, the dogs are led upstairs to be weighed again on an ancient industrial-size scale of the type used by butchers. Doc Murphy, an Alabama-born vet with Popeye-like forearms, examines the dogs for signs of illness or foul play. If dogs lose more than a few pounds between weigh-ins (evidence of "nervous slobbering" or the use of diuretics), Doc Murphy can disqualify them or, as is usually the case, run them earlier in the day, before they have the chance to grow lighter still. Paddock judge Ray Garcia checks inside each ear for the blue tattoo that identifies a dog by age, parentage, and number in litter, in order to ensure that a ringer hasn't been entered in the race. He also checks their paws and torsos against markings that are recorded for each dog on index cards according to a system of classification invented to identify murderers and thieves by Alphonse Bertillon.[2]

From the grandstand, the numbered blankets on the dogs recall

2. The Bertillon system was the first scientific methodology that allowed people to be classified by their physical traits like plants or insects so that they could be positively identified at a later date. Bertillon, the son of the French statistician Louis Bertillon, began his lifelong romance with physical measurement and classification as a lowly records clerk in the Paris police department, where he

the Ping-Pong balls used in televised lottery drawings. By the rail, though, the differences among the dogs become apparent. Dog No. 6 paws at the ground. Dog No. 2 and Dog No. 5 display a more curious temper, craning their necks through cagelike muzzles to sniff at the crowd, which numbers this evening slightly fewer than two thousand people. The High Stakes Derby Lane Band strikes up a propulsive tune, known in the trade as a "hurry" (short for "hurry to post"), the kind of music that once accompanied antic scenes in silent movies. The music stops, the dogs are pushed and prodded into the starting box at the far end of the track, and the gate slams shut. The lights dim, the mechanical rabbit approaches the box, and the dogs begin to howl. A buzzer sounds, and the dogs burst out from the starting gate, leaping, stumbling, and clawing at the sand.

---

grew dissatisfied with the ad hoc methods of identification that prevailed in central booking. Braving the ridicule of both inmates and guards at the notorious La Sante prison, Bertillon began to take measurements of various bony parts of the inmates' bodies, including the width of their skulls and the length of their feet and left index fingers. These measurements, along with notations about eye color, tattoos, scars, and other distinctive physical markings and personality traits were recorded on pieces of cardboard that measured six and half inches tall by five and a half inches wide. The resulting system, which Bertillon named anthropometrics—commonly known as "bertillionage"—allowed for the classification of human beings into 243 distinct categories which could be further divided into 1,701 subgroupings. Bertillonage was adopted by the Paris police in 1882 and spread like wildfire throughout police departments around the world. In 1887, Bertillon's system was introduced into the United States by Major R.W. McClaughry, warden of the Illinois State Penitentiary.

Using his fame as an expert in the field of criminal justice to expand into other fields where the scientific methods might be applied to apprehending wrongdoers, Bertillon appeared as a witness for the prosecution at the second trial of Major Alfred Dreyfus in 1899. Presenting himself as a handwriting expert, Bertillon claimed to have "scientific proof" that Dreyfus had written incriminating documents that were found in the wastepaper basket of the German military attaché Max von Schwartzkoppen; after Dreyfus spent five years in jail the documents were later proven to be forgeries written by Major Ferdinand Esterhazy, a French infantry officer of Hungarian descent. Bertillon's system of physical classification of criminals fell into disrepute several years later after a series of well-publicized cases in which innocent men were convicted of crimes they did not commit, and was supplanted by the much simpler method of taking and comparing fingerprints. The Bertillon system works just fine at the dog track, though.

No one cheers for the dogs by name. As they round the first turn in a frantic blur of speed to yells of "Six dog! Six dog! Two dog! Two!" the five dog tries to cut in front of the favored six, the two bumps the eight, the seven swings wide on the second turn, and the one dog languishes on the rail fifteen lengths behind the rest of the field. From start to finish, the race takes thirty seconds to run.

Tonight's winner, Bomb Threat, is a great favorite of the Derby Lane fans. Every muscle visibly outlined beneath his dun-brown coat, he stands apart from the other dogs, with his feet planted in the sand and his ears pricked up in an attitude of obvious pleasure. The rest of the pack heads for the rail to bury muzzles in the grass, where a hidden squawk box emits dog-friendly noises. The crowd goes back to smoking cigarettes, staring off into space, and fidgeting with pens and racing forms in a sea of crumpled Autotote betting slips and empty beer cups, consoled by the knowledge that the seventh race of the evening is only fifteen minutes away.

II.

Even the most sentimental and determined mourner would be hard-pressed to locate the tragic dimension in the death of a place whose most obvious purpose is the extraction of ready cash from the dwindling local population of retirees, single mothers, deadbeats, scam artists, and liars. Especially liars. In my time at Derby Lane I will meet many liars, from the young man in black leather with pin-wheel eyes who tells me that he has ridden to the track today from New Orleans, where he lives alone in a thirty-room mansion in the French Quarter, to the older gentleman in a navy-blue windbreaker who claims he once worked as an acrobat in the circus before moving to Phoenix, where he dated Stevie Nicks of Fleetwood Mac. But for the most part these people are not lying to me, or to one another, but to themselves. They lie about money, and about how much of it they have lost.

The presiding spirit of this place—an admixture of fear and what passes for hope among chronic gamblers—can be found in the basement beneath the grandstand, in a room populated by an old General Electric refrigerator, a tan couch, a wall of tan cabinets, a green rotary telephone, and a battered wood desk. Behind the desk, smoking Carltons and stubbing the butts out in an old ceramic ashtray from the now demolished Sands Hotel in Las Vegas, sits Jay Sizemore, a slight man with still, lean features and powerful glasses that magnify the darting, watchful eyes of a small woodland animal. Jay's official title—head of valet parking—gives little sense of his role at Derby Lane. He first came to the track in 1962, working his way up from parking-lot attendant to assistant manager to head of valet parking, all the while maintaining various business interests in the St. Petersburg area, including a junkyard, a mushroom farm, a drive-in movie theater, and Callahan Bail Bonds. He also owns a collection of over one thousand science-fiction novels, which he enjoys because they illustrate his more general philosophy of life. "I guess I like them because of the way they show human nature and the motivating force of money and greed," he says, "no matter whether it is now or out there in the future someways."

Every evening, just after the fourth race, Jay climbs the spiral staircase from his office to the grandstand, which his father, a carpenter, helped to build, and picks up an armful of programs to deliver to the dozen or so regular bettors who make their living playing the dogs. When times are good, the bettors employ runners to place their bets in exchange for $10 tips. There are also the ten-percenters, Jay explains, who cash winning tickets in exchange for 10 percent of whatever the ticket is worth so that the gamblers can avoid paying taxes on their winnings. "It takes a special breed to snake a living off the dogs," Jay explains, laying out the cast of regular bettors. "There was Strawberry Joe, Mobile Mike, Jim-Boy Mooney, New Jersey Joe," he says. "Mobile Mike was an attorney, and a hell of a man. He won the pick-six once, and someone followed him to a hotel room and beat his head in. He ain't never been the same since. You got Bear Cat and you got Flim-Flam Jimmy. There was Billy Duarte, who had a photographic memory and was the most intelligent man I have ever met in my life. You have men like Howie Lincoln out of West Memphis and John Robinson in Orlando, who chase the bigger pools via satellite. Of the ones who come to the track nowadays I'd say that Boston Jamie is the best. He spends about five and a half hours on every program. He used to work with Howie Lincoln when Howie was living up in the penthouse of Caesars Palace in Vegas and betting on everything—dogs, horses, sports, you name it. He'd ask Jamie how much it would take to win the Tri-Super, say, and Jamie would tell him $40,000 or whatever it was. Then he'd send the money the next morning via Federal Express."

As we emerge from the elevator on the fifth floor of Derby Plaza, Jay waves hello without breaking stride, scanning the crowd for the faces of the gamblers who merit the next day's program in advance. "It's the way they make their living," he says. "We give them tapes of the races too, so they can study at home and keep coming back." As he drops each program off in front of the gamblers, Jay nods and smiles, then says a few words and lays his hand on their shoulder.

"Billy Cairns," Jay continues. "A real nice fella. He's up and down. His son picks the dogs for him." We stop at a table full of well-dressed older Chinese and their handsome children, each with a Derby Lane program in front of him. "That's Chuck Wong, the noodle king," Jay says. "He's a good man. He provides noodles to all the Chinese restaurants in Florida. He's crazy for the dogs, and lately his dogs have been winning all the races here." Sitting alone at one of the tables downstairs, in the no-smoking area, is a man in a four-button vest from a tailored suit, the bottom half of which has been replaced by a pair of black spandex running shorts. His beard descends midway to his chest in a matching pair of skinny braids. "That's Richard Hens," Jay says. Richard lives in a shack that he built himself in the floodlands behind the track and often complains about the noise of the High Stakes Band.

Downstairs in the fourth-floor dining room, the gamblers cluster around several tables in front of the satellite feeds that show the races from Derby Lane, Jacksonville, and West Palm Beach, allowing the gamblers to chase the pools on exotic wagers like the Tri-Super (the first three dogs in order of finish in the first race combined with the first four dogs in order in the second) from track to track. Dogs, unlike horses, tend to run the same race every time out: some prefer to run on the rail, others in the middle or the outside of the track. A good dog player can therefore reasonably expect to predict the outcome of enough races to make a modest return on his bets over the course of a year. Today, however, the combination of capped betting pools (a maximum of $50,000 at both Derby Lane and West Palm Beach) and the availability of off-track betting, allowing dog players to bet any race they want anywhere in the country, has made it much harder for the handicappers to snake money. The gamblers on the fourth floor survive by pooling their bets and splitting the profits when they hit.

Everyone here seems to agree that Derby Lane is a terrible place and that the Weaver family, which owns the track, is busy running it into the ground with bad food, bad service, and such distracting promotions as the greyhound-adoption booth on the second floor of the grandstand and giveaway nights featuring fifty-cent hot dogs and lottery drawings for 24-inch color television sets that have no apparent connection to dog racing. Everyone agrees that the races are crooked, though the precise nature of the supposed fix varies greatly from bettor to bettor. "See the way they rip up the outside of the track?" asks one man, who identifies himself as a retired postal inspector from the Boston area. "That's so the outside dogs never stand a chance." Other gamblers hint of steroid use, or of more homey methods such as feeding dogs chocolate and coffee to make them go faster or buttermilk to slow them down. More sophisticated bettors cite the influence of "the syndicate," which they describe as a shadowy collective that buys up winning tickets through remote tracks in New Hampshire and South Dakota that give 5 percent or 10 percent of their wagers back whether or not the syndicate bettors win.

III.

Although the existence of a shadowy, all-powerful dog-betting syndicate appears to be a figment of bettors' imaginations, it is true that gamblers like Howie Lincoln and John Robinson do place their bets at remote off-track locations that lure big-time bettors with sizable discounts. By doing so, both the bettors and the tracks are simply taking advantage of the irrational economics of off-track dog betting. On an average weekend night, the "handle" at Derby Lane ranges from $700,000 to $1,000,000. Of that total, more than two thirds comes from off-track sites, which receive, on average, a 6 percent commission on bets placed. Off-track sites can give the lion's share of their percentage back to a handful of big bettors and still come out ahead. Belief in the existence of a fixed number of "winning tickets" for each race, on the other hand, is a symptom of the same kind of thinking that leads people to bet the dogs in the first place.

Up at the top of the Plaza, sitting alone at a table, is a dark-skinned man in a sweatshirt with a two-day beard and a saturnine expression that grows even darker as Jay begins his approach.

"Boston Jamie, I'd like you to meet my friend," Jay says, by way of introduction.

Boston Jamie does not appear charmed in the least. "Jay," he says, broadening his vowels even further than might seem necessary for the occasion, "will you please look at this, Jay, and explain to me why, for once, the goddamn programs can't be stapled correctly?" He unfolds yesterday's program, with its handicapper's hieroglyphics, and lays it down with an appropriate flourish on top of the program for this evening, tries to fit the two together, shrugs, and then tosses them back on the table. "Is it possible for the morons who run this track to do even the simplest little thing without screwing up?"

Jay lays a soft hand on his shoulder. "It's free, Jamie," he says.

Jamie plays the moment perfectly. He cocks his head, waits a beat, then slowly, reluctantly, rises to his feet. He puts his hands in his pockets, pulls out a clutch of Autotote tickets, and lays them on the table with an expressionless stare.

"It's not free," he says.

As we head back down to the basement, a stout black man in his early thirties beckons Jay into a corner, then counts off ten $100 bills from a roll in his pocket.

"That's five hundred more," Jay replies, folding the money and sticking it in his pocket in a smooth gesture that draws my attention to the bracelet on his wrist, a double-braided length of gold chain supporting a solid gold plate with the letters J-A-Y spelled out two inches high in diamonds. When I stare at the diamonds too long, Jay shrugs and says, "They use me as a kind of a bank, to borrow money and to pay their debts to each other." As we proceed to his office, it is clear that asking for any further explanation at this juncture would be unwise.

IV.

The only bettor I find at Derby Lane who does not complain end-
lessly about the track is Richard Hens, who has sat in the no-smoking area in Derby Plaza since 1986 with only a few complaints. The
most immediately noticeable thing about Hens is not his compla-
cency or the braids in his beard or his enormous shoulders but his
style of dress, with the formal vest, the bush shirt and tie, the black
spandex shorts, and the paper rings that decorate his fingers. "The
last time I shaved I was thirty-two years old," he says. "I am now
fifty-three. The way the braids came about," he says, when I ask,
"was that I was with some lady company one time, and the female
asked if she could braid my beard. For the last thirteen or fourteen
years, I would say that it hasn't grown at all."

On the subject of betting, Hens is all business. "I keep handwritten records in a large file that I have, and I see myself as a professor
of the subject you mention." He fixes me with a trained hippie stare.
"The way I see it, your money is the tool that you have." He reaches
into his pocket and pulls out a small wad of cash and counts through
the bills one by one. "This here is the nail," he says, pulling out a five.
"This is the level," he says of a ten. Then he holds up a twenty. "And
this is the hammer. The fifty, I call that the chalk-line." He holds up
his hands, stares, and slips the paper rings from his fingers and un-
wraps them without ever breaking his gaze. "The hundred-dollar bill
you see here, that is known to me as the toolbox."

Hens is known to the staff of Derby Lane as the track's most dedicated patron, having lived for the past four and a half years in the
small lean-to he built behind the track. As we sit and talk, a young
man with a truck-stop haircut, sometimes called a "mullet" or a
"neck-warmer," comes up to our table dragging a shy-looking
blonde behind him. He slaps Hens on the shoulder.

"Hey, Braids," he says. "What's the best dog in the race?" Hens
rubs his thumbs together and waits until a spark of inspiration finally
comes.

"I'd try the five," he suggests. The odds on the five dog, I notice,
are 13 to 1.

Although there are many people who dismiss Hens as a harmless
madman, he has also built up a considerable following among occa-

sional bettors at the track. At one point, I am told, he had over twenty people who would regularly come to Derby Lane to play his tips. I ask him to explain his reasoning on the five, which he does at length and with enough lucidity that I go up to the teller window and bet $10 on the five dog to win. When I return with $282.50 in hand, Hens is not at all surprised.

"I believe that I already told you that I have spent many hours observing the races," he says. "Over the course of my betting career I have made well over one million dollars."

What Hens and I have in common, it turns out, besides our interest in the dogs, is that we both like words. On the desk in front of him is a folded copy of the evening's racing form and a well-thumbed copy of the *Webster's New World Large Print Dictionary,* which is held together with electrical tape. The page to which the book is open reveals a number of carefully underlined words and definitions, including faux-naif ("artificially naive"), feather ("any of the soft, light growths covering the body"; the last three words of the definition, "of a bird," are not underlined), and form (among the underlined definitions are 6, "a way of doing something requiring skill"; 7, "customary or conventional way of acting"; and 9, "condition of mind or body"). As I flip through the dictionary, I am struck by the thought that Hens possesses a fractured version of my own familiar consciousness. When I ask him why he likes the dictionary, he looks off into space for a full minute and a half before he responds.

"I read the dictionary because it is pure and without distracting opinions," he says. "I have been reading this particular volume for nine months and have studied it completely. The print is large, and it features short etymologies, a general term which means 'pertaining to the origins of words.' I bought it back in '93. Before that I used to read a Random House dictionary, which I purchased after the divorce. I was thirty years old. I read that edition for approximately three years, but it was not as good as the *Webster's.*"

As we flip through his dictionary, I also discover that the word dog is not underlined or marked in any way. When I ask Hens about this omission, he grows pensive, and it takes him a moment to gather his thoughts. "Animals to me," he finally says, "such as the dog or the cat, mean very little. This is particularly true of dogs. Dogs bite people for no reason. Once I had to knock one out with a club. The dog is simply another low-life animal. They're like livestock. I like fish as much as I like dogs. I like birds the most, because of the word ornithology, the definition of which is 'the scientific study of birds.' I would be very grateful to you if you could use that word in your article."

V.

It is easy to portray Derby Lane as a relic of a bygone era in which state-sponsored theft from the poorer and more delusional elements of the population was sugar-coated with the sporting excitement of watching numbered dogs chase a mechanical rabbit around a quarter-mile track. Yet it is also true that, in the eight decades since it was founded, the track has taken on a half-life of its own as a central Florida working-class version of the magical kingdoms that populate the novels of Gabriel García Márquez. With this similarity in mind, I approach the Weavers, Derby Lane's royal family, who have owned and operated the track since 1925. I join Art Weaver, the family patriarch, his son, Vey, and his cousin Richard Winning, who hobnobs with the legislators and regulators in Tallahassee, for dinner at the Derby Club, where the Weavers eat nearly every night at precisely seven o'clock.

The Derby Club is a five-story pyramid of luxurious dining with a TV monitor on most tables showing the races and reruns of Seinfeld. The buffet boasts Gulf Coast shrimp and rare roast beef carved by a white-hatted chef who apparently is meant to distract diners from the glum parade of losers and terminal cases winding its way to the mutuel teller windows below. The fact that Derby Lane, like the majority of Florida's dog tracks, is owned and operated by a family like the Weavers is part of what more sentimental observers might refer to as the industry's charm. Names like "Richard Winning" also go some distance toward explaining why the Florida dog-track owners can so easily be mistaken for fictional characters: in addition to Richard Winning, there is Joe Love in West Palm Beach, Mike Hater in Tampa, and a man named Loser, who ran a dog track upstate.

Art Weaver is a bulky man in his mid-seventies, with a firm grip, an easy laugh, and eyes that linger behind nondescript glasses just a

few degrees off from the imaginary dotted line that might connect
his gaze to that of a curious reporter. He seems pleased that his track
is attracting the attention it deserves, and offers little response to my
suggestion that the track is doomed, or that the decline of dog racing
in Florida might serve as a window into the process of destruction
and renewal by which American culture is made. "I guess I'm not
sure exactly what you're after," he says. "Maybe the story of how we
came to own the dog track will interest you."

The story of how the Weavers came to own and operate Derby
Lane is a mix of chicanery and chance entirely appropriate to the peculiar empire to which it gave rise. It begins in 1891, when Art's
grandfather T. L. Weaver (whose crinkly visage now graces T. L.'s
Card Room on the fourth floor of the Derby Club), together with his
brothers, Samuel and John, began operation of a portable sawmill in
Whitfield and Murray Counties in Georgia. The success of the
sawmill begat the Weaver Brothers Lumber Company, which begat
in turn various logging and lumber operations in Clark County, Alabama, and throughout Louisiana by the turn of the century. The
Weaver brothers' methods of operation were simple.

"What they would do," Art Weaver says, looking kindly over his
glasses at the next generation of Weavers, "is they would come into
town, mortgage the land from the bank, cut down the trees, mill the
lumber, default on the loan, and move on. What happened in
Louisiana is that someone discovered natural gas on some land they
had already cut, which led the brothers to conclude that they were
better off buying the land instead of defaulting on their loans and
made them the outright owners of several hundred thousand acres."

The Weavers made their way to northern Florida and opened a
retail lumberyard, the Pinellas Lumber Company, in St. Petersburg,
a decision that allowed for a more sophisticated version of their former strategy, as families and businesses moved in to Pinellas County
during the great Florida land boom of the twenties. The Weavers
would buy land, cut down trees, mill the wood, sell the land, sell the
wood, and then, if the builder couldn't meet his payments, take the
land back with improvements and either keep it for themselves or
sell it all over again.

It was at this point in time that the acquisitive instincts of
T. L. Weaver (inevitably known by this point in his Snopes-like rise

as "the Captain") collided with the less easily explicable trajectory of a man variously known to posterity as "Oliver P. Smith" (*Encyclopædia Britannica*) or "Oliver B. Smith" (the *World Book Encyclopedia*) or, to the Weavers, as "Opie Smith" (a corruption of Owen Patrick Smith, his actual name), the son of a Memphis funeral-home director, who is variously reported to have come from Oklahoma, Arkansas, California, or Tennessee. He worked odd jobs throughout the Midwest until he arrived at Hot Springs, South Dakota, a town described, in the 1971 *Sports Illustrated* article that appears to be the only reliable account of his life—furnished to me by Louise Weaver, Art Weaver's cousin and Derby Lane's official historian—as "a small railroad stop in a region of ghost towns and worked-out mines near the Wyoming and Nebraska borders." In 1905, as secretary of the Hot Springs Chamber of Commerce, O. P. Smith was called on to set up a coursing meet, a popular turn-of-the-century entertainment in which dog owners would match their animals against a live rabbit in an open field.

It was then that Owen Smith discovered the elusive idea he would chase for the rest of his life: a cruelty-free version of coursing with regularly scheduled meets nationwide. By 1907, Smith was in Salt Lake City, experimenting with a decoy rabbit that could be dragged behind a motorcycle. By 1910, he had secured the first of his forty greyhound-racing-related patents, for a device known as the "Inanimate Hare Conveyor." It was not until 1919, however, that Smith ran the first full-scale test of his contraption, at a cost of over $40,000 to investors. When the Conveyor was finally in place, at a newly built track in Oakland, California, the Hare promptly jumped the rails, causing dog owners to protest that their animals would be ruined by the discovery that the rabbit was fake. Smith disagreed. He believed that greyhounds would chase anything that moved with little if any psychological damage. When the Oakland track closed down, Smith brought the Conveyor to Tulsa and then to East St. Louis, where the track went bankrupt after running up losses of over $100,000. By the early twenties, Smith was in Florida, where he acquired the backing of a former Al Capone associate named Eddie O'Hare to install a mechanical lure at a track in the town of Humbuggus, later known by the more tourist-friendly name of Hialeah.

In 1924, a dog track was built in St. Petersburg by a local promoter who bought his lumber from the Pinellas Lumber Company, with more or less predictable results. Over its nearly three quarters of a century of operation under four generations of Weavers, Derby Lane has played host to Babe Ruth and Joe DiMaggio and Marilyn Monroe, as well as to hundreds of thousands of bettors, touts, and hangers-on, not to mention the generations of dogmen who passed their livelihoods on to their children. There is E. J. Alderson, son of the Kansas dogman Perry Alderson and brother of Sonny Alderson, perhaps the most famous dog owner and handicapper in the history of the sport; E. J.'s daughter Jan Lesperance, who runs the Alderson kennel; and Sonny's son Jerry Alderson, who used to run dogs, became a gambler, went broke, found Jesus, and now works behind the mutuel window on the fifth floor of the Derby Plaza.

By the time we are ready for dessert I have only one question remaining: "What became of O. P. Smith?" Richard Winning smiles, his cherubic features wreathed in the smoke of a large cigar. His cousin Vey shrugs. None of the Weavers is able to answer.

VI.

The next evening I follow a well-worn path around the back of the tote board to a door that opens onto a space that looks like the wings of an abandoned theater, with wooden scaffolding above and discarded transformer boxes on the floor. I climb up the stairs and open the hatch to a small room divided by a plywood wall into two parts. In the first is a single cot covered by a ratty-looking blanket, with a collection of baseball caps on the far wall next to a framed picture of John Wayne and a television set belonging to Carl Edward Dodson, a friendly-looking, red-faced man in his late fifties with a walrus mustache. Most everyone calls him "Chubby." When I ask about John Wayne, his eyes light up. "He's my favorite," he says with a shyness that manifests itself in conversation as great enthusiasm for whatever question is asked. "He was a great actor and a hell of a man. He's an actor that's not too much of a love actor, no Tom Hanks, if you follow what I mean."

The far section of the room, which is called "the glass house," has floor-to-ceiling picture windows that look out onto the track. Beyond the track, the grandstand seems deserted. Red-white-and-blue bunting flutters on the rails. "I came here when I was twenty years old," Chubby says. "This is all I've ever done. I worked in valet parking, on the gate, I took care of the track, I sold mutuel tickets. I used to start the dogs from the box. I helped to build this little building that we're sitting in now, me and Roy Keene."

In front of the window is a metal device, standing approximately three feet high and bolted solidly to the floor, that differs very little from the Inanimate Hare Conveyor invented by O. P. Smith. The inside of the device, which looks like an ancient generator, is a stack of thin steel plates stamped in a delicate snowflake pattern. On top of the snowflakes is a thick metal plate with a crank on top. The farther you push the crank along the plate, Chubby explains, the faster the mechanical rabbit goes. "When they offered me this job," he says, "I didn't know if I'd be able to do it. I thought about that a lot. Because you'll have times when a dog will fall down or start back toward the rabbit. Once I saw a dog jump the rail and dive into the fountain there in the middle of the infield. One time I had a lead dog catch it. But that only happened once." In an average year Chubby will go through three rabbits. He estimates the top speed of the lure at approximately fifty miles an hour, though he rarely if ever runs it that fast.

The first race of the evening is now set to begin. Chubby flicks a switch that dims the grandstand lights, pushes the crank forward, and sparks fly out. As the rabbit begins its journey to the box, bouncing on the end of a long, thin pole, he pushes the crank forward to speed it up, then slows it down as it approaches the box so that the dogs can get a clearer look at the bait as they take off. He pushes the lever forward, and more sparks fly out as the dogs race down the stretch. In the silence of the glass house, broken only by the steady click of the tote-board odds, I ask Chubby if he has ever heard of O. P. Smith, the father of greyhound racing, who invented the machine he operates. He says no. Then I ask if the thought has ever occurred to him that he occupies, as far as the dogs and the bettors are concerned, a position not unlike that of God. He shakes his head no again.

If the metaphorical resonance of Chubby's occupation is hard to ignore, it is also a fact that every lure operator brings his own particular habits to the job. Chubby's predecessor in the glass house, he tells me, was a man named Bobby Harmon. "He was probably the greatest lure operator that there ever was," Chubby says. Harmon was a distant figure who liked the job because he could be alone. He rarely if ever spoke. "He never talked to Bobby Wagner," Chubby says, with a wondering expression, pointing to the squawk box that connects him to the judges' booth and to the trap where the lure ends up. As the years went on, Bobby Harmon grew more addicted to silence, muffling the paddock gate with electrical tape so that the latch could fall into place without a sound. "He didn't want you to call him, talk to him, nothing," Chubby recalls. For over thirty years, no one was allowed inside the glass house except for Bobby Harmon. One day he left his job and walked out of Derby Lane forever, offering no explanation that anyone at the track can recall.

I leave Chubby alone in the glass house and spend the rest of the evening in the Derby Lane bandstand, where between races I sit in the bandleader's office, a small room with a distinctive rotting-wood smell that reminds me of summer camp, and talk with Jules Levan, the piano player. A spry eighty-three-year-old whose career encompasses nearly the entire history of twentieth-century American entertainment, Jules accompanied the silent movies in the 1920s, played piano for the Miss America pageant in the 1940s, worked as the bandleader for Paul Anka ("a real bastard") in the early 1960s.

"We had the pleasure of playing the *Ed Sullivan Show* the first time the Beatles were here," he remembers, when I ask him about the highlights of his career. "We were on the same night. I remember they were rehearsing, and I leaned over to Paul Anka and said, 'They'll never make it.' "

I ask Jules whether he is happy to end his career playing the piano at Derby Lane, and he pauses for a moment to let the question sink in. Then he answers with an embarrassingly delicate balance of tact and pride that he doesn't really see himself as playing for the dogs per se, or for the empty grandstand, but rather for his fellow musicians, who are true professionals. "When I play, nothing bothers me except the arthritis," he says. "But my experience makes up for that. I'll play this gig until I die."[3]

---

3. As of this writing, Derby Lane has replaced the High Stakes Band with a program of piped-in music.

VII.

As far as the sport of greyhound racing is concerned, the questions of greatest public interest in Florida have less to do with T. L. Weaver and O. P. Smith and their various lineal and spiritual descendants than with a number of well-publicized incidents of animal cruelty that damaged the industry's reputation during the 1980s. Raising such questions at Derby Lane is a delicate business. Dog owners tend to respond with a mix of indignation, references to the track's greyhound-adoption program, and puzzlement as to what all the fuss is about. The dedication of dog-racing opponents to the cause of banning greyhound racing for good, on the other hand, is manifested in St. Petersburg in letters to the editor, leaflets, and numerous boycotts. The intensity of this opposition is hard to overstate. Pickets outside the track are led by an organization that calls itself the Greyhound Protection League, whose habit of parading starved-looking greyhounds outside the Derby Lane grandstand suggests the passion of the demonstrators who wave jars containing pickled human fetuses outside local abortion clinics

The more superficially gruesome causes, as well as the deeper psychic resonances, of this opposition are captured in an article entitled "Incinerator Taxed by Dog Deaths," which appeared in the September 10, 1987, *St. Petersburg Times:*

> So many dogs are put to death at a Northwest Florida animal shelter during greyhound racing season that a new incinerator is being run nearly day and night. . . . "It's enough that it's tearing up a $40,000 crematory," said Jimmy Dykes, manager of the Escambia County animal shelter. He said the shelter averages 25 dogs a week during the April–September racing season, but gassed 23 Tuesday alone.

The article ends with a comment from a shelter worker named Karen Hansen: "That's what happens when you don't win."

My own investigation of the conditions under which racing dogs live at Derby Lane begins at seven on Monday morning inside a sandy run at the Marriott kennel. The kennel enclosure, which is surrounded by a tall chickenwire fence, resembles a well-kept retirement community of whitewashed ranch houses with pickup trucks parked out front and fenced-off dog runs in back. There are twenty-three kennels at Derby Lane, each of which contains approximately sixty dogs, for a total of 1,400 or so dogs in all. When several kennels outlived their usefulness as dog shelters a few years back, they were donated by the track to a local private school for use as classrooms.

In the prime of their racing careers, the dogs in the Marriott kennel bear the same relation to your average house pet that Michael Jordan does to your average suburban dad. They have long, thin, intelligent-looking faces and anatomy-book-perfect bodies without a single visible ounce of fat. Most begin their lives on breeding farms in the Southwest—usually in Kansas, Texas, and Oklahoma—where they learn to run by the age of six months. Kennel owners travel to the farms and buy the dogs at auction: a good dog from a champion line costs between $5,000 and $10,000. The dogs stay on the farms until they are fourteen months old, when they join their appointed kennel and begin their racing lives, starting out on less competitive tracks and then working their way up to tracks like Derby Lane, where the competition is better and the purses are bigger. Racing twice a week, over a three-year career, a successful dog might earn upward of $50,000. A true champion, like Bomb Threat, can earn $300,000 or more.

At this moment, however, the Marriott kennel dogs are displaying their championship qualities by pinning me against the fence of their enclosure. As the dogs surge forward, they take turns leaping with their paws extended and hitting me full in the chest in what I interpret as a playful but concerted attempt to knock me down. I breathe slowly in and out while the pressure builds behind my eyes. As the dogs in back push toward the front, and the dogs in front worm their way in between my legs and up to my face, drooling, nuzzling, and sticking their warm wet tongues through their muzzles, I start to relax and enjoy the experience, which is oddly therapeutic in a way that I associate with swimming naked with dolphins or being buried up to my neck in mud.

Watching from the neighboring dog run is the kennel's owner, Chuck Marriott, a sunburned Army vet with an indecipherable tattoo on his forearm and the hardened, taciturn look I associate with circus people. The life of the kennel owners at Derby Lane is bounded by the daily routine of caring for their animals, waking up at 6:00 A.M., feeding sixty dogs, tending the injured, training the young. The economics of owning a kennel at Derby Lane are not encouraging. Over the course of a six-month-long racing season a top kennel can expect to gross approximately $300,000 in purse money. Of that total, almost half goes to expenses, including food and veterinary bills, two or three handlers, and commissions on dogs leased from other owners. Almost halfway through the season, the Marriott kennel has earned only $86,000.

When their fifteen minutes in the sun are up, the dogs are led back into their cages inside the kennel, which is permeated by the healthy-athlete smell of the dogs mixed with the smell of rotting carpet and the tangy, medicinal smell of Ben-Gay. For their first meal of the day, the dogs are given tin bowls filled with generous helpings of meat mixed with vitamins from a galvanized iron tub. The packaging of the meat, I notice, is marked "unfit for human consumption." As all sixty dogs throw themselves howling and barking against the sides of their cages, Marriott walks down the aisle with a bag of doughnuts from the 7-Eleven, which he distributes to his favorites. After a moment of consideration, he reaches into the bag and hands me a chocolate doughnut: the caffeine in the chocolate, he explains, might cause one of his dogs to be disqualified from a race.

With no maltreatment of dogs evident at the kennels, I spend the rest of my afternoon trying to locate the grandson of the track's former veterinarian, Doc Llewellyn, who I have been told is a leading greyhound activist in the St. Petersburg area. In a file I am directed to in the Derby Lane executive offices, under the heading "Animal Welfare," amid articles like "Hidden Shame of an American Sport" and "Death of Greyhounds Investigated," I find a letter from a "James E. Lewallen" of Largo denouncing "the ghastly greyhound death toll" and "an industry that directly results in the wholesale slaughter of tens of thousands of 'man's best friends.'" Unfortunately, the only vaguely similar name that I can find in the St. Petersburg phone book is a "Norma Llewellyn." When I call her she promptly disclaims any connection to "Doc Llewellyn" or "James Lewallen" before launching into a lengthy account of her marriage to a man named Frank Pause, who died of a heart attack in 1985.

"We had to move out of our home because he was still living there," she explains.

"He would walk around at night, flush the toilet, run the bath, and turn the TV on."

"And how did you meet Mr. Llewellyn?" I ask.

"He has a brain dysfunction the same as me," she explains. "So we really hit it off. He can't remember anything that happened in the past. In August 1985, I was pronounced dead. I've got the power of God in me," she adds. "I was combing my husband's hair the other day and it was growing out in my hands. The dishes were being rinsed and jumping into the sink by themselves. My husband wouldn't come close to me."

When I ask what she did then, Norma Llewellyn is quick to respond. "We went to the priest," she says, "and he told my husband, 'You don't have to be afraid. Your wife is one of the gifted ones.' "

VIII.

Greyhound racing is hardly a cruelty-free sport. What is most cruel about dog racing has less to do with how the dogs are treated, however, than with the belief system that is inculcated in bettors, which revolves around the demonstrably mistaken and often quite dangerous idea that if you try hard and believe in yourself the laws of chance will be suspended. In practice, there is nothing very mysterious about the laws that prevail in the closed universe of the dog track. The dogs never catch the rabbit. The odds always favor the house. Still, there is very little evidence that these lessons are actually learned by the people who come here night after night, like the woman sitting by the rail in a glow-in-the-dark T-shirt that reads IT'S NOT THE HEAT, IT'S THE STUPIDITY and who bets five dollars on the same three numbers in every race, a 6–2–4 trifecta, despite the fact that the mathematical odds of winning the trifecta are 512 to 1 and the six dog is—all other factors being equal—the least likely dog to ever win a race. Even the Weavers would seem well advised to park their money elsewhere. According to the track's treasurer, Steve Hlass, the family would make a great deal more money, with no risk at all, by selling the land on which Derby Lane stands and investing the proceeds in a passbook savings account.

The Weavers' current return on investment, he says, is approximately 3 percent per annum.

What little profit Derby Lane does generate always winds up in the same place at the end of the night, in a windowless room located behind the mutuel windows on the grandstand level and presided over by Larry Green, a thin, bearded man in his fifties. He is more than happy to show me around and tells me that he has worked here for nine years. The money, which he takes me to right away, is held in a closet-like room with yellow walls that looks much the same as it did in Captain Weaver's day. The walls are lined with wooden shelves on which sit tightly bound packets of ones, fives, twenties, fifties, and hundreds. On the floor is a squat, ancient-looking safe manufactured by the Mosler Safe Co. of Hamilton, Ohio. On the shelf above the safe is a rip-proof vinyl bag containing more than half a million dollars in cash.

I look at the bag and ask Larry Green whether working around so much money has changed his view of the world in any particular way. His answer is careful and deliberate, befitting a man who handles hundreds of thousands of dollars a night.

"Maybe it has changed the way that I keep my own money," he says. "Before I came to work here, I kept my money scrunched up in my pocket. Now I like to keep it in a neat and orderly fashion, back-faced, with all the bills facing in the same direction and turned the same way." He pauses to consider the question again.

"Money is awfully dirty, and it smells," he says. "I wash my hands five or six times a night. I wash them before I go to the bathroom. When I go home, I can smell it on my clothes."

I ask him to describe the smell.

"A musty smell," he says. "During the summer it gets particularly strong. Otherwise, it's kind of hard to describe. A very musty smell."

"A musty, inky smell," adds David Tiano, Green's boss, who has joined us in the money room.

Larry Green looks at him curiously for a moment. "That's true, I guess, of new money," he says. "New money, brand-new money, has an awful smell because of the ink."

As I put my nose to the money and breathe in, the musty old-money smell starts to deepen into something sour and stale, like the karmic equivalent of old sweat, made up of bettors' failed dreams and lasting compulsions that have been absorbed into the worn-out bills atom by atom and are passed on in turn to whoever holds the bills next.

Through an interior window, a Hal-like computer, a technological marvel of the early seventies, sits in a white-walled room, alone in a world of silent calculations. Off-track wagering totals on each race clatter from a nearby printer, a Morse-like code from the world of instant gigabyte data transfers that is fast making the sport of grey-hound racing obsolete. With more than two-thirds of Derby Lane's nightly take coming from off-track wagers, why bother coming out to the track? And given the superior odds at other gambling venues, from Vegas to sports to the horse tracks, why bother to bet on the dogs at all? The result of the process of rationalization powered by computers is that Derby Lane is no longer really a physical place but rather an abstract device for the production of odds that are, by any reckoning, unfavorable.

IX.

In the basement below the grandstand, Jay Sizemore has settled in behind his desk for the rest of the night. He offers me a Carlton and tells me stories about his service during the Korean War, about attending thirteen schools in fifteen years, and about his mother, who made him memorize his multiplication tables (one through fifty) and inculcated in him a respect for the laws of mathematics that has served him well ever since. Our conversation is soon interrupted by a tall, black-haired man in a red polo shirt with a Motorola pager hooked onto the belt of his jeans. He is sweating profusely.

"Could you do like you did for my daddy?" he asks. "Twenty percent by the end of the month?"

Jay considers this for a moment, looks him up and down, takes in the glazed expression in the man's eyes, considers again, and frowns.

"You got bills to pay, you can't go broke," he says in a sharp voice. "Think about what it is that you're doing." The man hangs his head but stays standing exactly where he is until Jay reaches into his pocket.

"Let me think about it until Monday," he says, as the man reaches forward. "Here's a hundred to get you started."

Throughout the evening they continue to come, with the same bright embarrassed gleam in their eyes, the same loser's slouch: amateurs, professionals, men with good jobs, single moms working in truck stops, a hospital nurse with a favorite grandchild, asking for money to buy food for their kids or to make payments on the car and the house.

Later, as we step out into the dark of the half-empty parking lot, ostensibly to make Jay's nightly tour of the valet-parking stands, the Florida air is cool but humid. Beneath the neon Derby Lane sign is Jay's car, a 1984 Chevy Blazer. There is something disconcerting about the inside of the car, the flat brushed-steel ring around the odometer, the empty spaces on the dashboard beneath which old cigarette butts overflow from the ashtray. It looks like a spaceship interior from *Star Wars*.

"I put about thirty-five hundred into this car," Jay says. He turns on the headlights and drives slowly up the ramp, talking all the while about people he has known who appeared to be honest but took his money and ran off. He talks about his older sister, who is dying of cancer. He tells me hard-luck stories about the valets, most of whom are young and work two or three jobs to support their families.

"Life is hard," he finally says, hunched over the steering wheel of his Blazer. "Life is unfair a good part of the time. And people love to feel sorry for themselves. They say, 'Someone did this to me.' But they love to hurt themselves too."

The reason people come to Derby Lane, Jay suggests, is to be with people like themselves. "It's like a family," he says. The softness of his eyes, the gravelly sound of his voice convey the impression of some knowledge of a particularly desolate world whose one saving grace is that its inhabitants are too weak and impatient to do much damage. His eyelashes flutter behind his thick, black frames. "You're supposed to learn from experience in life, but life's too short to learn from your own experiences," he adds. "So when I think about it, I guess I understand why you're here."

X.

My last night at Derby Lane is a warm and balmy evening with no rain and perhaps a thousand people in the stands. I have come to say my goodbyes. In the top row of the Derby Plaza, Boston Jamie is spending the evening with his daughter, who is in her mid-twenties and teaches kids in Tampa. Although she has been around the dogs all her life, she isn't much interested in the races. She is here tonight to spend time with her father, and she hopes to win enough money to buy herself a new computer. So far this evening she is up fifty bucks. Richard Hens fixes me with his hippie stare from the no-smoking section. He wiggles the bills on his fingers and does not smile. In the money room behind the grandstand, Larry Green has already begun stacking tonight's haul. Jay Sizemore is in a sober mood. He takes my hand, puts his other hand on my shoulder, and confides that he has just received word that the parking area behind the paddock will be closed and that he will have to lay off four more valets.

As the evening wears on I wander down by the rail to be nearer the dogs. Pack after pack runs by, and six dog after six dog fails to win. Some time during the ninth race I make the acquaintance of Bertha Lavoie, a "small owner," which in her case means that she owns exactly one dog, a class-D greyhound named Teedee's Dream that will be running for the Castellani kennel in the eleventh race tonight. Bertha is somewhere in her sixties and wears gold hoop earrings. The first time she ever visited a dog track, she says, she was seventeen years old. "I thought it was disreputable because people were betting," she remembers. "Never in a million years did I think that I would end up owning a dog of my own."

The story of how Bertha Lavoie came to own Teedee's Dream contains what I am now beginning to understand as the inevitable complements of tragedy and disappointment associated with the sport. "I have a friend who has a breeding farm," she says. "She introduced us to these greyhounds, my sister and I." Bertha's sister's name was Terry Daleb. On March 25, 1997, Terry died of a massive cerebral hemorrhage, and Bertha's friend, the dog breeder, offered her a greyhound as a gift in the hope that going out to the track would help cushion Bertha's loss. "I called him Teedee's Dream because my sister's initials were T. D., and it was always her dream to one day have a stakes winner," she says while keeping an eye on the tote board. "His dad was a top racer."

The odds on Teedee's Dream are rising precipitously, from 10 to

1 to 18 to 1, then 20 to 1. "Oh, Lord, here we go," Bertha says as the dogs are led out onto the track. She is obviously nervous, sipping from her beer and chain-smoking Merit 100's. She says that she feels closer to her sister when the dog runs.

The dogs are led into the starting box, and as Chubby's rabbit begins its bouncing run around the far turn Bertha starts to shout, "Come on, baby! Make me proud!" As the dogs leap from the box, and the crowd yells, the look on her face suggests that she should have known better than to expect something good to come of a bad situation.

"He's dead last," she moans. "Last again." Teedee's Dream falls farther and farther behind the rest of the field, loping ten, fifteen, then twenty-five lengths behind the leader. It is at this moment, standing by the rail, that I have my one true vision of Derby Lane. The dream that united O. P. Smith and T. L. Weaver, the dream that animated the ten thousand or more people who came out to the track with greed in their hearts, all dressed up in their sporting best on a Friday night, that dream died long ago. It was buried for good in 1988, the year the state lottery came in. It is inevitable that someday soon, the Weavers will sell the land, the great trumpet of progress will sound, and the tote board, and the grandstand, and the bandshell, and the other physical components of this strange universe will disappear, and the bettors, and the touts, and the twenty-three kennels of dogs, and the 500 or so people who make their living here will be lifted up by an invisible hand and transported across the pennisula to Orlando, where Derby Lane will live on forever as a theme attraction dedicated to our ancient ways of life. Fathers and mothers will buy tickets to watch the bettors and the touts test their luck before heading off to Space Mountain or the Hall of Presidents.

"Would you believe that the dog ran on the twenty-fifth, the anniversary of my sister's death?" Bertha Lavoie asks. "He lost that race too." As she contemplates this fact she takes another drag on her cigarette and her eyes take on a look that is equal parts tender and forgiving. "He just loves to be loved," she says. "That's his problem. That's what makes it so hard for him to win."

Source Notes

The pieces that appear in this collection were originally published in the following places:

"Woodstock 1999" was published as "Rock Is Dead" in the November 1999 issue of *Harper's Magazine*.

"Notes from Underground" appeared in the May 2000 issue of *Harper's Magazine*.

"The Spaceman Falls to Earth" is a (slightly altered) version of an article that appeared in the September 2001 issue of *GQ*.

"The Making of a Fugitive" appeared in the March 21, 1999, issue of the *New York Times Magazine*.

"In the Age of Radical Selfishness" appeared on October 17, 1999, in the "The 'Me' Millennium," a special issue of the *New York Times Magazine*.

"Rehab Is for Quitters" is a revised version of "Saying Yes to Drugs," which appeared in the March 23, 1998, issue of *The New Yorker*.

"400,000 Salesmen Can't Be Wrong!" appeared as "The Golden Pyramid" in the April 23/30, 2001, issue of *The New Yorker*.

"A Prince Among Thieves" appeared as "Prince Paul" in the September 2000 issue of *GQ*.

"Bringing Down the House" appeared in the July 1997 issue of *Harper's Magazine*.

"On Message" appeared in the January 2002 issue of *Harper's Magazine*.

"Buried Suns" is a revised and more heavily footnoted version of the article with the same title that appeared in the June 2005 issue of *Harper's Magazine*.

"Being Paul McCartney" appeared as "The Beatles 1" on February 7, 2001, in the online magazine *Nerve*.

"Sleeping on Roads" is a revised version of the article with the same title that appeared in 2002 in *Surface*.

"Life Is Full of Important Choices" is a (slightly altered) version of "Crossing Over," which appeared in the autumn 2004 issue of *The American Scholar*.

"Marginal Notes" appeared in the summer 1999 issue of *The American Scholar*.

"The Light Stuff" appeared in the June 9, 2003, issue of *The New Yorker*.

"A Fistful of Peanuts" appeared in the March 2004 issue of *Harper's Magazine*.

"The Blind Man and the Elephant" appeared in the June 2006 issue of *Harper's Magazine*.

"Only Love Can Break Your Heart" was published as "Going to the Dogs" in the February 1999 issue of *Harper's Magazine*.